SUCCESSFUL INVESTING

A Complete Guide to Prudent Investing for Safety, Income, or Capital Growth

Fifth Edition/Revised and Updated

BY THE STAFF OF

Babson-United Investment Advisors, Inc.

Editor **CAROLYN F. FINNEGAN**

A FIRESIDE BOOK
Published by Simon & Schuster
New York, London, Toronto, Sydney, Tokyo, Singapore

F

Simon & Schuster/Fireside
Simon & Schuster Building
Rockefeller Center
1230 Avenue of the Americas
New York, New York 10020

Designed by Irving Perkins and Associates
Manufactured in the United States of America

10 9 8 7 6 5 4 3 2 1
10 9 8 7 6 5 4 3   PBK

Library of Congress Cataloging-in-Publication Data

Successful investing: a complete guide to prudent investing for safety,
    income, or capital growth.—5th ed./rev. and updated by the staff of
    Babson-United Investment Advisors, Inc.; editor, Carolyn F. Finnegan.
        p.   cm.
    Includes index.
    1. Investments.   2. Finance, Personal.   I. Finnegan, Carolyn F.
    II. Babson-United Investment Advisors.
HG4521.S823   1991
332.6′78—dc20   91-3280
                                                                     CIP

ISBN 0-671-72835-0
    0-671-74232-9 (pbk)

Contents

6 / Contents

Editor's Note

SUCCESSFUL INVESTING IS an art as well as a science. First, though, before the artistry can be acquired, the science of investing must be mastered. To invest successfully requires time, patience, and a willingness to dig out information. The beginner must learn the fundamentals; the seasoned investors must keep abreast of new developments.

In this book we present basic information on all aspects of investing to acquaint the novice with this fascinating world. For the old hand we delve into the hows and whys of some arcane new and not-so-new securities. We also demystify a few of the more involved investment strategies. Whether your investment goal is safety, income, or capital growth, you will learn how to invest successfully to attain these goals. We cover in detail how our complex tax laws affect investment and financial planning decisions.

Compiling a book such as this and keeping it current with changes in the investment world and in tax law requires the expertise of many people. We have approached the task on a team basis. The members of the professional staff of Babson-United Investment Advisors who have contributed to this work bring to it a diversity of backgrounds.

In addition to their experience in the field of investments, the contributing authors have impressive credentials. One has a doctorate in economics. Several have master's degrees in business administration. Many are Chartered Financial Analysts, and one is a Certified Financial Planner. Collectively these authors have more than 275 years of experience in the fields of business, investment, finance, and academia.

While we have attempted to avoid material that will become dated, it is virtually impossible for a truly useful reference book to elude this trap. We do not venture opinions on the investment potential of any specific company. References to particular corporations are included for the purposes of illustration and emphasis.

Happy reading . . . and successful investing.

Carolyn F. Finnegan, *Editor*

The charts appearing in this book are from Securities Research Company, a division of Babson-United Investment Advisors, Inc.

How to Use This Book

THE EFFECTIVENESS OF a reference book can be nullified if the user can't quickly and easily find the information he or she seeks. Recognizing this, we have provided you with a detailed table of contents and a thorough and extensive index. A quick scan of the table of contents shows you the breadth of the subjects covered in this book. The index pinpoints any references to subjects that interest you.

The book is arranged in broad segments, each containing several chapters. A beginner would be wise to start at Chapter 1 and work his or her way through to the end. Experienced investors may prefer to use this book as a reference source. The table of contents will help the latter find sections that cover subjects on which they need information. Each chapter and segment leads the reader in a logical sequence to the next.

Here is a synopsis of each of the book's eight sections:

Part I—The Art of Prudent Investing—can best be described as an expression of investment philosophy. Summed up in this section are the investment theses that have shaped the company's advice for over 70 years. Buy for the long term. Buy common stocks for capital growth. Buy them for increasing dividend patterns. Select your investments with care, then hold them. Avoid fads. Be content to amass capital slowly—but surely.

Part II—Evolving Markets—covers the major trends of the market in the 1980s and their effects on investors. Chapter 4, written by David McClain, Henry A. Walker Distinguished Professor of Business Enterprise at the University of Hawaii and economic advisor to Babson-United, treats the capital markets and the economy from his special perspective as an economist.

Part III—Your Investment Alternatives—describes each of the various securities from which you may choose: stocks, bonds, convertibles, Treasuries, municipals, mutual funds, options, futures, index and financial futures, gold, and real estate. In these chapters we explain how each of these securities works, which investment goals they facilitate, and their advantages and disadvantages.

Part IV—How to Make Your Choices—discusses the various investment analysis tools used by professionals. You discover how the various market averages are compiled and in what ways they differ. You can learn how to read charts and economic indicators.

Annual reports are dissected for your edification. To select stocks, you should first know something about industry groups. Several chapters are devoted to industries—from smokestack to high tech, from food to water. In addition, we tell you about other sources of investment information.

Part V—Mastering the Strategies and Tactics—this "how-to" segment shows you when to use options, and how to capitalize on overseas investment opportunities. The functions of the exchanges, brokers, and investment bankers are outlined; the various types of buy and sell orders are explained. We also give you five succinct investing rules to follow.

Part VI—Taking Care of the Housekeeping—explains how to decide whether you need a discount or a full-service broker. It also tells you what to do if you lose a stock or bond certificate. Dividend reinvestment plans and other periodic investment plans are detailed. The relationship between taxes and your investment program is clarified.

Part VII—Investments and Your Financial Plan—helps you plan for your future financial security. You learn what needs to be done in advance of death to assist survivors. Planning programs for a secure retirement are included. The advantages of employee benefit, IRA, and Keogh plans are detailed, especially in light of the Tax Reform Act of 1986. Highlights of the Revenue Reconciliation Act of 1990 are included. The hows and whys of annuities are explained. You can learn about several techniques for estate and family financial planning.

Part VIII—Speaking the Language of the Bulls and the Bears—is an extensive glossary of investment, economic, business, legal, and financial terms.

PART I

The Art of Prudent Investing

CHAPTER 1

Overview

IF THERE IS one observation that has remained true through-out the five editions of this book, it is that most people want to remain poor, and do. They deliberately avoid financial prosperity. Think of the number who rent apartments instead of buying houses, for example, when everyone alive today should know that home prices have risen every year since memory began, except for a brief period during the Depression of the 1930s, and in more recent spells of tight money or soaring interest rates, or both, and most notably in the recession of late 1990 and 1991. But these interruptions in the long-term rise in real estate prices are of short duration and limited scope.

The mortgaged householder can deduct his interest payments and real estate taxes from his income before taxes, so Uncle Sam is really helping him pay his "rent." The real rent payer pays his share of his landlord's interest and taxes but gets no deduction; the landlord gets it. The landlord gets the profit on the apartment or house as it rises in value. So does the homeowner. What does the rent payer get from a boom in property values? An increase in rent.

Yet millions of people pay rent, by preference. Other millions borrow but once. They take out a mortgage to finance their first home, because there's no other way to get a home, then bear down to pay off that mortgage. "Neither a borrower nor a lender be," advised their mothers, so they push to retire the mortgage early. Think of all the World War II GIs who sacrificed to get rid of their GI mortgages and the 4 percent rate they carried. What do mortgage lenders now demand? Double and triple that amount. Few of us today are likely ever to see a 4 percent mortgage rate again.

Lessons Not Learned

Even those who have profited from the post–World War II plunge into real estate have not learned much of a lesson. How many people do you know with two houses, one for living and one for investment? The writer had a friend with a paid-off mortgage and a swollen passbook account. When the house next door came on the market we urged the friend to borrow and buy it for investment. The advantages were easy to see—deductible tax and interest costs, plus depreciation and a steady flow of rental income. Long term there was the virtual assurance of profit through capital gain.

What was the response? A sardonic smile and the cynical remark, "No thanks, and I suppose the next urging from you will be to buy stocks instead." True, that's what we did urge, the point being to buy something, for the road to wealth must in great part be traversed via the ownership of things—real estate, businesses, equities, and the like. The more you buy with bank money the more leverage you have, and the faster the progress can be. But buying things with borrowed money does involve risk, and we'll talk more on that later in this book.

Why don't people buy things? Why do they tend to squirrel money away into "safe" places like the local savings and loan association? Why do they determinedly turn their backs on the chance to make money? Because they are pessimists. They fear the future. They don't believe things will work out. They give everything a negative interpretation. They lack faith. "I would never open a store on that corner." "Convertibles are too dangerous. What if you rolled over?" (How many convertibles have you seen roll over? How many sedans, for that matter?) "Flying scares me." "The weather has been so bad this winter that corporate earnings are sure to suffer—and if this cold weather does break, the floods could be disastrous."

There is no shortage of worries. The Japanese will own the United States. Inflation is heating up again. The savings rate is too low. Consumer debt is too high. The budget deficit will surely swamp us. Who can afford to buy a house or car at these prices?

There is always something to worry about, and concentrating on such uncertainties or unfavorable possibilities prevents action. Fears are fueled by media gurus—as was seen in the coverage of the Gulf War—who dwell on every negative event while glossing over positive happenings. And certainly such momentous events as the recent war in Iraq made investors nervous.

The Power of Positive Thinking

The optimist, statistically a rare bird, has a leg up. He assumes from the start that as America was here when he was born, it probably will be when he dies. If he's wrong in this main assumption, he will lose more important things than his money. He looks around for opportunities. When the dollar is at an all-time high against European currencies, he takes a trip to the Continent and buys a Mercedes while there—a bargain! He doesn't simply mutter darkly, "Foreign trade has had it," and keep his cash in the bank.

Consumers generally do exactly the opposite, which is the very worst thing for them to do. When inflation threatens, they cram their extra money into bank accounts. If the stock market falls, optimists look for bargains while the pessimists are predicting even lower prices. Most people never seem to learn from the turtle that you cannot make any progress unless you stick your neck out.

The optimist can, and often does, go too far. He might expect to get rich quick. He often thinks he can pick stock market winners, and has been known to get so far out on a borrowed-money limb as to be cut off by a falling stock market or interrupted cash flow. Despite experience that tells him there are no wizards on Main Street, he frequently believes there are some on Wall Street.

For you, the key is to think positively. But temper your optimism with prudence. Weigh the possible gains and risks, then go ahead, making haste slowly. That's the road to riches.

People tend to think alike. When times are prosperous, everyone feels good, usually too good, and lots is done to excess. Too much borrowing, spending, and speculating often bring on a corrective recession of some sort in business, and folks turn to living sensibly. But they feel worse. They don't feel as if they are living sensibly, but more as if they are being forced to live at penurious levels.

The truth is, the future is always impossible to foresee. Who could have predicted double-digit inflation, the dominolike collapse of communist governments in Eastern Europe, or a savings and loan bailout bill that is expected to exceed $500 billion?

30 YEARS OF P/E'S ON THE DOW INDUSTRIALS

1982 P/E-100.0

PRICE/EARNINGS
(scale left)

DJIA (scale right)

Throughout it all our big corporations and their shareholders have prospered, a fact that was reflected in the performance of the Dow, which reached a peak in August 1987, then collapsed, only to reach a new peak two years later. This prosperity should continue in this decade. Meantime, as the preceding chart shows, stocks are still historically undervalued as measured by the price-earnings ratio on the Dow Jones Industrial Average.

Be Positive, Be Patient

The moral is, of course, to think positively (with prudence), and when everyone else is waiting for the future to become obvious, buy the good stocks you see on the bargain counter. But you must be patient, too. Sometimes the stocks you buy will move up rapidly, but more than likely they won't. The time factor is always unknown. Just buy the shares of a company that has a good record and seems to have as good a prospect, and sit with it. In short, buying and holding beats trading over the long term. Below are a couple of true-life examples of what one sensible lady did with her patience and positive thinking.

She bought 100 shares of Dresser Industries in March 1954 for $2,339. This was split two for one twice, giving her a total of 400 shares. She bought another 300 shares in September 1966 for $7,590, and another 200 in March 1974 for $9,950. The total holding was then 900 shares. After she had given away 200 of her lowest-cost shares, her remaining 700 were split two for one, giving her 1,400 shares with a total value of $56,000 as of the end of 1977. Another two-for-one split in 1980 meant 2,800 shares, worth $50,400 at the market's bottom in 1982, and $58,800 three years later when she sold the shares. Her net cost was $18,700.

Her experience with Emerson Electric was even more impressive. She bought 100 shares in December 1949 for $1,200 and another 100 through rights in April 1953, for $1,810. After several stock splits, she had 7,296 shares by early 1990 worth $294,000. Her annual dividend of $9,193 was more than three times her total cost of $3,010.

She always told us she was too busy running the farm to trade. "I just buy and hold," she said. Too bad more people don't do likewise.

Where Should You Invest Your Savings?

Let's look at some of the options. First, the passbook account. Great for the beginning. The interest rate is modest, but you can have the money anytime (with the passbook and proper identification, of course). The savings bank is perfect for the dollar you may need tomorrow or next fall. But for the long pull, forget it.

Inflation takes the joy out of saving. When this writer joined the working world four decades ago, the clerical starting wage in Boston was around $32 per week. Today it is over $225 and one could suspect that today's beginner is not much wealthier than yesterday's. Thus, the poor soul who squeezed a dollar out of a meager pay envelope 40 years ago for a savings account would be withdrawing a dollar worth 15¢ today. So the savings account, whatever its other blessings are, is no long-term investment.

Neither is insurance, and for the same reason—inflation. Insurance is for protection, whether from the premature demise of the principal breadwinner in the family or the flaming destruction of the family home. So buy it that way, for protection against financial loss and not as an investment, and you'll be OK.

Real estate can be a good investment. However, to make wise individual investments in real estate, you have to know the territory, and for the average person that generally is limited to his own backyard. Thus, for practical purposes, most of us buy the house we live in, and maybe one in the country, but that's about it, and properly so. We have more about real estate later on in this book, but for now we can probably agree simply that it is not a major investment preoccupation for most of us.

There are other choices for those with miserly inclinations. French peasants buy gold napoleons and bury them in the backyard, a relatively tiresome practice for the average

American family that moves every few years. Furthermore, there is no interest income here and an obvious risk of theft in this break-and-enter society of ours. Certainly you have read of the man who kept his packages of tens and twenties in an old stove until a kindly neighbor came in and used the stove to burn the trash.

The small investor can have difficulty with bonds, if only because they tend to come in relatively large dollar amounts. Bond dealers prefer to work with $25,000 units and really jack up the price when you talk about anything under $10,000. But the larger investor should review the opportunities in the bond market, particularly when income is of paramount concern.

We'll deal in depth with all sorts of bonds—corporate, government, municipal, convertible, deep-discount—later in this book, but for now we'll treat them generally as one savings option. Bonds are a loan by you to the issuer. That issuer agrees to pay you a fixed rate of interest and to give you your money back on a certain future date.

This means that a bond has much the same weakness as a savings bank account. It leaves you vulnerable to the ravages of inflation. The dollar you get back is nowhere near as good as the one you originally lent or deposited. It won't buy as much. A good bond will usually give you a better return than the savings account, but the bond will move up and down as interest rates fluctuate. So the savings account and a quality bond are at about a standoff and, because of their vulnerability to inflation, are not particularly attractive for very many of your long-term savings dollars.

Why You Can't Ignore Stocks

Short of diamonds, art, or some other esoteric storehouse of value, there's not much left in the way of choices for the saver but common stocks. Lots of people stay away from common stocks because they always go up and down in value, sometimes with alarming speed. Stocks can also at times fall to zero and disappear, a most disheartening experience for the holder.

All of us have heard of people who "lost everything" in the great stock market crash of 1929. Few of us hear of the good solid investment gains enjoyed by thousands upon thousands of sensible buyers of good common stocks. Like a happy family life, a good investment experience does not make prime-time TV.

So we tend to hear the horror stories of stock ownership, and, unless educated to the contrary, we stay away from common stocks. It is a shame, for the investment in common stocks is about the only way most savers can hope to offset inflation. Sometimes stocks do not rise enough to match the loss in purchasing power of the dollar, and sometimes in a roaring bull market stock values soar far ahead of the inflation rate.

Folks tend to overlook the fact that the intrinsic values behind good stocks go up along with dividends. As the economy of this country grows, so do the sales and earnings of our leading corporations. Gross national product, for instance, amounted to $286 billion in 1950. Forty years later, the figure was $5.3 trillion. Part of this impressive change was inflation, of course, but part also represented incredible industrial growth and a huge surge in the standard of living.

Naturally, business participated in this growth. Some would even claim that business created this materialist surge. In any event, stockholders participated in it, while savings bank depositors did not. Emerson Electric, for example, reported revenues of $23 million and net income of $1.4 million in 1947, versus revenues of $7.1 billion and net of $588 million for the year ended September 30, 1989. Small wonder that the stock sold at 33¢ (adjusted for all splits) a share then compared with $40 at the end of 1989. Yet the stock was selling at a reasonable multiple of 15 times earnings.

Other companies have fared as well or better. Consider the random sample (shown opposite) of the performance of some well-known blue chips from 1979 to 1989. Note how values rose for these companies. Yet, in some cases, stock prices have not increased commensurately with the gains in revenues and profits.

Of course, having determined that common stocks repre-

	Revenues*		Earnings†		Stock Price‡	
	1979	*1989*	*1979*	*1989*	*1979*	*1989*
Abbott Labs	$ 1,683	$ 5,380	$0.74	$3.85	10	65
Anheuser-Busch	2,776	9,481	0.53	2.68	4	39
DuPont, E.I.	12,572	35,534	2.14	3.53	13	40
Merck & Co.	2,385	6,551	0.84	3.78	12	79
Minnesota Mining	5,440	11,990	2.80	5.60	25	80
Procter & Gamble	9,329 §	21,398 §	1.75 §	3.56 §	37	68

* Millions of dollars.
† Per share, adjusted for all stock dividends and splits.
‡ At year end.
§ Year ended June 30.

sent your best long-term investment savings option, you shouldn't just trot down to your corner broker and start investing in stocks. You can, to be sure, but you shouldn't. You need a plan that accommodates such variables as your income, your family responsibilities, your housing needs, reasonable insurance protection, short-term spending protection (savings accounts), and long-term investment objectives (college, retirement, and so forth).

Rough these figures out and you'll have an idea of what part of your spending stream is savable, and how much of that you will likely have available for the purchase of common stocks over the years ahead.

CHAPTER 2

Investment Risks—
Defined and Contained

"I ABHOR RISK," wrote the senior legal type for a large life insurance company. "I want to know that a dollar saved today will be around tomorrow and the day after that." So his savings plan was strict and sober—straight life, paid-up annuities, and, of course, plenty in the local savings bank. "No use putting all your eggs in one basket." That is the picture of the supercautious saver.

If risk is inevitable, it is worth studying. What sorts of risks are there, how should they be offset, how much can you take in the way of chance, what is tolerable and intolerable as far as risk is concerned, and is one man's risk another man's opportunity? In this chapter we will run through some of the typical risks all of us face today. Then we will show you some ways to balance them. We'll also try to show you how to recognize your risks and opportunities and, more important, how to determine just how much risk you can and should assume.

The Inflation Risk

First, what sorts of risks are there? The biggest risk to anyone, of course, is his own mortality. This the intelligent soul tries to keep under reasonable control with moderate living habits, good medical care, and, if he's inclined, prayer. But financial risks are more complicated. Savers are perpetually on the horns of this dilemma. If they buy securities, the market for them may go down, and their savings will shrink. If they don't buy securities, if they just hold their dollars, they'll stand a good chance of seeing those dollars shrink in purchasing power, if not in number.

Inflation is *the* enemy. It is the biggest and surest risk most of us ever face, for no currency in the financial history of mankind has failed to lose purchasing power over the years, sometimes at a furious rate, as in Argentina and Brazil in the 1980s, and at other times quite sedately, as in the early 1950s in this country, when the dollar lost only about 2 percent of its value annually to higher prices. In fact, during that period the late Professor Sumner Schlicter of Harvard Business School argued for more inflation as an economic stimulant and a producer of a faster rise in the standard of living.

It is unlikely that even Dr. Schlicter would have liked the raging inflationary pace of the post–Vietnam War era, when the nation struggled with inflation rates up to 13 percent. It is equally unlikely that we'll ever again get back to the Eisenhower era's 2 percent, which became so dull to some. Even an annual 4 to 5 percent rate means some real problems.

The table here shows what a 5 percent rate will do over a 25-year period.

	Start*	After 25 Years
Bread	$ 1.35	$ 4.57
Rib steak, per pound	3.29	11.14
Potatoes, 5 pounds	1.49	5.04
Milk, ½ gallon	1.40	4.74
Toilet paper, 4 rolls	1.10	3.72
Man's suit	250.00	846.59
Woman's dress	95.00	321.70
Home, 3-bedroom	145,000.00	491,021.47
Chevrolet, Cavalier	8,000.00	27,090.84
Gasoline, 1 gallon unleaded	1.05	3.56

* Florida prices, 1990.

To keep pace with this, a $5 hourly wage would have to reach $16.93 in 25 years. Clearly, investments that did not have a chance to move along too would be disastrous.

The Interest-Rate Risk

Though inflation is the major risk, there are other, usually smaller, risks in setting out to defeat or even partially offset that primary threat. Prices of stocks and bonds fluctuate, for example, and when they fall below your purchase price, the loss seems real even though it is only on paper. Some people can't take such losses—even temporary ones, on paper. Our "I abhor risk" friend is one. Others can, and thus they are able to use stocks and bonds to beat inflation.

Let's take a look at the risk in bonds. First, a bond is simply a certificate that represents a loan you have made to a company, say General Motors, or to the United States government, a state, or a city. One obvious risk is that the borrower might not pay you back. Given the nature of the borrowing organizations above, this is unlikely. But it can and does happen with institutions of less stellar quality. However, because bonds are rated, you have a good idea before you buy of the issuer's financial condition and ability to repay principal and interest.

The real risk in a bond is a rise in interest rates. Bonds are issued initially at a fixed rate of interest. But from there on—until they are close to maturity—they trade at a price where the current yield is equal to that of the bond market generally. A bond with a 9⅝ percent coupon rate and nearing maturity will sell at 100 if interest rates generally are running close to the 9⅝ percent coupon rate (or the $96.25 annual interest payment on the $1,000 face value bonds). But if rates rise to 12 percent generally, the bond price will fall to around 93½ ($935), so the $96.25 payment will represent a 12 percent yield to maturity for a new investor adding such a bond to his portfolio. Conversely, if interest rates should fall to 7 percent, the bond would rise to 109 ($1,090) or thereabouts, the increase needed to make the $96.25 interest payment produce a yield to maturity of 7 percent.

Since the prospect of profit is not a very scary one, we'll

concentrate on the risk of loss of principal due to rising interest rates. This risk can be greatly reduced by keeping the maturity of the bond you buy short. This means you get the bond's face value back in a few short years, regardless of where interest rates are then. Thus, if interest rates are up between the time you buy and the time the bond matures you can simply ignore the paper loss, knowing that when the maturity date comes you will get your money back.

The Market Risk

Everyone knows that the risk in common stocks can be enormous. We have already noted how the stock market crash of 1929 beggared many investors overnight. In fact, most people think the risk in stocks is so great that buying stocks is just like betting on horses. They believe that savers go to the bank and gamblers to the stock market. While nearly everyone is familiar with the 1929 experience, how many of them know that thousands of investors who held common stocks in 1929 still held them in 1939 and were doing very well indeed? That is because good stocks—the shares of our leading corporations, such as Abbott Labs, General Electric, and Emerson Electric—go down in a bad market, but not out. When investment sentiment, the business cycle, or whatever improves, good stocks come back.

If the big risk in stocks is a rising and falling market, it can largely be offset by long-term holding. Don't worry when the market goes down. It will eventually come back, and your good stocks will come with it. A second risk in stocks is the soundness of the companies they represent. Stocks vary widely in appeal, popularity, price stability, and dividend characteristics, as well as in risk and reward. Before entering the stock market with your dollar saved, you should review these differences carefully, for on Wall Street what's good for the goose isn't necessarily good for the gander.

How Much Risk for You?

Which brings us to you and your risk-taking ability. If the money you save is small in amount and your needs pressing and near-term, you have to be a lot more careful than if you are in the opposite and more enviable position. If you barely have your son's tuition in hand and the bill is due in six months, you don't put the money in *any* common stock, not even a blue chip. Who knows what surprise could come around the corner to upset the stock market, albeit temporarily, and leave your tuition fund badly dented?

On the other hand, if you have your son's tuition in hand and he's only seven years old, you would be foolish not to buy some Merck or GE with it. By the time he gets to college, it could be two or three times as big (so also the tuition bill). Better yet, you may have saved even more, so you can let your stocks ride to even higher long-term levels.

In the final analysis, the amount of risk you take depends on you and your circumstances. The richer, younger, and less depended upon by others can take bigger chances than the poorer, older, and more leaned on, obviously. The commission salesman should save more carefully than the tenured academician. The fellow with six kids has to play it safer than the man with none and a working wife.

Put another way, invest in stocks only that money you do not expect to need in the foreseeable future. Start with the shares of the best companies, picking those that represent the fastest-growing areas of the economy, rather than the clearly more mature industries—drugs rather than rails, for instance.

Spreading Your Risks

By all means, diversify. This means spreading your money over a number of different companies and industries. You never get rich quickly this way, for one stock will sag when another soars. Neither will you go broke, for the same obvious reason. A Wall Street tycoon once said the way to make money was to put all of your eggs in one basket and then to "watch the basket like hell." Well, maybe it worked for him, but for the rest of us diversification is a must.

It makes saving more fun, too. To hold the shares of a number of companies is entertaining. It makes you feel like part of the big world. You can stick out your chest when "your" company comes up with a promising method for treating cancer, and can shrink in shame when your company is caught polluting the shoreline with oil. Owning stocks puts you right out there in big business with the millionaires, tycoons, and corporate brass who make things happen.

There are other risks within the stock market beyond that of price or rising and falling markets. There is the risk of obsolescence—of corporate management or products. Things go out of style. LP records became rapidly outdated when the compact disk (CD) came into its own. The Telex is now a dinosaur, having been replaced by the FAX machine.

There is risk in too much of a good thing. The first discount stores were highly successful. Soon they became chains, then more chains. After a while there were too many of them and lots went under. If an industry appears to be "the rage," stay away. Political shifts can add risk, too. It's one thing to make pharmaceuticals in England, France, or Germany. It's quite another to mine copper in Peru, drill oil in Indonesia, or refine chrome in Zimbabwe.

Politicians are important at home, too. Electric utilities know this all too well. All of them have to appeal to various governmental agencies for rate increases. The company with a friendly regulatory climate is usually a much better investment than one in the opposite situation. Similarly, think twice before investing in an industry whose product runs counter to national policy. Producers of nuclear generators, asbestos, and some chemicals have suffered as a result of this in recent years. Last, remember, politicians have an unnerving way of reversing themselves, to the endless discomfort of some companies and their shareholders.

No discussion of risk is complete without an avuncular admonition to common stock buyers that life itself, as well as the stock market, is risky. Don't worry about a sharp drop in the Dow. Don't be rattled by the television anchorman's sonorous announcement on the evening news that "stocks fell sharply today on Wall Street." Just remember that if you buy the "best," stay reasonably diversified, and hold for the long pull, you are bound to win. The country is growing, the economy is expanding, and our leading companies are going right along, too. So also will their shareholders, with ever-rising dividend income and stock prices.

PART II

Evolving Markets

CHAPTER 3

The 1980s, a Period of Change

CHANGE WAS THE ICON of the 1980s. During this decade the Communist party was overturned in one Eastern European country after another. Congress enacted four major tax revisions, deregulation was in vogue, the stock market plummeted 508 points in one day, the federal debt surpassed $3 trillion, and for the first time, human consumption of oats surpassed that by horses.

The government split Ma Bell into seven pieces, yet leveraged buyouts were merging other companies at a fever pitch. Although the savings and loan industry was in a shambles that will cost taxpayers more than $500 billion, the economy managed an unprecedented peacetime period of recession-free growth lasting over seven years. Some of the new millionaires of Wall and LaSalle streets ended the decade by swapping business suits for prison garb. Unbridled greed was their undoing. Another trend that gained momentum in the '80s and continues in the present decade is foreign investment in, and ownership of, America.

Winners and Losers

The decade began with the prime rate hitting 21 percent and ended with it at half that level and heading lower. Late in 1986, the prime stayed at a low 7.5 percent for six months. Gold followed a similar path, starting the decade at its all-time peak of $850, ending it 50 percent lower. The Dow Jones Industrial Average more than tripled in those 10 years, moving from under 900 to within touching distance of 3,000. In spite of the crash in 1987, those investors who rode out the storm by staying in their stocks did very well. Some made spectacular gains—Marion Merrell Dow was up over 4,000 percent for the decade, while Wal-Mart Stores and Lin Broadcasting did almost as well. Excellent though less extraordinary gains were achieved throughout the market. The compound annual return on the S&P 500 was 17.4 percent. Small company stocks enjoyed a compound annual return of 16.1 percent, while stock mutual funds gained 15.3 percent annually from 1980 to 1990. By comparison the compound annual growth rate was a modest 5.1 percent for inflation and 8.9 percent for residential real estate.

Because the rate of inflation slowed, oil and precious metals stocks were losers rather than winners during the period. The taming of inflation was also a contributing factor in slowing the pace of real estate price escalation.

Wall Street wasn't the only stock market to sparkle. Market indexes in Japan, Sweden, Italy, and Denmark were all up more than 500 percent in the decade. In the United Kingdom, Belgium, France, and Spain the gains were in the 300 to 400 percent range. For the U.S. investor, currency exchange rates can alter overseas investment results in either direction. For example, the Hong Kong market was up 269 percent between the end of 1979 and 1989, but in U.S. dollars, that gain translated to only 132 percent. Conversely, the Japanese market increased 567 percent, but this would be equal to a 1,000 percent rise in U.S. dollars.

Participate and Profit

On the whole, individuals didn't participate in the growth of the securities markets during the 1980s. According to Federal Reserve figures, only 19.6 percent of U.S. households held stocks in 1988, compared with 43.4 percent in 1968. However, indirect investment, through pension funds, did increase—from $800 billion in 1980 to $2,350 trillion in 1989. Many of those hardy souls who continued to be direct participants in the stock market through the 1980s were scared off by Black Monday in October 1987. The institutional dominance of the market, the exaggeration of normal market swings when program trades kicked in, and the distortions created by concurrent option and futures expiration dates left the individual investor out in the cold.

Market traders and institutional investors tend to move in concert, dumping large blocks of stock when company earnings are less robust than anticipated. Despite these roller-coaster rides, long-term individual investors who can steel themselves to ignore the market's ups and downs, who buy and hold, generally achieve excellent results. A $1,000 investment in General Electric at the beginning of the decade was worth $4,800 at its end. In addition, dividends generated a yield of 3 percent or more for each of those 10 years. A similar investment in Merck, the largest U.S. drug maker, was valued at $6,600 on December 31, 1989; General Mills at $5,846; H. J. Heinz at $12,000; and Walt Disney at $10,000.

Merger Mania

The merger fever began in earnest in 1984, when takeovers amounted to $16 billion. By 1988—the peak year— some $576.5 billion worth of deals were announced. The following year mergers in progress had dropped to $388.3 billion. Of those, $6.5 billion or 158 transactions involved foreign companies buying U.S.-based corporations. The largest of the takeover companies, Kohlberg, Kravis, Roberts & Co. (KKR) acquired 35 companies over a 14-year period. KKR spent $303 billion to buy RJR Nabisco, Owens-Illinois, Safeway, Beatrice, Jim Walter, and Stop & Shop. According to one study, mergers and stock buybacks shrank equity markets by 4 percent in 1988 alone. To defend against takeovers many companies repurchase their own shares. Between 1985 and 1990, $48 billion worth of shares had been repurchased in 347 stock buyback programs. There will be more on the ramifications of mergers and the debt used to finance them in Chapter 4.

Tax Changes, a Constant

Starting with the Economic Recovery Tax Act of 1981 (ERTA), four other major acts were passed during the decade: the Tax Equity and Fiscal Responsibility Act of 1982 (TEFRA), the Tax Reform Acts of 1984 and 1986, and the Technical and Miscellaneous Revenue Act of 1988 (TAMRA). Five less ambitious revenue measures were also enacted, some to correct the most glaring errors in previous, hastily enacted legislation and others to raise additional revenues.

Unfortunately, a constantly changing Tax Code does little to encourage long-term investment. A real estate project that appears to have economic merit when conceived may have lost that profit edge by the time it is completed because of one or more changes in the Tax Code.

Most of the tax revisions in the 1980s had a negative impact on investors of all types—business, real estate, and corporate. The securities investor lost the capital gains rate advantage. He also stood to lose at least part of the deduction for interest paid to finance those investments. The real estate investor could no longer offset all of his rental losses against ordinary income. Real estate developers involved in low-income housing and historic rehabilitations suddenly lost part or all of the liberal tax advantages that had been factored into their plans. Businesses were first given tax credits, then denied them. Depreciation rules were liberalized, only to be tightened again. Estate plans that had been put in place for the future had to be redrawn, then revised again.

Changes in tax rules will most surely continue as long as any tax benefits remain for Congress to eliminate. This is one area where change itself is the constant.

The Selling of America

High interest rates, an expanding economy, a rising stock market, and a strong dollar attracted more than $1 trillion in foreign investments to the United States during the 1980s.

Stocks, bonds, real estate, and corporations became the property of foreign nationals, particularly the British and Japanese. Because of prohibitive real estate prices at home, the Japanese have been major buyers of properties in the United States, especially in California. In 1989, Japanese companies and private individuals had direct investments of close to $70 billion in the United States, up from only $5 billion in 1980.

At the end of the decade, Western Europeans (companies and individuals) had direct investments in the United States worth $262 billion, while Canadians had $31 billion, and Latin Americans had over $21 billion. All told, direct foreign investments in the United States had reached $625 billion, with $135 billion of it in U.S. Treasury securities. Foreign governments held $337 billion of U.S. securities.

Although the average American is less aware of foreign ownership of securities than of real estate or companies, foreign holdings in U.S. stocks and bonds represent a considerably larger amount of money. With the economy moving sluggishly and the national debt reaching staggering proportions, these outside investors are a very necessary addition to the economy. When those funds dry up, the lack of buyers at Treasury auctions drives up interest rates, compounding the potential problems of inflation and recession. These factors, which continue to plague the nation in the last decade of the century, are further complicated by the recent war in the Gulf.

CHAPTER 4

The Financial and Real Economy, into the 1990s

THE FINANCIAL MARKETS of the 1990s bear little resemblance to the markets of 15, 10, or even 5 years ago. The wave of deregulation that swept the markets in the 1980s, leaving behind it new financial products and techniques, increasingly leveraged corporations, and failed financial institutions, is being reevaluated and reassessed. Advances in communications technology have bound regional and national financial markets more tightly together. For investors, the computer has become more relevant and the clock less so.

Radical Changes in the Real Economy

The economic environment underpinning the financial markets also has changed dramatically. The pace of technological change has accelerated with biologically based products and processes promising the same kind of quantum advance that attended the inventions a generation or more ago of the transistor, ferrite-core memory, and the semiconductor. New technological information is more quickly diffused, placing a premium on research and development, and tending to create more homogeneous industrial structures in the United States, Europe, and Japan. Technological ad-

40

vances also have permitted better control of inventories and, along with a continuing evolution of national economies from manufacturing toward service industries (which have no inventories), have made the business cycle a less frequently observed phenomenon.

Technological diffusion and the completion of the post–World War II catch-up phase have propelled first Japan and more recently a reunified Germany and greater Europe to the fore, matching and sometimes exceeding the traditional economic and financial power of the United States. The European Community is forging a new economic and political identity, while Eastern Europe and the Soviet Union are in the throes of an even more radical transformation. Meanwhile, the newly industrializing countries (NICs), particularly in East and South Asia, are continuing their development surge. Latin America still languishes under a mountain of debt, while Africa seems to be falling farther and farther behind.

The economic promise of events in Europe had been tempered, however, by the intransigence of the leadership of the People's Republic of China. And with the Gulf War, the availability and price of energy became subject to speculative excesses, both on the up and down sides. Another concern, that for the environment, has reappeared as worries over global warming, depletion of the ozone layer, and a massive oil spill in the Persian Gulf have mounted.

Finally, the economic growth in the industrial world is increasingly constrained by the lack of skilled labor, the consequence of the baby bust that followed the postwar baby boom. With population growth still spurting in the developing world, pressures to solve the industrial world's labor shortage via immigration are increasing. Immigration-fueled growth also would provide the income to care for the increasingly aged population of the industrialized countries.

Financial Deregulation—Causes

Against this background of profound change in the real, goods-and-services economy, the domestic and international financial systems are seeking to reestablish some sense of equilibrium after the pell-mell rush to deregulation during the 1980s, and in the wake of the global stock market crash of October 1987.

The deregulation binge in a variety of industries generally derived its impetus from the poor economic performance that characterized the 1970s. In particular, in the United States financial inflation in the mid-1970s resulted in the inability of regulated interest rates to offer investors a fair return on their money. Via the Depository Institutions Deregulation and Monetary Control Act (DIDMCA) of 1980 and the Depository Institutions (Garn–St. Germain) Act of 1982, interest and loan rate ceilings were lifted and the line of business restrictions that separated commercial banks from thrift institutions (savings and loans) was blurred.

Financial Deregulation—Consequences

As in other deregulated markets, the change in the law was quickly followed by a rush of banks into the thrifts' mortgage lending business and of the thrifts into the banks' traditional consumer and industrial loan business. Inevitably, because the number of new entrants exceeded the number who could make sustainable long-run profits, many failed. Part of the problem was the difficulty the thrifts have had in matching the maturities of their assets and liabilities. Because they borrow short and lend long, thrifts have always been vulnerable to rising interest rates. Many thrifts and some banks sought to become more profitable by taking more risks—investing their assets in real estate and junk bonds.

So-called *junk bonds* are simply non–investment-grade securities. They rose to prominence in the 1980s as a vehicle to finance often hostile takeovers and leveraged buyouts (LBOs—purchase of a corporation by its managers or employees using debt). In an LBO or a takeover, the bonds are issued in conjunction with the sale of the issuing firms. Repayment is intended to come from selling some of the acquired firm's assets after it is restructured by its new owners to increase profitability. For some time, analysts maintained that the default rate on junk securities was sufficiently low that investors came out ahead owning these high-yield bonds. But after the junk-bond market collapsed in the fall of 1989, following a plunge in the stock market, it became clear that only the savviest of investors should own non–investment-grade bonds.

Similarly, the oil price slump of 1986 exposed the excessively risky character of real estate investments in the Southwest. As the decade ended, the overbuilding of commercial structures and diminished demographic support for residential housing caused the real estate slump to spread nationwide.

Deposit Insurance and the S&L Crisis

Some S&L and bank failures were expected as part of the deregulation process. What Congress and President Reagan did not fully appreciate was the excessive risk-taking incentives created by federal deposit insurance, which of course remained in force as it had since 1935. Depositors sure of getting their money back (up to $100,000; if you had more, you simply spread it around among several banks) paid little attention to the investment policies of institutions where they placed their money. Federal appropriations for bank examination also were insufficient to meet the needs of a newly deregulated industry.

With no check on risk taking, the number of thrift institutions and banks that failed far exceeded initial estimates. The result: the savings and loan crisis, in which the federal government has taken over hundreds of failed institutions, paid off depositors, and tried to recover its losses through the sale of these institutions' often worthless assets. The bill to the taxpayer, as we mentioned in Chapter 3, is estimated at over $500 billion over 30 years. Fears that a similar catastrophe could affect the banking industry are given substance by the currently rapid rate at which the FDIC fund is being depleted.

Junk bonds are only the most visible evidence of the additional debt taken on in the 1980s by households, corporations, and the American government. Unquestionably, a more deregulated financial structure has made this possible. Whether the new debt levels are excessive depends on the time-honored principle of ability to service the debt. This in turn depends on how the borrowed purchasing power is put to use.

For equity investors, a higher level of debt in the companies in their portfolios means the potential for greater returns. It also means greater risk, since earnings per share fluctuate more with changing economic conditions, owing to the fixed-charge nature of the interest obligations. For such high-leverage firms, high-quality investment research will pay even greater dividends.

More Volatile Equity Markets

Another outcome of deregulation is the increased numbers of new animals in the financial product menagerie. A number of these are described elsewhere in this volume. However, several of them have achieved notoriety as a consequence of their widespread use by professional money managers, and their perceived culpability in the market volatility in the latter part of the 1980s.

One of the so-called culprits—program trading—is the use of computer programs to place buy and sell orders for large numbers of stocks. With the professional money manager able to execute huge transactions with electronic speed, many market watchers fear that the individual investor will be whipsawed by the excess market volatility caused by one program triggering another.

The tandem use of two program strategies—portfolio insurance and index arbitrage—was a destabilizing influence on the stock market during the 1987 crash. Portfolio insurers, seeing stock prices drop, would sell stock index futures, driving down their price. This made the S&P 500 futures cheap relative to the underlying stocks (in the index), which triggered the stock index arbitrageurs' programs. They bought futures and sold the underlying stocks, pushing stock prices further down. This decline in stock prices set in motion a second round of selling by portfolio insurance programs; that unleashed another purchase of index futures and sale of stocks by the arbitrageurs, and so on.

When all this selling activity hit the exchanges, the antiquated and undercapitalized specialist system didn't have enough liquidity to continue to make a market in the affected stocks, so trading ground to a chaotic halt. Only the Federal Reserve's timely interjection of credit into the markets, and some support buying on the Tokyo exchange, prevented a complete meltdown. Portfolio insurance has lost its luster as an investment product for the simple reason that selling in a down market works only if no one else is selling. But index arbitrage continues, amidst debates over whether it contributes to market volatility.

Certainly there continue to be free-fall days in the market, when the bellwether Dow drops 50 to 100 points. In mid-1990, the NYSE adopted a series of formal "circuit breakers" that provide for a limited time-out on the exchange in the event of a sharp fall in the Dow. Encouragingly, these are coordinated with circuit breakers on the futures markets in Chicago. Thus, in normal times the efficiency benefits of index arbitrage are allowed to occur, while in too volatile sessions both markets are given a cooling-off period.

Despite these reassuring developments, the markets remain subject to abrupt and frequent moves. The already cited specialist system is one reason; it is likely to be replaced during this decade by more computerized means of trading. A second source of rapid movement is globalization of the securities markets. Capital can flow into and out of American markets at a moment's notice. And while stocks and futures circuit breakers are now somewhat coordinated, the harmonization of national stock market regulation across countries is in its infancy.

Market Regulation Fragmented

Also worrisome is the continuing fragmentation of market regulation in the United States, with Chicago adopting the free market point of view and New York favoring a more regulatory approach. The Securities and Exchange Commission, which is more allied with New York, has been seeking to wrest regulatory control of stock index futures away from the Commodity Futures Trading Corporation, Chicago's parent.

For the buy-and-hold investor, one following the recommendations in this volume, the additional stock market volatility of recent years is an annoyance, but little more than that. Under the pressure of continuing improvements in telecommunications technology and the growing interdependence of national economies, the markets will continue to instantly reflect the ebb and flow of financial and economic news. The deregulatory excesses of the 1980s are likely to be followed by a period of regulatory retrenchment in the 1990s, in which political considerations, as well as economic ones, will ensure that the interests of the small investor receive a hearing.

Policy Issues in the Decade Ahead

Capital markets in the 1990s will be influenced by a series of regulatory compromises, reflecting conflicting tensions of globalization, efficiency in the allocations of scarce savings, the enormous added financial burden of the recent Gulf War and the rebuilding of Iraq and Kuwait, and the need to rectify the excesses of the 1980s.

In the United States, debate over the repeal of the Glass-Steagall Act and the advent of nationwide banking will dominate the political agenda. In Japan, the Glass-Steagall analogue is called Article 65; there too, a dissolution of the barriers between commercial and investment banking is under consideration. In both nations, however, hard times in the securities business and the troubles of commercial banks have taken legislative action off the fast track. Nonetheless, developments in Europe may force both the United States and Japan to act sooner rather than later.

Financial Integration of Europe

The 1982 initiative in the European Community includes a number of directives aimed at realizing a single market in financial services across Europe. In particular, European authorities are looking to apply some form of reciprocity rule, under which foreign banks would have the same privileges in Europe as European banks enjoy in the foreigners' home markets. Under the German example of universal banking, in which commercial and investment activities are commingled, the EC may move more quickly than either Washington or Tokyo to break down the walls separating the two kinds of activities. If it does so, America and Japan will be forced, in some fashion, to follow suit—though existing foreign banks in Europe will be "grandfathered."

The European Community is the scene of another grand financial experiment, monetary union. Since 1979, the European Monetary System has covered a portion of Europe's economy with its "parity grid" of nearly fixed exchange rates between the major currencies on the Continent. The EC's unit of account, the ECU (European Currency Unit)—essentially a basket of European currencies—has come to be widely used by consumers and firms alike in denominating claims and liabilities. Now the EC is planning to move further along the road to monetary union, either by replacing all EC currencies with the ECU or by having it circulate publicly in parallel with existing currencies.

The willingness of the nations of Europe to subordinate their economic policies to the direction of a higher, "Euro-Fed"–style authority reflects the fact that in large part, in the 1980s, the growing integration of Europe's economies has meant that economic policy is relatively powerless to influence employment and output anyway. In the case of the European Community, it is more than conceivable that the prospective steps toward monetary union will lead to a new, more powerful political unit. One thing is sure: The prospect of a more competitive Europe has caused multinational firms in America and Japan to rethink their global strategies.

One World?

The growing integration of all the economies of the industrialized world has led to greater monetary and exchange rate policy cooperation in recent years. The Plaza Agreement of

September 1985 found central banks working in concert to push the overvalued dollar lower. The Louvre Accord some 17 months later signaled their belief that the process had gone far enough. After the October 1987 stock market crash, American, Japanese, and European authorities again coordinated their monetary policy responses. And in response to the continuing international debt crisis, they have promulgated a harmonized set of bank capital regulations, scheduled to take full effect in 1993.

While coordination in matters financial has become more typical in the past several years, protracted debate and grudging concessions have been the norm in affairs commercial. The global restructuring of production in the past decade has kindled protectionist sentiment in North America and Europe. To blunt these concerns, legislators have passed tougher anti–free-trade laws. The latest round of trade liberalization talks under the auspices of the General Agreement on Tariffs and Trade (GATT)—the so-called Uruguay Round —brought less agreement among the parties than had been expected.

The lack of success in this multilateral setting has forced national governments—most notably the United States and Japan in their celebrated Structural Impediments and Initiative (SII) talks—to resort to bilateral means to settle trade disputes. Here too, despite politicians' claims of victory, success has been limited and protectionist pressures remain.

The global economy of the 1990s will thus be an environment of change and upheaval, with competitive forces more Darwinian than before and national political and regulatory authorities scrambling to keep pace. Investors who understand these new international realities and who possess a global outlook stand to profit handsomely from the world's continuing rush toward economic development.

PART III

Your Investment Alternatives

CHAPTER 5

Equity Investments: "A Piece of the Action"

IF EVER THERE was an affordable and convenient way for most of us to participate directly in the free enterprise system, it is through the acquisition and holding of common stocks. Your single share of General Electric represents an actual ownership stake in that industrial behemoth. As even a most fractional owner, you enjoy certain rights—and you assume certain risks. We'll get into those rights and risks in this chapter as we explore the pros and cons of investment in common stocks. We'll also introduce you to ways other than common stock ownership to establish equity positions in a company: preferred stock, convertibles, warrants, rights, and put and call options.

The Concept of Ownership

Let's expand a bit on the ownership concept, zeroing in first on common stocks. Your share of common stock represents something of intrinsic value, a piece of equity in the company. As that intrinsic value rises and falls, so does the worth of your investment. You have committed a portion of your wealth to the fortunes of the company. If you have chosen the company wisely—or fortuitously—each dollar invested has the potential of rising exponentially in value as the company prospers. You are not merely being paid for the privilege of letting the company borrow your dollars, as you are with bonds.

Because your investment is in something of inherent value, you have in effect untied it from monetary value. When you convert it back to monetary value by selling it, you will get what it is worth in current dollars—or at least what a buyer perceives as its worth. This is completely without regard to what it was worth in dollars when you acquired it. If the company has been growing as fast as the economy in general, or faster, the intrinsic value likewise will have grown. The dollars you receive when you sell will have buying power equal to or greater than that of the dollars you used to purchase the investment.

Contrast that with the situation when you merely lend your dollars to the company via purchase of a corporate bond. In effect, when you redeem your "loan," you get the same number of dollars back. In the meantime the buying power of those dollars may have shrunk, leaving you with less valuable dollars.

It is important that you have a firm grasp of the equity concept and comprehend the difference between being an owner and being a lender in order to understand the value of common stocks as a hedge against inflation. By being an owner, you tie your investment more closely to economic conditions, whereas by being a lender you keep your dollar tied to a post sunk into the ground on the day you made the loan. Lending can go only as far as its short leash allows.

You should also understand the risk-reward differences between ownership and lending. As an owner, just as you stand to gain when the business prospers, you stand to lose your stake if it should collapse. You are also at the mercy of the market when you sell your equity, for, in the final analysis, it is worth what the market *says* it is worth, regardless of its intrinsic value.

As a lender, your assets are protected against such loss (unless, of course, the business fails completely and defaults on the loan), but you replace that risk with the risk that the worth of your dollar and what it earns will not keep pace with rising prices.

Common Stocks: Rights and Risks

A corporation offers shares of its common stock to the public as a means of raising capital. If it is a company's initial offering, or if it is an offering of previously unissued shares, it is called a primary issue. Shares that are outstanding and offered in a block by one or more holders are referred to as secondary offerings; proceeds of these do not accrue to the company. In return for your investment, you receive a stock certificate that along with providing evidence of ownership has other legal characteristics. The certificate contains a serial number, the name of the registrar or transfer agent, and the par or stated value of the stock. It should be noted here that in the case of common stocks, par value has little, if any, relationship to the market value of the stock. The certificate also informs you that as a shareholder you have no financial obligation to the corporation. This means that should some corporate liability arise, that liability would not extend to you.

Along with certain legal protection, you enjoy various rights as a shareholder. First, unless you hold stock that is specifically designated as nonvoting, you have voting rights, meaning you are entitled to vote on such things as the selection of an accounting firm and merger proposals. Most of these matters are dealt with at a company's annual meeting. You may either enter your vote at the corporation's annual meeting or use the proxy statement you receive by mail to register your preferences. The proxy statement is a legal document that permits another (a proxy) to vote for you. It is mailed to the stockholder, along with information pertaining to the particular matters to be voted on.

As a shareholder you are also entitled to receive dividends on a pro rata basis. A corporation is not legally obligated to pay a dividend on its common stock, but when the directors declare a dividend, every shareholder receives an equal amount per share of the stock.

Also, as a stockholder you retain the right to protect your proportionate interest in the corporation. For instance, if you own 100 shares of a company that at some point, say, decides to increase the amount of its outstanding stock by 15 percent, you have a preemptive right to purchase 15 additional shares. If you decide to exercise this right, your initial proportionate share of ownership in the corporation has not been reduced despite the increase in the number of shares outstanding. Those rights, by the way, have a value of their own; should you choose not to exercise them, you can sell them to someone else. This usually must be done within a certain time or the rights expire. More on rights and their cousins, warrants, later.

Finally, although you have no legal financial obligation to the corporation, in cases of bankruptcy or liquidation the corporation has an obligation to its common stockholders. In such cases, the corporation's first responsibility is to its creditors—to those who have lent it money. After they have been paid, the holders of preferred stock are entitled to the par or stated value of their shares; that's one reason it is called "preferred" stock. If anything remains, it is then divided among the common stockholders on a pro rata basis.

Picking the Right Stocks

OK, you ask, now that I know what a common stock is, how do I go about choosing from the thousands of stocks available? How do I determine in which corporations I want to own shares?

The answer is the key to successful investing—choosing stocks that meet your individual investment needs. It is not an altogether simple task, as any professional analyst, portfolio manager, or investment advisor will tell you. However, in the case of common stocks, understanding a few basic characteristics can help you make your investment decisions.

First, you should know that the two most important aspects of a common stock's value are quality and earnings. Determining the quality of a common stock is more difficult than determining the quality of, say, a bond. But a common stock is usually graded on the basis of the corporation's historical earnings performance as well as its future earnings outlook. Has it shown healthy growth in the past? Have earnings been stable? What are its prospects in the years ahead? The stock's performance in the market is an important criterion, too. Does its price tend to remain relatively stable or does it tend to be volatile?

Watch Dividend Performance

Of more than passing interest to the common stockholder, naturally, is the company's performance on dividends. As we said earlier, a corporation is not legally required to pay dividends on its common stock. However, since the regular payment of dividends increases the attractiveness of its stock, a corporation tries to provide them whenever possible. The most common form is a cash payment. Such payments are usually made quarterly, but they can also be made more or less frequently. The corporation's directors decide how much will be paid.

At this point it might be helpful to define some of the terms that are used in conjunction with dividend payments. First, the directors *declare* a dividend of a specific amount. The dividend is said to be payable to *holders of record* (in other words, owners of the stock) as of a certain date. The *payment date* is the actual date that you, as a shareholder, will receive the dividend. The *ex-dividend date* determines whether the buyer or the seller receives the dividend.

As a shareholder, you should also be aware of two other types of distribution: the *stock dividend* and the *stock split*. Neither of these actually changes your proportionate ownership in the corporation. A stock dividend is stated as a percent dividend. For example, a corporation declares a 2 percent stock dividend. If your initial holding amounted to 100 shares, you would own 102 shares after the dividend was paid.

How Stock Splits Work

Now take the case of a stock split. Say a corporation declares a two-for-one split. This means that if you were originally holding 100 shares you would have 200 shares after the split. But since all the other shareholders would likewise have twice as many shares, your relative ownership position would remain the same. The value of your investment would not change, either, for the new shares would trade at half the price of the old ones. Reducing this trading price, in fact, is the main reason for stock splits; a corporation generally uses a split to trim the stock's price to what it considers to be a more marketable trading range. It is important to keep in mind that when you receive a stock dividend or when your stock is split, your interest in the corporation has been neither increased nor decreased. Also, the total value of a company's stock has not been affected, nor has its earning power been diminished.

How to "Value" a Stock

How can you place a specific "value" on a common stock? How do you determine at what price you should buy? When can it be considered overvalued and best sold? Let's talk more about a point we mentioned earlier—the discrepancy that sometimes exists between a stock's "intrinsic" value and the value that the stock market places on it. In determining a stock's intrinsic value, you look at such things as the corporation's balance sheet (assets, liabilities), its debt, capital requirements, earnings, dividends, future prospects, and management. In choosing a stock, you try to pick one whose intrinsic value appears greater than the value placed on it by the market. Other factors sometimes used to evaluate a stock are book value (net worth), liquidating value, and price-earnings ratios.

Be Aware of the Risks

Let's now talk more about some of the risks involved in investing in common stocks. One of the largest is also the most difficult to combat, for it frequently is fickle, unpredictable, and illogical. That factor is market psychology. As a rule, prices trend upward when investors are optimistic about the economy, politics, or social conditions. Declines occur when investors take a pessimistic stance. Shifts in the direction of the stock market often reflect a change in investor psychology.

A particular stock's price also will be affected by such things as earnings, dividends, and future prospects. The risk is that these elements change and that unforeseeable events occur. For example, within days of the announcement of the gas leak at Union Carbide's plant in Bhopal, India, the stock had lost 40 percent of its market value. More recently stocks have been bounced around by takeovers—rumored, successful, or abandoned.

So you can see how abruptly the tide may turn for certain corporations. Of course the higher the quality of the stock, the lower the inherent risk. High-quality stocks tend to be much less volatile, and while "quick" profits will probably not be forthcoming, what is saved on the nerves might be worth it to some investors.

Preferred Stocks

The more conservative investor might be better able to sleep at night with preferred stocks instead of common. Preferred stocks reside in a sort of no-man's-land between bonds and common stocks. Some would say these hybrids embrace the least favorable characteristics of both, for they have neither the enforceable claim of a bond nor the share in profits of a common stock. Although preferred stock is an equity security representing ownership in a corporation, holders do not have a vote (except under certain conditions), nor do they have preemptive rights.

"Preferreds" must have some redeeming features, or they long ago would have passed into oblivion. For individual investors, that appeal is seated in the generous returns usually available in preferreds. Though the dividend may not enjoy the same guarantee that bond interest does, it takes preference over common stock payments. This is a right that usually is stated in the issuing company's charter, as is the right of the preferred holder to corporate assets in liquidation ahead of the common stockholder. But for the corporate investor, new-money preferreds (those issued since 1942) offer a tax break. In order to avoid double taxation, a taxable corporation may deduct 80 percent of dividend income derived from investments in other taxable corporations.

Adjustable-rate preferreds, a more recent innovation, have proved very popular with corporate investors. These hybrid securities pay dividends that are tied to a Treasury index and are adjusted quarterly. The payment rate has a floor below which it won't fall and a ceiling determining the highest amount that will be paid. So these preferreds, although still classed as fixed-rate investments, pay a variable rate.

The market behavior of straight preferreds and adjustable-rate preferreds is much the same as that of bonds; both are fixed-income investments and therefore are interest-rate-sensitive. This is not the case with convertible preferreds. Their market price pattern more closely follows that of the common stock because they may be exchanged for shares of common. We mentioned above that preferred shareholders in certain cases may be allowed a vote. That generally happens when the preferred dividend has been omitted for a stated number of quarters. Still other types of preferred stock may accumulate unpaid dividends that have to be cleared before common dividends are paid.

More recently, utilities—the principal issuers of this genre—have offered preferred stocks with sinking funds, giving holders the illusion of eventually getting their money back. Under the terms of the sinking fund, the issuing corporation will retire a stated percentage or dollar amount of the total issue each year until the entire issue is retired. This fund may be satisfied by open-market purchases made when the issue is trading well below par value. The shares are held in the company treasury to satisfy future sinking-fund requirements. Thus, a shareholder could hold the preferred to the bitter end without a single share's being called early. Of course he would be free at any time to sell the shares on the open market.

Rights and Warrants

In counterpoint to the staid preferreds is an array of more speculative equity-related investments—rights, warrants, and options. Let's look first at rights and warrants. As is true of common stocks, a corporation issues rights and warrants to obtain additional capital. To obtain it quickly, a rights offering is usually made. Under the terms of a rights offering, a shareholder is entitled to purchase a limited amount of additional stock at a preferential subscription price during a fixed period of time (usually within a month of issuance). During this period the stockholder can either exercise his rights and buy the stock, or he can sell his rights to others, who, in turn, may exercise them or sell them. Or, if he is careless, he can merely allow the rights to expire unexercised or unsold. Money down the drain. It is in the buying and selling of rights and warrants that the speculation occurs.

Warrants, like rights, give the shareholder the privilege of purchasing additional shares of stock at a fixed price for a specific period of time (usually several years in the future). As mentioned previously, common stock prices tend to fluctuate widely over a period of time. There is considerable risk involved in trading either rights or warrants, but because rights involve a shorter period of time, they are of a less speculative nature.

Here is an example to help you understand how warrants work and how they are evaluated by the market. XYZ Corporation's common stock has a current market price of $40 a share. XYZ issues warrants that permit owners to purchase one share of common at $35. At these prices the warrant has a theoretical value of $5 (current market price of common minus subscription price). If the common should double in price to $80 a share, the warrant should be worth $45 ($80 less $35). As you can see, a far greater percentage gain would have been made if you had owned the warrant (800 percent) than if you had held the common (100 percent).

In rising markets warrants generally sell at premiums over their theoretical value, reflecting their greater leverage. By the same token, if the common begins to fall, the warrant generally falls at a more rapid clip.

As a buyer of warrants, you assume all the risks without the benefits of the common stock ownership. You are entitled to no dividends; you have no voting rights or any of the other rights of the common stockholder. In other words, you do not participate in the ownership of a corporation. Any return you receive on this type of investment is based solely on price appreciation.

Puts and Calls

Now let's look at another method of investing also linked to the price action of common stocks: put and call options. A put is an option to *sell* a specified number of common shares at a specified price (the striking price) during a specified period. A call is an option to *buy* a specified number of shares at a specified price within a specified period of time. Put and call options may be both sold (written) and bought, and we discuss them in greater detail in Chapter 14.

The major attraction of option trading is the great leverage it provides. An option can be bought or sold at a fraction of the cost of its underlying stock (usually 3 to 8 percent), and small swings in the price of that stock can generate larger gains or losses for the option trader. The field, therefore, has been a magnet for speculators.

But conservative investors, if they know what they are doing, can make use of options, too: in guaranteeing market position and obtaining stock at what may amount to a discount price, in hedging against unpredictable turns in an uncertain market, and in generating greater income.

As a general rule, we think your best bet in staking out a position in the equity markets is through common stocks. In the next two chapters we give you more specific information about how to find the stocks you need to fulfill your investment aims.

CHAPTER 6

How to Find Growth Stocks

LET'S ASSUME THAT at this point in your life you do not need any extra income, and you are beginning to think about building funds for the kids' college education and your own retirement. With the evils of inflation hacking away at your hard-earned savings, you want today's invested dollars to grow sufficiently to meet your future needs. What you are looking for is a good growth stock.

"Fine," you say. "How do I tell good growth stocks from any other stocks? Where do I look for them? How do I evaluate them?"

What Makes a Growth Stock

Let's take a look at some of the characteristics that distinguish a growth stock from the other general categories of stocks—those that emphasize dividend payments (income stocks) and those whose prices tend to rise and fall in line with the economic cycle (cyclicals). For a start, we can tell you that growth stocks are generally found in companies that offer products and services with particularly favorable long-term growth potential. Their managements tend to be aggressive and are constantly searching for new products and eyeing growing markets. They place a good deal of emphasis on research and new-product development. Also, they generally exhibit an ability to achieve consistent and above-average sales and earnings growth.

On the other hand, dividends may be modest because a good portion of earnings is plowed back into the company rather than paid out to investors. It should be pointed out, however, that a low yield today could mean a higher return tomorrow. By reinvesting its earnings, the company hopes to increase its profits over the years, which in turn means higher dividends for investors. For instance, between 1975 and 1990 Walt Disney increased its dividend payment at a compound annual rate of 22 percent, yet the stock's current yield remains below 1 percent.

Growth Stocks and Economic Trends

One of the most difficult tasks in choosing a growth stock is knowing what areas of the economy do in fact possess unusual growth potential. It's difficult, but by no means impossible. In the absence of a crystal ball, you have in your daily newspaper one of your best information sources. What phases of life does it discuss the most? What are people talking about? What trends are developing in our society? What deep-rooted changes are emerging?

One increasingly obvious example of an expanding technology is the area of data processing. Automatic Data Processing, a $1 billion concern, is the largest independent purveyor of data services in the country. Currently in its twenty-eighth successive year of uninterrupted growth, ADP has succeeded largely by concentrating on the service sectors of the economy—banks, insurance agents, securities brokers, auto and truck dealerships, and repair shops. The company provides payroll, accounting, reporting, and other services to small- and medium-sized businesses on a client-to-client basis. Its revenue stream is steady and continually growing, and its markets far from saturated.

The company's success—earnings have grown at close to an 18 percent compound rate in the 15 years from 1975 to

1990—has not gone unnoticed. The stock is widely held by institutions and its price-earnings ratio is above average.

So, through just this one example—and there are countless others—you see the rewards that can be reaped from finding an area with promise and being patient enough to stay with it.

Timing Your Buys

With growth stocks, as with any other investment, timing is an important key to success. You have to determine the best time to buy—and to sell. While there is no sure formula, a few considerations should prove helpful. The ideal time to buy is when a company is still in its early stages of development. There is, of course, more than average risk involved, since emerging companies are smaller and less known, and their success has not been firmly established. But their stocks do tend to be more reasonably priced than those of companies that have carved a niche.

On the other hand, a company's chronological age is not necessarily significant. Some well-established corporations fit the criteria for a growth stock because of their proven ability to introduce new product lines and find new markets. A good example is Philip Morris. For years its growth had been based on cigarette sales. Then in 1969 it embarked on an expansion program, acquiring Miller Brewing. Within a decade this cigarette maker had taken over three more companies—a wine maker, a paper company, and the Seven-Up soft-drink bottler. Philip Morris applied its skills as a marketer of consumer products to these new lines, boosting the company's growth rate from 15 percent to more than 20 percent annually. More recently Philip Morris entered the food-packaging business in a big way, acquiring giant General Foods in 1985 and Kraft in 1988. The company's growth rate over the next few years should continue in the 19 to 21 percent range. This example vividly demonstrates that a company's growth has less to do with its age than its ability to recognize growing product areas and then to capitalize on them.

Of course an investor must be willing to pay a premium for a well-established growth company, such as Abbott Labs, Merck, Procter & Gamble, and Walt Disney, which sold at 25 to 45 times earnings in 1972. But these same companies are also sensitive to market declines—as amply demonstrated by their price-earnings ratios, which fell to around 10 a decade later. The key is to choose a stock with an above-average growth record that is selling at a reasonable multiple of earnings. While this takes a bit of searching, it can be done.

Finding the answers to a few simple questions should make the selection easier. Does the company have a product or service with exceptional long-term potential? Does management reinvest earnings? Is a reasonable return on capital realized? Is capitalization of a size that will allow for future expansion? Does management have a piece of the action via stock ownership? What portion of net goes to research and development? Is the price-earnings multiple reasonable vis-à-vis that of other companies in the industry and its own record and potential? If most of these questions rate a positive answer, you may well have uncovered a worthwhile growth situation.

Timing Your Sells

Even long-term growth stocks should be sold at certain times and in some situations. Performance of the market as a whole is not generally one of the criteria. Major market turns are difficult to spot and they seldom coincide with the tops and bottoms in an individual issue. The October 1987 crash hit all stocks hard, but quality growth stocks recovered to hit new high ground within 24 months. What you should be on the watch for are changes in the prospects for a firm—new competition, new laws, new products. If something in the fundamental outlook for a corporation develops, a switch may be indicated.

There are many examples of this principle at work, but one of the best was Scott Paper back in the 1960s. Scott was the foremost maker of premium tissue and toweling. The company's record was one of dynamic growth. The stock was a blue chip growth favorite and sold at lofty price-earnings ratios. The company had a huge and growing market pretty much to itself. Then Procter & Gamble moved in. It bought a Midwestern outfit named Charmin and took off after Scott's tissue and toweling customers. This shook the Scott management at the time. To have the expert marketers at P&G after its customers would scare anyone.

Here, then, was a perfect example of fundamental change. Scott went from being virtually alone in a rich market to being eyeball to eyeball with one of the world's toughest competitors. The market saw this and the Scott price-earnings multiple tumbled. Investors who sold then were doing the right thing for logical reasons. The fundamentals of Scott had changed.

In conclusion, if your investment objective is to beat inflation, then growth stocks could be the route for you. But remember, patience may be required. The table here illustrates comparative short- and long-term performances of cyclical and growth stocks in the 1980s. As you see, the rewards for perseverance can be great.

| | *Price* | | | *Price* | | |
	Aug. 1982	Oct. 1983	% Change	Jan. 1980	Jan. 1990	% Change
Growth Stocks						
Abbott Laboratories	17	26	+ 53	10	66	+ 560
Capital Cities Comm.	75	150	+100	46	540	+1074
Heinz, H.J.	11	17	+ 55	7	32	+ 357
PepsiCo Inc.	14	12	− 14	8	64	+ 700
Philip Morris	7	9	+ 29	4	40	+ 900
Wal-Mart Stores	4	10	+150	1	47	+4600
Average			+ 79			+ 938
Cyclical Stocks						
Aluminum Co. Amer.	29	46	+ 59	31	70	+ 126
Dow Chemical	16	24	+ 50	20	68	+ 240
General Motors	24	38	+ 58	25	44	+ 74
Int'l Paper	21	28	+ 33	19	51	+ 168
Union Pacific	38	57	+ 50	38	80	+ 111
USX Corp.	18	28	+ 56	17	34	+ 100
Average			+ 51			+ 131

CHAPTER 7

Common Stocks for Income

IN THE PREVIOUS chapter you learned the benefits of investing in growth stocks. But what if your prime objective is income —you're looking for a little extra "bread money"? Many retired people with fixed incomes find themselves in this category. While bonds and preferred stocks are popular investment vehicles for those seeking income and safety, you should not make the mistake of ignoring common stocks as a valuable means of obtaining extra income. Many of these issues provide high current yields and have the potential for future dividend increases as opposed to the fixed returns on bonds and preferreds. They offer the possibility of some capital growth as well.

Although the need for additional income might be of the utmost importance, with the cost of living constantly edging upward, albeit at changing rates, you should not pick a stock solely on the basis of current dividends. You won't gain any ground by purchasing one of today's high yielders if there is little potential for future dividend increases.

Look Beyond Current Yield

There is, of course, more risk involved with a common stock than, say, a bond, but the risk can be reduced by choosing stocks that have exhibited steady and dependable earnings and dividend growth over the years. The key, again, is not just to look at current yield. You must look to the record, too. Is there a long history of consistent dividend payments? What has the dividend growth record been like? What are the prospects for dividend growth in the future? Again, careful attention must be given to price. What is the stock's price-earnings ratio? Is it high or low in terms of current earnings and prospects and in terms of other stocks in its industry? Like any other common stock investment, an income stock should be chosen on the basis of quality and growth, and not just because it is enjoying a high level of current income.

Actually, choosing income stocks is a relatively easy matter compared to selecting growth stocks. First you look for a business that is steady, something that by nature tends to do well despite the prevailing economic climate.

Get a Line on Telephone Stocks

The telephone business is a fair representative of this type of industry. People tend to use the telephone as much in bad times as in good. With the rapid pace of technological progress in the last decade, the communications field is expanding into several new and growing areas—cellular communications, FAX transmission, and mobile telephone systems. Concurrently, the field is experiencing steadily increasing demand for its basic services.

The only major problems the telephone business encounters come from inflation and politics. The former pushes up costs of both labor (through increases in wage levels) and capital (through higher interest rates). Politics enters when the company seeks rate relief from the squeeze of rising costs. In the wake of the consumer movement, regulatory authorities frequently think first of the consumer's reluctance to pay more for telephone service and second, if at all, of the stockholder's right to a fair return on his investment. After all, in the popular lexicon, the user is poor, the stockholder rich. But these problems have been surmounted time and again, so the earnings-dividend experience of telephone companies' shareholders has been passing fair.

Politics also resulted in the 1982 antitrust agreement between American Telephone & Telegraph and the Justice Department. It divided huge Ma Bell into one high-tech communications concern and seven regional telephone holding companies in order to encourage competition in both areas. As a result of the divestiture, income investors have seven more telephone utilities from which to choose.

In addition to the former Bell System affiliates, some of the independent telcos are attractive. Increasingly, telephone utilities are at the forefront of cellular communications both in the United States and overseas. Because this is a high-margined and potentially lucrative field, mergers are frequently used to expand a company's cellular franchise. As a result of this consolidation, some of the independents have been absorbed. So when you are putting together an income portfolio look at all the possibilities. Some well-situated telephone companies are:

ALLTEL Corp.   Southwestern Bell
Bell Atlantic   United Telecommunications
GTE Corp.

Plug into Electric Utilities

Like telephones, electric utilities are attractive choices for income investors. We say this even though they are having trouble these days from environmentalists and from nuclear-plant shutdowns, skyrocketing construction costs, and consumer-conscious public utility commissions. In spite of these problems, the industry's leading companies have enviable dividend records.

The following table lists dividend payments for TECO Energy over a 15-year period. It shows why utility stocks have appeal for income investors. Year after year the dividend increases, even if the stock fails to behave.

In short, a buyer of TECO in 1975 would have seen his dividend payments increase every single year to more than triple the rate originally paid. During the 15 years, the dividend compounded at an 8.2 percent annual rate while the consumer price index moved ahead at a 6.0 percent annual compound rate.

Year	Dividend	Year	Dividend
1975	$0.50	1983	$1.00
1976	0.55	1984	1.08
1977	0.57	1985	1.16
1978	0.65	1986	1.24
1979	0.71	1987	1.32
1980	0.77	1988	1.40
1981	0.84	1989	1.50
1982	0.92	1990	1.62

This type of inflation-beating dividend growth has been exhibited by several other of the companies listed below. If electric utility stocks appeal to you as income possibilities, any of these perennial favorites would bear investigation.

Central and Southwest
Central Louisiana Elec.
Houston Industries
Kansas Power & Light
New England Electric

Nevada Power
Potomac Elec. Power
SCEcorp.
TECO Energy
Washington Energy

Tap a Water Company

One little-known and often overlooked group that offers steady income plus some hope of profit over the long pull is the water utilities. Just as certain as death and taxes is our steady uptrend in water consumption. This has been regularly reflected in a similar annual increase in water utility revenues and, in most cases, earnings. Of course, water company profits per share are unlikely to explode, but no matter how bad the times, neither are they likely to dry up. Water is just about the last commodity we would forgo. While consumer activists often oppose rate increases requested by telephone, electric, and natural gas utilities, water service is generally too cheap to get excited about. The fact is, however, that water rates have been rising at a much faster pace than inflation recently. The rate increases reflect higher levels of capital expenditures, maintenance costs, and treatment expenses necessary to keep up with increasing demand.

After years of ignoring the group, investors have begun to take a second look. They see not only a conservative management, but also an underlying value in the group's real estate holdings. Yields on the water-service stocks are not as generous as those of other types of utilities. But with dividends rising at an 8 percent to 10 percent annual pace, a shareholder should be well satisfied. The following water companies are worth checking:

American Water Works	Philadelphia Suburban
Consumers Water	United Water Resources

Other industry groups come and go as candidates for an income list. When in disfavor, stocks in some industrial groups can sell to yield more than twice what they do when they have caught the public favor. It's perfectly logical to buy temporarily unpopular stocks for income as long as you can be reasonably certain that the dividend is safe and that the company has a good earnings-dividend record. Do not, however, buy a stock for high yield when the earnings-dividend performance is erratic, for that very irregularity may account for the temporarily generous return. The market will be telling you in those instances that it "ain't safe."

Inflation and Income Stocks

A word is warranted at this point on how inflation affects income stocks. One of the reasons income stocks return a high yield in times of rising prices is inflation itself. When inflation intensifies, stock prices fall at first, particularly those of income-type stocks. They fall with the bond markets as lenders say, in effect, "If you want my money now you will have to pay me a decent return, plus what those dollars will likely depreciate per year."

A high prime rate reflects just this equation—so much for a "real" return and so much to offset inflation. The income group generally comes to terms with current inflationary reality. For instance, the yield on many electric utilities was less than 5 percent for years. But when inflation reached the double-digit level, yields on utilities rose to 10 and 15 percent. Even after inflation had cooled to 4 and 5 percent and stayed there, yields on utilities were slow to return to their earlier level. Thus, inflation expectations were factored into utility returns for several years after the fact.

CHAPTER 8

Corporate Bonds

A GOOD MANY conservative investors have long believed that the only really "safe" security is a corporate bond, and would never think of putting their money into anything else. Nevertheless, many common stock investors still blanch at the thought of investing in bonds, and one reason is that fixed-income securities represent unfamiliar territory. We shall seek to span that knowledge gap in this chapter. There is no real mystery to bonds. Neither are bonds always as "safe" as they seem, and we'll get into that a bit here, too.

Simply Stated, Bonds Are Loans

Stripped of their esoterica, bonds are no more than credit instruments and merely represent a loan by the investor to the issuing company. When a corporation wishes to build a plant or finance equipment purchases, it may do so by floating a bond issue, which is no more than taking out a loan composed of tradable evidences of debt.

There are several reasons why a corporation will choose to sell bonds rather than offer shares of common stock. For one thing, the registration procedures and expenses of issuing bonds generally are less burdensome than those involved in issuing stock. For another, the company might not wish to dilute any further the equity of outstanding common shares. Or the company's assessment of the existing investment and economic climate might tell it that bonds would be easier to sell than stock, or less costly in the long run.

Corporate bonds come in several styles. They can be mortgage bonds backed by liens on specific assets. They can be issued for specific purposes, as when railroads or airlines float equipment trust certificates. Most frequently, however, they are in the form of debentures, which means they are backed solely by a pledge of the earning power of the corporation rather than by a lien on specific corporate property. Mortgage bonds, trust certificates, and debentures have many common characteristics. They are tradable evidences of debt; they usually come in denominations of $1,000, and thus can be readily traded by investors; they generally carry a fixed interest rate (coupon) on the face; and they have a predetermined expiration date when the loan must be repaid. That date is known as the bond's maturity date.

The precise nature of the bond and the specific terms of the "loan" agreement are contained in the bond indenture. Besides noting the type of bond being issued and fixing the coupon and maturity date, the indenture might also reserve the issuing company's right to retire, or "call," the bond at a specified date and price in advance of maturity. It might also note whether all bonds of the particular series will mature at once or serially, that is, in stated amounts annually. It would give specifics on how the bonds could be called. Sometimes, if an entire issue is not called, those bonds chosen for retirement are picked on the basis of serial number; often they are chosen by lot. The indenture also will give the name and address of the trustee, usually a bank. The trustee administers and oversees the bond issue, making sure all terms and conditions are met, interest payments are made on time, and the like.

The "Mechanics" of Bonds

Bonds may be issued in "registered" form, which means the name and address of the current owner are kept on file by the corporation. The issuer sends periodic interest payments directly to the owner, and no one else may offer the bond for sale or redemption. The registered owner of a called bond is notified directly. This is the safest and most convenient way for you as an investor to hold bonds. Although bonds can no longer be issued in "bearer" form, there are thousands of older issues still available. Bearer bonds, in effect, are owned by whoever has them in his possession. Thus, they are virtually the same as cash. No proof of ownership need be demonstrated to redeem them or to collect interest. Interest payments are collected by clipping the attached coupons from the bond certificate and presenting them to a bank for payment. Because ownership of bearer bonds and interest payments on them are difficult for the IRS to trace, these bonds have been used by the unscrupulous for tax avoidance. Congress therefore banned the issuance of bonds in bearer form after 1982.

Bonds are issued and traded in $1,000 denominations and quoted in terms of "par" (100). Thus, a bond quoted at 98 sells at $980, one quoted at 101½ sells at $1,015, and so forth. Since interest rates on bonds are fixed, the market adjusts the price it will pay for the bond, to align with current interest rates. Occasionally such an adjustment is made before issuance. For example, a company may prefer to offer a bond with a 6 percent coupon rather than one paying the going rate (6.25) of interest. To compensate, the bond is offered at $960, a price at which it will yield the current 6.25 percent rate. Bonds offered at less than par are called original issue discount bonds. At maturity, the owner will collect the full $1,000 par value. The difference between the par value and the issuing price is reported as income ratably over the life of the issue, with the holder's cost basis rising each year by that amount of reported income.

Marketplace Determines Yield

Once the bond has been issued, whether it sold initially at par or at a discount, the marketplace takes charge of its price fluctuations. Suppose you buy a bond at par that pays 7.5 percent interest. Each year as long as you hold the bond you will receive a $75 interest payment. If bond yields in general rise to 8 percent, your 7.5 percent bond will drop in current value to $940, because that's all a potential buyer would be willing to pay, in order to reap the 8 percent he could get elsewhere. On the other hand, if bond yields generally dropped to 7 percent, you could get $1,070 if you sold your bond. For the sake of simplicity these examples ignore the effect that years to maturity may also exert on the price of a bond. A bond that sells below par is said to be selling at a "discount." One that sells above par is said to be selling at a "premium."

In order to avoid paying out the high rates of interest prevalent in the early 1980s, corporations began offering deep-discount bonds with zero coupon rates. For example, J.C. Penney, the first company to exploit this idea, brought out a bond priced at $332.47, which provided initial investors with a 14.25 percent yield when it matured at face value in 1989. However, because the bond holder is taxed on a portion of the discount each year, as if it were earned income, these bonds are suitable for individual investors *only in tax-sheltered accounts,* such as Keogh plans and individual retirement accounts.

Yields Fluctuate

Over the past four decades, the overall trend in bond yields definitely has been upward. Back in 1950, Moody's Aaa Corporate Bond Composite Index returned less than 3 percent. By 1982 that yield had jumped to nearly 17 percent, reflecting expectations of continued inflation. Since 1986, the yield on this high-quality bond index has moved between 6.5 percent and 10.5 percent. There are times when interest rates go down sharply, usually when the economy enters a recession. Then bond prices move up just as rapidly. When interest rates stop falling, the advance in bond prices slows and then stops.

International political and economic conditions are playing an increasingly important role in bond prices and interest rates. Currency fluctuations facilitated by floating exchange rates, and our inevitable entanglement in the web of world-wide politics and economic cycles, will pose uncertainties.

How do you as a bond buyer protect yourself in such an investment and economic climate? One way is to buy short-term bonds, sticking pretty much to those with maturities of 10 years or less. Such bonds tend to hold price fluctuations to more moderate proportions. Try to keep your portfolio heavily represented in bonds with coupon rates closely approximating prevailing interest rates.

Rating the Risk

How do you judge a bond's quality? If you're up to it, you can examine the corporation's debt structure, its financial statements, its credit rating, and other complex factors and make an assessment on your own. More likely you'll do what most of the rest of us do—you'll look to the rating services and bow to their judgment. There are two that are widely quoted: Moody's Investors Service and Standard & Poor's.

Both use similar criteria in determining the relative quality of bonds available for public sale, those representing the least risk to the investor being rated highest. Consequently, U.S. Treasury issues backed by the federal government's awesome taxing power are at the top of the pile. Close behind are those of the various federal agencies, which, though they are not specifically backed by the government, carry the weight of moral obligation of the government not to allow them to go into default.

Some corporate bonds carry the highest AAA or Aaa rating —Exxon, General Electric, IBM, and some of the Bell System spin-offs. Since 1985 more credit ratings have been lowered than have been advanced. Credit quality has deteriorated, particularly in the corporate sector, in response to junk-bond-financed takeovers. These LBOs—leveraged buyouts—were slowed drastically by an increase in bankruptcies. As bonds go down the rating scale, risk rises. In compensation for that added risk, investors demand a higher yield. The higher the bond's rating, the more closely its yield will tend to reflect changes in interest rates in general. On the other hand, yields on bonds carrying lower ratings will be much more heavily influenced by changes in the credit rating or profitability of the issuer.

This table shows you the rating scales used by Standard & Poor's and Moody's (in addition each uses qualifiers, + or − for Standard and Poor's, and 1, 2, or 3 for Moody's):

Standard & Poor's		*Moody's Investors Service*
AAA	Highest quality	Aaa
AA	High quality	Aa
A	Good quality	A
BBB	Medium grade, some speculative aspects	Baa
BB ⎫ B ⎭	Speculative, but with some defensive qualities	Ba
CCC ⎫ CC ⎭	Highly speculative	B
C	Bonds on which no interest is being paid or which already may be in default	Caa
D	Lowest rating	C

Both rating services are highly regarded in the financial community, and either one can be relied upon as you make your bond-buying decisions. However, for the purposes of uniformity, we shall use the Standard & Poor's ratings throughout this book.

Generally speaking, most investors buying for income should go no lower than BBB-rated bonds. If you go lower than that, you could put your capital in jeopardy; and, after all, the primary reason you're interested in investing in bonds is to protect that capital. Examining authorities, for example, consider issues carrying one of the top four ratings to be suitable for bank investments. Trust departments, being more conservative, stay with bonds rated A or better. Any additional yield provided by more speculative issues would be more than offset by the additional risk undertaken.

Different Kinds of Yields

As we noted earlier, bonds are issued with a specific interest rate printed on the face of the certificate. This is called the "stated," or "nominal," income. However, as we also noted, the price you actually pay for the bond, whether at its issue or in the aftermarket, determines the true yield the bond is earning for you. This yield, the amount of annual interest payment in relation to the price you paid, is called the "yield on cost." Another important figure is "current yield"—the coupon rate divided by the current trading price for the bond. If a bond stands a chance of being called before maturity, there is a "yield to call date" to consider. Finally, there is a "yield to maturity."

If you buy a bond at par when it is issued and hold it until it matures or is called and you get your principal back, all four yields will be the same. However, that's not a likely sequence, so you have to apply one or another of the available yields to your investment to determine its standing in your portfolio.

Generally speaking, the current yield will give you the truest reading, for it tells you how much income that holding is generating in comparison with other income investments.

If you hold the bond until it is called or until it matures, the yield to call date or yield to maturity will be of some consequence to you. That's because these figures take into account the premium or discount at which a bond is trading and the fact that this premium or discount must be amortized from purchase date to maturity.

For instance, if a bond trades at 107, you pay a $70 premium. When the bond is called or matures, you will sustain a $70 loss, since you will receive only the $1,000 face value of the bond for which you paid $1,070. That $70 may be offset against the income you will receive over the life of the bond. On the other hand, if you buy the bond at 93, you will receive a $70 profit when the bond is retired.

These yield-to-call or yield-to-maturity figures allow you to make a quick comparison of the bond's possible return to the potential return of all other bonds carrying an endless variety of coupon rates, maturity and call dates, and prices. The computation is more involved than most of us want to bother with, so we consult tables that have been especially constructed to provide this information. Your broker should be willing to look it up if you ask. These yields, as well as current yields, are frequently included in a newspaper's listing of bond quotations.

Bonds—Why and When?

Bonds have appeal, despite their tendency to fluctuate in price as interest rates change, because they do offer better defensive qualities than common stocks; hence, they really can represent an anchor to windward in your investment program. Because their return is fixed, they can provide a firm dollar foundation on which to build an income portfolio. That fixed return is useful, too, if you should wish to use securities as collateral for a loan. Often bankers will lend you a greater percentage of the market value of a bond than they will of the common stock of the same corporation.

But the fixed return of bonds also represents their greatest drawback. This is particularly so in an inflationary environment such as we have seen in recent years and which we can expect to continue into the foreseeable future. The continual erosion in the dollar's purchasing power has raised havoc with fixed-income investments, and today's investor cannot begin to keep pace with rising prices if he stakes his entire claim on fixed-income securities. That's why it is our judgment that bonds should compose no more than a modest portion—perhaps 30 percent at most—of your portfolio.

Because conditions change, no bond, not even those of the very highest quality, can be put away and forgotten. Contrary to many investors' impressions, bond holdings should be watched closely, less for changes in quality or interest-payment reliability than for shifts in the overall level of interest rates. Federal Reserve policy, the availability of credit, the volume of bank loans, corporate liquidity, and a host of other outside factors all have an important bearing on the prevailing level of interest rates, and these have a far greater and more frequent impact on high-grade bond prices than changes in the interest-paying ability and credit rating of the issuer.

Consequently, if you choose to include bonds in your investment program, you have to remain alert and ready to shift positions according to your perception of overall interest rates and bond market trends.

CHAPTER 9

Convertible Securities

SOME STOCKS, AS we have seen, offer the double attraction of good yield plus moderate capital gains potential. So does another form of investment security—the convertible.

Logically enough, the convertible derives its name from the fact that it can be converted into, or exchanged for, another investment security—common stock in all but the rarest of cases. Also, it can come in the form of a bond or preferred stock. In either event, the convertible can be swapped for a specified number of common shares—often within a specified time period, after which the conversion privilege is "no longer" and the bond or preferred sells on its merits as a fixed-income investment.

To some degree, at least, the convertible enables the investor to have his cake and eat it, too. If the common stock goes up, the convertible will go up, though probably at a slower gait, assuming the common isn't selling well above the conversion price. Of course, stocks also move in the other direction. Then, because the convertible usually provides a better yield than the underlying common, it has greater downside resistance. If the yield is sufficiently generous, it can even provide a "floor" through which the convertible won't penetrate, no matter what its common counterpart does.

This is a rather esoteric area of investment, abounding with terms such as "conversion basis," "conversion value," "premium," and "parity." It's really not very complicated, but much of it seems to be a mystery to the average investor —the person who just might find the convertible much to his liking if he understood what it was all about.

How Convertibles Work

So, let's try to unravel the mystery. Below we have tabulated four convertibles—two bonds and two preferred stocks —using prices and yields that were prevailing in mid-1990. The table is of the type you can expect to find whenever convertibles are touted by investment advisors, brokers, and the like.

First of all, remember that the Fleet Financial and IBM bonds, like all bonds, are quoted on the basis of 100, though they bear face values of $1,000; hence, one of each of these bonds would actually cost $1,000, not $100. Now let's look at the individual columns in the table.

| | Convertible | | Common Stock | | Conversion | |
	Price	Yield	Price	Yield	Basis*	Value†
Bonds						
Fleet Fin. 8½ 2010	100	8.5%	19	7.4%	50.3	95½
IBM 7.875s 2004	100	7.9	121	4.0	6.508	79
Preferred Stocks						
Arkla, Inc. $3.00	46	6.4%	23½	4.5%	1.7467	41
Baxter Int'l 3.50	78	4.5	26	2.5	2.976	77½

* Number of common shares that would be acquired if conversion privilege were exercised.

† Market price of common stock multiplied by number of shares to be obtained in conversion.

Price and yield, of course, require no explanation. Under *conversion basis*, we have the number of common shares you will receive for each bond or each preferred share if you convert. In the case of the IBM bonds, each can be swapped for 6.508 shares of common. The holder of the Baxter International $3.50 can convert each preferred share to 2.976 shares of common.

The *conversion value* is simply the number of common shares you can acquire through conversion (or conversion basis) times the price of the common. In other words, it's the value of what you will get if you convert. Again, in the case of IBM the conversion value is 79 (6.508 times 121, the market price of the common). With Baxter common selling at 26, the conversion value of the preferred is 77½ (2.976 × 26).

Common stock yields, as seen in the table, are lower than the returns generated by the convertibles listed above. If the yields were higher, in all likelihood it would pay you to convert.

The Conversion Premium

Before we get into the techniques of converting, the conversion premium should be explained. The premium is simply the percentage by which the price of the bond or preferred exceeds its conversion value. If the price is equal to conversion value, then the convertible is selling at conversion parity. If by some quirk the bond or preferred is trading below its conversion value, it is at a discount.

Therefore, the premium is just that. It's simply what you pay for the conversion privilege, over and above the value of the common stock into which you can convert. For Baxter preferred, you pay 78 for the right to swap for stock worth 77½. Thus, the conversion premium is less than 1 percent. You are also paying a premium for the higher yield offered by the preferred. The 4.5 percent yield on Baxter preferred is almost double that on the common.

In buying convertibles, the size of the premium is always an important consideration. Generally it isn't a good idea to pay a premium of more than 20 percent, but there are no ironclad rules. For example, IBM 7.875s are selling at a 21 percent premium (100 − 79), yet the bonds still have investment merit. The 7.9 percent yield is about double that on the common. The premium at which Fleet bonds are selling over their conversion value is a modest 4.5 percent, reflecting in part the modest yield differential between the bond and the common.

Generally speaking, a convertible is not much better or worse than the stock it can be swapped for. While such factors as premiums, yields, and expiration of conversion privilege must be carefully weighed, it is the investment appeal of the company and its common stock that overshadows everything in importance.

How and When to Convert

Converting a bond or preferred isn't a very complex process. Most convertible certificates carry on their reverse sides a small section that the owner must fill in and sign (everything is well explained) and then send along to the company's transfer agent—the address of which is given. If there is no such section on the back of the certificate, the holder can either contact the company directly or turn it all over to his broker.

As to *when* it's best to convert, it pretty well boils down to this: So long as the convertible provides better income, stay with it. But when dividends on the common stock are raised to the point that you can improve your income by converting, then do so. Of course, there is no guarantee that dividends will continue to be paid at the new higher rate. That's up to the company directors from quarter to quarter. But if prospects are good, as they should be if dividends have just been increased, it's most likely that payments will be maintained at the new rate.

A good example of a time-to-convert situation was provided by Westinghouse Electric in 1990. After the stock split two for one in May, the dividend was boosted to 35 cents quarterly. With the bond convertible to 64.6 shares, conversion would result in a greater return for the holder. Each bond paid $90, whereas 64.6 common shares would generate $90.40 annually. Bondholders were advised to convert following the semiannual interest payment in August.

There is, of course, another time when conversion is called

for, and that's when the conversion privilege is about to expire. This may happen when an issue is called for redemption, but in some cases the convertible "lives on" as a straight bond or preferred after the exchange period has run its course.

Again, an example might clarify matters. In the summer of 1990, Southwestern Energy called for redemption its 8½ percent debentures, at a price of $1,051, plus almost $31 of accrued interest per $1,000 face amount. Bondholders had the option of converting into 30.89 common shares then worth about $1,060. The investor's course of action was dictated by his investment objective. If income was the primary aim, conversion would mean accepting a much reduced yield from the common.

The Uses—and Limits—of Convertibles

Convertibles, like stocks, come in all sizes and colors. Some are issued by strong, growing companies and carry high-quality ratings. Some are highly speculative. Clearly, a bond or preferred selling closely in line with its conversion value is much more appealing than one that is selling well above this value. In the latter case, the conversion privilege may never be of any real value. The attraction of convertibles —which are, after all, fixed-income securities—may also be influenced by the current level of interest rates.

Well-chosen convertibles can provide inflation protection, long-term growth, relatively better price protection on the downside, and, in almost all cases, greater income than the underlying common stocks. A successful investor once described them as "like spinning a coin and saying, 'Heads, I might lose a little; tails, I could win a fortune.' " Maybe that's an overly rosy assessment, but convertibles certainly deserve consideration by the patient investor.

CHAPTER 10

Investing in Uncle Sam

You would be hard put to find anyone but an unrecon-
structed pessimist to argue with the statement that obligations of the United States government are just about the
safest investments in the world as far as preservation of your
dollar is concerned. As long as Uncle Sam retains control of
the presses that print the money, there is virtually no doubt
that interest and principal on these obligations will be paid
when due.

The safety of "Governments" in terms of preserving the
buying power of that invested capital is quite another thing.
When inflation ran at annual rates of 9 percent and upward,
and yields on these government securities remained moderate by comparison, the purchasing power of the assets committed to them continued to shrink. In other words, you pay
for one kind of "safety" with another. It's that trade-off of
risks we talked about in earlier chapters.

An understanding of these risks and trade-offs is necessary
if you consider U.S. government obligations as candidates for
your investment program. Sometimes they do indeed have a
valid place—because you want some safety of capital, or you
want an assured rate of return for a specified period, or you
have a tax problem they can help solve.

When the New York Stock Exchange was founded in 1792,

its main business was dealing in U.S. government issues. Ever since then, they have been actively traded and enjoy the best market of any security in this country and probably in the world. In fact, in recent years the Japanese have been major buyers of U.S. government securities, as pointed out in Chapter 3. Millions of dollars' worth can be bought and sold in a few minutes. Most of the trading is now done in the over-the-counter market, though these issues are listed on the New York Stock Exchange.

How "Governments" Work

"Governments" come in a wide variety of sizes, shapes, and styles. Before we get into their specifics, let's take a short detour and explore the structure through which they are issued and administered. All securities that are issued directly by the federal government come from the Department of the Treasury. Hence, they are also frequently called "Treasuries." The Treasury sells these securities to raise money to pay its bills, either in anticipation of tax revenues or because such revenues are insufficient to cover the bills.

The government buys as well as sells these securities to help control the supply of money floating around in the economy. But that job is done by the Federal Reserve Board, a fiefdom unto itself, charged with the well-nigh impossible task of keeping the country's monetary and credit machinery running smoothly, while maintaining a balance between too much growth and too much inflation. When the Fed wants to shrink the size of the money supply, it sells securities, thus taking out of circulation the money investors use to buy those securities. Conversely, if it wants to expand the money supply, it buys up these obligations, releasing dollars into the nation's spending stream.

The Fed also acts as the nation's central banker. It does this through the 12 Federal Reserve banks spread out around the country. These banks administer the Federal Reserve Board's monetary, credit, and banking policies. They also serve as the "bank" for the Treasury Department by handling the details of selling and purchasing its various marketable securities. You can deal directly with your nearest Federal Reserve Bank if you wish to buy or redeem U.S. government obligations.

Bills, Notes, and Bonds

Back to those securities. Although they provide an almost endless variety of yields, maturities, and denominations, Treasury obligations are divided basically into three categories: bills, notes, and bonds.

Each week the Treasury auctions off 13- and 26-week bills and, every four weeks, 52-week bills. The bills are sold at a discount from par, the difference representing the interest to the buyer. Until 1970, these bills came in denominations as low as $1,000. But when a surge in short-term interest rates lured millions of dollars from savings accounts into Treasury bills that year, the minimum denomination was jacked up to $10,000 to keep small investors from draining thrift institutions dry. Because of their relatively short maturity, T-bills present practically no market risk.

If you can't come up with the $10,000 entry fee for bills and you find Treasuries attractive for short-term investments, take a look at Treasury notes. They range in maturities from 2 to 10 years. Although the minimum denomination varies with each offering, four-year and longer-maturity notes are issued in denominations as low as $1,000. Their yields, too, are generally comparable with those provided by bills.

For longer-term investment, Treasury bonds are available. They are issued in varying maturities longer than 10 years, depending on the Treasury's financing needs at the time of offering. They come in book-entry form and in denominations ranging from $1,000 to $1 million. (The book-entry form has now replaced the older coupon and registered forms.) The owner is listed in a Treasury computer file as the owner; he receives a receipt showing his purchase.

Some U.S. obligations are callable at par before maturity, on four months' notice. This fact is indicated in their description—for example, the 4¼s of 1987–92.

Besides these marketable issues, the government offers a

variety of other special-interest securities. The most common are U.S. Savings Bonds. If you're old enough, you'll remember them as the "war bonds" of World War II. For many years these were available in the E and H series, but now they are issued only in EE and HH series. HH bonds are no longer marketed, but are still available in exchange for EEs.

Sales of U.S. Retirement Plan bonds were discontinued in mid-1982. Interest on those Retirement Plan bonds still outstanding is compounded semiannually and is payable when the bonds are redeemed. In accordance with Keogh, SEP, and IRA rules, redemption may not take place before age 59½ without tax penalties to the owner, unless he can demonstrate complete disability. Federal income tax is deferred on these issues until they are redeemed. They are exempt from state and local income taxes.

Hold That Tiger

In response to investor acceptance of the zero-coupon bond concept, several large brokerage companies offered similar investments, using Treasury bonds. Merrill Lynch's Treasury Investment Growth Receipts (TIGRs) were the first to come on the market and their acronym caught on, so now these securities are known as "tigers," "cats," and "lions." You buy the tiger, maturing in 6 to 20 years, at a substantial discount from face value. These receipts are backed by Treasury bonds, so they are considered safer than their corporate counterparts. At maturity you receive face value, and the difference between that amount and cost is treated as income. Because taxes are payable annually on that future interest, tigers are suitable for tax-sheltered investments, such as IRAs and Keoghs.

The Treasury STRIPS

Early in 1985, the Treasury initiated its own program of stripping and selling 10-year notes and bonds. The acronym STRIPS stands for Separate Trading of Registered Interest and Principal of Securities. Individuals can't buy these zeros directly from the Treasury but must obtain them from a bank or other depository institution. STRIPS are sold in book form only, in a minimum denomination of $1,000, which represents the maturity value, not the cost, per bond. Current quotes on these and other Treasury securities are listed daily in *The Wall Street Journal* and other financial publications.

Federal Agency Bonds

In addition to these direct obligations of the United States, there are a wide variety of securities called "instrumentalities of the United States government." These are securities issued by official or quasi-official offshoots of the government called federal "agencies." These agencies were first used in the 1920s to provide capital for federally sponsored activities or federally guaranteed programs outside the regular budgetary structure.

Their growth mushroomed in the 1970s and continued to accelerate in the 1980s. As recently as 1965, interest-bearing obligations of agencies and government-sponsored enterprises amounted to about $17 billion. Only eight years later, in 1973, the total had soared to more than $70 billion. By 1986, it had passed $536 billion and was still climbing.

Many obligations of these agencies do not carry a direct federal guarantee. But a strong moral obligation is attached to honoring them, and it is improbable that the government would ever allow a default on any of them, a point that was tested during the farm crisis in the late 1980s. Therefore, from the standpoint of safety of principal, they are virtually as solid as obligations specifically guaranteed by the government.

The government-sponsored enterprises are Farm Credit System, Federal Home Loan Banks, Federal Home Loan Mortgage Corporation, Federal National Mortgage Association, Student Loan Marketing Association, and the U.S. Postal System. Federal agencies include the Export-Import Bank, General Services Administration, Government National Mortgage Association, Maritime Administration, and the Tennessee Valley Authority.

In 1973, Congress created the Federal Financing Bank in an attempt to bring a measure of order to the chaotic structure of federal agency financing. Its aim was to provide a single vehicle through which the smaller agencies could raise capital. Debt issued by the FFB was $4.5 billion in 1974, its first year of operation; it had reached well into the hundreds of billions by the end of the next decade.

At times these quasi-governmental securities have provided noticeably higher yields than direct obligations of the United States. When this occurs, investors should consider these issues. Generally, though, the yield spread is rather narrow.

In 1985, the farmer-owned Federal Farm Credit System reported a $2.7 billion loss for 1985 and nonearning loans of $5.3 billion (8 percent of its loan portfolio). Despite its shaky financial condition, long-term System bonds were yielding only 50 to 75 basis points (½ to ¾ of 1 percent) more than comparable Treasuries. Short-term issues were just a few basis points higher. Before Congress voted to allow the Farm Credit System to tap the Treasury for bailout funds, the spread had been as high as 130 basis points. Once the government's backing was assured, the market saw no undue risk in System bonds, so the yield spread narrowed.

A Word on Taxability

Before leaving Governments, we should take note of the tax implications. Income earned on them is fully taxable at the federal level. However, interest on Treasuries and most agency obligations is exempt from state and local income and property taxation. Interest on Federal Home Loan Mortgage Corporation, Federal National Mortgage Association, Government National Mortgage Association, and Export-Import Bank obligations isn't exempt from local taxes. Taxability at the state and local level is a point to consider when comparing Governments with corporate bonds and other taxable securities, particularly if you live in a state with a high tax rate.

Although their income may escape state and local taxes, U.S. government and agency securities are subject to excise, gift, estate, and inheritance taxes levied by the states. They are also subject to federal income tax on capital gains and gift and estate taxes.

Flower Bonds Still Bloom

We should mention here a class of Treasury bonds that bears a special privilege with regard to federal estate taxes. This feature, which allows them to be applied at par against the estate tax obligation even if they were bought at a discount, has earned them the nickname of "flower bonds." Although law prohibits issue of any new bonds carrying this special feature and none have been issued since 1971, there are still several outstanding, should you wish to acquire some in the course of your estate planning. The following flower bonds are still outstanding:

4¼s of August 1987–92	3s of February 1995
4s of February 1988–93	3¼s of November 1998
4⅛s of May 1989–94	

Since government obligations are at the top of the quality list, their market action depends wholly upon fluctuations in interest rates. The volatility of a particular security is determined largely by the amount of time to its maturity. The shorter the maturity the narrower will be the price swing. As a bond approaches maturity, its price will begin to stabilize right around par. Prices of obligations subject to call are influenced by that factor. For example, in times of falling interest rates, high-grade bonds tend to rise in price but their call price also limits the extent of such advances; noncallable issues are not under such constraints.

To preserve investment flexibility, we recommend that if you include Governments in your portfolio you choose those with maturities of 10 years or less. This will help minimize the market risk should you find it desirable or necessary to sell them before they mature.

But keep in mind that despite the ultimate safety of U.S. government and agency obligations in terms of marketability and preservation of capital, they possess the same serious drawbacks in protecting against inflation as do other bonds, because both income and principal are fixed.

CHAPTER 11

Investing in Tax-exempts

THE MUNICIPAL BOND market was irrevocably changed by the Tax Reform Act of 1986. This law placed narrow limitations on the amount of tax-exempt bonds that could be issued to fund state-sponsored projects. However, existing restrictions on the stripping of municipal bonds were removed by TRA '86. Consequently, several new municipal bond products have been introduced, giving this market a whole new look. In addition to the tried-and-true tax-exempt municipal bonds, there are now taxable municipals, stripped municipals, annual-payment M-CATS, and munis collateralized with Treasuries. The tax exemption on "munis," as they are collectively known, provides a means for state and local governments to raise capital at lower interest costs. Because munis are tax-exempt they are attractive to investors in higher tax brackets despite their below-market interest.

When Are Tax-exempts Profitable?

When does it become more profitable for you as an investor to buy tax-exempts than to hold taxables? The answer depends on three things: your tax bracket, the prevailing yield on taxable securities, and the going rate on tax-exempts. A table and a simple mathematical formula are presented below to help you decide when you should switch to munis.

When we say tax bracket, we do not mean the percentage of your income you actually pay to Uncle Sam, but the amount you would pay on every dollar earned above your present taxable income, based on the Internal Revenue Service tax tables. Thus, if you are in the 31 percent bracket, 31 cents of your next dollar of income will go to pay federal taxes.

Besides your own tax bracket, the relationship between yields on taxable and nontaxable securities will determine their relative merits. On average, tax-exempts yield somewhere around 70 percent of what taxable bonds yield. The following chart traces the relationship between taxable and tax-exempt bond yields.

Although this relationship was fairly stable during the pe-

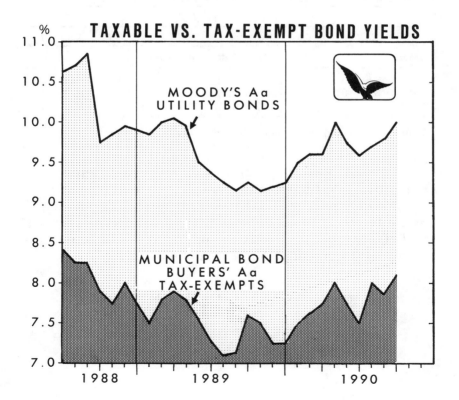

TAXABLE VS. TAX-EXEMPT BOND YIELDS

MOODY'S Aa UTILITY BONDS

MUNICIPAL BOND BUYERS' Aa TAX-EXEMPTS

1988   1989   1990

riod depicted on the chart, there have been times when this was not the case. In the 1975 aftermath of New York City's near default, tax-exempts took a real beating, pushing their yields to within 85 percent of those on taxable bonds. This stimulated widespread investor interest in munis. To accommodate those lacking the wherewithal to buy bonds outright and those who wished to diversify assets, tax-exempt unit trusts sprang to the forefront. Bond funds with their portfolios of tax-exempt bonds did not appear until a propitious change was made in the tax laws that allowed the funds to pass through the tax exemption for interest to fund holders.

There remains the broad question of deciding when tax-exempts are of value in your portfolio. The table below shows how the advantages of tax-exempt securities are increased by a tax-bracket increase.

TAX-EXEMPT AND TAXABLE YIELDS COMPARED

Tax bracket	*Tax-exempt Yield of*									
	5.5	6.0	6.5	7.0	7.5	8.0	8.5	9.0	9.5	10.0
	is equivalent to taxable yield of									
28%	7.6	8.3	9.0	9.7	10.4	11.1	11.8	12.5	13.2	13.9
31%	8.0	8.7	9.4	10.1	10.9	11.6	12.3	13.0	13.8	14.5
38%*	8.9	9.7	10.5	11.3	12.1	12.9	13.7	14.5	15.3	16.1

* Assumes a combined federal and high state tax rate.

If you want to work the figures out for yourself, here's how. Divide the stated interest by 1.00 minus your tax bracket to calculate the taxable yield that is equivalent to the municipal bond rate. Thus, for someone in the 31 percent bracket a yield of 7 percent from a tax-exempt bond would be equivalent to a 10.1 percent yield on a taxable bond.

$$\frac{0.07}{1.00 - 0.31} = .101$$

What Kinds of Municipals Are There?

The safest of all tax-exempt securities are those offered by municipalities under the Department of Housing and Urban Development (HUD) and guaranteed by federal subsidies. Don't confuse these bonds with those issued by the various state housing authorities, which have neither federal nor state backing.

General obligation bonds, also called "full faith and credit bonds," are next safest because they have the full taxing power of the state or municipality behind them. However, they run the gamut from safe to moderately speculative, depending on the solvency of the issuing body.

Revenue bonds, which depend on such things as tolls and user fees for their income, are more risky because they do not have taxing power behind them. If their fees do not generate the necessary income to service the obligations, they can go into default.

Tax revenue bonds and tax anticipation notes are offered by communities in expectation of incoming revenues. They are usually short term and have low interest rates. However, their short maturities and high quality make them attractive to commercial banks. Generally, they trade at roughly half the rate available on taxable commercial paper.

Industrial revenue bonds (IRBs, also called industrial development bonds) are first cousins to revenue bonds. IRBs are issued by a state or community authority to build a facility for a company whose lease payments cover interest and principal. The corporation puts its credit on the line but in return gets financing at tax-exempt rates. They were created to provide incentives for investment in local economic development projects and particularly to attract capital for installing pollution-control equipment in existing plants. Because corporations are easier to analyze than municipalities, IRB offerings generally are snapped up quickly.

The popularity of industrial revenue bonds with both issuers and investors led Congress to restrict their use. Too many questionable projects were being funded with tax-exempt bonds at the expense of federal revenue. Now only a limited amount of so-called private-activity bonds can be issued tax-exempt annually. The cap for each state is the greater of $150 million or $50 per resident. Above these limits, municipalities have to fund projects with taxable bonds. However, all municipal bonds issued before mid-August 1986 retain their tax-exempt status. Public-purpose municipal bonds—those serving a bona fide public need and issued after that date—also are fully tax-exempt.

New Muni Bond Types

Private activity municipal bonds are also known as AMT bonds because the interest paid on them is a preference item for individuals who are subject to the 24 percent alternative minimum tax (AMT). While most of the offerings are sold to institutional investors, they have some appeal for individuals since the yield on them is often higher than that on similarly rated offerings. However, the availability of AMT bonds is limited since these bonds represent a very small portion of the total municipal market.

Stripped municipal bonds were permitted for the first time by the technical corrections segment of TRA 1986, which removed prohibitions on their stripping. With this stricture lifted, Wall Street began scurrying to offer stripped or zero coupon tax-exempts. Interest income on these deep-discount zero coupon bonds is not received until they mature. Zero coupon municipal bonds are attractive investment alternatives for parents who must pay tax on the unearned income of their children aged 14 or under.

Annual-income stripped municipals are another innovation from the staff at Salomon Brothers. Coupons are stripped from a municipal bond selling at a premium. One of the two semiannual interest payments will be made to buyers of these annual-income issues. The remaining coupons stay with the principal. This maneuver converts a bond selling at a premium into one that sells at par. Since most investors prefer not to pay a premium for municipal bonds, annual-income muni strips have investment appeal.

Collateralized municipal receipts are packaged with serial

maturities of one to "X" number of years. The offering municipalities collateralize the bonds with Treasury issues in order to take the debt off their books before the bonds can be refunded. Thus, the receipts are backed by prerefunded bonds. Muni receipts are suitable for individuals seeking high quality and safety.

Marketability Can Be a Problem

There is no central marketplace for the half trillion dollars' worth of outstanding municipal debt. Bonds are traded by telephone among countless brokerage dealers. There are no commissions, but neither are the prices of most bonds listed anywhere. You are completely at the mercy of the dealers, who inventory bonds for their own accounts and have a major stake in profiting from markups and discounts.

Moreover, there is no strict definition of a round lot in this market. It is whatever amount is large enough to get the dealer to narrow his spread between bid and asked prices. Although $25,000 is considered a round lot, sometimes $50,000 or $100,000 is the standard.

With many thousands of issuing entities continually floating and retiring bonds of varying maturities and interest rates, the factors affecting these securities reach infinite proportions. Because institutional and individual investors frequently purchase and hold these securities for long periods, the market is not nearly as liquid as that for common stocks or corporate bonds.

Potential municipal investors should consider marketability in making purchases. Generally speaking, it is best to avoid small-town securities that might be difficult to sell without a price concession should you need to dispose of them prior to maturity.

Issues floated by larger state and local authorities are rated by Moody's and Standard & Poor's. They also appear regularly in the Blue List, an inventory of bond offerings published each trading day by Standard & Poor's and circulated among municipal bond dealers. The obligations of many smaller towns, school and utility districts, and authorities, on the other hand, will appear in the listings only infrequently. Generally speaking, any muni bearing a rating of A or better may be considered safe.

Insured Bonds

In the early 1970s, AMBAC Indemnity Corp. began offering bondholders protection against the risk of default. Since then several other companies have entered the field, and municipal bond insurance has become a well-accepted feature in the industry. Today more than 25 percent of all tax-exempt bonds are issued with insurance protection.

There are three major insurers—American Municipal Bond Assurance Corporation (AMBAC), Municipal Bond Insurance Association (MBIA), a subsidiary of Continental Corp., and Financial Guaranty Insurance Company (FGIC). Each is backed by a consortium of other insurers or financial companies. Citicorp, Stephens Inc., Johnson & Higgins, and Xerox are backers for AMBAC. Behind MBIA are five major insurance companies, while FGIC is backed by GE Credit Corp., General Re Corp., J. P. Morgan, Merrill Lynch, and American Express's Shearson Lehman Brothers.

These three insurers are rated triple A by both major rating services. Therefore, bond issues underwritten by them carry a similar rating. However, the underlying bond, if uninsured, could carry a lower rating. It is important for the buyer to know the rating of the municipality offering the bond, since the insurance only guarantees continued payment of interest. It is unlikely that the municipality would fail to repay principal. Insurance is not without cost to the investor. Yield differentials on insured bonds have shrunk in recent years to about 15 basis points, or the difference between a yield of 7.65 percent and 7.80 percent.

Insurance Isn't a Panacea

If the insurer falls on hard times and is downgraded, ratings on bonds insured by the company are also lowered. The trading price on bonds insured by the firm also will fall, even though the municipality continues to pay the interest. No major catastrophe has truly tested the insurers. However, when Washington Public Power Supply System (WPPSS) defaulted on two of its bond series, its insurer, AMBAC, paid off.

How Do You Judge Munis?

There is a great deal more to picking municipal bonds than selecting the largest yield and collecting income. Auditing standards for municipalities are inferior to those of the corporate world. Though financial statements are improving, issuers frequently publish inadequate reports. Moreover, ratings can sometimes be unreliable measures of credit risks.

Therefore, you are much more on your own as you evaluate tax-exempts than you are with corporates. Good information is hard to find, so the rating services are a helpful starting point. But you should get a prospectus on any bond you are considering for purchase, and you should watch financial statements for news of litigation or legislation that might influence the quality of the bond.

Beyond that, what should you look for in a municipal bond? With general obligation debt, the object is to discover how heavily indebted the issuing municipality already is relative to its real assets and its economic power. Important considerations must include an assessment of the area's largest employers and taxpayers, population growth, personal income levels, and operating revenues.

If you look at revenue bonds, pinpoint the sources of income. As a rule of thumb, be sure there is at least $1.20 in income for every $1.00 in debt service (interest costs). If revenues tend to be highly cyclical, you might want to add a larger cushion. Then try to determine the order of liens, see what is pledged to whom.

Revenue bonds include water and power issues backed by receipts from users (industrial, commercial, and residential customers of the utility). Besides a company's financial track record, you must also assess the rate-relief history of the state's regulatory agency.

Revenue bonds, bridge and turnpike bonds, airport and

sports-complex bonds, and local housing authority bonds fall within the private-purpose category. Tax exemption of interest on such issues already in existence before the passage of TRA 1986 is grandfathered. However, the interest on some newly issued private activity bonds is taxed under AMT.

Bonds floated by hospitals, which historically have derived about 90 percent of their revenues from Medicare and Medicaid programs, now entail increased risk. With the institution of congressionally mandated cost cutting in these health care programs, hospital revenues have been hurt. Skyrocketing malpractice awards are another cloud on the horizon. Increasingly, hospitals are being taken over by private hospital management companies, thereby reducing supplies of these bonds.

We should not proceed without mentioning specifically the bonds of Puerto Rico. Its economy has strengthened in recent years; unemployment rates are down and production up. Puerto Rican bonds possess a feature that should not be overlooked: Income from them is exempt not only from federal taxes but also from taxes in all states and municipalities. Look for A- or AA-rated issues when selecting them.

Which Munis to Buy?

Once you've decided that tax-exempts belong in your investment program, you're faced with the decision of how to stake your claim. Do you want to hold the bonds themselves or leave the selection to the professionals? If you choose to go with the pros, do you want an unmanaged unit trust or a managed municipal bond fund?

If you don't feel confident of your expertise and you have no advisor to consult, or if you have less than $25,000 to invest, you might do best to stick with the funds. Many offer minimum investments as small as $1,000, and for that you get a broadly diversified portfolio, which minimizes your risk.

Bond fund or unit trust, what's the difference? A bond fund has no set expiration date; maturing bonds are sold or replaced and the fund continues in existence long after its original portfolio has matured or changed. Not so with a unit investment trust (UIT), which consists of a set portfolio split into $1,000 units. As the components of its portfolio mature, unit holders receive their prorated share of the principal.

If you are going to invest in tax-exempt bond funds or unit trusts, you should try to reap the fullest measure from the tax exemption. This means you must explore your own state's and municipality's tax treatment of them. All states but Illinois, Iowa, Kansas, Oklahoma, and Wisconsin exempt interest generated by bonds issued within the state. If your state is one that exempts interest only on its own bonds, you should try to find home-grown bonds, issued by your state or by local municipalities within it. If you live in Indiana, New Mexico, South Dakota, or Utah, interest is state-tax-free on *all* municipals, regardless of the issuing state.

You have to watch this angle when investing in unit trusts or bond funds. While these funds are allowed by federal law to pass the tax exemption on to you, some state and local governments have not gone along. This means they tax all the income generated by the fund—including that from bonds issued within your state. If local or state law penalizes you on that score, then you should buy the bonds themselves instead of a bond fund. An alternative would be to invest in a unit trust holding a portfolio composed of bonds issued only by your state and its municipalities.

Single-state municipal unit trusts are getting increasing attention from sponsors and investors alike. State tax bills will account for a larger share of individuals' tax burdens now that federal tax rates have been lowered. Therefore, investments that help reduce the state tax take are of interest to many taxpayers. However, with sponsors vying with one another for a shrinking pool of tax-exempt municipal bonds (as a result of the previously discussed tax law changes), these UITs may be heading for problems. Single-state UITS are only available for states with a high tax rate.

When Shouldn't You Use Munis?

There are times when municipal bonds do not fit the investment needs even of those whose income is most heavily taxed. Since munis are subject to gift, estate, and inheritance taxes, they may cause some estate-planning problems. A forced sale in an estate settlement could result in loss of principal, particularly in the case of municipal bonds for which no ready market exists. Younger beneficiaries might rather have investments with greater appreciation potential.

Taxpayers who are subject to the alternative minimum tax should choose tax-exempt bonds with care. Interest on non-essential function tax-exempt bonds issued after mid-August 1986 is a tax preference item. And for Social Security recipients, tax-exempt interest is added to adjusted gross income to determine whether a portion of the SS benefit is taxable.

If your income fluctuates a great deal, tax-exempt bonds might help you one year but hurt the next. However, if you anticipate substantial growth in your income over the next several years, you might want to acquire municipals during times of high interest rates, when their yields are attractive.

In the final analysis, though, tax-exempts are vulnerable to the same criticisms we voiced earlier about other fixed-income investments. If they possess any protection against inflation, it is strictly limited. In fact, in a highly inflationary environment, they can lose ground. The prospect so alluring to many taxpayers—depriving Uncle Sam of some tax revenue—must be weighed against the possibility of obtaining greater gains elsewhere. Giving Caesar his due can frequently be more profitable in the long run.

CHAPTER 12

Mutual Funds

THE CONCEPT OF forming a company to execute in collective investment the pooled assets of like-minded investors is a relatively recent development. As early as 1823 a New England life insurance company possessed features that resembled those of an investment company. The first recorded precursor to what we know today as mutual funds was organized a few years later by King William I of the Netherlands.

But it wasn't until 1868 that the first bona fide "mutual fund" came upon the scene. In that year the Foreign and Colonial Government Trust was formed in London to provide "the investor of moderate means the same advantages as the large capitalists, in diminishing the risk of investing in Foreign and Colonial Government stocks, by spreading the investment over a number of different stocks."

If the mutual fund idea was rooted in Europe, it blossomed into full flower across the Atlantic. The first bud appeared in the United States in 1893 with the appearance of the Boston Personal Property Trust. It was followed in 1904 by the Railway and Light Securities Company. Both were organized as closed-end investment companies. In 1954, the latter converted to an open-end investment company and became the Colonial Fund, under which name it still operates. We shall distinguish between closed-end and open-end funds and de-

105

fine other terms in a moment. First let's put it into historical perspective.

The early 1920s witnessed the appearance of the mutual fund as we know it today, offering a self-liquidating feature, prudent investment policies and restrictions, diversification, a published portfolio, and an uncomplicated capital structure. Massachusetts Investors Trust, the first of the modern genre, was introduced in March 1924. Then came State Street Investment Corporation, also in 1924. These were followed in 1925 by Incorporated Investors, now Putnam Investors Fund. From modest beginnings, these three funds have become giants with assets in the hundreds of millions of dollars.

By 1929, there were 19 open-end funds with assets totaling only about $140 million. Growth was slow through the Depression of the 1930s, so that by 1940 combined assets of mutual funds were less than $500 million. The next three decades witnessed phenomenal growth, and by the end of 1972 net assets of the industry had mushroomed to $60 billion, representing more than 10 million shareholder accounts. Falling markets and net redemptions served to lower the total to only $34 million in 1974. By early 1987, industry assets stood at $464 billion, well above the $137 billion figure of a year earlier. Money-market funds and short-term municipal bond funds had another $244 billion in assets. Mutual fund sales in early 1986 were at record levels, with much of the buying coming from IRA investors.

It should be noted that while the mutual funds have been credited from time to time as having a significant influence on the direction of the stock market, their assets generally have accounted for a very modest percentage of the market value of all stocks listed on the New York Stock Exchange.

What Is a Mutual Fund?

Now let's get a handle on what a mutual fund is—and what it isn't. Legally speaking, there is no such thing as a "mutual fund." That's merely a name coined to embrace a variety of investment companies and investment trusts created for the mutual investment under professional management of assets contributed by several individuals. A mutual fund—or, more technically, an investment company—is a corporation, and as with other corporations, the individual investor's interest in it is represented by shares of stock. If the assets under management increase in value, the investor's capital will increase accordingly. Should the assets' value decline, the prorated net value of each share will likewise decline.

A mutual fund thus is basically different from, say, a savings account, where a depositor is guaranteed a fixed rate of return and will be able to withdraw all of his principal when he desires. A mutual fund investor is an owner, not a lender; he shares in the profits and losses and in the income and expenses.

However, there are some differences in the way they are taxed that distinguish investment companies from other corporations. Where all of the income from a conventional corporation is subject to federal income taxation, investment company income that is passed to shareholders is not taxed at the corporate level. In order to qualify for investment company status, a fund must comply with the provisions of the Investment Company Act of 1940. That comprehensive piece of legislation provides the foundation for regulation of the mutual fund industry and establishes standards of income distribution and diversification of assets.

Briefly, to operate as a regulated investment company and enjoy the tax benefits attached thereto, a fund must distribute at least 98 percent of its capital gains or earned income each year to its shareholders. The remainder is used to cover operating expenses and other overhead and is subject to corporation taxes. Shareholders pay income taxes at their own individual rates on the income passed along to them.

To assure diversification and to prevent the possibility that an investment company would acquire a controlling interest in a corporation, the law prohibits it from investing more than 5 percent of the value of its total assets in the securities of any single company or from holding more than 10 percent of the voting securities of any one company.

Closed-Ends and Open-Ends

The first mutual funds were closed-end funds. Closed-end funds, which today are known as publicly traded investment funds, differ in a number of respects from open-end funds. The primary difference, though, is in the way the shares of the fund are created.

In a publicly traded fund, the number of shares to be offered for sale is fixed at the outset; the fund operators may not create new shares on demand. An open-end fund, on the other hand, may create and sell its shares on a continuous basis; if an investor wishes to purchase fund shares, the new shares are created as needed.

Another important difference is that open-end funds stand ready to buy back, or redeem, outstanding shares at a price based on the market value of the portfolio at the time of redemption. Publicly traded funds do not buy back their shares from investors. Investors, in fact, have no direct buying or selling contact with the publicly traded fund except when reinvesting distributions in additional shares. Instead, they buy and sell fund shares on a securities exchange or in the over-the-counter market, just as they would do with any common stock. The broker who handles the transaction charges the same commission as he does for any similar transaction involving common stock.

Load Versus No-Load Funds

Open-end funds fall into two major categories: load funds and no-loads. However, the industry's terminology also includes low-load funds, which usually carry nominal sales or redemption charges. Load and no-load funds resemble each other in every way but one. Load funds are sold with a sales commission (the "load"), which can reach as high as 8.5 percent. This figure is expressed as a percentage of the total purchase price; that is to say, net asset value plus the sales charge. Thus, as compared with stock commissions, which are based on the sums actually invested, the sales charge for mutual funds is understated. For example, if you purchased shares in a load fund for $1,000, only $915 would actually be invested in securities. The remaining $85 would go to the sales organization. If you divide that $85 by $915, the amount invested, you get 9.3 percent. Looking at it another way, if you want a full $1,000 in securities earning money for you, you must pay the fund a total of $1,093.

In respect to performance, studies show that there is no appreciable difference between that of the load funds and that of the no-loads. Why, then, should you as an investor pay the load? Mutual fund salespersons will proffer any number of arguments to justify the load. Probably the most common is that over the long run the growth of the fund will reduce the effective cost of the sales charge to a minimum. In rebuttal, you can't always count on such growth, even over a relatively long period. Even if you amortize the load over a nine-year period, it amounts to about 1 percent a year. And over time, the sales charge actually becomes more and more detrimental to performance because of the effect of compounding. The longer you plan to hold your mutual fund investment, the greater the advantage of purchasing a no-load. Because of compounding, the no-load will produce a significantly higher total return over the long haul.

Another argument put forth in defense of the load is that it carries an element of service for the investor. The salesperson or broker to whom the load is paid stands ready to answer questions, give advice, and help iron out any kinks that might develop with regard to your fund account. You have to ask yourself whether the cost of such an implied service is justified. In the final analysis, the price of a fund, whether you pay a sales commission or not, is secondary to choosing a fund with a good long-term performance record and investment aims in accord with your own.

Advantages of Mutual Funds

There are a number of sound reasons why small investors and large investors lacking access to investment counsel should explore the advantages of buying and holding mutual funds. Among them:

PROFESSIONAL MANAGEMENT. When you buy a fund you benefit from the expertise of full-time money managers who watch over the fund's portfolio and make all the necessary decisions about what to buy, sell, or hold. Of course, the experts can make mistakes—some of them are beauties—and, as is true among doctors and lawyers, some mutual fund managers are bright, others are not. On balance, however, most leading funds are run by high-caliber people with substantial experience in investments.

DIVISION OF RISK. A typical fund spreads your investment dollar over many different industry and company stocks and securities. Thus a disaster in any one or a few of them does not mean a calamity for the fund as a whole. For example, a fund such as T. Rowe Price Growth Stock, with about $1.5 billion in assets, invests in some 175 to 200 different stocks, none of which accounts for more than 5 percent of the fund's total market value at the time of purchase.

INFORMATION. How a mutual fund has performed is a matter of record. Mutual funds are unique in that they publish information about their performance and it is readily available. Thus the layman, by reading the prospectus and shareholder reports, can compare one fund with another and decide which to buy. This is not the situation, say, with bank trust departments and stockbrokers.

FREEDOM FROM EMOTIONAL INVOLVEMENT. All too often the individual investor is swayed by the influence of one or a few well-motivated but poorly informed friends who are only too free with their stock market advice. Also, lacking expert knowledge, the individual may make investment decisions at times on the basis of headlines, rumors, and the fears and emotions of the moment. Investing in the stock market is for cool heads only, and it is one place where a little of the wrong knowledge can lead to big losses. When you buy good mutual funds, generally you can sit back and relax and, to paraphrase the Greyhound ad, leave the driving to them. The time and effort needed to choose and follow a good fund and keep on top of its fortunes, compared with the time and effort required for keeping track of individual stocks, is as minutes are to hours.

FREEDOM FROM HOUSEKEEPING. Aside from the emotional aspect of investing, there is the problem of mechanics. If you own stocks, you have to protect the certificates unless your stocks are held by your broker in "street name." There may be proxies to sign, rights to exercise, decisions to exercise or sell warrants, and on and on. Then there is the headache at income tax time. At the end of each year, mutual funds provide shareholders with information about the total of dividends and other distributions made during the year and certain pertinent tax information. On a day-to-day basis, the status and value of your mutual fund account can be determined at a glance from the mutual fund quotations in your newspaper.

AUTOMATIC REINVESTMENT OF INCOME DIVIDENDS AND CAPITAL GAINS DISTRIBUTIONS. One of the advantageous features of mutual fund investment is that dividends can be automatically converted to additional shares, thus compounding your investment. Contrast this with the situation when you own a few thousand dollars' worth of each of several stocks. The dividend checks might be so modest that it would be difficult or expensive to reinvest them in additional shares. All too often dividend checks are frittered away, and the investment loses the benefit of compounding. The reinvestment feature of mutual funds can be a driving force in a successful investing program over the long run.

INSTANT DIVERSIFICATION. It often takes as little as $250 to start a mutual fund account. Additional investments can likewise be made in small amounts and at any time. When you buy shares in a mutual fund you buy a pro rata share of many different corporations in a number of different industries. To achieve similar diversification as an individual investor even in a small way would entail considerable time, to say nothing of commission expenses. Furthermore, funds purchase stocks in such large quantities that they almost always qualify for minimum sales commissions.

EXCHANGE PRIVILEGES. Most of the larger investment companies sponsor a variety of funds, which offer a broad range of investment objectives, services, and programs. Thus a shareholder whose investment goals have changed may be able to switch part or all of his principal from one fund to another within the same "family." In addition, this exchange may be done by mail, telegram, or even telephone. The exchange privilege is only one of a number of shareholder services that make mutual funds an increasingly useful adjunct to financial planning. Tax-sheltered retirement plans and systematic investing and withdrawal plans are other features of the modern mutual fund, making it a comprehensive and convenient investment for the individual of moderate means.

Cost of Ownership

Every form of investment has its negative side, mutual funds included. Fund ownership is no free ride; there are costs and fees. We've already discussed the sales charge in the case of load funds. Not so obvious are management fees, which average about 0.75 percent per year of assets for load and no-load funds alike. In some instances the management fee is reduced as the fund's total assets expand. Besides the management fee, there are a number of smaller charges for administrative services, directors' compensation, shareholder servicing, custodian fees, legal fees, reports to stockholders, and the like.

The total of the management fee and the housekeeping costs expressed as a percentage of net assets constitutes the fund's expense ratio. These ratios vary considerably depending on the size of the fund and other factors. For example, at T. Rowe Price Growth Stock they have averaged about 0.6 percent annually in recent years. Aside from efficient management, the low expense ratio reflects the benefits of size, for this is a fund with assets in the hundreds of millions of dollars. Contrast that with the 1.8 percent five-year average for the $12 million Nautilus Fund. Since many expenses are fixed, they understandably represent a larger portion of the cost of running a small fund than of a large fund. What you look for is a declining trend in the expense ratio as assets grow over the years. Otherwise the fund is not managed efficiently, and expenses may become a heavy drain on performance.

When a No-Load Isn't a No-Load

Recently many funds that began as no-loads have been reborn as low-loads. A low-load fund typically charges a fee of 4 percent or less. Low-load fees are used to cover the costs of marketing the fund to new investors; they are not used to pay brokers' commissions. Increasingly all funds, loads and no-loads alike, have added several fees and charges of which you should be aware.

DEFERRED SALES CHARGE. Also called a back-end load, this fee is used by funds to discourage frequent exchanges or early liquidation of shares. Sales charges are assessed when shares are sold before a certain time period has elapsed. For example, Dean Witter charges a deferred load of 5 to 1 percent when shares are liquidated within six years of purchase. The fee is eliminated after six years. Deferred sales charges are often used to pay brokers' commissions on portfolio transactions.

REDEMPTION FEE. This fee, generally 1 to 2 percent, serves to inhibit switching of the fund shares. Redemption fees can disappear after the first year of holding.

12b-1 PLAN. Since 1980, a plan called *12b-1* has been used to help investment companies underwrite the costs of marketing and distributing their funds. The fee can also be used to pay brokerage costs. Although fee amounts are not often disclosed in a prospectus or financial statement, the fact that a 12b-1 is used will be noted somewhere in the prospectus.

There is a maximum allowable charge of 1.25 percent per year under these plans, but generally fees are less than 1 percent of assets per year. Be forewarned that 12b-1 plans often are used by companies that levy deferred sales charges.

Reading the Prospectus

The Securities Act of 1933 requires delivery of a prospectus (essentially an abbreviated form of registration statement) before or with any solicitation of an order for mutual fund shares. The prospectus "tells it all"—something about management and its background, such unfavorable facts as there may be, including litigation and problems with the Securities and Exchange Commission, as well as a host of figures relating to income and expenses, dividends and gains (or losses), portfolio turnover, assets and liabilities, and the portfolio of investments.

In most cases, the funds have taken great pains to word their prospectuses in such a way that the average investor, with careful reading, can find out more about a fund's potential than he can glean from a similar reading of the annual report of an industrial corporation. Only when you buy a new issue, with its accompanying prospectus, are you in a position to learn as much about a corporate common stock.

The prospectus opens with a statement about the fund's primary objective. Thus the prospectus of Financial Industrial Income Fund states:

Financial Industrial Income Fund, Inc. (the "Fund") pursues its investment objective of seeking the best possible current income while following sound investment practices by investing its assets in securities which will provide a relatively high yield and stable return and which, over a period of years, may also provide capital appreciation. Capital growth potential is a secondary factor in the selection of portfolio securities of the Fund. The Fund invests in common stock, as well as convertible bonds and preferred stocks.

The prospectus also elaborates on the fund's investment aims and gives information about the minimum starting investment ($250 in the case of Financial Industrial Income) and the minimum subsequent investment, which is generally $50 or less. Early in the prospectus is a statement of per-share income and capital changes for each of the past 10 years. That will give you an idea of the fund's investment income and expenses, its dividends, and its net realized and unrealized gains (or losses) on securities. The statistical tables that accompany this information show changes in net asset value and various financial ratios, such as the ratio of expenses to average net assets, and the ratio of net investment income to average net assets. It usually shows annual portfolio turnover.

The prospectus, coupled with the fund's "Statement of Additional Information," outlines the fund's investment parameters. For example, near the beginning of the Statement of Additional Information of the Financial Industrial Income Fund it is stated that the fund may not "sell short or buy on margin unless it is a temporary measure for clearance of purchases of securities. . . . buy or sell commodities, commodity contracts, or real estate (however, securities of companies investing in real estate may be purchased). . . . invest in any company for the purpose of control or management. . . . buy other than readily marketable securities. . . . purchase securities if the purchase would cause the fund to have more than 5 percent of the value of its total assets invested in the securities of any one company, or to own more than 10 percent of the voting securities of any one company (except obligations issued or guaranteed by the U.S. Government)."

Next comes information about the fund's investment advisor, plus the names and backgrounds of officers and directors. Information on the "how-to's" follows: how to purchase shares, how to redeem shares, how to exchange shares, and how to transfer shares. Then come statements about the fund's dividend policies, dates dividends are paid from investment income if and when earned, and perhaps a few remarks on the tax status of dividends and capital gains distributions.

The Statement of Additional Information ends with a statement about the fund's investments, including a breakdown of the proportion of the portfolio in common stocks and bonds as well as the number of shares and the market value of each holding as of the statement date. The prospectus may also provide the cost of each investment, thus enabling the reader to see at a glance how the portfolio is doing. Other statements about assets and liabilities, along with notes to the financial statements, bring up the rear.

The Pulse of Portfolio Turnover

The frequency with which securities are bought and sold is a vital measure of a fund. By itself, however, it does not tell all you need to know to evaluate a fund's prospects. You might call it a financial heartbeat. A rapid heartbeat may be shown by a vigorous individual enjoying healthful exercise, and in someone else it may be symptomatic of a morbid condition. Similarly, a performance fund may show a substantial portfolio turnover rate and good performance all at the same time; a similar turnover rate for a fund that never goes anywhere suggests both poor portfolio management and a heavy drain on net assets from brokerage commissions and related expenses. The table on the next page will give you some idea of the wide variation there is among funds as to expenses and portfolio turnover rates.

An Important "Don't"

There is nothing to be gained by acquiring mutual fund shares immediately before dividends or capital gains distributions. On the contrary, to do so can hurt you.

Here's how: Apart from the ups and downs of the stock market, asset value gradually increases to the extent that portfolio securities can be a source of interest and dividend income to the fund. When portfolio holdings appreciate, so much the better, for this also builds asset value. To the extent such appreciation is realized, it becomes a source of capital gains distributions. Dividends from investment income and capital gains distributions are paid to the shareholder who buys the shares before the ex-dividend date. In other words,

1989 FACTS ON 25 REPRESENTATIVE MUTUAL FUNDS

Fund	Total Assets*	Fund Type†	Expense Ratio	Turnover Rate	Maximum Load‡
Alliance Quasar	$303.3 mil.	AG	1.73%	89%	5.5
Amer. Capital Harbor	373.8	CV	0.76	94	5.75
Columbia Growth	261.5	G	0.96	166	NL
Delaware Decatur II	347.9	GI	1.24	60	4.75
Eaton Vance Nautilus	12.9	ST	1.88	114	4.75
Evergreen Fund	711.8	G	1.11	40	NL
Fidelity Equity-Income	4,688.5	GI	0.63	68	2.0
Fid. High Yield Tax-Free	1,702.9	TE	0.58	71	NL
Fidelity Magellan	13,176.9	AG	1.08	87	3.0
Franklin U.S. Gov't. Sec.	11,233.0	FI	0.52	26	4.0
Guardian Park Avenue	247.1	G	0.79	48	4.5
Legg Mason Value Trust	808.8	G	1.96	30	NL
MFS MMB Trust	1,304.8	TE	0.64	199	4.75
Merrill Lynch Pacific	246.6	IF	1.05	18	6.5
Mutual Qualified Income	1,342.6	GI	0.70	73	NL
Mutual Shares Corp.	3,151.0	GI	0.65	72	NL
Nicholas II	393.2	G	0.74	8	NL
Northeast Investors Tr.	291.9	FI	1.33	34	NL
OTC Securities	291.9	G	1.14	33	4.75
Pioneer II	4,340.5	GI	0.77	34	8.5
SteinRoe Special	369.6	AG	0.96	205	NL
Strategic Silver	24.6	S	1.49	0	8.5
Templeton World	4,403.2	G	0.59	16	8.5
Twentieth Century Select	2,862.7	G	1.00	93	NL
Vanguard Wellesley Income	835.2	FI	0.45	23	NL

* Assets as of March 31, 1990.
† AG—Aggressive Growth; CV—Convertible Securities; FI—Fixed Income; G—Growth; GI—Growth & Income; IF—International Fund; S—Specialized; ST—Technology; TE—Tax-Exempt.
‡ NL—No-Load.

the ex-dividend date is the day on and after which the buyer of a share is not entitled to a previously declared dividend.

An investor who purchases fund shares shortly before an ex-dividend date will receive the dividend, to be sure, but it will be a hollow benefit. The pitfalls are spelled out in the prospectus, but while some funds take pains to explain the matter in some detail, others slough it off as a minor detail. This is unfortunate, because in a strong market the payments can be big and the tax consequences important.

Here's how one fund explained it:

Prior to purchasing shares of a fund, the impact of dividends or capital gains distributions which are expected to be announced or have been announced but not paid should be carefully considered. Any such dividends or capital gains distributions paid shortly after a purchase of shares by an investor prior to the record date will have the effect of reducing the per share net asset value of his shares by the amount of the dividends or distributions. All or a portion of such dividends or distributions, although in effect a return of capital, are subject to taxes. The individual should consult his own tax advisor for any special advice.

No one wants to pay taxes on someone else's gains, yet that is the situation if shares are purchased just before a capital gains distribution. Moreover, in the case of a load fund, the sales charges could be needlessly high.

Funds in Your Future?

There you have some of the basics of mutual funds—where they came from, how they work, what to look for in evaluating one, how to read a prospectus. As you must have concluded from the foregoing, it's not exactly a matter of running your finger down a list of funds, finding one whose name intrigues you, and buying it to hold for keeps.

As with any investment decision, you have to know first what your own objectives are. Then you must find the proper vehicle—or, more frequently, vehicles—for meeting those objectives. Mutual funds can and do play an important part in achieving the investment goals of millions of Americans. How well funds do for you as an individual investor depends in large measure on how skillfully you have chosen the funds in your portfolio.

Just as you must evaluate other investments as to quality and the type and extent of risk each embodies, you must do the same with mutual funds. Some funds are better managed than others. Some place more emphasis on safety of principal than others. Some trade off quality of their holdings for higher yields or the chance of greater growth.

What Kind of Fund?

If you are a risk taker at heart and like a fast ride for your buck, look at the high-performance funds, generally referred to as aggressive growth funds. If you buy for the long haul and have in mind a nest egg for retirement many years hence, you should stick with the sound-quality growth funds. If you want some current income while waiting for the day you cash in your shares, you should try to find funds that combine good current income with a potential for growth, that is, growth and income funds. Finally, if income is all-important and you are willing to settle for little or no growth in the process, funds with a focus on fixed income may be for you.

Often people find that their investment objectives change over time. Different stages of life—young adulthood, child rearing, midlife, retirement, old age—make different financial demands. Mutual fund families offer a ready method of accommodating changing investment needs. A family is a group of funds, each with a different objective, sponsored by a single investment company; three well-known ones are Fidelity, Vanguard, and T. Rowe Price. Most load-fund sponsors allow exchanges from fund to fund at minimal (usually $5) charge. Fund switching can also be used to take advantage of stock market cycles. And a money-market fund can be used to give conventional mutual fund investments added liquidity. When you need to cash in shares, a process that normally can take five days or more, simply instruct the fund sponsor to move the desired amount from the stock or bond fund to the money-market account. The transferred funds are then accessible by writing a money-market check.

Closed Funds and Clones

As a mutual fund attracts investments, it gets larger and larger. Eventually it may become so sizable that its management may have difficulty moving in and out of stock positions at satisfactory prices. Fulfilling the fund's investment objectives can become tough sledding. For this reason some popular funds have been closed to new investors. Present shareholders' money continues to be managed as before. Dividends can be reinvested, and new money may be added to their accounts. Sometimes the fund will reopen after a time, or the sponsor may simply opt to start a clone. A clone is a mutual fund whose investment objectives closely resemble those of some other, established fund from the same sponsor. Clones often sport familiar names onto which Roman numerals have been tacked to indicate generation: Pioneer II, Nicholas II, and Olympus Option Income Portfolio II are examples. Once spawned, the offspring may or may not mimic the performance of its parent. Also worthy of note, clone fund management may differ from that of the predecessor fund.

A SAMPLE OF MUTUAL FUNDS BY INVESTMENT OBJECTIVES

Quality Growth

Acorn Fund

Babson Enterprise

Evergreen Fund

Guardian Mutual

Nicholas II

OTC Securities

Templeton Growth

Fixed Income

Fidelity High Income

Fidelity High Yield Municipals

Franklin U.S. Govt. Securities

Northeast Investors Trust

Pacific American Income

Wellesley Income

Growth and Income

American Capital Harbor Fund

Decatur Income

Evergreen Total Return

Fidelity Equity-Income

Mutual Beacon

Aggressive Growth

Alliance Quasar

Fidelity Magellan

Janus Fund

Price (T. Rowe) Capital Appreciation

SteinRoe Special

Tudor Fund

Twentieth Century Select

Again . . . Diversify

For the same reason you choose a mutual fund to diversify your portfolio and thereby spread your risk, you should not put all of your investment eggs in the same mutual fund basket, either. By avoiding that trap, you will cut your losses should a fund you are holding undergo a management crisis, lose its "magic touch," or just plain hit a patch of poor luck.

CHAPTER 13

Special-Purpose Investment Funds

COLLECTIVELY, MUTUAL FUNDS compose a dynamic, ever-evolving industry. Sponsors have been resourceful in bringing out new products to fit changing market conditions and investors' desires. In recent years, new types of funds have been devised, particularly in the income area—with narrowly aimed industry-specific or geographically limited funds also coming on the scene.

This section is devoted to a rundown of funds that meet specialized investment objectives. Few of these funds should stand alone in an investment program, but they can be used with other funds or securities to tailor your portfolio to your particular financial needs.

Convertible Funds

Though convertible bonds and preferred stocks are insignificant in number of issues compared to Wall Street's aggregate, mutual funds investing in these securities offer reliable income and the potential for healthy capital gains. *Convertible bonds* are securities that, at the option of the bondholder, may be converted into the common stock of the issuing corporation. This conversion takes place at a prescribed price or ratio. *Convertible preferred stock* is likewise convertible

122

into common shares of the issuer. The market for convertibles is generally strongest when stocks are rising and interest rates are high. But during weak markets convertibles offer special appeal because they retain their value better than the underlying common stock.

It makes sense to purchase convertible funds after the underlying stock prices have fallen. That's when the bargains are found. There are several funds that have a sizable percentage of their assets in convertible securities, among them AIM Convertible Yield Securities, American Capital Harbor, Calmos Convertible Income, Fidelity Convertible Securities, Putnam Convertible Income-Growth, Value Line Convertible, and Vanguard Convertible Securities.

Gold Funds

Some investors choose gold stocks as a hedge in times of war, social upheaval, inflation, or other dire distresses. During 1973–74, when inflation was rampant and foreign exchange rates fluctuating, gold-bullion and gold-mining shares lured large numbers of speculators and individuals seeking to protect the purchasing power of their savings. Aside from their disaster-hedge value to pessimists, gold and gold-fund shares have little usefulness except as speculation on the value of gold itself. Gold funds are volatile, heaped with political and economic hazards, and burdened with the unpredictability of the production process itself. In fact, the performance of gold funds is ragged, generally even poor. But if an investment in gold will give you peace of mind, or if gold-market timing is your interest, try Blanchard Precious Metals, Fidelity Select American Gold, Franklin Gold Fund, Keystone Precious Metals Holdings, Lexington Goldfund, Oppenheimer Gold & Special Minerals, United Gold Shares, USAA Gold Fund, or Vanguard Special Gold & Precious Metal.

Foreign Funds

An investment made on a foreign stock market can produce gains in two ways. The first is by a simple increase in the price of the foreign shares. Often foreign markets are out of step with American ones. The Japanese economy, for example, grew twice as fast as the American economy from 1953 to 1983. Because foreign market cycles frequently lag American ones, they often heat up when the U.S. market is cooling down, and therefore provide additional opportunities for investors. The second means of profiting from foreign investments is through disparities in the relative exchange rates for U.S. and foreign currencies. If an American investor puts $2,000 into the German stock market and the value of the deutsche mark rises by 10 percent relative to the dollar, then the value of the German shares rises to $2,200 when converted back into U.S. dollars. As you can see, such exchange-rate windfalls have nothing to do with the underlying value of stocks themselves. When the dollar is rising relative to a foreign currency, foreign investments will lose value when translated into dollars; when the dollar falls, they will gain value in U.S. dollars.

The two components, share value and exchange rates, must be considered together to determine whether a foreign investment is a money-maker. During 1984 many foreign stock markets outperformed the U.S. market in terms of their own currency. For the American investor, though, the strength of the dollar effectively wiped out most of the very large overseas gains. But for those who hung on, 1985 was a different story; a declining dollar permitted the favorable conversion of profits acquired the year before.

Since foreign markets are often remote, volatile, and less closely regulated than Wall Street, one of the better ways for most people to participate in them is through an international mutual fund. Such funds may either hold stocks from the most promising markets around the globe, as do Templeton's World and Putnam's International, or they may be composed of stocks from one region or market, as are the Japan Fund and Merrill Lynch's Pacific. Other leading foreign funds include Templeton Growth and Global II, Fidelity Overseas, G.T. Pacific, and Vanguard World International Portfolio.

The recent breakdown of political and economic barriers has resulted in a torrent of new investment dollars flowing into funds with overseas operations. International mutual funds could prove to be one of the more lucrative fund arenas for the 1990s.

Ginnie Mae Funds

When interest rates are down, Ginnie Maes heat up. But Ginnie Maes, often touted as offering unbeatable safety and yield, are both more complex and more unpredictable than they seem at first glance. The Government National Mortgage Association (GNMA), or Ginnie Mae, as it is affectionately known, specializes in mortgage pass-through certificates backed by the full faith and credit of the U.S. government. Ginnie Maes represent shares in pools of mortgages, issued either by the Federal Housing Administration or the Veterans Administration and insured by GNMA. GNMA guarantees the homeowners' mortgage payments, both principal and interest, and passes them through to investors each month, even if a homeowner defaults. A growing number of fund sponsors, recognizing the popularity of Ginnie Maes, have begun offering GNMA mutual funds. Because the yield on government-backed Ginnie Maes is often 2 percent higher than the yield on an equivalent Treasury issue, they are attractive to many income investors.

A Ginnie Mae mutual fund is the easiest way to invest in these certificates for several reasons. First, the average minimum investment in a Ginnie Mae fund is substantially less than $25,000 for a GNMA certificate. Then, too, the professional management of a mutual fund is especially advantageous in mortgage security investing because the average investor has neither the time nor the expertise to analyze and track rates on different Ginnie Mae pools. Also, since mortgage-backed securities, unlike other fixed-income investments, return dribbles of principal along with monthly interest payments, reinvestment can be irksome. Ginnie Mae funds automatically reinvest these payments of principal and they will reinvest interest, too, upon request.

The following funds invest solely in GNMA certificates: Franklin U.S. Government Securities, Lexington, Price (T. Rowe), Scudder, and Vanguard GNMA funds. Other funds—

Alliance Mortgage Securities, Fidelity Mortgage Securities, USAA Income, and Van Kampen Merritt U.S. Government— invest in Federal National Mortgage Association (FNMA) and Federal Home Loan Mortgage Corporation (FHLMC) issues in addition to GNMAs. While FNMA and FHLMC are federally chartered, their securities, which aren't government backed, offer slightly higher yields.

Index Funds

The Vanguard Group introduced the first index fund to be offered to the public, First Index Investment Trust, in August 1976. This fund seeks to provide investment results corresponding to the price and yield performance of the Standard & Poor's 500 Composite Stock Index. To achieve this end the trust holds all of the issues in the S&P.

Although First Index Investment Trust tracks the S&P, there are some mutual funds that have outperformed it over the long term. If you are content to ride the coattails of the Standard & Poor's 500 and have no expectations of doing better than this average, then an index fund may be satisfactory. However, if you have loftier goals and a conviction that good judgment pays off in above-average performance, then your investment dollars may be better off in a managed mutual fund.

Money-Market Funds

A soft stock market and hefty returns of 10 percent or more combined to give money-market funds a lot of appeal when they were introduced in 1974. Two dozen or so were started that year, and investors salted away more than $3 billion in them by the end of 1975. Increasingly, small businesses, corporations, and individuals found these funds convenient repositories for their cash reserves. In terms of sales, number of funds, and total accounts outstanding, the growth of the money-market fund has no parallel in the investment industry. At year end 1974, there were but 15 money-market funds, with total assets of $1.7 billion. By 1991, there were over 700 such funds (including institutional funds), holding assets totaling in excess of $540 billion. Among the largest of the conventional money mutuals are Merrill Lynch's CMA Money Fund, Merrill Lynch Ready Assets, Dreyfus Worldwide Dollar, Dean Witter/Sears Liquid Assets, Fidelity Cash Reserves, Fidelity Spartan, and SLH Daily Dividend.

What makes money-market funds so attractive to so many? Safety of principal. Money-market funds are the only investment vehicles that maintain a constant price, usually $1.00 per share. To obtain this constant share value, money funds use various investment means, including bank CDs with short, often two-week, maturities, U.S. Treasury bills, bankers' acceptances, and prime commercial paper. Some funds, which take slightly more risk for the chance at slightly higher yields, use repurchase agreements (repos), nonprime commercial paper, letters of credit, and Yankee and Euro dollars (domestic deposits in foreign banks).

Besides safety of principal, money-market funds have two other attractive characteristics. They provide automatic dividend reinvestment and cashlike liquidity. Check-writing privileges make money-market investments as easy to tap as conventional checking accounts—although most funds have a $500 minimum per check. Also, exchange privileges with other mutual funds in the same fund family—for example, Fidelity's Cash Reserves may be exchanged for shares of another Fidelity fund or vice versa—allow investors to implement changing financial objectives and to gain access to equity fund assets easily.

If the promise of tax-free income is worth sacrificing a point or two of yield, a tax-exempt money-market fund may be the answer. Such funds invest in short-term issues by, or on behalf of, state and local governments. Tax-free yields are available from Merrill Lynch CMA Tax-Exempt, Fidelity Tax-Exempt MMT, Dreyfus Tax-Exempt, and Municipal Cash Reserve Management, among others.

When ironclad safety is a must, a fund that invests solely in Treasuries is your ticket. Capital Preservation Fund, Dreyfus Money Market Instruments Government Fund, Merrill Lynch USA Government, Neuberger & Berman Government MF, and T. Rowe Price U.S. Treasury MF are just a few of the Treasury-only funds. Other funds, which invest in agency as well as Treasury debt, include Cash Equivalent Government Securities, Dean Witter/Sears U.S. Government, Liberty Government Money Market Trust, and SLH Government & Agency Fund.

Municipal Bond Funds

Until the Tax Reform Act of 1976, there was no way a conventional mutual fund could pass along to investors the tax-exempt status of interest earned on municipal bonds held in their portfolios. Unit trusts, reviewed below, were able to pass through this tax exemption, but it was necessary to change the tax laws to cover conventional mutuals. Once an appropriate law was passed, mutual fund sponsors lost little time in introducing managed municipal bond funds. Within a few years, more than 30 such funds were offering shares to the public. Today there are more than 150 muni funds, with total assets in the tens of billions.

The tax-exempt bond mutuals have drawn their share of critics. Some say that they are not the straightforward, safe investments they were at their inception. Seesawing interest rates and huge numbers of poorly rated bonds have introduced new risks into these vehicles. Today municipal bond funds fall into a variety of risk categories ranging from ultra-conservative *insured* to high-yielding *"junk."* Low-risk funds include Merrill Lynch Municipal Bond Fund Insured Portfolio and the Vanguard Insured Long-Term Portfolio. Both purchase munis insured by AMBAC Indemnity Corporation and the Municipal Bond Investors Assurance. At the price of assuming a little more risk, slightly higher yields can be obtained from the SteinRoe Tax-Exempt Bond Fund and MFS Managed Municipal Bond Trust. These funds invest primarily in municipals rated A or better by Moody's or Standard & Poor's. Most volatile, but highest yielding, are "junk" funds, which invest in low- to medium-quality municipal issues. Two such funds are Colonial Tax-Exempt High Yield and Fidelity High Yield Municipals.

Another variation on the municipal bond fund theme is the single-state or single-city fund, which is exempt not only from federal taxes but also from the issuing state's or city's taxes. These have become very popular in heavily taxed states such as California or municipalities such as New York City.

Municipal bond mutual funds are available in no-load, low-load, and load varieties (commonly charging 4 to 4¾ percent). Dividends accrue daily and are distributed monthly or quarterly or are automatically reinvested, whichever is elected. Many also offer exchange privileges with their other funds.

Option-Income Funds

The primary investment objective of option-income funds is to provide shareholders with a high level of current income. To achieve this goal, the funds write covered call options on a diversified portfolio of common stocks, the majority of which are dividend paying.

When a mutual fund writes such an option, it agrees to sell by a certain date shares of its stock to the purchaser for a specified price in excess of the market price at the time the option is written. These options often expire without being exercised, because the stock fails to reach the exercise price by expiration date.

In exchange for this promise to sell, the fund receives a premium from the purchaser of the call option. Premiums are distributed to shareholders on a quarterly basis and are considered to be short-term capital gains. When these premiums are added to the portfolio's common stock dividends, the total return can exceed 14 percent per annum.

You've seen how you can win with option income. Now let's look at how you can lose. Option writing imposes a sharp limitation on potential profits. If a fund sells options during a rapidly rising market, the income earned from premiums is often far less than the amount forfeited through missed stock appreciation. As a simple example, consider a mutual fund that owns 100 shares of General Electric selling at $53 per share. To earn extra income, the fund decides to write an option at $55 on its GE holdings for a premium of $275. If the stock's value rises above the prearranged price of $55 before the expiration date, the option will undoubtedly be exercised (the fund will have to deliver its 100 shares). While the fund will pocket the difference between the amount at which it purchased GE and the price at which it was called away plus the premium received for selling the call, it will not share in the capital gains should the stock continue to climb in value.

When stock prices are falling, writing covered calls can help offset a portfolio's losses. Option-income funds are far less volatile than the market as a whole. However, the premiums paid for options are at their lowest during bear markets. The environment in which option-income funds perform best is one that is relatively stable—rising or falling only gradually.

Leaders in this category include Putnam Option Income I, Kemper Diversified Income, Colonial Income Plus, Olympus Option Income Plus II, and Zweig Option Income.

Sector Funds

Sector funds invest in the stocks of a single industry or market segment. Fidelity's Select Portfolios Fund, first introduced in 1981, is the father of the portfolio-type sector mutuals. It gave investors the choice of four different portfolios and the ability to switch among them. By late 1986 the number of funds in Select Portfolios had swelled to 25. Other mutual fund companies, Vanguard and Financial Group among them, have joined the sector game.

Sector fund investing is risky; it is best reserved for the knowledgeable, active, aggressive investor. These single-industry funds are becoming more and more specialized. The sector supermarket now spans the alphabet from air transport to utilities. So although Fidelity and Vanguard may nearly always have a sector fund or two in the top 10 performers, very rarely are they the same ones from period to period. If the potential for huge profits and the ability to control your investments are irresistible to you, we suggest investigating Fidelity's original six sector portfolios: Energy, Financial, Health Care, Precious Metals, Technology, and Utilities. They are more diversified than newer ones and require less day-to-day vigilance.

In order to profit from market segment funds, one must be savvy enough to invest in a sector before it heats up and disciplined enough to get out before it loses steam. How does one get in and out at the right time? The majority of investors and professionals have learned that they don't, at least not with any degree of consistency.

If an investor believes a particular industry group has long-term growth potential, should he purchase a corresponding sector-portfolio fund? Probably not. When one sector is hot, its assets generally increase, and when it is not, shareholders abandon it for the current darling. This ebb and flow of money can cause the portfolio manager to sell a stock prematurely to cover redemptions, or he may be forced to hold too much cash. Neither scenario bodes well for the long-term investor. For long-term holding, a sector fund that is not part of a portfolio is a better bet. Technology enthusiasts might try Alliance Technology or Merrill Lynch Sci/Tech Holdings, "A." Price Science & Technology and Putnam Health Sciences Trust are good choices for the health/medical industry investor.

Social-Action Funds

A number of funds have emerged that cater to investors' wishes to take political stands or precipitate social change. Such funds use a predetermined philosophical screen to select stocks for their portfolios. Commonly such funds will not invest in companies doing business in South Africa, using nuclear power generators, or manufacturing armaments. In the past these funds have had returns generally similar to or better than those of the Standard & Poor's 500. Leading social-action funds include Calvert Social Investment Managed Growth Portfolio, Dreyfus Third Century Fund, Fidelity Select Environmental Services, New Alternatives Fund,

Parnassus Fund, Pax World, and Pioneer Fund. Calvert and Working Assets also manage socially responsible money-market funds.

Unit Trusts

Unit trusts are similar to conventional funds in that they allow investors to obtain a share of a widely diversified portfolio, thereby benefiting from lower risk through diversification. However, they differ in one very important respect. The portfolios of unit trusts are fixed; no new bonds are added after the initial offering. No trading of the portfolio bonds is allowed—the funds exist as self-liquidating trusts until all or most of the bonds reach maturity or are retired.

The proceeds from trust securities that mature or are called are distributed rather than reinvested. Unit trusts offer monthly, quarterly, or semiannual distributions or income reinvestment in a money-market mutual fund or open-end bond fund managed by the sponsor. The trustee also furnishes statements for tax purposes. Pay careful attention to these, as trust distributions can represent a return of principal as well as interest income. Return of principal is not taxable and should usually be saved for future reinvestment.

Shares in the trusts are called units. Unit prices will fluctuate with interest rates and market conditions and will reflect portions of principal that have been called or have matured. Unit trusts yield an average of 1 to 2 percent more than comparable diversified municipal bond funds because trust expenses are lower. Although they are under no obligation to do so, sponsors maintain a secondary market in their units. Should a unit be redeemed before maturity, its value is generally based on the bid prices of underlying bonds.

Taxable corporate and federal tax-exempt municipal unit trusts are regularly launched by brokers and dealers such as Merrill Lynch and John Nuveen; minimum investment amounts range from $1,000 to $5,000. When a unit trust comes to market, its stated return takes into account both a front-end sales charge ranging from 3.9 to 5 percent and estimated annual expenses per unit. Unit trusts are available both as intermediate-term investments, with bond lives from 5 to 15 years, and as long-term investments, having 15- to 40-year maturities. Because the trusts are self-liquidating, over time the ever-smaller portfolio will reduce income payments.

Unit trusts, like municipal bond funds, are offered in single-state and insured forms. The single-state tax-exempt feature is a boon in high-tax states. Insurance is an expensive balm for the skittish. But if insurance appeals to you, be sure to purchase a product, like Nuveen's insured trusts, in which each bond is permanently insured by the Municipal Bond Investors Assurance (MBIA). Such bonds receive AAA ratings from Standard & Poor's. This kind of insurance is called "insured to maturity" and is superior to "while-in-trust-only" coverage. "While-in-trust-only" coverage ceases when bonds are sold, and thereafter cast-off bonds are priced according to their intrinsic credit worth.

CHAPTER 14

Options

TO UNDERSTAND OPTIONS and to be able to employ this knowledge for profit is to be the object of awe among the uninitiated who mill and churn in the courtyards of the temples of investment. To presume to do so without proper understanding is to invite almost certain financial disaster.

Fewer still are those who possess the capacity to convey this esoteric and mysterious wisdom by means of the spoken or written word. It is thus with due humility that we embark on this chapter.

The first step in your rite of passage is an introduction to the colorful language of options. Puts. Calls. Strips. Straps. Straddles. Spreads. Naked Options. Naked short puts. Trapezoidal hedges. The list goes on.

The basic concept of options is simple enough. They are used in many businesses as a matter of course. Option contracts are nothing more than obligations to buy or sell a given piece of property at a stated price within a specified time period. A real estate purchase and sale agreement is something like an option contract, and if you've ever bought or sold a house, chances are you used one.

CBOE: Order from Chaos

Until the Chicago Board Options Exchange (CBOE) opened its doors in April 1973, trading in puts and calls was a haphazard venture. Each contract was individually negotiated by brokers for the buyer and seller. Once an investor was into a contract there was little opportunity for his transferring it to a third party.

Initially, the CBOE traded only call options, and those on only 16 stocks. By mid-1977, it was listing options for stocks of more than 100 companies, each offering three expiration dates and at least as many different striking prices. We'll define these terms as the explanation proceeds.

Investors, always eager for new ways to make a killing, latched on to options with such enthusiasm and with such obvious profit to the CBOE that other exchanges soon were clamoring for a piece of the action. By 1980, the American, Pacific, and Philadelphia stock exchanges were sitting comfortably on the options bandwagon. The Big Board, a latecomer to the field, lists puts and calls on fewer than 50 issues, compared with around 200 each for the CBOE and ASE and around 125 apiece for the two other option exchanges. In addition to equity options, the five exchanges actively trade options on stock indexes, interest rates, and foreign currencies. All told, puts and calls are listed on around 700 issues.

The CBOE introduced, and the four option exchanges adopted, a systematized method of setting striking prices and expiration dates for contracts. The exchanges also provide liquidity and visibility for options transactions. The trading of options on multiple exchanges is being adopted in stages as a new computer system called Public Investor Privileged Express (PIPE) linking the exchanges is fully operative. PIPE enables brokers to place the orders with exchanges offering the best price, greatest liquidity, and lowest execution costs.

Purchases and sales are handled in much the same way as they are for common stocks. An order is placed with your broker and is executed on the floor of the exchange. Once an order between a buyer and seller is matched, their connection is severed and the Options Clearing Corporation steps in to become buyer to the seller and seller to the buyer. In this way both parties to the contract are free to take whatever subsequent action they choose, independent of each other. Thus, contracts may be closed out at any time before expiration by making an offsetting trade. Furthermore, the Options Clearing Corporation, which serves all the option exchanges, guarantees that stock will be delivered if the option is exercised *and* that the seller will be paid.

While the various option exchanges are auction markets, not all of them use the CBOE system of competitive market makers. This was a major innovation of the new exchange. The two functions normally handled by the specialist were separated. A board broker took over the brokerage function of executing limit orders placed by floor brokers. Competing market makers were assigned to take over the specialist function of trading for their own accounts to stabilize the market. This tends to make the CBOE a more efficient market, with premiums cleaving closely to supply and demand balances.

Two-Year Options Introduced

Late in 1990, the CBOE and the American Stock Exchange opened trading in two-year options on 25 blue chips. Known as "Leaps"—Long-Term Equity Anticipation Securities—on the CBOE and as long-term stock options on the Amex, they came to market during a period of declining stock prices. Needless to say their reception was less than enthusiastic. One month after introduction open interest amounted to only 6,000 contracts. These long-term options are similar in every way but longevity to previously existing option contracts. Because long-term options have a longer life, the premiums on them are greater than those on short-term options.

Call Options

A call is an option to buy 100 shares of the underlying stock at a specified price, known as the "exercise price" or "striking price," within a specified time period. Unless the Options Clearing Corporation makes a change to reflect a stock split, one option contract is for 100 shares of the underlying security. Striking prices are set at 5-point intervals on or around the trading price for stocks selling below 50 and usually at 10-point intervals for those above 50. A new option series is initiated nine months before its expiration date, so that at any given time three contracts with the same exercise price are available on one underlying stock, with maturities three months apart. Options with the same expiration date may be offered with several different striking prices.

When the striking price is above the current trading price, the call is said to be trading "out of the money." A strike below market price would mean the call was "in the money." When market and striking prices jibe, the option is "at the money." Although premiums—the price you actually pay for the option—generally run from 5 to 12 percent of the price of the underlying stock at the time of the option's introduction, this figure then varies with supply and demand and with time. Options are a wasting asset; that is, they have a value for their limited life span, beyond which they are worthless.

If the premium, which is paid to the seller (also called the "writer") of the option, and the option striking price are equal to the current price of the stock, that option is said to be trading "at parity." The premium tends to move point for point with the share price only when the option is at parity. Before that the premium rises less than point for point, since the leverage value is reduced at parity and thus the demand for that call dries up.

In a rising market, the demand for options increases as the number of sellers decreases. This increase in demand under normal circumstances tends to enlarge the premium. In a declining market, the reverse is true, causing the premium to narrow.

The relationship between the striking price and the stock price has an important influence on the size of the premium. A call with a striking price of 40 on a stock trading at 50 is understandably worth more than a call with a strike of 60. A call approaching its expiration date with little chance of being exercised at a profit will move down in value and expire worthless.

Another factor that influences the call premium is an approaching ex-dividend date. It is just before this date that options are most frequently exercised by option buyers eager to collect the dividend. In order to prevent the stock from being called away, the writer may buy an offsetting call to close out his contract. This tends to enlarge the premium before the ex-dividend date as demand exceeds supply.

These various influences can be clearly seen in the chart below of a common stock and two of its call options.

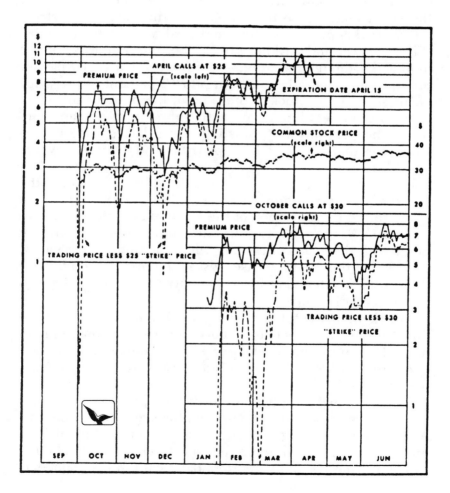

The space between the dashed and solid lines represents the amount by which the call is trading above parity, or its tangible value. The effect of time is obvious; the "fat" in the premium is trimmed away as the calls approach expiration. In fact, the April call traded below its tangible value (parity) about a month before expiration, a clear warning to option writers that exercise was a strong probability. The October call, trading well above its parity value until June, shows very succinctly the vital influence of time in the level of a premium.

When to Buy and When to Sell Calls

The call option *buyer* is looking for a rise in the price of the underlying security. If the stock moves up, he may choose to exercise the call and buy the stock at its strike price, which would then be below the current market price. Or he could liquidate the call by selling one bearing the same date and striking price. It is the latter transaction that is most commonly used, since this does not entail the expenditure of additional capital.

If the option is covered before expiration, a short- or long-term capital gain is realized, depending on whether the holding period exceeds six months. However, if the buyer chooses instead to exercise the option and actually acquire the shares, no taxable event will have occurred as long as he keeps the shares. But his cost basis for these shares will be increased by the premium paid for the option. Thus, if the call was bought at a premium of 5 and exercised at 30, the cost basis will be 35 and the exercise date becomes the purchase date for tax purposes.

When the underlying security moves contrary to expectations and it becomes clear that a loss is inevitable, the call buyer is usually best off to take some action rather than allowing the option to expire worthless. He should make a closing sale transaction in order to reduce the extent of the loss. However, he should be sure to make his move before the proceeds from the sale sink below what he would have to pay the broker in commissions. Either an expiration or a closing sale is a short- or long-term capital loss. A covering transaction that would reduce the loss may or may not be possible, depending on whether a buyer exists for that particular series.

A *writer* (seller) of covered options is generally interested in generating a greater return from his long-term holdings than would be possible from dividends alone. When a call is written against securities already owned, it is referred to as "covered."

Writing "naked" options, where the underlying stock is not owned by the seller, is quite another matter. This highly speculative technique will produce a profit if the stock declines or remains constant, but the profit is limited to the amount of the premium received. On the other hand, if the stock rises, the potential for loss is unlimited, as it is on a short sale. Then the writer must either make a closing purchase transaction to liquidate his contract or buy shares at market to cover when the call is exercised.

The premium paid to an option writer is not reported as income when received. If the option expires unexercised, the premium is taxed as a short-term capital gain in the year of exercise. If a covering option is bought, the difference is a short-term gain or loss. However, under certain special circumstances, a loss on a covered call may be long term.

Options and Margin Requirements

Option-writing programs, covered or otherwise, are executed in margin accounts. Margin agreements give the broker a lien on the assets in the account and assure the proper delivery of shares or cash as required. Options currently have no loan value in a margin account. Writers of naked options must maintain sufficient cash or loan value in their accounts to fulfill their obligation in the event of a call.

In a sideways or declining market, when profits are difficult to come by, an option-writing program can generate additional cash flow from a portfolio. However, the market does not always perform as expected, and the call writer may be faced with delivering securities he would prefer to hold.

Rather than incurring a large capital gains tax liability, he could purchase new shares to satisfy the call obligation.

Avoiding Unwanted Exercise Notices

A call can be exercised at any time up to expiration; the writer has *no* choice in the matter but to give up the shares he promised to sell. If he really doesn't want to sell, he can watch for and heed certain early warning signals. The odds that a call will be exercised are highest just before an ex-dividend date, since the buyer will want to own the stock and collect the dividend. Also, as a call reaches parity, the likelihood of exercise increases, and, of course, a profitable call would never be allowed to expire unexercised.

To avoid having to deliver shares, an investor must make a closing purchase transaction in the same call series before an exercise notice is received. Exercise notices are assigned on a random basis and delivered to member firms by the Options Clearing Corporation. Brokerage firms may use a random selection method or may assign exercise notices on a first-in, first-out basis. You should check to find out which method your broker uses, since it could have a strong bearing on when to close out a questionable option. Once an exercise notice is received, the writer's choices are narrowed—the underlying stock must be delivered, be it shares already owned or new shares purchased to cover. At that point, the call can no longer be liquidated by executing an offsetting option transaction.

It is usually more profitable to write call options in a declining or trendless market than in a rising market. An up market favors the call buyer. While an "in-the-money" call may earn the writer a larger immediate cash advance, this type of contract stands a greater chance of being exercised. Similarly, for a call buyer an "out-of-the-money" option is the least costly but also the most likely to expire worthless.

Balancing these risk-reward factors when there may be a dozen or more choices for one stock is not easy. One good rule of thumb is not to reach too far but to settle for the middle of the road, particularly in writing calls.

Put Options

Four years after call option trading was initiated, the exchanges won permission from the Securities and Exchange Commission in June 1977 to begin a pilot program of offering put options. Initially trading was limited to 24 issues, but puts are now available on the same issues that have listed call options.

Contrary to what you might think, puts are not simply the reverse side of calls. They are totally separate and distinct transactions. Where a call option gives the buyer the right to purchase shares of the underlying stock from the writer, a put option gives him the right to sell (or "put to") the writer those shares.

Let's take a closer look at how puts work. A trader who expects the stock market to decline might buy a put option on stock he holds to limit his potential loss. Remember the put gives him the right to sell those shares at a specified price. Generally this is done by buying the put with a striking price at or above the current market price. If the market price declines below that level, he can exercise the put to cut his losses. Of course in his expectation of a market decline he could have written a call option on the stocks he was holding, as we explained in the preceding section. Conversely, should the trader expect a rise in the stock market, he could write a put or buy a call.

Buying Puts—When and Why

Buying a "covered" put—one purchased against stock actually owned—allows the trader to put a floor on his losses should the market decline, a point we made a moment ago. However, he might also buy a put without actually owning the underlying shares and make money in a falling market. In this case, if the market declined according to his expectations (before his initial put expired) he would sell a put of the same series and expiration date. At that point, the put he sold would be commanding a higher premium than the premium he paid at purchase. The difference in these premium prices would represent his profit.

In exercising a covered put, a buyer need not necessarily deliver the shares he actually holds, though of course he has the right to do so. If he expects the market to recover and wishes to retain his position in that stock, he might do as the buyer of the uncovered put did and write a put with a higher premium to close out his contract.

If the market goes up contrary to the put buyer's expectations, the loss is limited to the cost of the put—the premium. Just as the buyer of a call option need not let it expire worthless, a put buyer may limit his loss if the stock rises by selling the put at a lower premium than he originally paid. In general, this is a prudent policy. In this case the loss is limited to the difference between the premium paid and the premium received on the covering trade.

There are tax implications in put trading that you should understand before embarking on such a program. Ask your accountant or investment advisor to explain how this type of trade would affect your tax liability.

Writing Puts

The risk for the writer (seller) of a put is that the market may move down against him. In this event he will be required to take delivery and come up with the cash for shares at a price well above market. This disconcerting situation could occur at any time up to the expiration date of the option contract. The cost basis on these shares will be the exercise price minus the premium received.

The put seller may be motivated by a desire to generate cash in a trendless market. The put expires worthless and the writer pockets his premium. He may also wish to acquire stock at a price below the current market. In this case he writes a put with a striking price at market and pockets the premium. When the stock drops, the put buyer exercises his option to deliver the shares. Thus, the writer acquires stock below market, the cost being the strike price minus the put premium. Puts should only be written against sufficient cash to purchase the shares when exercise occurs.

Unlike call premiums, which rise as the share price rises, put premiums rise when the share price drops. Thus, for a put to be "in the money" the strike price must be above the market price, and to be "out of the money" the strike price must be below the market price for the shares. Premiums tend to be higher for the more volatile stocks, which also holds true for call premiums. Time has the same value with puts as with calls.

A Growing Market

Although widespread institutional participation is a major factor in the growth of options trading, this was not always the case. Aside from the strictures that were placed on money managers and pension fund administrators by the prudent man provisions of the Employee Retirement Income Security Act of 1974 (ERISA), institutions theretofore had been held back by tax considerations. Mutual funds must derive at least 90 percent of income from investments to qualify for pass-through tax exemptions. Until the Tax Reform Act of 1976, option premiums were treated as ordinary business income, not investment income. After that, such premiums were specifically classed as capital gains. This development cleared the way not only for institutional option-writing programs but also for the introduction of a new group of mutual funds called "option income funds."

Summing Up

Broadly speaking, options may be used to guarantee market position, to obtain stock at below-market prices, to limit losses, to hedge against unpredictable turns in an uncertain market, and to generate income or cash flow.

To help you get a handle on these somewhat confusing trading techniques and to help clarify for you the risk-reward parameters of options trading, the table opposite places these concepts in perspective.

Using options as a part of your investment program can be conservative investment strategy. Conversely, it can be as speculative as short selling, with an unlimited loss potential. It is not a technique that should be attempted without full understanding of its uses, values, and risks.

Market action necessary for profitable option trades:

Call Options	*Put Options*
Buyer: Rising market	Buyer: Declining market
Seller: Declining or sideways market	Seller: Rising or sideways market

Market action that will result in losses on option trades:

Call Options	*Put Options*
Buyer: Sideways or declining market	Buyer: Sideways or rising market
Seller: Rising market	Seller: Declining market

The amount of risk or reward in a given option position:

Option Contract Position	*Possible Loss*	*Possible Gain*
Call buyer	Cost of premium	Unlimited
Call seller, covered	Cost of buyback*	Premium received
Call seller, naked	Unlimited	Premium received
Put buyer	Cost of premium	Unlimited
Put seller	Cost to buy in*	Premium received
Spreads, straddles, or combinations	Unlimited†	Unlimited†

* For the writer of a covered call or a put, the extent of the loss may be limited by making an offsetting sale. If no covering option is purchased, the loss is more a matter of lost opportunity than of cash loss; the option seller cannot participate in a rise on the call side and must take delivery of shares at a price above market on a put.

† Depending on type of spread, straddle, or combination transacted.

CHAPTER 15

The Futures Markets

MENTION THE WORD "commodities" or "futures," as they are now called, to the average investor, and if there isn't a totally blank look on his face, chances are his reaction to the topic will be strongly negative. Either he will know someone who has lost heavily, or he will regale you with a horror story or two about a hapless investor who awoke one morning to find a truckload of pork bellies or a few thousand bushels of grain on his doorstep. He may even have read about the great salad-oil swindle, the losses in cocoa and silver trading that destroyed an American-owned Swiss bank, or the shellacking a large U.S. grain exporter took in the soybean market. He may even have lost money himself on a flier.

To our Mr. Average Investor, the futures market is a hot ticket and not for him—and quite possibly he is correct. After all, many of these stories are rooted in fact. Tino DeAngelis did bankrupt one of the leading brokerage houses of the day (Ira Haupt) with his watered-down salad-oil tanks back in 1963. In the process, he gave the American Express Company a major fright as well. Paul Erdman became a successful author after his Swiss subsidiary of the United California Bank of Los Angeles lost 200 million Swiss francs—$80 million at the exchange rates of the day—trading in cocoa and silver in 1969–70. An American grain company, Cook Industries, dropped $60 million in the soybean pits in 1976–77—running neck and neck with the Hunt family, who a few years later lost hundreds of millions of dollars when the silver market collapsed, destroying one of the great family fortunes. Moreover, many an untimely delivery, although not on anyone's front doorstep, has bloodied a speculator or two caught napping. So if our average investor gets just a little nervous thinking about futures, it is understandable. There are few quicker ways to part an investor from his money than the futures market.

Man's urge to speculate, however, is well documented throughout history. Thus, while the average investor is quite right to stand at arm's length, those among us willing to apply common sense, a good deal of discipline, a little scholarship, and some spare cash will find the futures game not beyond their ability. They will also find it highly exciting, potentially very profitable, and in some cases not much more dangerous than the stock market. Now let us look more closely at this wild horse called the commodity or futures market and see what it is all about.

Historical Evolution

The futures market that is so widely traded today in reality is an offshoot of the cash or "on-the-spot" market that traces its roots back to the early Greek and Roman trading empires or perhaps further, since there is evidence that the Sumerians had a rudimentary system of credit backed by grains or metals 3,000 years before Christ.

Many of the basic rules of futures trading are clearly traceable to the law merchants' code that evolved out of the well-organized European medieval fairs. Highly complex futures trading systems also existed in Japan in the 1600s. But the rapidly expanding commerce of the city of Chicago in the 1850s was the primary catalyst for the development of the modern commodity exchange and the popularity of trading in "time" or "forward" contracts.

The Civil War was a particularly important formative period. Rising grain demand and price fluctuation stimulated use of forward contracting on the Chicago Board of Trade, a cash grain-trading exchange formed in 1848 to handle and promote Chicago's booming commerce.

Time or forward contracting was not an idea born in the United States, however. It evolved from "to arrive" contracts, which, in turn, were refinements of *lettre de faire* documents used in the twelfth century and earlier. Forward contracting was not quite futures trading, although the distinction is slight. The earlier types of contracting, including forward contracting, were entered into for the express purpose of receiving title at some specified date to the actual goods. The parties to these documents were connected to the business, and nearly all such financial agreements ended in transfer of titles and delivery of the base commodity.

When war, harvest glut, and winter shortages of grains began to create large price fluctuations as well as highly attractive profit situations, it was only natural that the more adventurous investors outside the commodity business would be attracted. They were. But then the game changed. The new players were not interested in making or taking delivery, but rather in assuming a risk to reap a profit. As a result, each contract passed through many hands. Thus the concept of trading for purposes other than taking title became firmly, though unofficially, established in Chicago during the Civil War years. With speculators now involved, and deliveries the exception rather than the rule, forward trading became the futures trading of today.

In late 1865, shortly after the end of the war, the Chicago Board of Trade passed its first rules on the subject of time trading, providing, among other things, standardization of delivery, margin deposits, and prescribed terms of payments. In practice, if not in name, forward or time contracting merged into futures trading and the era of the modern futures exchange had begun.

The Futures Exchange

The modern-day futures exchange and futures trading have evolved over a long period to fit the developing commercial needs of the country. Each exchange, however, evolved on a separate, if somewhat parallel, track, and each is highly individualistic. Generally, the older exchanges are state chartered. The Chicago Board of Trade was chartered by the Illinois State Legislature in 1848 and is the oldest and largest of the U.S. exchanges. The newer exchanges are organized under membership corporation laws.

Despite the individualistic nature and variety in size of the dozen or more active domestic exchanges, they are all fundamentally similar. The primary objective of the modern commodity futures exchange is to provide and regulate a marketplace for members to trade in futures contracts. Basically this entails providing the physical trading space, establishing the rules and regulations to conduct trading, setting the operating hours, providing the information for the standardized contract, seeing that prices and market information are recorded and disseminated to guarantee the financial obligations of exchange members in connection with futures commitments, and settling disputes between members. In addition to their futures trading activities, some exchanges also provide extensive cash market services such as sampling, grading, weighing, and inspection.

Organization of the Exchanges

U.S. futures exchanges are voluntary associations of persons interested in buying and selling futures. Whether the exchange is state chartered or corporately organized, in the United States only individuals are eligible to become members. There are no company memberships. In practice, companies often do control a membership. Many members are employees of large companies whose businesses are closely linked to exchange futures—large brokerage houses, grain processors, meat packers, and exporters. The company furnishes the money to purchase the membership provided the individual agrees to give it up if he leaves their employ.

Only members can trade on a futures exchange, and therein lies one of the two principal reasons for buying a seat on an exchange—access to the trading floor. The floor trader pays only clearing costs (which will be explained later) and receives a commission from nonmembers to fill orders. The other reason to purchase a seat is economic, provided one is a large enough trader to justify the costs involved. Membership for trader-members unable or unwilling to become floor traders entitles them to a reduced commission rate.

To provide the facilities and services required, futures exchanges need some source of revenue. U.S. exchanges are nonprofit organizations that exist only to facilitate futures trading of members, not to make money. But they do have expenses to meet, and must remain as solvent as possible. This is generally accomplished through a combination of investments, dues, fees for services, and, if necessary, member assessments.

The Clearinghouse

Guaranteeing the financial commitment that each member makes when buying or selling a commodity futures contract is an important but difficult task. To do this, exchanges have developed corporations called clearinghouses to take the opposite side of all trades and to guarantee all contracts. The clearinghouse, in effect, becomes the buyer to all sellers, and the seller to all buyers. By so doing, it is able to ensure that each contract will be honored. The section on margins later in this chapter explains how the clearinghouse maintains financial integrity for each contract.

The clearing procedure continues throughout the trading day. All exchange members send their trading cards to their respective clearing member. There is a card for each side of a transaction containing the details of the trade. The clearing member posts this information on a computer and forwards the information to a clearinghouse. The clearinghouse takes the computer run from all the clearing members and matches up each purchase and sale for names, prices, delivery months, and quantities. The match-up must be exact. If there are any discrepancies, the clearinghouse makes up a list of unmatched trades, called *out-trades,* and sends it, via computer, back to the clearing member firm. All discrepancies must be resolved before trading begins the following day or the trade is rejected. If this occurs, one of the two parties involved (usually the one with the greatest financial exposure) will fix the extent of the loss at the opening the next day. The disputed trade is then sent to the exchange's arbitration process for final settlement. The exact procedure for the various exchanges may vary, but in principle, this is how futures trades are handled between clearing member firms and clearinghouse.

Not all members of an exchange belong to the clearinghouse, but all clearinghouse members must be members of the exchange. The clearinghouse is a stock company, and clearinghouse members buy stock in relationship to the amount of clearing business they do. All trades must be cleared through a clearinghouse member. In addition to purchases of stock, a substantial cash deposit must be made to the guarantee fund of the clearinghouse corporation. Like the exchange itself, the clearinghouse is a nonprofit organization and generates its operating capital through fees and from interest on invested capital.

The Standard Futures Contract

Another, equally important creation of the exchange is the standard futures contract. "To arrive" trading, the forerunner of forward and then futures trading, was replete with pitfalls for everyone. Shipments came in all sizes and grades, depending on what the seller happened to have on hand, and settlement was a nightmare. Each transaction needed to be individually negotiated as to the specific terms of payment, delivery point, and so on.

To put everyone on an equal footing and to simplify trading, the standardized contract was developed. Traders now only need to be concerned with the price and number of contracts during trading hours.

In brief, each commodity contract represents a firm legal agreement between the buyer or seller and the exchange's clearinghouse. The buyer agrees to accept delivery on a specified amount of a commodity when the contract is tendered (delivered). Conversely, the seller agrees to deliver the commodity detailed in the contract sometime during the delivery month. In some of the financial-based futures, most notably stock index contracts, settlement for both buyers and sellers is made in cash, not in the underlying commodity. Only a small percentage of contracts are actually delivered, since most traders in futures contracts are either speculators who have no need for commodities, or hedgers (producers or consumers of the commodity) who are using the market to shift risk temporarily to the speculator. Indeed, the risk-shifting function of the futures market is one of its main economic justifications.

With few contracts being settled by delivery, a method is needed to dissolve the contractual obligation. A simple one is used. The buyer or seller takes an equal, but opposite, position in the same delivery month. Called offsetting, it negates the original purchase or sale. It can be done at any time before the contract goes off the board (terminates). During its lifetime, a futures contract, despite its deliverability, is merely a bookkeeping entry. A futures contract, therefore, is not a tangible item like a stock certificate, and when you first buy and then sell or sell and then buy the same contract, the net result is zero.

There are many futures traded; each has specific requirements to maximize its usefulness to the people who are in the cash business—the farmers, packers, manufacturers, and others, collectively known as the "trade." This is an important consideration even though most contracts are offset before delivery. No one is 100 percent sure of what makes one cash commodity a successful futures market while another fails. There are guidelines: a large supply and demand that is uncertain, adaptability to standardization and grade, relatively free flow of supply to terminals, and a low degree of perishability, to mention a few. But there are exceptions to these guidelines, especially with regard to perishability. One thing is clear, however; trade acceptability is a significant factor for success. If the trade cannot economically use the contract to hedge, it is less likely to survive.

The details vary for each commodity, but in general a contract will cover the following items: (1) the quantity (trading unit) being traded; (2) the grade; (3) termination of trading and delivery date; (4) daily minimum and maximum price fluctuations allowed; (5) description of par delivery grade, the grade of commodity specified for delivery; (6) premiums and discounts for nonpar delivery; (7) trading limits (number of contracts that can be bought and sold in one day); (8) position limits (the number of contracts a trader can hold in one single delivery month, and in all months together); (9) delivery points. Essentially, every facet of entering into, making, and taking delivery of or exiting from the commodity futures market is covered in a standard contract.

Margins

In the earlier description of exchange operations, the subsidiary clearinghouse emerged as the party to all commodity transactions; that is, it became the buyer to all sellers and the seller to all buyers. From this vantage point, the clearinghouse can and does control the financial integrity of its members and their contract commitments. We have already mentioned that each clearinghouse member buys stock and deposits a large amount of cash into the corporation's guarantee fund. Each member is also required to post a performance bond to the clearinghouse for each net open position. This payment is called margin and affects not only clearinghouse members but nonmembers as well.

There are four basic classifications of margin. The first is called *standing* or *original margin* and is the amount of money a clearinghouse member keeps on deposit (to assure settlement of the contract) with the clearinghouse for each net open position (long or short) at the end of the trading day. If the member firm, for example, has 500 long May copper and 500 short May copper, its net position is zero and, theoretically, no standing margin is required. (In practice, a clearinghouse member would always keep a sizable deposit in his account whether it is needed or not.) On the other hand, if there were only 400 long May copper, the firm would be net short 100 contracts and would be required to post standing margin to cover this net open position. Standing margins are fixed by the governing board of the clearinghouse and must be current before each day's trading begins.

The second type also affects the clearinghouse member and is called a *variation margin*. If a market is particularly active and moves against the member's position, his standing margin would have to be supplemented to keep it at full value. The clearinghouse can call for variation margin money at any time to cover price changes, and the member must provide the money by certified check within one hour.

Like most cost-of-business items, margins are passed through the system to the nonmembers of the clearinghouse and on to the nonmembers of the exchange. Although the clearinghouse sets the rate that member firms pay, what they in turn request from individual traders is left to their discretion. This, incidentally, accounts for the differences you will encounter when asking different brokers about margins on the same commodity.

Use of the word "margin" to describe up-front money in futures differs significantly, by the way, from its use in the stock market for speculator-investor accounts. Stock margins are the minimum amounts of money an investor can put down to buy shares. He then must borrow the balance of the cost of the stock from the broker to complete the transaction. As a result, the stock investor pays the broker interest on the borrowed funds until the position is terminated or the "loan" is paid off.

In contrast, futures margins at the brokerage level are similar to those at the clearinghouse level—they are primarily a performance bond to assure proper settlement of the contract. The futures broker does not put up the difference between margin and the value of the contract as does the stockbroker, so no interest is required of the futures investor.

The first level of margin at the customer end is called *original margin*. Unlike a stockbroker, a futures broker will not buy or sell before he has your money in hand; there is no five-day settlement period. Typically margins will run between 5 and 10 percent of the face value of a contract. But they can be much higher, depending on its volatility and how close the specific contract is to expiration. For example, most margins are increased when the contract reaches its delivery month.

Since it would be inconvenient for brokers to demand hourly variations in margin from their clients, but since it could be dangerous for them not to adjust for adverse price changes, brokers usually take a range approach. At the upper end is the original margin, and at the lower end is *maintenance margin*. You need original margin to initiate the trade, but the broker will not ask for additional money until your account falls to the maintenance level. At that point the broker will send a written notice, or margin call, to you requesting enough money to bring the entire position back up to the original margin level. If you are unable or unwilling to meet the margin call, the broker can close out the position.

Leverage

The margin system is a particularly important aspect of futures trading, for it provides the main attraction for speculators—leverage. With a margin rate of 10 percent, it takes only a 10 percent change in the commodity's price to give the speculator a 100 percent gain or loss in his trading equity. The speculator is also permitted to use equity gains in open trades to purchase additional positions at no cost. For example, assume the margin on one hog contract (30,000 pounds) is $1,200, and the current commodity price is 40¢ a pound. If the price of hogs should advance to 44¢ a pound, the equity gain would be $1,200. Until the trade is offset, the $1,200 would be only a paper profit. However, if he wishes, the trader can buy a second hog contract at 44¢ without adding any extra money. The paper profit would cover the second margin requirement. With two positions working for him, the hog market need only advance to 46¢ a pound to give the speculator enough for a third position. Leverage, of course, is a two-edged sword. A decline of 3¢ a pound would leave the trader with virtually no gain; a decline of 4¢ would leave him with a loss.

Open Interest

When a trader buys or sells a contract, until he offsets the trade or settles it through delivery, he is said to have an "open position." In each market there will be a number of these open positions, and collectively they are referred to as the future's "open interest." Open interest is reported along with the volume of sales and the prices each day. Since there are always two sides to each contract—a long interest (representing contracts that have been bought) and a short interest (those that have been sold)—a figure of 100 for open interest would mean there are 100 longs and 100 shorts currently holding positions in that commodity.

Hedging

We have talked mostly about the speculator up to this point. But futures markets are real, not just artificially created arenas for gambling. They are backed by cash markets, and grew out of the need of the producers and manufacturers engaged in processing the commodity to protect themselves from adverse price changes. The use of the futures market by the people in the business or trade is called hedging, and is the backbone of the industry. A hedger, then, is an individual or company that either has the actual commodity to deliver or wishes to receive delivery of it. Whether they actually make or receive delivery is immaterial. A hedge, or hedging, is taking a position in the futures market that is equal to but opposite from an existing or soon-to-exist position in the cash market. This is also true of financial-based futures. Although they are not processed in the same way as a conventional commodity, large cash markets exist in bonds, stocks, and other financials. Individuals or companies (banks, pension funds, and so forth) with long positions in bonds, for example, would be considered hedged if they sold an equivalent amount in the futures market. To facilitate hedging activity, a must for a successful futures market, exchanges usually set margins for bona fide hedgers below those for speculative accounts, give them lower commission rates, and eliminate position limits.

Because hedging involves the cash market, the hedger is not concerned with changes in the futures price per se. His interest is in the relationship between the cash price and the futures price. This mathematical difference between the two prices is called the "basis." Usually, the basis is given as an amount above or below the futures prices. If a farmer can get $2.50 per bushel for corn at his local elevator, and corn for December delivery is selling for $2.75 on the Chicago Board of Trade, the farmer's basis that day would be "25 under."

In a normal or carrying-charge market, the difference between the cash prices and the delivery of grain in the futures (the basis) will reflect insurance and interest costs. Occasionally an agricultural futures market will be inverted; that is, the cash price will be above the futures. This generally occurs when there is a near-term shortage in the commodity and buyers are willing to pay a premium to obtain supplies.

Hedging is an extremely complicated topic—and beyond the survey nature of this chapter. However, generally, a hedger is interested in eliminating as much of the risk associated with price fluctuation as he can, and he does this by putting on long or short hedges in various combinations. So that you will have some idea of what a hedging operation is about, we have conjured up two highly simplified hypothetical examples to illustrate a short and a long hedge.

The Short Hedge

It is July, and farmer Jones has planted 1,000 acres of corn that he expects will be ready for harvest in September. The weather has been good, and his yield history suggests that he will get 100 bushels per acre, or 100,000 bushels by harvest. His production costs are running about $2.00 per bushel. Unfortunately for our farmer, the crop looks good all over the state, and it appears that prices will fall by harvest time. Currently the local elevator is buying corn for $2.35 per bushel. Farmer Jones looks at the futures market and sees that corn deliverable in December is selling for $2.55 per bushel. That makes his basis 20 under.

If the forecasters are correct and corn does fall, Mr. Jones could end up, not only with less profit, but possibly with no profit at all if the market dips below $2.00 per bushel. To protect his current margin of profit of 35¢ a bushel (production cost of $2.00 subtracted from elevator price of $2.35), farmer Jones decides to put on a short (selling) hedge. He sells 20 contracts (grain contracts are in units of 5,000 bushels each) of December corn at $2.55 per bushel. Now, no matter what happens to the actual price of corn, if the basis holds up, farmer Jones will have his 35¢ a bushel. If the cash market falls, what he loses at the elevator or terminal when he sells his corn will be offset by an equal gain in his short futures position. If the price of corn should go up, the loss in the futures position would be offset by the gain in the cash price. The table opposite illustrates the principle.

The Long Hedge

Assume once again that it is July. ABC Milling has just landed a large contract to supply a local bakery with flour. A price has been agreed upon for the flour, but the baker wants half of it delivered next January. ABC Milling based production costs and the flour sales price on the current cash wheat price of $2.75 per bushel. January delivery, however, means ABC will need to buy additional wheat in December. To protect itself against adverse price changes over the five-month period, the milling company turns to the futures market. The price for a December contract is $3.00 per bushel, which gives ABC a basis of 25 under. By purchasing (long hedging) enough December wheat contracts to fulfill its raw material needs, the milling company, like farmer Jones, can eliminate much of the risk of changing prices.

The two examples assume that the basis is flat and that the hedges performed perfectly, although in practice they seldom do. As the price goes up and down, the basis also changes, sometimes narrowing, sometimes expanding. These contractions in the basis can be quite costly if they move against the hedger's position. Furthermore, the above examples assume the hedger is seeking only protection from price changes. Recent studies indicate hedgers expect to profit from a hedge in the same manner that a speculator expects to

PROFIT-LOSS EFFECT ON A SHORT HEDGE UNDER VARYING MARKET CONDITIONS

(This illustration assumes that corn costs farmer $2.00 per bushel to produce.)

Unhedged	Profit (Loss)	Hedged — Effects of a hedged position in a changing market if basis* remains stable	Profit (Loss)	Effects of a hedged position in a changing market if basis* changes	Profit (Loss)
Sale now at market price of $2.35	35¢	Cash price $2.35	35¢	Cash price $2.35	35¢
		Futures price $2.55	0¢	Futures price $2.60	(5¢)
				(basis: 25 under)	
		Net	35¢	Net	30¢
Sale in December at market price of $2.10	10¢	Cash price $2.10	10¢	Cash price $2.10	10¢
		Futures price $2.30	25¢	Futures price $2.25	30¢
				(basis: 15 under)	
		Net	35¢	Net	40¢
Sale in December at market price of $2.60	60¢	Cash price $2.60	60¢		
		Futures price $2.80	(25¢)		
		Net	35¢		
Sale in December at market price of $1.95	(5¢)				

*Basis is difference between market price and futures price.

159

profit from an outright futures position. Thomas A. Hierony-
mus makes a convincing argument that hedging is, in fact,
another form of speculation (*Economics of Futures Trading—
For Commercial and Personal Profit*, Commodity Research
Bureau, New York, 1971).

The Trading Floor

Naturally, the trading area for each commodity will differ
from exchange to exchange. Nonetheless, they all have common elements. On the floor will be a specific area where each
commodity trades. These individual trading areas within the
larger complex are called "pits" (or sometimes "rings"), and
there is only one to a commodity. Some are elaborate octag-
onal platforms with ascending steps on the outside and descending steps on the inside. Others are simply handrails
formed into a circle. There is a telephone area near the pits
for floor brokers (or their telephone people) to receive orders
from the firms they represent. There is, in close proximity, a
table or platform containing one or more market reporters.
Their job is to monitor the changing price picture, then to
transmit it to the exchange's quote board system and to the
ticker services, which send prices all around the country and
abroad. There is a quote board system—easily viewed panels
or blackboards containing the size and price of the last trade
for each contract.

Now that you are familiar with the structure of a modern
futures exchange, let us look at what happens when the bell
rings and commodity trading's special brand of pandemo-
nium takes over. For the sake of simplicity, the following
description of a futures trade is a composite of several markets. Procedures differ from exchange to exchange, but the
path an order takes is basically similar in all markets.

It all begins when trader Joe decides to enter the futures
market. We will assume he is not a member of the exchange
and that he wants to buy 10 contracts of May XYZ commodity
at 45. His first step is to call his account executive and give
him the buy order. The AE writes out the buy slip for 10 May
XYZ at 45 and then sends the order ticket to the brokerage

firm's order room. The order room time-stamps the slip and then calls or wires the information to the exchange that handles XYZ futures. At the exchange, the order is received, time-stamped, and passed on to the floor broker's telephone person, stationed at one of the many phones on the trading floor. The phone attendant writes up the order and sends it by messenger or hand signal to the floor traders. All futures trading is done by public outcry. Needless to say, with several hundred brokers on the bigger exchanges aggressively shouting at one another, it is sometimes difficult to execute orders. To supplement the yelling, therefore, hand signals are also used. There are hand signals for both prices and quantity. The combination of shouting and hand waving often gives the pit a frantic look, but it is remarkably orderly and efficient.

The floor broker, with order in hand, then goes to the necessary pit and via voice and hand signal makes trader Joe's bid. Fortunately for trader Joe (or possibly not), another floor broker has a matching sale order and shouts or signals, "Sold." Meanwhile the market reporter notes the transaction and sends it off to the quote board, and to the ticker system if it is different from the last trade. The two brokers get together and fill out their trading cards before moving back into the pit to fill another order. Trader Joe's floor broker also sends the completed order ticket to the floor phone person, who sends it back through the system to trader Joe. The time between the receipt of the order and its execution is only a few minutes.

Government Regulation

Where large sums of money are at stake, man can be very creative and devious in his pursuit of it. Thus, along with the advantages of having a futures market for agricultural products, Americans also have suffered through an assortment of abuses, most notably those involving the cornering of markets and manipulation of prices by wealthy traders.

The first federal foray into regulating the commodity futures market came in 1884. Since then, there has been a steady stream of legislation passed largely on a "crisis" basis; when the horse has bolted, Congress has locked the door. The Grain Futures Act came in 1922. This act was amended and strengthened somewhat in 1936 and renamed the Commodity Exchange Act; it also extended federal regulations to nongrain commodities. The act created the Commodity Exchange Authority (CEA), which applied its rather limited powers to futures trading until 1974. That year Congress created a stronger watchdog, one modeled on the Securities and Exchange Commission, which regulates the stock market.

Called the Commodity Futures Trading Commission (CFTC), this regulatory agency is armed with a much broader mandate than its predecessor, and over the past few years it has slowly been expanding its authority into every aspect of the futures industry. The latter, meanwhile, has not been idle. The futures industry has set up the National Futures Association (NFA) along the lines of the National Association of Securities Dealers, the watchdog of the securities industry. The NFA became operational on October 1, 1982, and it has steadily expanded its responsibilities. At present this self-regulatory organization looks after the standards of professional conduct and the financial health of the various individuals and organizations that make up its membership. This includes all segments of the industry, since members are not allowed to do business with nonmembers. Thus, people or organizations that do not remain qualified for NFA membership are prevented from dealing with the public in a business that involves buying and selling futures or futures option contracts.

CHAPTER 16

Index Futures and Other New Investment Products

OVER THE YEARS, Wall Street and the futures markets have developed a number of arcane financial products. One statistics-minded market follower claimed that between 1986 and 1989 more than 600 new financial products came to market. While many of these hybrid securities are of limited interest to the average investor, some, as they became better understood, proved useful tools. What are these products? They include futures contracts, options, and futures options on a variety of stock market indexes, currencies, Treasury securities, bank CDs, and interest rates. Described in earlier chapters are the junk bonds and zero coupon debt issues. They also include schemes that sever stocks into two or three parts, each representing a different part of the stock's value. The separate parts would represent the appreciation, the residual value, and the dividends. Americus Trust, with its units, SCORES and PRIMES, was the first to appear. Then an even more complex hybrid was publicized, the unbundled stock unit (USU). This never made it out of the box.

The Early Days of Financial and Index Futures

The Chicago Mercantile Exchange formed a branch in the early 1970s, the International Monetary Market (IMM), to introduce and initially trade futures on British, Canadian, and Japanese currencies. The IMM introduced futures on Treasury bills first in 1976. The Chicago Board of Trade (CBOT) got into the act with futures on Treasury notes in 1979, then added GNMA and bank CD futures two years later. The Kansas City Board of Trade broke the ice early in 1982 with its two index futures on the Value Line Index. Next the Chicago Mercantile Exchange introduced contracts on two Standard & Poor's indexes. The New York Futures Exchange (NYFE) opened trading for futures on the NYSE Composite Indexes. This exchange, which is owned by the NYSE, was established in 1980, but has since fallen on hard times. Its volume accounts for less than 1 percent of the futures traded in the United States.

Since 1982 financial futures and options have proliferated as a result of the increased institutional interest in them. In one of the largest futures markets, the Treasury bond pit of the CBOT, the value of contracts traded daily is more than twice the volume on the bonds themselves. The extensive use of computer-driven program trading has been explosive for the volume of S&P 500 futures. On some days index arbitrage trading in these contracts has accounted for up to 45 percent of Big Board volume in the underlying issues. Today investors can choose from a growing assortment of these derivative products. In addition to those already mentioned there are technology stock index options, short- and long-term interest rate options, Eurodollar, sterling, and muni bond index futures. In 1990, the American Stock Exchange began trading put and call warrants on the Nikkei index of 225 Japanese stocks. The Philadelphia Stock Exchange plans to list similar warrants on the Deutscher Aktieindex (DAX) of 30 blue-chip German issues.

The Mechanics of Futures

Each index future functions essentially as does a hog, silver, corn, or any other futures market. Although originally a standardized contract was established at $400 times the underlying index, smaller $250 and $100 contracts were subsequently introduced. Thus, a one-point move in the index means a $500 ($250 or $100) change in the value of the future contract on it.

Since each market index is composed of several hundred stocks, normal delivery, in kind, would be difficult. Therefore, these futures, unlike other futures markets, are settled in cash. But cash delivery does not mean that the entire price of the contract (around $80,000 for Value Line Index, $70,000 for S&P 500, and $40,000 for NYSE Composite) is required for settlement. Rather, only an amount equal to the change in value on the final day of the contract actually changes hands—a two-point price change times the standard $500 would mean a settlement of $1,000.

The entry fee for trading in these markets varies, typically from 5 to 10 percent of the value of the contract. This can range anywhere from $2,000 to $6,500, depending on the futures market in which you are dealing. However, should the market go against you, you may get a margin call and have to add more cash along the way. Big-league pros use financial futures, and more recently index futures, to hedge their positions. Banks may employ them as a means to protect themselves against future interest-rate changes. Portfolio managers turn to the futures market to protect clients' assets against precipitous market declines. And speculators may trade index futures, rather than stocks, while holding portfolios of low-risk Treasury securities.

Informational Tools

How can you use these contracts? Even if you choose not to put up your cash, you can still derive use from the futures market in the form of information. A typical day's listing might look like this:

	S&P 500	NYSE Composite
Sept.	358.25	195.55
Dec.	362.62	197.95
Mar.	366.36	—
Actual	*355.91*	*194.55*

You will note that the futures are selling at a premium to the actual indexes, reflecting the fact that owning them is more convenient than owning the equivalent stocks. When this premium disappears it may indicate that investors are bearish. When the more distant months are selling at a significant premium to near months, it indicates rising investor expectations. Similar inferences can be gleaned from the fixed-rate financial contracts. You can use these markets as a bellwether of investor expectations, but keep in mind that investors are not always reliable prognosticators.

Program Trading Causes Volatility

Institutional trading in the derivative instruments has increased to the point that it is leading the market. Computer-driven arbitrage strategies seek to benefit from price differentials between a market index and the futures and options on that index. The program triggers buying or selling of index futures or options and selling or buying a basket of stocks that have the greatest weight in the underlying index. A NYSE study by a panel was commissioned after the 191-point plunge in the market in October 1989, when institutions dumped $600 million or 14.7 million shares of S&P 500 stocks in 30 minutes. The panel was composed of eight persons who were program traders or favored program trading but only four critics of programs. The panel concluded that arbitrage programs were not undesirable but it favored installing a temporary trading halt (circuit breaker) to help curb excess volatility. A circuit breaker was credited with cutting short a 107-point, 90-minute drop in the market on July 23, 1990. The SEC has instituted a pilot program that would tighten existing "circuit breaker" rules. A one-day move of 50 points triggers a rule allowing index arbitrage orders to buy S&P component stocks only at a price equal to or above that of the preceding sale.

Regulatory Authority in Dispute

During most of the 1980s, jurisdictional disputes between the Securities and Exchange Commission and the Commodity Futures Trading Commission (CFTC) seethed. The sharp plunges in the market in 1987, 1989, and 1990 have focused even more attention on the issue of regulation. Several bills in Congress would, if passed, determine whether the CFTC would remain the overseer of stock-index futures or whether this duty would be ceded to the SEC. The CFTC reauthorization is one of the bills awaiting passage. Central to the issue is margin-setting authority, which has been held by the commodity exchanges. The securities industry would like to have this authority held by the SEC, although some have suggested that the Federal Reserve should hold that power. The latter body does not want this authority, although the Fed does set margins on stocks. Traders of futures have a preferential margin requirement of 5 percent versus 50 percent for stocks. This and other trading rules differences give the program traders advantages. The futures industry stands four-square for keeping regulation with the CFTC and margin-setting authority at the exchanges.

New Equity Products

In October 1983, Americus Shareowner Service Corp. launched the Americus Trust for American Telephone, the first in its series of 30 trusts, to a singularly uninterested market. But as more of the trusts began to trade, investors started to take notice of the possibilities of these products. Now they are accepted as one of the many ways for investors to participate in the market. Shearson Lehman Brothers (owned by American Express) recruited Goldman, Sachs & Co. to help in the marketing of its unbundled stock units, scheduled for introduction early in 1989. American Express, Dow Chemical, Pfizer, and Sara Lee shares were scheduled to be split into three parts—a bond, a preferred, and an equity appreciation certificate. Unless holders of 5 percent to 14 percent of the outstanding stock could be convinced to tender their shares, the plan would fail. But in the end the Securities and Exchange Commission killed the deal over the issue of voting rights for the units.

How Americus Trusts Work

The units have two component parts—PRIMES or Prescribed Rights to Income and Maximum Security and SCORE or Special Claims on Residual Equity. Holders of PRIMES collect all dividends of less than 5 percent of the unit's net asset value and a termination claim to net asset value when the trust terminates; most of the trusts expire in 1992. Because of a change in the tax laws no new trusts are expected to be offered. Holders of the SCORE segment are entitled to the net asset value that exceeds the PRIMES termination value. The combined units, as well as the PRIMES and SCOREs, are actively traded on the American Stock Exchange. If the stock languishes and the PRIMES fail to reach their termination value, they are redeemed at their market value and the SCOREs will expire worthless. The trust will redeem recombined units at any time, but will not redeem the two segments separately.

PRIMES' high yields make them attractive to income investors. Because they sell at a discount to their underlying stock and holders collect all but five cents per share of the dividend, PRIMES yield more than the stock on which they are based. SCOREs are priced well below the common shares, allowing the holder to speculate on a rise in the price of the underlying shares at a much smaller cost.

Junk Bonds

Although junk bonds—bonds that are unrated or carry very low ratings—have been around forever, they came into prominence late in the 1980s as mergers and acquisitions proliferated. One estimate places the size of the junk bond market at $210 billion. The use of debt instruments of questionable quality to fund leveraged buyouts (LBOs) increased geometrically as did mergers. Furthermore, the public's voracious appetite for high-yield mutual funds—the yields generated by portfolios of junk bonds—provided a ready market for more and more unsecured debt. Among other factors, junk bonds played a less than heroic role in the collapse of the savings and loan industry. As a result of this fiasco and reduced buying of junk bonds by the mutual funds and insurance companies, the price of these bonds was driven down, upping yields to almost double that of medium-term Treasury bonds.

The viability of these bonds varies widely; not all junk is real junk. Some of the more secure issuers, those who still had cash available, jumped in when prices dropped to buy back their junk at attractive discounts. Companies that issued bonds with what is known as a reset feature are facing potential problems. The reset bond guarantees that at some point the interest rate will be raised (or lowered) to maintain the bond's value. Many of the $12 billion in outstanding reset bonds have no cap on the interest rate, which potentially could drive the issuer into bankruptcy. In the decade of the 1980s, junk bonds accounted for 70 percent of the corporate bond defaults.

A Silk Purse from a Sow's Ear?

To make junk bonds more palatable to the market, investment bankers have packaged them as collateralized bond obligations (CBOs). Two years after these appeared in 1988, some $3.7 billion CBOs had been packaged, and in 1990 close to $4 billion more had been sold. Junk bonds of multiple issuers are pooled and interest and principal payments are allocated to tiers of investors. The top tier of investors gets a lower yield than all other tiers. The maturity for this group is also shorter. The second and third tiers get increasingly higher yield and longer maturity. The top tier of some pools have earned A and even AA ratings.

While these new products offer sophisticated investors new and flexible ways to play the market, they should not be approached without knowledge or, failing that, expert guidance. Some brokerage houses are incorporating the use of futures hedges in managed accounts. However, these generally have a minimum account level of $300,000 or even more.

CHAPTER 17

Gold, Inflation, and Your Dollars

GOLD HAS BEEN popular with humankind almost as long as the species has existed. It has been used to beautify, buoy, and bribe for centuries. It has been at center stage in the human drama from time immemorial. "Saint-seducing gold," Shakespeare called it in *Romeo and Juliet*. "Though wisdom cannot be gotten for gold, still less can it be gotten without it," said Samuel Butler a couple of centuries later.

The chance for finding gold opened up the American West, and the subsequent preoccupation of this nation with the yellow metal gave William Jennings Bryan the opportunity to declaim, at the National Democratic Convention in Chicago in July 1896, "You shall not press down upon the brow of labor this crown of thorns. You shall not crucify mankind upon a cross of gold."

The Gold Standard

Enhancing the elevated status of gold has been the low status of official money, particularly paper money. Thanks to the widespread inability of governments to live within their incomes, currencies have always depreciated, and often even disappeared. The German mark did so twice within one human lifetime. The runaway inflation in Germany after World War I simply eliminated the hardworking, rigorously saving middle class and paved the way for social and political disasters of far worse proportions. More recently the value of the currencies of Argentina and Brazil dropped alarmingly, leading to Draconian countermeasures by these governments.

Anyone who has had the foresight or ability to convert bank deposits or currency to gold during such periods of financial holocaust has survived. Those who "trusted" the system and its money perished. Small wonder, then, that the financial vicissitudes of the twentieth century further elevated gold in the minds and hearts of men. It was tangible, had "intrinsic value," and was a permanent haven for wealth.

So strong was the faith in gold and so weak the trust in paper money that the latter had to be tied to the former to have any credibility. Europe and the United States went on a so-called gold standard, meaning that a dollar, pound, or franc was worth a specific amount of the metal. As long as this was the case, the paper money became as good, or almost as good, as gold. The trouble with the gold standard was the cost it exacted in terms of economic, social, and political upheaval.

Here's the way the gold standard works, in theory. As a nation prospers on the upside of a business cycle, domestic wages and prices tend to rise to a point where some other nation has a competitive advantage in the domestic market. Domestic consumers then begin to buy imported products. The exporting nation exchanges the currency received from the sale of its goods for gold, which it takes home.

As the domestic market loses gold—the base of the domestic money supply—that money supply shrinks. A smaller money supply turns the business cycle down, a depression ensues, and wages and prices fall as unemployment and the number of idle plants rise. Domestic prices then become competitive in foreign markets and domestic companies begin to prosper by selling in those foreign markets.

Foreign currencies are swapped for foreign gold, which is brought home and monetized. Paper money is printed to match it, and the money supply is increased, which leads to boom conditions again. Wages and prices move up as prosperity returns, only to make domestic products vulnerable to foreign competition once again, and the boom ends in another bust.

Obviously, no social or political fabric could stand one wrenching depression and soaring boom after another. Thus, the gold standard was really honored more in the breach than in the observance early in this century. The Great Depression really did it in, and the United States under President Franklin D. Roosevelt finally abandoned it in 1933.

Gold and the Dollar

The United States led the Western world out of the Depression, whether thanks to FDR or thanks to the consequences of Hitler's imperialistic designs for Germany. The dollar was the world currency, having replaced the British pound during World War II. It was pegged to other currencies and to gold at $35 per ounce. Any foreign nation that did not want the dollars earned from sales of goods to us could turn them into gold. Few did. It was American products they wanted, first to rebuild their war-shattered countries, then to give them the consumer prosperity we had long taken for granted.

During that period we could, generally speaking, go wherever we wished, using the English language and the American dollar almost as handily in Manila or Madrid as in Muncie or Mamaroneck. In addition, we sold our excess steel and radios to the world's "natives" and bought what we wished of their coffee, copra, and copper. If we failed to buy enough from them, their prices fell and near starvation followed. Even Europe was sufficiently dependent on the U.S. economy to give credence to the statement that "when the United States gets the sniffles, Europe gets pneumonia."

U.S. trade dominance immediately following World War II produced a flow of gold to this country. The yellow metal was a luxury Europe could scarcely afford when its citizens were clamoring first for food, clothing, and shelter, and later for autos, dishwashers, and color TVs. In the years following

World War II, we had most of the world's gold in expensive underground quarters at Fort Knox, Kentucky. Even big gold-producing countries such as South Africa and the Soviet Union turned their gold into dollars so they could buy U.S. products and technology. So in those years, when a few foreign countries sidled up to our gold window with some excess dollars to swap, no one paid much attention.

But things began to change in these early postwar years, too. First came the Marshall Plan, which funneled U.S. dollars into the rebuilding of European facilities.

Second was the "trade, not aid" philosophy developed by the Eisenhower administration, which encouraged our purchase of European and "third world" products as a way of stimulating those countries' economic growth enough to diminish their need for our aid. All of this worked, helped in no small way by the unswervingly hard work of the ordinary men and women of Germany and Japan. Thanks to their "grit" and our enlightened economic policy, Europe and Japan rose from the rubble of war to economic heights in a far shorter time than anyone predicted. It wasn't long, in national terms, before Germany and Japan became real competitors with the United States in world markets.

During the decade or two immediately following World War II, we sold, or exported, much more than we bought, or imported, in the world marketplace. This excess of exports over imports was used to finance U.S. troops stationed in Europe. We also used the excess to finance the building of Caterpillar Tractor plants in Scotland and Burroughs facilities in France. But as the prosperity we had encouraged, and in part financed, waxed, the need for our dollars to buy goods from us waned.

Our so-called trade surplus—the excess of exports over imports—narrowed and financed less and less. By the time the Vietnam War had escalated, we were spending more for foreign military actions than the U.S. economy earned in the world market. Our balance-of-payments surplus became a deficit. This meant a growing number of dollars were being held abroad, dollars that foreigners increasingly had no need to spend here for the things we made.

Thus, the move to exchange dollars for gold steadily

gained momentum. Our gold reserves sank drastically, causing great alarm. The first to panic were those with no trust in "paper money." As far as they were concerned, erosion of the U.S. store of gold was fast reducing the value of dollars to mere paper.

Then came the smart money men. These were the financial experts in the big multinational companies who dealt daily in large amounts of pounds, yen, lira, and marks, as well as dollars. If the dollar was losing its international appeal, they reasoned, why shouldn't we keep as much of our working capital in other, more popular, and stronger currencies? So they swapped dollars. Then came all sorts of speculators, big and little, all trying to "make a buck" (if you will!) selling dollars.

The Dollar Is Cut Free

By the summer of 1971, the dollar was in real trouble. The Nixon administration realized this and did three things. First, it closed the gold window. Second, it unpegged the dollar. From now on, said the White House, in effect, gold buyers can pay what they wish for the yellow metal; the price of gold will have no bearing on the dollar. The price of both gold and dollars in foreign currencies fluctuated according to the dictates of supply and demand. Third, it slapped controls on domestic wages and prices in a frontal assault on the raging inflation that was plaguing the U.S. economy. This was in part to help consumers at home, but also to show Europeans and others that we were facing our inflation and balance-of-payments problems.

Because of this inflation at home and the adverse balance of payments, the dollar had really become overvalued. In part, too, the dollar had started out overvalued after World War II to help our "trade, not aid" policy. An overvalued currency is one that buys more in a foreign country than it does at home. By 1971, this overvaluation of the dollar had become so obvious that everyone had to recognize it, and did.

Gold rose immediately from $35 an ounce, the price for

nearly four decades, to $42 or so, a gain of 20 percent. Also escalating were the West German mark, the yen, and most other free-world currencies. The dollar was allowed to move with supply and demand instead of being artificially adjusted by the high priests of the international monetary world, the central bankers.

Recurring "panics" occurred, including a substantial one in early 1973, when Treasury Secretary George Shultz announced a major easing of wage and price controls, following a big jump in farm and food prices for two months in a row. This immediately rekindled fears in the hearts of European central bankers of more inflation here, and the dollar fell apart. Gold leaped to around $126 an ounce or more, and Wall Street got the jitters.

The United States on the Bargain Counter

Sink the market did, although the declining dollar was far from the only reason. For the next few weeks the dollar became truly undervalued—you could buy more of life's needs in New York with dollars than you could with an equivalent amount of marks in Frankfurt or francs in Paris. This was a good thing for us. Detroit sold more cars; West Germany sold fewer.

Everything we had here really ended up on the bargain counter for foreigners, all because the dollar "collapsed." The dollar remained free to float at levels dictated by supply and demand, clearly the healthiest thing for the economy. Finally the stock market took heart, or at least began to worry about other things as investors saw that a declining dollar did not hurt them. Meantime, gold stocks—the shares of gold-mining companies—had gone through the roof.

When Washington unpegged the dollar from gold in 1971, gold-mining stocks nearly doubled in price within a couple of years. A glance at the accompanying chart shows what happens when supply and demand are allowed to set the price.

Gold Investments Legalized in the United States

In 1974, the U.S. Congress made it legal once again for Americans to own gold. Currency speculators rushed out and bought a lot of yellow metal, pushing the price of gold to almost $195 an ounce by the end of 1974 and giving the mining companies a nice surge in earnings. Then the gold-bullion bubble burst, as bubbles always do, and prices plummeted to a low of $103 in August 1976. Obviously, gold wasn't much of an inflation hedge in that 20-month period.

Gold went through another cycle in the late 1970s and early 1980s. This one sent the yellow metal to an incredible price of $850 per ounce for a few minutes in January 1980. This proved to be the high-water mark. The price of gold began to ebb and by mid-1982 it had dropped to under $300, about one-third of what it had been at its peak. After rising to around $500 in early 1983, the price of the yellow metal moved gradually lower. By early 1985, gold was again at $300, a low from which it took three years to recover to near the $500 level. Since the late 1987 top, gold has continued to trace its volatile path, eliciting excitement among the gold bugs when it pushed above $400 in late 1989.

The price of gold could explode just as readily as it could wither, depending on how the political winds are blowing.

Twice in 1989 the price of gold fluctuated by as much as $50 an ounce within a couple of weeks. Massive sales by the Soviet Union or Middle Eastern nations depress the price: a flareup of global tensions, particularly in the Middle East or South Africa, and the price of gold surges. The state of inflation, interest rates, and oil prices also have a strong influence on gold prices. Surprisingly, as the Iraq-Kuwait imbroglio unfolded, gold went up only modestly, to a little above $400 in August 1990, despite a 35 percent rise in the price of crude. A decade earlier, the threat of a Middle East war pushed gold up threefold. Yet, in the more recent Middle East crisis and the subsequent outbreak of hostilities, the price of gold rose initially, only to fall back to its prewar level of just under $400.

The yellow metal is a commodity now, just as corn, copper, or cocoa are. Admittedly, gold differs from other commodities in the way people are willing to squirrel it away. Most above-ground gold is just that, hidden away for a rainy day. Who among us would be willing to store tons of corn or copper ingots forever? If people should ever lose this mystical love for the yellow metal, the price could plunge over the long term, for industry uses only a fraction of the available supply. Nevertheless, gold will tend to move up when inflation fears are rampant and down when world finances appear to be under control. All the hoarders are not yet gone. The long-term balance of market forces favors higher gold prices.

Industrial demand for gold (which accounts for one-third of U.S. consumption) flows and ebbs in line with the economic ups and downs in the United States and other Western nations. Gold is an excellent electrical conductor and a well-nigh indispensable ingredient of the supersensitive electronic technology of our times. Therefore, gold-mining shares are likely to continue in a volatile pattern, reflecting the many factors that influence the price of gold.

The market performance of the shares will be enhanced by inflation jitters and depressed by labor and political turmoil in gold-producing nations. They will reflect generally the things that help or hinder all freely traded common stocks. One might guess that earnings progress for this industry, given the problems of dirty and dangerous working conditions, might be substantially slower than that for companies in computers, health care, banking, and brewing.

Investment Outlook: Volatile

Generally speaking, therefore, gold-mining company shares have no more than average appeal. However, if you wish to speculate in gold, if you prefer the yellow metal to greenbacks, do so in mining-company shares rather than gold bullion itself. There is a ready market for gold stocks, easy storage of the certificates, and, usually, dividend income. Owning gold bullion, on the other hand, is expensive. You must pay to store and insure it. It represents negative income, if you will. It offers no dividends and is much more difficult to market when you want to sell.

If you still want a stake in gold you might consider buying shares of one of the North American gold-mining companies. However, gold-mining stocks are affected by the price of gold, currency fluctuations, profitability, extent of reserves, and myriad other factors, many of which are beyond the company's control. Unless you are willing to live with the volatility of gold prices, as reflected in the trading levels of the mining company stocks, you had best put your investment dollars elsewhere. An alternative might be one of the mutual funds that specialize in gold. This type of investment has the advantage of professional management and, because its portfolio contains numerous companies, diversity.

The Risks in "Kaffirs"

Not satisfied with the risks inherent in NYSE-listed gold-mining stocks or gold mutual funds, some traders and eternally gullible investors are tempted by shares of South African gold producers. Our advice, in a word, is *don't!*

These stocks, called "kaffirs" (for the native tribes in the area), offer all the same risks plus a still potentially explosive racial situation. Despite some recent concessions to its black population, South Africa remains committed to its outdated apartheid policies. In a move that underscores the political uncertainty there, South Africa—based diamond producer DeBeers Consolidated moved the control of its assets to Switzerland. The possibility that a future South African government would impose a punitive tax or nationalize the assets of companies operating there makes investments in "kaffirs" highly speculative. In addition, reliable current information on reserves, taxes, and routine operating statistics is hard to come by.

The Krugerrand, Eagle, Maple Leaf, and Others

Until November 1985, the Republic of South Africa offered for sale gold-coin-shaped ingots weighing one-tenth, one-quarter, one-half, and one troy ounce, the basic weight on which gold prices are quoted. Subsequently, the South African government suspended minting of the Krugerrand because of a large surplus of the coins. The surplus resulted from bans on the importation of the coins imposed by the United States and many other countries as a protest against South Africa's apartheid policies.

What do the boycott and the suspension of Krugerrand minting mean to individuals who already own the gold coins? Not much. Many coin dealers still handle Krugerrand trading. So if you decide to sell the coins you now own, and there really is no need to do so immediately, you should obtain a price at or near that day's gold trading price.

In order to take advantage of the void created by the Krugerrand boycott, the United States has begun minting gold coins in four weights, from one-tenth to one ounce. Canada has for some time offered its gold maple-leaf coin in these same weights. Other gold coins include the Mexican 50 peso, the Austrian 100 corona, and the Hungarian koruna, each of which weighs about an ounce. The Austrian four-ducat coin weighs about half an ounce. You can frequently purchase these coins at a premium from dealers in the 15 states that exempt gold coins from sales tax.

In general, gold coins offer little appeal as a serious investment. They generate no income and are subject to relatively wide price swings. Coins can be lost, misplaced, and stolen. Our opinion is that if you want some of these coins just to possess, wear as jewelry, or otherwise enjoy, fine, but limit your expenditures and understand their limits as an investment.

CHAPTER 18

Real Estate

"OF ALL MILLIONAIRES, ninety percent became so through owning real estate," Andrew Carnegie, the steel tycoon, once observed. He went on to advise: "The wise young man or wage earner should invest his money in real estate." This country's history is generously peppered with examples of the fortunes that can be made in pursuit of that investment. John Jacob Astor became the richest man in America in the early 1800s as the "landlord of New York." William J. Levitt foresaw the need for low-cost housing for GIs returning home from World War II and mass-produced houses for them into the Levittowns that have become a part of our landscape and language, making himself comfortably well off in the process. William Zeckendorf fathered scores of flamboyant real estate projects, wheeling and dealing himself into and out of several fortunes.

Not all of us need aspire to such heights to enjoy the fruits of real estate investment. Even if you confine your involvement to owning your own home, you stand to add substantially to your net worth as you dutifully make mortgage payments over the months and years. Home ownership, in fact, is the most common form of real estate "investment." For most homeowners—more than 60 percent of American households own their own home—their house represents their largest single asset. Furthermore, it is likely to be an appreciating asset in dollar terms, for it represents a tangible entity with intrinsic value. It tends to hold its true worth, regardless of what inflation does to the buying power of the dollar. In many cases it tends to rise in "real" value as well, particularly if it is well located and of a type eagerly sought by potential buyers. In fact, Census Bureau figures show that the prices of new and existing houses have risen every single year since 1972.

Another type of home ownership that is gaining in popularity, particularly with the rise in housing and energy costs, involves taking a stake in multifamily residential property. There are two basic forms: cooperative apartments and condominiums. With a cooperative, you own a share of the entire property. Whatever tax considerations apply to the whole package apply to you as well. With a condominium, you own your unit outright, just as if it were a single-family residence, and have your own individual tax considerations. In addition, you hold a joint interest in the common parts of the property. In both a cooperative and a condominium, you share in the maintenance costs of the common property through assessments, which you have a legal obligation to pay. As with a single-family house, you build equity as you make your monthly mortgage payments, and if the property is well maintained and favorably situated, your stake should rise in value over the years.

But beyond the appeal of home ownership, one basic reason for the popularity of real estate as an investment vehicle is the federal government's use of its powers to provide incentives for good-quality housing for all. Recent legislative history is dotted with incentive-inducing provisions. The Housing Acts of 1949, 1965, and 1968, for example, provided mortgage insurance programs, rent subsidies, and the massive urban renewal programs. In 1978, Congress enacted a 10 percent tax credit for investments in historic rehabilitation, which it upped to 25 percent in 1981. As a result of the generous tax credit, some $11 billion has been invested in restoring 17,000 buildings. The 1986 tax revision eliminated most incentives for all but historic rehab investments, but even these were reduced. The tax credit was lowered to 20 percent and is denied to investors whose income is $250,000 or over. Furthermore, the interaction between various aspects of the tax code limits the credit that an investor can take on his tax to $25,000. The new rules will be fully phased in by 1994.

Successes—and Failures

There have been astounding successes and resounding failures in real estate investment in recent years. Two of the strongest areas—farmland and the single-family home—have provided, over the long term, excellent protection against a sharply rising cost of living. When the economy softens nationally, or even regionally, so too does the price of real estate. Farmland went through its boom and bust cycle during the 1980s and many overleveraged farmers lost their family land. But by the end of the decade, good times had restored, at least partially, land values in the Farm Belt. In recent years, home values have weakened more in response to the economy in the region than in response to national trends. Home prices in the Midwestern "Rust Belt" sagged and remained depressed long after those in the rest of the country had rebounded following the 1980–81 recession. When home values in New England and other areas had eased in the late 1980s, Midwestern real estate remained healthy. When the media note that the value of homes is declining, they fail to mention that the decline may be a very small percentage and from an overinflated price level. Between late 1988 and 1989, a typical new single-family home in the Northeast dropped less than 1 percent in value, according to the National Association of Realtors.

Favorably located real estate has always been a profitable area of investment. It should become even more so in years to come as the earth's resources continue to shrink in proportion to its population. Demographic factors indicate that a strong demand for housing will continue into the 1990s. Some of the demand will come from replacement of aging or dilapidated homes, urban renewal, and the acquisition of second homes.

Regardless of your investment objective, real estate can be a contender for inclusion in your portfolio. The following paragraphs discuss some of the more important forms and their investment characteristics.

Investing in Raw Land

Land investment can encompass anything from the most arid prairie land to fertile farming acreage. Speculation in land has provided magnificent fortunes—but also sizable losses. A speculator in land is looking ahead to some possible change in the use of the piece of property. Either it must be seen to have potential for homes or it must promise to provide some form of future income. Potential industrial, commercial, residential, or recreational uses can have a major impact on land values.

Speculating in raw land is extremely difficult, and dreams of quick profits can obscure the all too numerous pitfalls. Raw land not only provides no current income but for such things as financing and taxes, it entails additional costs while it is being held. This means that such an investment must appreciate in value by at least 10 percent a year just to break even. That can be an especially tall order. Furthermore, raw land is an extremely illiquid investment and should never be purchased with funds that might be needed quickly. In addition to these drawbacks, you may find you have to work hard to make your speculation succeed. You might have to exert influence over zoning or even a community's total master plan.

If you are undeterred by these potential obstacles, your best approach is to buy close to home, where you can more easily appraise development and growth prospects. There are land development companies that purport to provide real estate investments for you. These programs have been sprinkled with more than their fair share of development problems. At times promised amenities have been nonexistent or slow in coming or have been delayed or stopped altogether by environmental concerns over the proposed development plan. Government regulation has not always fully protected investors. Do not expect that your investment in raw land will be a quick road to riches.

Rental Property

Apartment living offers an appealing life-style for a growing number of Americans who are discouraged by the ever-rising cost of owning a residence or who simply prefer the convenience. Investing in rental property thus constitutes a large and expanding market that ranges all the way from leasing a single-family home to participation in large apartment complexes with all the amenities—swimming pools, tennis courts, and sauna baths. Investment in rental property can bring substantial economic benefits, even though it may entail management headaches as well. As a landlord, you face the problems of keeping up with maintenance, finding tenants, collecting the rent, and handling complaints about the all-night parties in 4B. If you're not up to those tasks, you can hire someone to manage the property for you, but this cuts into your profits and may have unfavorable tax implications.

In seeking a rental property, it is well to keep in mind the rule of thumb that monthly rental income should total about 1 percent of the purchase price—as a bare minimum. This effectively removes most single-family homes and as a practical matter makes it hard to justify anything less than three units.

There are some distinct advantages to this form of investment. Apartments can generally be financed with a relatively small down payment of 20 to 30 percent of the purchase price, affording considerable leverage on the investment. The down payment is generally smaller if you make the building your home, too. Indeed, leverage is one of the major benefits of investing in rental property, for it magnifies your rate of return on the appreciating value of the property.

In purchasing rental property, make your selections carefully. Avoid those that show evidence of structural flaws or other conditions that might cause hefty maintenance expenses later on. Location is another important consideration. The deterioration of a neighborhood could seriously erode your capital and diminish the property's earning power. Don't be afraid to get a professional appraisal of the property's worth, either.

You should study the rental market in the area you are considering to be reasonably sure you won't be stuck for long with empty units. There will be vacancies from time to time, to be sure, but too many will play havoc with your bottom line.

Finally, study the tax rules in light of your financial and tax situation to determine whether you can gain any advantage from investing in rental property. If your income exceeds $150,000, rental losses in excess of rental income can't be used to offset other income. Loss of this tax break could make the difference in whether the rental investment is feasible.

Business Property

Investing in business property takes several forms. Office buildings, shopping centers, and warehouses are among the most familiar alternatives. When considering these investments, bear in mind that overbuilding has depressed this market. Business property provides certain advantages over rental apartments. The commercial tenant is generally more stable and is looking for a location around which he can build a profitable business. He takes better care of his property and, barring extreme financial emergency, pays his rent on time. Some of the drawbacks include the more expensive maintenance services you as a landlord must provide. Vacancies are usually harder to fill and may require such things as the dismantling of a customized office.

One approach to investing in business property is to buy and convert a marginal suburban retail operation into an office building. This has worked successfully for a good many real estate investors. Some developers have gone one step further. When conditions warrant they then convert the rental offices to condominiums, selling the space to their former tenants or to new occupants.

In the past the potential for tax recapture from using accelerated depreciation has had to be taken into account on this type of conversion. However, on new investments, only straight-line depreciation taken over a 31½ year life is allowed for nonresidential real estate, so recapture is no longer a threat.

Business property investments in regional shopping centers can be profitable. The largest of these can encompass one million square feet or more of store area and serve a customer base of about 250,000 people. They usually have a magnet store or two to act as the main drawing card. Smaller community-type shopping centers may cluster around a supermarket and a drugstore. Reasonably priced land close to rapidly expanding outlying areas can offer the speculator a good opportunity.

The shopping-center owner attempts to build a long list of good-quality tenants with long-term leases. His compensation is generally in the form of a minimum rent plus a certain percentage of gross sales above minimum volumes. Because of the specialized nature of this field, shopping centers are best left to professional developers, though smaller investors can frequently invest through participation in joint ventures and limited partnerships (more on them below). A bad experience with a particular key tenant, such as when Zayre's and then Ames closed many of their outlets, can seriously cut into profits.

Investment in shopping centers is also possible through common stock ownership. A handful of companies specialize in the field, but Rouse Company is the best known.

Real Estate Investment Trusts

Real estate investment trusts (REITs) allow individuals to participate indirectly in real estate and thereby avoid management headaches. Like mutual funds, REITs sell shares to the public to raise their capital; but, instead of investing in a portfolio of stocks and bonds, as do mutual funds, they invest in real estate and mortgages. REITs, like publicly traded investment companies, do not redeem their shares; rather, the shares are bought and sold over the counter or on the stock exchanges.

REITs come in two basic forms—equity trusts and mortgage investment trusts—or a combination of both forms, commonly known as a hybrid trust. Equity trusts own property outright and seek their profits from rental income and capital gains. Mortgage investment trusts make long-term mortgage loans to large real estate buyers and intermediate and short-term construction loans to builders and developers.

The main attraction of REITs is that they are able to pass on all the tax advantages of real estate ownership to their investors. By law, a REIT must distribute 95 percent of its taxable income to shareholders each year. Since the trusts are not allowed to reinvest their earnings, they rely heavily on borrowed funds to provide growth. Typically mortgage-type REITs' capitalization will be 65 percent to 75 percent long-term debt, with the remainder composed of equity. The capitalization of those REITs that concentrate on real estate ownership is in almost directly reverse proportions—equity 70 percent to 85 percent and debt 15 percent to 30 percent. For those REITs with large amounts of short-term debt, tight money has made debt rollover either impossible or ruinously expensive. As a result, one firm filed for protection under Chapter 11 of the Bankruptcy Act and a second has gone through major restructuring.

The popularity of mortgage trusts reached faddish proportions during the late 1960s and early 1970s. Promoters, eager to cash in, put together projects of dubious merit that were snapped up by equally eager investors. As long as the economy remained robust, they could survive. But between 1973 and 1975 they collapsed like so many houses of cards. Indeed, even the strongest of the REITs took some hard knocks under the barrage of shifting long- and short-term interest-rate relationships, rising unemployment, soaring operating costs, and rent control. Rapidly rising short-term interest rates played havoc with financing arrangements and spelled doom for many of the highly leveraged REITs. Overbuilding during the early part of the decade also fueled the bust. Bankruptcies hit the industry, share prices plummeted, dividends dried up, and investors were left hanging.

As a result of this drubbing, REITs got a bad name in the

investment community. It wasn't until 1980 that they staged a comeback. Then investors saw REITs as bargains, since they were trading below their breakup values and real estate markets had moved from an overbuilt to an underbuilt condition. By the end of the decade the balance had shifted back toward being overbuilt.

As you can see, there is more to investing in REITs than merely picking one off the shelf. You have to evaluate the merits of individual trusts by a careful study of a number of factors, including examination of past performance, capital structure, investment objectives, and management. Equally important is the vacancy rate experienced at the trust's properties. Since 1986, the vacancy rate for office space in 49 major cities has been in the 16 percent to 17 percent range. You should realize that although REITs have a potential for high return, they have a similar potential for risk.

Taxation of REITs did not change materially under the Tax Reform Act of 1986. Because Congress determined that REITs were portfolio investments rather than limited partnerships, passive loss limitations do not apply to them. Therefore, if an investor sustains a trading loss on a REIT, it can be used to offset up to $3,000 of ordinary income.

Real Estate Syndicates

The syndicate, or group participation form of real estate investment, usually is organized as a partnership, occasionally as a corporation. Syndicates raise capital by selling participations or shares. This capital is then used to pay off debts and even to pay tax-free dividends. In the past, accelerated depreciation has helped these syndications reduce investors' taxes. When property held by the partnership is fully depreciated, it is sold and the investors realize a profit. With the capital gains rate at 28 percent, that isn't a very big advantage. Real estate syndicates are also used as vehicles for property development and land speculation.

Most of them take the legal form of limited partnerships rather than general partnerships. Under a general partnership, all partners bear equally in the risks and rewards of the venture. This means all partners can be held liable for losses in excess of their actual stake in the project. Under a limited partnership, on the other hand, the limited partners are liable only to the extent that they are invested in the project. A general partner puts the deal together and manages it for a consideration, which he is paid regardless of how well or how poorly the venture goes. However, a well-conceived and properly managed project can bring highly expert management to bear, with rewarding results for the limited partners.

The 1986 revision of the Tax Code virtually did away with the tax-sheltering effects of these limited partnerships. This was accomplished by eliminating the capital gains rate, replacing accelerated with straight-line depreciation, and stretching out the depreciable life of a building to 31½ years. Moreover, a previous tax change limited the amount of loss that partnership investors could claim to the amount they are at risk. The '86 tax law defines income and losses from limited partnerships as passive. Passive losses can be used only to offset passive gains, not investment or wage income. For individuals whose limited partnership investments were held on the date the law was enacted (October 22, 1986), the passive loss limitation was fully effective in 1991.

Real Estate Investments and Taxes

Real property has intrinsic investment value, as we discussed earlier. It has had, in addition, special tax benefits that have made it especially attractive to high-income taxpayers. But Congress has a penchant for restructuring our tax laws fairly regularly. So an investment made solely for tax reasons may turn sour when those tax benefits disappear. The Tax Reform Act of 1986 laid a heavy hand on the real estate industry. It eliminated or reduced some tax benefits that had been enacted only a few years earlier and others that had been on the books for decades.

Some of the tax benefits of real estate ownership have been retained. Homeowners who itemize may deduct mortgage interest and real estate taxes from their federal income tax.

This also holds true for a second, or vacation, home. Although these deductions have withstood the depredations of a revenue-hungry Congress in the past, they may be limited in the future.

When a second home is rented as well as being used by the owner, tax treatment is a bit more complex. If two or more vacation homes are owned and used by the owner more than 14 days a year (or 10 percent of the time the property is rented at a fair rate), then the home on which the deductions are greater should be claimed as the second home. Rental income does not have to be reported on a vacation home that is rented two weeks or less annually.

A home that is rented and is used less than two weeks a year by the owner qualifies as rental property. Because rental income and losses are classified as passive by the 1986 tax act, they are subject to the same rules and limitations as income and losses from limited partnerships. However, when the owner actively manages the property and his or her adjusted gross income (AGI) is less than $100,000, then $25,000 of losses may be used to reduce income. For those with AGI over $100,000, losses are reduced by $1 for each $2 of added AGI. When AGI reaches $150,000, the rental loss exception is exhausted. If your financial and tax situation is such that you are able to claim rental losses against other income, then all expenses associated with the property—taxes, mortgage interest, utilities, depreciation, and so forth—are included. These "expenses" must first be used to offset rental income, then any excess can be used to offset other income.

When a principal residence is sold, the gain on that sale can be rolled over and added to the cost basis of the replacement home, so that the tax on the gain is deferred. This nonrecognition of the gain can go on for years, through two or two dozen home sales. Once the homeowner reaches age 55, a residence can be sold and up to $125,000 of the gain excluded from income. Conceivably, a taxpayer could parlay $10,000 into $125,000 tax-free using these two tax strategies.

What Can Go and Has Gone Wrong

A sizable increase in interest rates is a perfect example of what can go wrong. If you owed a large real estate loan at 1 percent over prime when that rate was 5 or 6 percent, or even 10 percent, imagine your horror when the prime rate escalates to 20 percent, as it did in 1980. That jump could wipe out many a real estate investor.

Another example of what might go wrong was the sharp rise in California real estate values. This was accompanied by escalating property taxes. California homeowners on fixed incomes were often forced to sell or to take out second mortgages. When the upward spiral in home prices broke in the early '80s, a lot of people suffered, including banks and mortgage companies that had written mortgages based on inflated values.

Changing and deteriorating neighborhoods, demographic shifts, and rezoning can affect real estate investments. The revamping of tax laws, as discussed above, is another factor that can go wrong. An investment that makes sense under existing tax laws may prove to be a loser when those rules change. While present investors are sometimes protected by grandfather clauses, new investors are not. Thus, the value of real estate can be adversely affected.

PART IV

How to Make Your Choices

CHAPTER 19

Forecasting with the Cyclical Indicators

FORECASTING IS A complicated process. Even the most expert forecasters are sometimes quite wrong, and ordinarily they are only partially accurate. Yet, like eating, forecasting is something that has to be done. Every action that each of us undertakes implies a forecast. Buying the week's groceries involves forecasting family needs and implies certain expectations about price behavior during the week. The actions of buying, selling, or even holding stocks all imply certain forecasts about stock prices.

The decision, then, is not between forecasting and not forecasting. Investors must forecast, and in so doing they must rely heavily on the work of others, at least for the needed data, and ordinarily for interpretations of those data.

Newspapers and business publications frequently carry reports of forecasts, with the fall of the year usually the most popular time for such reports. Investment advisory services, in most cases, carry forecasts, at least in summary form, throughout the year.

A forecast that appears each month is the one implied in the government's *composite index of leading indicators.* This forecast results from the efforts of a few economists to find a group of economic indicators that tend to move up or down in advance of the movements of general business. The reports of the current behavior of this index are widely watched, and the individual investor can advantageously pay some attention to these reports. However, the index is far from infallible, and most professional economists consider it to be only one of several forecasting tools available to them.

The index of leading indicators now being used by the U.S. Department of Commerce turned down 3 months before the 1953–54 recession, 20 months before the 1957–58 recession, 10 months before the 1960–61 recession, 8 months before the 1970 recession, 8 months before the 1973–75 recession, 15 months before the 1980 recession, and 3 months before the 1981–82 recession. The index also turned down in 1950–51, 1962, 1966, 1984, and 1987. None of those downturns was followed by a full-fledged recession, although the 1966 economy was often referred to as a mini-recession and the 1989–90 economy as "sluggish." The declines in the leading indicator index mentioned here were all drops lasting several months. A chart of the index also displays other, meaningless, short-term movements.

Actually, the particular index now in use wasn't even in existence on most of the dates cited above. The present index, introduced in 1975, is an improved version, which, when computed historically, produced the above-mentioned results. The leading indicators are flawed by the exclusion of an index tracking the output of the service sector of the economy. Services now constitute about 70 percent of the country's output.

Leading Indicators: 11 Precursors

The revised index of leading indicators has 11 components, all tested for historical reliability in moving ahead of periods of general business expansion and contraction. The data for the components are gathered monthly and assembled into a combined index. The combined index measures departures from the base-year (1982) value of 100. However, when the combined index is first published, data for all the components are not available. Also, revisions in some of the individual components are made over a period of several months, leading to revisions of the combined index on those occasions.

The 11 Leaders

Average weekly hours of production or nonsupervisory workers in manufacturing

Average weekly initial claims, state unemployment insurance

Manufacturers' new orders in 1982 dollars, consumer goods and materials industries (bil. dollars)

Vendor performance—slower deliveries diffusion index (percent)

Contracts and orders for plant and equipment in 1982 dollars (bil. dollars)

New private housing units authorized by local building permits (index: 1967 = 100)

Change in manufacturers' unfilled orders in 1982 dollars, durable goods, smoothed (bil. dollars)

Change in sensitive materials prices, smoothed (percent)

Stock prices—S&P 500 Stock Index (index: 1941 − 43 = 100)

Money supply—M2 in 1982 dollars (bil. dollars)

Index of consumer expectations (index: 1st Q 1966 = 100)

SOURCE: *Business Conditions Digest*, monthly publication of the U.S. Department of Commerce.

The leading indicators are statistical measures that tend to foreshadow movements in the coincident group discussed later in this chapter. This is quite apparent in the indicators that report on new orders for consumer goods, on contracts and orders for plant and equipment, and in the index of housing permits. Movements in these indicators may be expected to be followed by movements in employment, production, incomes, and sales.

Other leading indicators generally have a rationale for their particular place in the timing sequence of economic measures. The stock market, for example, is sensitive to changes in the state of confidence concerning future business activity and profits. Improved confidence about the future often leads to higher stock prices, and deteriorating confidence brings stock prices down.

Changes in sensitive prices of crude materials—excluding foods, feeds, and fibers—reflect variations in demand-and-supply pressures for particular raw commodities. Thus a rise in this index could reflect rising levels of demand and, hence, expectations of increased business activity, while a drop in the index could signal the reverse.

The money supply, measuring the total of currency plus demand deposits and expressed in 1982 dollars, is another measure that often can be expected to precede, in its ups and downs, changes in the general level of business. Increases in the money supply tend to fuel expansion of business activity, while contractions in supplies of money tend to have a dampening effect on levels of business.

In recent years, investors, and especially stock market traders, have devoted a good deal of attention to short-term movements in the money supply (without adjustments for price level changes). The weekly money-supply reports come out late in the afternoon every Thursday. Some observers interpret consistent increases in money as a signal that the Federal Reserve Board may feel compelled to restrict monetary growth and thereby tighten credit. Thus stocks often drop on Friday when the Thursday report shows a sharp rise in the money supply. If the report shows no gain or even a reduction in the money supply, the expectation sometimes develops that the Fed will ease the money supply and credit, and, accordingly, stocks may rise on Friday. This interpretation of money-supply movements is not only short term but also fails to take into account the serious problems in the collection of the data. The role of the money supply in the leading indicator index depends on the actual movements of money rather than expectations of how money is going to move.

It is not generally a good idea to pay much attention to the movements of the leading indicator index for any single month. One reason for this caution is that movements of the index over short periods sometimes reflect the influence of random events, such as strikes or unusual weather patterns. The initial report of a small decline in the indicator could be revised in the subsequent months to a modest increase. The initial data have been temporarily distorted by a serious delay in the dispatching of tax refunds. Also, as previously noted, the index is oriented toward production and doesn't give proper weight to the increasingly larger role played by the service industry.

The leading indicators are actually part of a family of economic indicators. The two other branches of the family tree are the *roughly coincident indicators,* which are generally the economic measures being led by the leading indicators, and the *lagging indicators,* which tend to bring up the rear, but which also have an importance of their own.

Roughly Coincident Indicators: Four Track Broad-Based Activities

The roughly coincident indicators are those that move with general business conditions, that is, those that move up and down with the swings that pervade most sectors of the economy. In general, one would expect the coincident indicators to encompass measures of employment, production, incomes, and sales, on the basis that these activities reflect the broad movements of the economy. As it turns out, these four aspects of economic activity are exactly the components of the index of coincident indicators.

The particular measure of employment used in this indicator is the monthly report on the number of employees on nonagricultural payrolls. This tests out better than other possible employment (or unemployment) measures as a reporter of the general ups and downs of business. One reason for this is that the payroll reports upon which this number is based reflect a markedly larger sample than does the household survey upon which the monthly labor force, total employment, and unemployment data are based.

The income measure included is the monthly report on personal income. It is expressed in constant 1982 dollars, with transfer payments (Social Security benefits and other nonwage government "transfers" of funds into the hands of individuals) deducted. These adjustments improve upon the performance of the personal income figure as a measure of cyclical behavior, which is what is desired of a coincident indicator.

The third coincident indicator is the monthly index of industrial production prepared by the Federal Reserve Board. This index measures activity in manufacturing, mining, and electric and gas utilities. Manufacturing activity tends to be cyclical and represents a declining share of the gross national product. However, the industrial production index reflects important activities and is still worthy of inclusion in the index of coincident indicators.

The final component in this index is a combined figure for manufacturing sales and wholesale and retail trade sales, expressed in constant 1972 dollars. This figure provides a comprehensive report on distribution and consumption activities

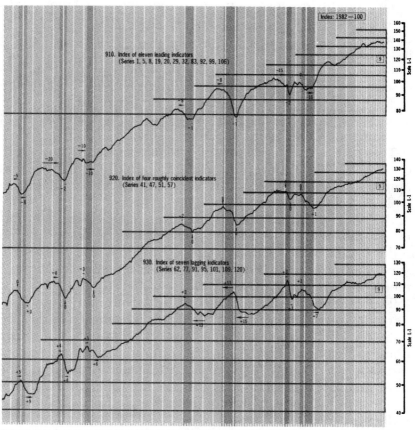

and, like the personal income measure, is one from which the inflation influence has been removed.

A notable exclusion from the list of coincident indicators is the most comprehensive of all measures. This is the gross national product, the total dollar volume of the nation's output of goods and services. It is not included because it is available only quarterly, rather than monthly, and is subject to rather frequent revision.

The four coincident indicators are combined in a single index of coincident indicators, again using the year 1967 value of 100. The combined index tends to follow movements of general business quite closely, a result that is not surprising, given its broad composition. Although the combined index has a slight tendency to lead general downturns by a couple of months, its upward movements tend to coincide in timing with upswings in business.

The Roughly Coincident Four

Employees on nonagricultural payrolls (thous.)
Personal income, less transfer payments, in 1982 dollars
  (ann. rate, bil. dollars)
Industrial production, 1977 = 100
Manufacturing and trade sales in 1982 dollars (mil. dollars)

SOURCE: *Business Conditions Digest*, U.S. Department of
  Commerce.

Lagging Indicators: Seven Tend to Trail Behind

The third member of the indicator triad is the group of lagging indicators, those that rise or fall after the general upward or downward movements of the economy have appeared. For example, since 1950 the index of lagging indicators has turned down, on average, five and a half months *after the peaks* in general business and turned upward, on average, 10 months *after the low points.*

The lagging indicators, however, are more than faithful followers. A sequence exists among the three groups of indicators, so that the lagging indicators turn down before the leading, and later the coincident, indicators turn up.

The Seven Laggards

Average duration of unemployment (weeks)

Ratio, manufacturing and trade inventories to sales in 1982 dollars

Change in index of labor cost per unit of output, manufacturing, smoothed (annual rate, percent)

Average prime rate charged by banks (percent)

Commercial and industrial loans outstanding, in 1982 dollars (mil. dollars)

Ratio, consumer installment credit outstanding to personal income (percent)

Change in consumer price index for services, smoothed (annual rate, percent)

SOURCE: *Business Conditions Digest*, U.S. Department of Commerce.

Since the lagging indicators tend to make their moves before the leading indicators make theirs (in the reverse direction), the former have a place in the forecasting scheme. One would not expect the leading indicators to signal an upward or downward move until the lagging indicators had made a downward or upward move.

The family of leading, coincident, and lagging indicators forms a useful tool in the forecaster's kit. It is important, however, not to draw conclusions from observations pertaining to just one or two months. Unfortunately, the indicators don't foretell much about the severity or duration of business movements. Nor do they purport to forecast stock prices. But since the monthly reports on the leading indicators are widely published, it is easy for the general reader to follow them and thereby get some clues concerning the direction in which the economy is headed.

CHAPTER 20

Measuring the Market's Ups and Downs

THE MARKET IS "up." The market is "down." The market is in a sustained "rally." It is moving "sideways." The daily stock market reports make it sound as if all 1,700 or so issues that trade regularly on the New York Stock Exchange, plus the 800 or so on the American Stock Exchange, the 4,000 on NASDAQ, and the 15,000 others that trade on regional exchanges, Autex, and over the counter, are all moving in lockstep up, down, and sideways.

Obviously that's not the case. Just as obviously it would be an impossible task to provide a daily analysis of the aggregate price movements of all stocks. Yet investors, corporate money managers, stockbrokers, economic forecasters, government policymakers, and others concerned with the pulse of investment and business must have some way of keeping a running check on the investment climate.

So they have devised various averages to keep tabs on both the general trend and the present status of the market. Since the "market" is such a huge and diverse agglomeration, even the averages frequently have difficulty in agreeing on precisely what the trend and status of the market are at any given moment. Furthermore, just as the presence of a television news team can sometimes affect the outcome of the event it is covering, the averages themselves can have an impact on the extent and duration of a market movement. If the averages, particularly the more widely followed averages, say the market is "rising," investors perk up and start buying. If the averages say the market is "declining," they start selling to nail down profits or to trim losses. Other elements play their parts, of course: the general strength or weakness of business, the availability of credit, the cost of borrowing money, the needs of corporate finance. In recent years, market swings have been exaggerated by program trading. These computerized buy, sell, and arbitrage systems initiate transactions when the market moves up or down a predetermined number of points. Unfortunately one program triggers another and cumulatively, they can cause a major break in the market. The factors affecting stock market movement and the movement of individual stocks are virtually limitless, and many of them defy analysis or rationality. Measurement of the stock market thus is an imprecise undertaking.

How to "Build" an Index

There are many ways to go about constructing an index of stock market activity. You could take a relatively small sampling of tried-and-true blue-chip companies and compute a simple, arithmetic average of their stock price activity on a day-to-day basis. You would have something like the Dow Jones Industrial Average. You could take a larger group of what you consider to be representative stocks and apply the same simple arithmetic averaging. You'd have something like the Associated Press and *New York Times* averages.

If you decided that such a simple price-weighted arithmetic average would not provide sufficient accuracy because it did not measure the impact of the stock's price on the total market volume, you could construct a so-called value-weighted average. You would factor in the differences in size of the components of your index by multiplying the price of each by the number of shares outstanding in each case. You would then average these resulting market-value figures and express them as a percentage of some base figure. Standard

& Poor's, the New York Stock Exchange, American Exchange, and the National Association of Securities Dealers Automated Quotation (NASDAQ) indexes are figured by this method.

This approach might not satisfy you either, because the largest components exert much more influence on the total than the smallest. You might regard this as a situation that unduly distorts the bottom line. So you would take still another tack. You would apply equal dollar investments to a fairly large group of stocks. The resultant index would be called an unweighted or equal-weighted average. You would need a firm grasp of mathematics, for you would then apply some rather complex geometric calculations to the daily price changes in order to come up with a result. Your index would resemble the composite index published by Value Line, an investment advisory company. In 1988, Value Line also introduced an index on the stocks in its composite index using an arithmetic averaging technique.

Different Indexes Yield Different Results

As you might suspect, these different approaches yield different results. For the most part, the differences are not so much in direction as in extent and occasionally in timing. The point is best demonstrated with a chart of three diverse averages—the 30-stock Dow Industrials, the S&P 500, and the Value Line Composite (geometric), which tracks close to 1,700 issues. For our chart, on the following page, 1973 equals 100, making 1973 the base year for all three indexes. Value Line, the broadest-based of the three, includes many secondary stocks, which makes it very volatile. In bull markets its rises are usually higher and last longer, while its bear market declines are more precipitous than those for the Dow and S&P 500. During the bull markets of 1980–81 and 1982–83, VL far outperformed the other two indicators, reflecting its representation in the high-technology industry.

Whereas by 1980 the VL and S&P averages had moved above their 1973 highs, the Dow took until 1983 to reattain its high of a decade before. This sluggish performance reflected the concentration of cyclical issues in the Dow in those years. Now the DJIA follows closely behind the S&P 500 Composite. The chart shows very clearly that secondary stocks, as represented by the VL Composite, didn't fully participate in the bull market enjoyed by blue chips and top-tier growth issues in 1990. This fact is further exacerbated by the fact that the VL index gives each stock equal weight regardless of its trading price and capitalization. The VL index peaked late in 1989, well shy of its 1987 high.

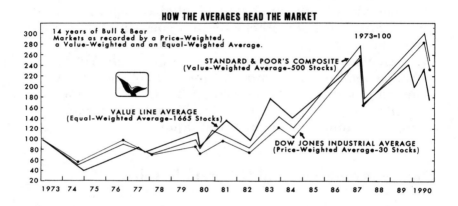

HOW THE AVERAGES READ THE MARKET

14 years of Bull & Bear Markets as recorded by a Price-Weighted, a Value-Weighted and an Equal-Weighted Average.

1973=100

STANDARD & POOR'S COMPOSITE (Value-Weighted Average-500 Stocks)

VALUE LINE AVERAGE (Equal-Weighted Average-1665 Stocks)

DOW JONES INDUSTRIAL AVERAGE (Price-Weighted Average-30 Stocks)

The "Dow"

The Dow Jones Industrial Average is the granddaddy of today's stock market measures. It's also probably the best-known and most widely quoted. The "Dow" dates back to 1896, when it contained an even dozen stocks, none of which remained on the list continuously. In 1916, another 8 were added, bringing the total to 20. It was not until 1928 that the average assumed its present shape. Not only were 10 stocks added, but a new method of computation was adopted, which it still uses.

Before 1928, stocks that were split were adjusted by multiplying the split price by two or three, or whatever the split was, to make the price consistent with the presplit value. Adjustments made since 1928 take into account stock dividends, rights, and mergers, as well as splits.

Here are the 30 stocks that made up the Dow Jones Industrial Average in 1990. Dates in parentheses indicate the company's first appearance in the average. Only General Electric was in the original average, though it has been in and out several times since.

Allied-Signal (1925)
Aluminum Co. of America (1959)
American Express (1982)
American Telephone & Telegraph (1916)
Bethlehem Steel (1928)
Boeing Corp. (1987)
Chevron Corp. (1924)
Coca-Cola (1987)
DuPont (E.I.) de Nemours (1924)
Eastman Kodak (1928)
Exxon Corp. (1928)
General Electric (1897)
General Motors (1915)
Goodyear Tire & Rubber (1930)
Int'l. Business Machines (1979)
Int'l. Paper (1901)
McDonald's Corp. (1985)
Merck & Company (1979)
Minnesota Mining & Mfg. (1976)
Navistar Int'l. (1925)
Philip Morris Cos. (1985)
Primerica Corp. (1916)
Procter & Gamble (1932)
Sears, Roebuck (1924)
Texaco Inc. (1916)
Union Carbide (1928)
United Technologies (1933)
USX Corp. (1914)
Westinghouse Electric (1916)
Woolworth Corp. (1924)

What is now known as the Dow Jones Transportation Average boasts an equally long history. Until 1970, it was known as the "Railroad" Average; the name was changed when other types of transportation companies were added to the list that year. The 20 stocks that were originally used were all rails, some with names that are still familiar. But many others have succumbed to mergers and bankruptcies. The Dow Jones Utility Average made its debut in 1929. The initial list of 20 utilities included both electric and gas companies, as well as American Telephone & Telegraph, International Telephone, and Western Union. Today the list has been whittled to 15 electric and gas utilities. The Dow Jones Composite Average was begun in 1933 as a compilation of the stocks used in the three individual averages. The utility, transportation, and composite averages are computed in essentially the same way as the industrial average.

For several reasons, the historical significance of the Dow industrial average is subject to question. Until 1928, no adjustments were made for stock splits of less than 100 percent. Furthermore, when the new issues were added, the continuity of the average was disrupted. Substitutions in the names of companies in the list were frequent in the early days; through 1939, more than 60 were made. While this probably made the list more representative of the current market, it also produced a historical bias.

Another complaint frequently lodged against the Dow, and one that has some justification, is that it is an elitist sampling of the market. Only 1.5 percent of the stocks listed on the New York Stock Exchange appear in it. Even when you consider that these issues constitute 25 percent of the total market value of Big Board issues, they are still an extremely narrow representation of all the issues regularly traded on all the exchanges and over the counter. Criticism of the Dow's heavy cyclical weighting has been put to rest in recent years with the addition of growth stocks such as Coca-Cola, McDonald's, Merck, and Philip Morris.

The S&P 500

Aside from the Dow, the most familiar average is the Standard & Poor's 500. This broad average is widely used by institutional investors and mutual fund managers as a yardstick against which to compare their own performance. In fact, some funds and institutions have adopted investment policies that restrict their holdings to those in the S&P 500 list, thereby giving up any attempt at outperforming this index.

Standard & Poor's also publishes separately the various component averages that make up the 500-stock composite. These are the 400 industrials, 40 utilities, 20 transportation companies, and 40 financial stocks. These new indexes were begun in 1957 to replace the original series started in the 1920s. As we noted above, the S&P averages are weighted. They are also expressed as a percentage of the base market value in 1941–43 = 10.

Other Indexes

The New York Stock Exchange Composite Stock Index uses as its base December 31, 1965 = 50, which approximates the average price of a share on the Big Board then. Thus, if the index stands at 60, it indicates that the market has advanced 20 percent above its value on December 31, 1965. The NYSE Index should not be confused with the figure cited daily by newscasters, the average price of a share on the New York Stock Exchange. The latter is simply the average price for all the stocks that traded on a particular day on the Big Board. There is no day-to-day continuity in this figure, for not all issues trade every session; neither is any attempt made to adjust for splits or other changes.

The American Stock Exchange Market Value Index is composed of all the common stocks and warrants listed on the ASE. These are weighted according to market value and indexed to 1973 = 100.

Indexes Are Useful—to a Point

Are market indexes useful tools for the average investor? Yes, up to a point. Certainly the person who plunges in and buys a stock with a high price-earnings ratio after the averages have recorded a steep and prolonged advance is asking for trouble. The investor who gets discouraged and sells stocks he has been holding through a protracted decline in the market is equally unwise. In other words, the averages are valuable as rough guidelines for timing your transactions.

Using the market averages as forecasting devices, although a favorite pastime of the technicians, can be tricky and unreliable. Complex formulas, involving virtually every conceivable variable, have been devised by serious students of the market, mathematical wizards, and charlatans. While some may prove accurate from time to time, no one has ever come up with a forecasting device of any kind that is always correct. If such an infallible formula exists, it is surely being kept under wraps by its originator, who is busy reaping his own fortune.

In trying to gauge market timing by consulting one of the market averages, you should use an average that represents the type of stocks you own or plan to purchase. The Dow Jones Industrial Average will be of little help if you are interested in utilities, glamour stocks, or rails. Junior growth stocks would more closely parallel the action tracked by the Value Line or AMEX indexes.

By keeping in touch with the general trend of the stock market averages, you should develop a better understanding of the action of your own portfolio. Many investors operate in a vacuum. Their holdings are down and they grow panicky, overlooking the fact that the entire market is in the doldrums. Then, too, keeping an eye on the market rather than on a few individual stocks helps you keep things in proper perspective. If one of your stocks diverges suddenly from the norm, you are more likely to spot this countermovement, investigate, and take the indicated action. Use the averages, by all means, but use them judiciously.

CHAPTER 21

Getting the Picture from Charts

CHARTS, QUITE SIMPLY, are devices that can be valuable aids to investors. They translate into graphic form—with bars or lines—information that could also be presented in tabular form. The basic usefulness of a chart is the picture presented, its conciseness, and the ability to portray relationships that would not be visible in a table. A two-month tabulation of the daily highs, lows, and closes for the Dow Jones Industrial Average follows on page 214.

Just about any set of data can be depicted graphically, and the result is a "picture" that can be quickly comprehended. The chart on page 215, top, shows the same information contained in the table, plotted on a simple arithmetic scale. This particular chart is a "bar chart," and its purpose is to show a range. In this case, the top of each bar represents the high price for the day, the bottom represents the low, and the cross line represents the close.

If the data to be plotted do not involve a range, the result would be a line connecting each of the points. Such a chart is called a "line chart," as depicted at the bottom of page 215. As will be noted throughout this book, many charts combine bars and lines, the better to portray the data, or picture, desired.

213

		High	Low	Close			High	Low	Close
April	1	930.27	919.55	927.36	May	2	934.02	923.00	931.22
	4	926.70	913.48	915.56		3	939.70	929.27	934.19
	5	920.88	909.74	916.14		4	944.96	929.44	940.72
	6	922.12	910.07	914.73		5	949.46	934.53	943.44
	7	921.21	910.57	918.88		6	943.27	932.24	936.74
	11	928.85	916.47	924.10		9	938.52	928.77	933.09
	12	940.98	924.69	937.16		10	941.40	930.55	936.14
	13	942.76	927.49	938.18		11	937.84	923.85	926.90
	14	956.07	943.69	947.00		12	930.04	917.74	925.54
	15	953.10	941.74	947.76		13	932.58	923.17	928.34
	18	951.32	939.28	942.76		16	938.43	926.73	932.50
	19	944.28	934.79	938.77		17	939.45	925.20	936.48
	20	948.69	933.43	942.59		18	947.34	935.46	941.91
	21	949.37	933.43	935.80		19	945.13	933.34	936.48
	22	935.13	923.59	927.07		20	937.16	925.71	930.46
	25	924.02	910.45	914.60		23	928.17	915.03	917.06
	26	922.74	910.36	915.62		24	917.83	906.55	912.40
	27	928.34	913.08	923.76		25	916.72	901.46	903.24
	28	931.14	919.78	927.32		26	910.45	899.17	908.07
	29	931.99	922.32	926.90		27	909.60	896.29	898.83
						31	904.77	892.55	898.66

Practical Application

Here are some practical examples of how charts can be useful in conveying information. In the chart on price-earnings ratio (page 216) you can tell at a glance how the price-earnings ratio for the stocks that make up the Dow Jones Industrial Average compares with the status of the Dow itself. You can see that the price-earning ratio was below 10X in 1981, indicating that stocks were not being realistically valued by investors. In late 1982, when the Dow rallied sharply, P/Es soared to unrealistically high levels, but reason returned and by 1984 the ratio was in a more normal range. After only a short breather the market and P/Es took off, reaching a high point in August 1987. Following the collapse later that year, P/Es worked down to the 11X to 13X level where they remained until 1990, when the line moved cautiously closer to 15X.

The chart showing mutual fund cash position (page 217) is another example of how figures can be more quickly grasped when they are presented graphically. The percent of assets

BAR CHART

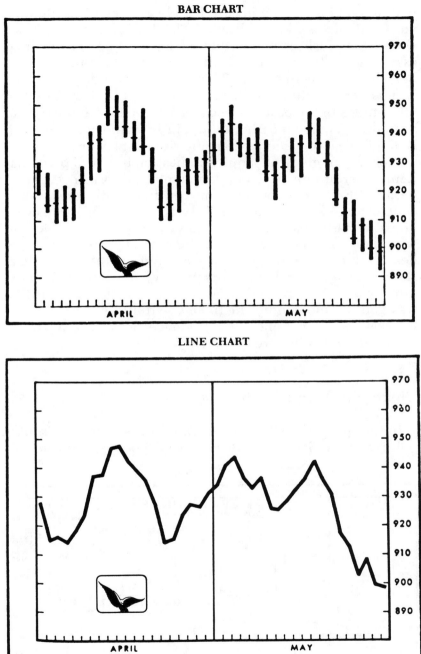

LINE CHART

that mutual funds hold in cash has always been considered a very reliable market indicator. The last plot on the chart shows that cash assets accounted for 11.3 percent of fund assets, down from 12.5 percent the previous month (remember, this scale is inverted). This is a bullish indicator, as the cash is being built up for future investment. In fact, only two other times in the past two decades has the fund industry had a similar 12 percent cash buildup, in 1974 and again in 1982. Both of these preceded a dramatic rise in stock prices.

A chart can give you a quick indication of how a particular item is performing now in relation to its performance in past periods. From that picture you can frequently draw some conclusions about the future. Take the next chart, on private housing starts (page 217). It shows the long-range picture, with housing starts declining from 2 million in 1978, a healthy rate, to about half that amount in 1981 and 1982. After recovering in 1983, starts moved sideways for the next three years. But in 1987, housing starts began a slide that was gaining momentum in 1990. Overbuilding, a less-than-vigorous economy, and high mortgage rates have all taken their toll on this important industry.

Charts and Your Investments

In the quarterly *SRC Blue Book of 5-Trend Cycli-Graphs,* published by Securities Research Company (a division of

Babson-United Investment Advisors, Inc.), there are over 1,100 stock charts and about 40 industry charts, as well as various business and market-average charts. The stock charts contain plottings of monthly price ranges, volumes, relative performance line (Ratio-Cator), plus earnings and dividends over a 12-year period. There are *one million or so* plotting points in one book of 288 pages. Much of the book may be scanned in a fairly short time, though a real study would take much longer. Imagine how many volumes would be required to show this information in tabular form, how long it would take to comprehend the material, and the difficulty that would be encountered in comparing one company with another.

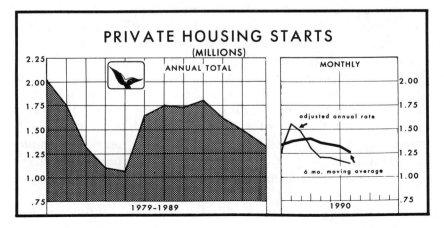

You don't have to possess a lot of investment expertise to draw some conclusions from the typical *Cycli-Graphs* chart shown opposite. It shows you that this hypothetical growth stock, ABC, Inc., rose almost steadily from 1979 to 1990, with only moderate downturns along the way. The chart tells more. It shows that earnings have risen consistently quarter by quarter along the way. Of considerable significance to the long-term investor, dividends have been increased annually.

The Ratio-Cator line indicates a stock's performance in relation to the Dow Jones Industrial Average. Periods when ABC raced ahead of the Dow and when its performance lagged that average are very easy to spot by looking at the Ratio-Cator Line.

Plotting the Percentages

You have probably noticed that the *Cycli-Graphs* chart looks somewhat "different" in that the vertical scale figures are not evenly spaced. That is because it is a "semi-logarithmic" or "ratio-scale" chart. Its purpose is to present everything on the chart in proportion. If a stock moves from 2 to 4, it has appreciated two points, or 100 percent. If it rises another two points, from 4 to 6, the gain is 50 percent. Another 100 percent move would have required a gain from 4 to 8. Even though the number of dollars or points may be greater at higher levels, the principle remains the same—the stock must move from 20 to 40 or from 200 to 400 to achieve a doubling, or 100 percent rise. The logarithmic scale is formulated so that any move of a particular percent uses the same vertical linear distance on the chart, regardless of where it may occur. Thus, for example, a move of 10 percent takes the same amount of space on the chart regardless of whether it occurs in a stock selling at 60 or one selling at 6. Furthermore, the use of a standard logarithmic scale permits the comparison of any one chart with any other so that movements may be perfectly related without fear of distortion.

The more familiar arithmetic-scale chart does not work in this manner. A move from 2 to 4 looks exactly the same on such a chart as a jump from 4 to 6, or even an edging up from 98 to 100. Obviously, two points have greater significance when a stock is selling at 2 than when it is selling at 98, but the arithmetic scale conceals this. The extent of a price movement, large or small, is easily hidden, and comparisons of one stock with another on such a chart are difficult to make and can be deceptive.

Charts can also be something of an eye-opener. Over a period of time you might have become accustomed to the current price action of a certain stock, while losing sight of what happened in the past. A glance at a chart, particularly if the stock used to be a high flier, can be edifying and, sometimes, sobering. Similarly, when a stock is rising sharply, you might easily forget the base from which the rise was initiated, an important consideration in making an investment decision. A chart will furnish the relationship.

A good example of this sort of illumination might come from the chart in the previous chapter showing the performance of three market averages. The Standard & Poor's 500 is a value-weighted average. The Dow Jones Industrial Average, a simple price average of 30 different stocks, is somewhat biased by its component blue-chip giants. The Value Line Composite is equal weighted. As explained in that chapter, a value-weighted index gives the most heavily capitalized companies the greatest weight. While this may reflect total market *value*, it does not tell us what the total market of all *stocks* may be doing. That is what the equal-weighted averages try to correct. In effect, they give one unit of value to a stock, regardless of whether it is a General Motors or a small company that is a fraction of the size of that giant.

Not Only for Technicians

Charts are basically a tool, one of many, that the investor may use to determine his investment action. There are myriad charts available, showing not just a stock's price action but market details, business statistics, interest rates, money supply—you name it. What a chart does is show the quantitative factors involved in the study of the market, a company, or an industry. It does not show the various qualitative considerations involved. In a manufacturing company, for example, these might concern management, product line, plant efficiency, labor relations, and many other items impossible to quantify, although they may be reflected to a certain extent in specific or general price action.

Many people tend to think that if someone uses stock charts in his investment decisions, he is a technician. Actually, the fundamentalist has just as much use for charts. The pictures they show and the amount of information they provide help to make the task of investment selection much easier for the busy person.

CHAPTER 22

Technical Analysis

Definitions

FUNDAMENTALIST. One who bases his investment analysis and decisions primarily on basic factors such as economic conditions, supply and demand, labor, products, earnings, and dividends.

TECHNICIAN. One who bases his investment actions and decisions upon a reading and interpretation of chart formations or compilations of statistics.

The discussions in this book are principally oriented toward the fundamentalist. This chapter is intended to furnish an introduction to the technician and some of his methods of analysis and must be very general in nature. To some, technical analysis is not a valid investment approach, perhaps because some of the technical theories seem too "far-out." Yet technicians will argue that their record certainly is no worse than that of the fundamentalists, and, in view of the number of those attracted to technical analysis, it may possibly be better.

There is no one method of technical analysis. In fact, there are so many methods and interpretations and there is such a wide variety of data and relationships developed that it is unlikely that any one person could become well versed in all. Certain methods use common data, but others are individual and unique. Some technicians base their market and investment decisions wholly or partly on the study of chart formations. Others may depend wholly or partly on statistical compilations and work relating one series of data to one or more other series. Using models of behavior based on prior study and experience, the technician derives from chart patterns and relationships and from statistics the material he needs to make his decisions.

Once the technician has created his models and his chart or statistical relationships, he must stick to them. He may refine them, but he cannot allow emotional considerations to influence his decisions. That is where many technicians go wrong. They allow their technical findings to be swayed by other factors. Perhaps this is because they are not completely convinced of the validity of their method, or perhaps their signal has been received far ahead of others. Thus, the technician may be alone and exposed with his findings. And that solitary position makes him wonder whether he has made a correct interpretation of his charts and data. He cannot entertain such doubts. While his method may not always work out —none is infallible, after all—it faces a greater risk of failure if he is influenced by exceptions, emotions, and outside considerations.

More Than Charts and Figures

People tend to think of technical analysis as meaning chart formations such as flags, pennants, channels, and heads and shoulders, but it involves much more. With the advent of computers, the technician may now tear apart stacks of statistics to obtain relationships, actions, and reactions over long periods of time—material that previously might have been too difficult to obtain. These studies permit the technician to determine a series of likelihoods and probabilities—of rises, declines, and side movements. They do not necessarily project the magnitude of the moves, only that a move will take place. Like any other analyst or investor, the technician is attempting to ascertain the optimum time to make his buys and sells.

The advantage of chart analysis over the fundamental approach is in calling a turn. Often the basics of a situation may look good, but for some unperceived reason the technical picture turns weak. It is at this point that technical analysis does better than fundamental. The lines often tell something more than the fundamentals may indicate, and it is this failure of the latter on many occasions that has led more people into technical analysis, not just of stocks but of all sorts of economic factors. Actually, fundamental and technical analysis seem to be coming closer together in investment decision making. However, if the technical approach shows weakness in a situation and the fundamental does not, the former should be followed, because the fundamental will confirm too late. For example, look at the chart of Stock A (on page 224).

Despite rising earnings, trading weakness developed after the shares peaked in August 1989. Earnings continued in a generally rising pattern and the stock turned upward for the next six months, challenging but not breaking the previous peak. The relative performance line moved sideways in this period, demonstrating the stock's weakness in relation to the Dow. The fundamentalist might have said the outlook remained favorable and the stock should be held. The technician, however, seeing weakness developing in the earnings and relative action, would have suspected that something was amiss and recommended sale of the shares.

In the chart of Stock B (page 225) we show an example of a rising price trend. Here we have a picture of declines that are accompanied by reduced volume and where rallies occur with increased volume. In addition, the stock's performance indicates relative strength at important highs. Accompanying this are the rising earnings trend and dividend increases.

Some Technical Indicators

There are various popular indicators used in attempting to determine market direction. Some, which are best shown by charts, are (not necessarily in order of importance):

MARKET AVERAGES. The chart patterns of averages such as the Dow industrials, the Standard & Poor's 500, the New

York Stock Exchange Composite, the Value Line Composite, and others are studied for clues to future action.

TRADING VOLUME. This information, in figures or as plottings on charts, is important to determine whether strength or weakness accompanies various price movements.

SPECULATIVE INDEX. This is the relationship of American Stock Exchange volume to New York Stock Exchange volume and is expressed as a percentage. The theory here is that since most of the issues listed on the AMEX tend to be of lower or more speculative quality than those on the NYSE, they will be slow to participate in the earlier stages of a bull market and will be very active in the later and declining phases. Thus, the lower the figure, the closer the market presumably is to a bottom, and, conversely, the higher the figure, the closer it is to a top. In the past, this indicator has fluctuated within a 20 to 60 percent range. In more recent times, it has dropped to as low as 10 percent. The rising volume of options trading is blamed for the decline in AMEX volume and the value of this indicator.

ADVANCE-DECLINE INDEX. This index may be started at any point in time and is the net result of all the advances and declines on the New York Stock Exchange since that starting point. The significance of this line is its comparison with the Dow industrials or other market averages to detect any divergence. Thus, in a bull market this line will often start down while the averages are still rising and, conversely, in a bear market will start to rise while the averages are still declining. It can be an early signal of a change in general market direction.

A ratio derived from relating advances to declines provides an overbought-oversold index, which, when substantially above or below 1.00, indicates one of those conditions.

UPSIDE-DOWNSIDE VOLUME. This is a tabulation of the shares traded on the NYSE at prices higher or lower than the previous day's close. The trend of either line may be used to confirm the movement of a market average, and the crossing of the lines is interpreted as possibly indicating a change in market direction.

NEW HIGHS—NEW LOWS. This is another indicator of market strength or weakness. In a strong market, the new highs should greatly exceed the lows and follow the market averages. The opposite is true in a weak market. It is when either line diverges from the averages and when the lines cross that an indication is given of a change in direction. A line representing the differential between these figures will perform similarly to the advance-decline index in peaking while the market averages continue to rise and in bottoming when the averages are continuing to decline.

ODD-LOT TRADING. This is the buying and selling activity of the small investor who deals in units of less than a round lot (100 shares). The extent to which this investor buys or sells has been used to indicate turning points for "informed" selling or buying. To greatly simplify the theory, the small investor is said to buy or sell at the wrong time, and the extent to which he does so provides a signal to the smart investor to do the opposite. Thus, odd-lot selling may peak around the bottom of the market, and odd-lot buying may reach its maximum around the top. The odd-lot index is the relationship of sales to purchases, and the higher the percentage, the more bullish the indicator. Thus goes the general theory.

A more recent study claims the odd-lotter has been maligned and has been more attuned to market action than was generally believed. Thus, at major bottoms he is seen to have been a buyer and at major tops he is often a seller.

To further refine odd-lot indicators, odd-lot *short* sales are related to odd-lot sales. The resultant figure is considered a significant indicator, since the small investor does not usually sell short, and when he does so it is under rather extreme conditions. Once again, he purportedly picks the wrong time. While there may be some difference of opinion concerning these figures, when the odd-lot short-sales figure is up around 10,000 and the ratio is in the 4 to 6 percent area, a major bottom may be signaled; on the other hand, when short selling is low and the ratio is around 0.5 to 1 percent, a top may be indicated. But the whole theory, or its importance, has been diminished by growth in options trading.

SHORT INTEREST. This is the total number of shares sold short. The higher this figure, the more bearish are investors (frequently at the wrong time). But since the stock that has been sold must be bought back, it provides a good cushion of buying power when the short sellers seek to cover their short contracts. When the market is at its top, short selling has usually diminished to a fairly low figure, reflecting the general optimism. Member and specialist short selling are also looked at for sensitive market signals.

SHORT INTEREST RATIO. This figure is obtained by relating the monthly short interest to the average daily trading volume in the period concerned. When the ratio moves up to two or more, it is generally considered a bullish sign, and when it declines to one or lower, the signal is bearish.

BARRON'S CONFIDENCE INDEX. This is a relationship between the yields of high-grade and intermediate-grade bonds on the theory that informed investors will put their money into the former during periods of market uncertainty and into the latter during better times. A decline in this index indicates that more investors are seeking refuge in high-grade issues, and a rise indicates a more optimistic attitude. The value of this index is that presumably the stock market will follow the same pattern, but usually at a somewhat later date.

An indication of how some of these data look when plotted and related to each other is shown in the charts that follow.

TECHNICAL INDICATORS

Irregular Forecasting Methods

There are many other methods of predicting market action. They are not especially technical but they are far from fundamental. Here are a few:

Years ending in seven tend to have an upward trend.
National election years have certain patterns.
The first year of a new presidential administration is likely to be
down or to be the worst of the four years of that administration.
An up or a down January sets the tone for the year.
The first 10 days of January set the tone for the month and the
year.
There is usually a summer rally.
A poor July-August market is usually followed by a rally in
September.
The direction of the market is indicated by whether General
Motors makes a new high or new low within four months of a
previous high or low.
Strength or weakness of sunspots will affect the market.
A strong indication of bearishness or bullishness by investment
advisory services is a sign that the market will move in the
opposite direction.

It is obvious there are nearly as many ways to "forecast" the market as there are those willing to express an opinion, and the variety seems limitless.

Interpreting Chart Patterns

When it comes to technical analysis of individual stocks, you will find a variety of formations and interpretations. While some of these formations are rather easy to identify, others tend to be more obscure. Sometimes the technician must strain to identify the pattern that makes his point. Also, formations vary with the type of chart used—daily, weekly, or monthly, arithmetic or logarithmic—so that what shows up on one chart will not necessarily appear on another for the same stock. The technician then must decide which charts make him most comfortable and confident, and proceed accordingly.

The discussion of formations which follows is intended only as a brief explanation of the most common terms.

SUPPORT LEVEL. A price area in which the demand for a stock is sufficient to keep the price from dropping below it on repeated occasions. Once there is a breakout below the area, a new support level is created.

RESISTANCE LEVEL. A price area that attracts selling sufficient to keep the price of a stock from rising above it on

SUPPORT LEVELS

repeated occasions. However, once it has been broken through on the upside, the old resistance area becomes a new support level.

CHANNELS. These are drawn by connecting a series of highs and a series of lows to make parallel lines. Characteristically, the stock will trade within the ascending and descending channels, indicating a sell at the top of the channel and a buy at the bottom. A confirmed breakout in either direction would mean a buy on the upside and a sell on the down.

DOUBLE TOPS AND BOTTOMS (M AND W FORMATIONS). These are formations in which the stock fluctuates, hitting the same top or bottom on two, and sometimes three or four, successive occasions. The breakout from such a pattern is the clue to the action to be taken. The chart on page 234 is an example of an attempted upside breakout from the W formation, followed by a clear violation of the three successive bottoms.

HEAD AND SHOULDERS. This formation's name is derived from the appearance given by the pattern of a head and right and left shoulders (page 235). The important thing here, if one has not previously sold on the higher head level, is to take advantage of the rally that forms the right shoulder, because price deterioration on reduced volume can set in very quickly.

Other patterns that may be drawn by connecting a series of highs and lows, usually during short time spans, include flags, pennants, triangles, wedges, and rectangles, all of which may give a message to the technician. And then there are bowls and saucers, and variations thereof, as well as trading volumes, which also tell a story. You must remember that none of these patterns is exact and perfection is impossible. However, the astute and perceptive student may achieve a high percentage of successful interpretation.

RELATIVE STRENGTH. This is the relationship of the price of a stock to the price of the Dow Jones Industrial Average or perhaps to one of the other major market averages. The resulting percentage, multiplied by a factor to bring the plotting closer to the price bars on the chart, shows by the direction of the curve whether the stock is performing better, worse, or the same as the market average used. The line is studied for trends as well as for variations of direction from that indicated by the price ranges. For example, the price of a stock may reach a new high but the relative performance line may not, a possible indication of weakness. Similarly, strength may be observed when the price drops to a new low but the relative strength line does not. Charts of stocks "A" and "B" printed earlier in this chapter provide good examples of how effective the relative performance line (Ratio-Cator) may be on the downside and the upside, respectively.

MOVING AVERAGES. One of the popular indicators for determining market and individual stock strength or weakness is the moving average. This is obtained by adding the prices for a certain number of days and dividing the total by the days involved to obtain an average. For the next figure, the price for the earliest day or week is dropped and the current one is added. A moving average rounds out the ups and downs, and the investor is then able to derive buying and selling signals from the action of the price in relation to the moving average curve. These figures are easily plotted, or

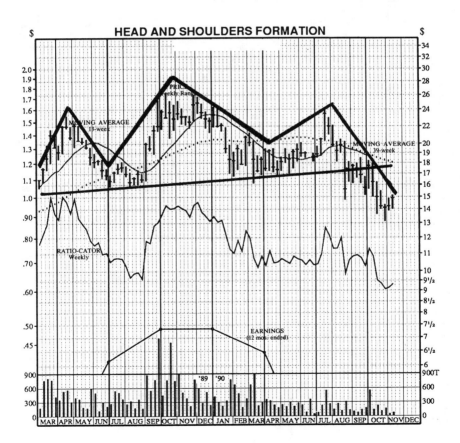

they may be conveniently used in tabular form. The following chart plots moving averages for three different time periods and can be referred to for an indication of short- and long-term market direction.

The most popular time period for individual stocks appears to be 200 days, or roughly 40 weeks, although some investors prefer a much shorter span to achieve a greater degree of sensitivity. The moving average gives a quick indication of where strength or weakness may lie, but, as with all other formations, the user must follow certain rules to avoid false moves.

While all the charts used in this chapter include a moving average, the chart of stock "C" opposite is a specific example of the moving average–price range relationship. It portrays one of the interpretations of a moving average that holds that a buy signal is indicated when the stock price is above the moving average, declines toward it but fails to penetrate, and starts to move up again.

STOCK "C"

POINT AND FIGURE ANALYSIS. This method of interpretation of price movement has its own dedicated devotees. Basically, these charts are designed to show strength of price movement and to emphasize changes in direction. Just as with bar charts, formations are created by the plottings, and these form the basis for interpretation and analysis.

The Dow Theory

Most of the foregoing approaches to technical analysis involve the use of charts. One that does not, and one that certainly should be included in any compendium of technical analysis, if for no reason other than its wide following, is the Dow Theory.

The Dow Theory was developed around the turn of this century by the editors of *The Wall Street Journal.* It was never clearly stated in its original form, and it has been bent, twisted, distorted, and elaborated on for most of its existence by those who seek to apply it in their own fashion. But its basic tenet is that a trend should be expected to continue until a reversal is definitely signaled. For investors, this means that profits will be made by taking advantage of the primary trend, not by resisting it.

The Dow Theory assumes a bull market trend is in progress as long as each successive market advance continues to a higher peak than the one preceding it, and each successive secondary reaction stops at a higher bottom than the last. Conversely, a bear market trend is defined when each successive decline carries to a new low and each interim rally ends at a point below the previous one.

The Dow Theory also holds that these moves must be confirmed by similar action in different averages within a short period. The averages most frequently used as reference and confirmation points are the Dow Jones industrial and transportation averages. If the Dow industrials signal the start of a bull market, the faithful wait for the transportation index to move similarly, and when it does, they begin buying stocks.

On paper, the Dow Theory allows profits to continue indefinitely, while it restricts the extent of losses. In practice, it has been successful only some of the time. One reason is the wide divergence in interpretations of the same signals by different Dow theorists. Another reason is the great difficulty in pinpointing the moves that are indeed the true turning points of the market. Finally, the effectiveness of the Dow Theory has been diminished somewhat by its wide following.

In Conclusion

The analysis of the stock market as a whole or of individual stocks, whether by the technician or the fundamentalist, is not an easy task. You must endure a good deal of trial and error as you build up your own background and experience and as you develop the methods that make you most comfortable. It is often a slow and painstaking process. Except for the very lucky or those who are highly intuitive, success can come in no other way.

CHAPTER 23

How to Read an Annual Report

THOSE SLICK PAPER, photo-enhanced, multipage annual reports that are mailed to shareholders each spring have a wealth of information between their covers for those recipients who are willing to dig it out. The purpose of this chapter is to help you mine that lode of information. Understanding how to interpret the financial data, read between the lines of the stockholders' letter, and translate the footnotes will make you a wiser investor.

Annual reports are easy to obtain. A company listed on the New York Stock Exchange, for example, is required to send one to each shareholder every year. In addition, many companies will send them to anyone who asks; address your request to "Investor Relations."

An even more detailed and comprehensive document is the 10-K statement that large, publicly owned companies are required to submit each year to the SEC. Some companies will send copies of the 10-K to shareholders and others on request. The 10-Ks are also available either in print or on microfilm at many large public and business school libraries.

In Tres Partes Divisi

Most annual reports have three main segments—a review of the year by management, information about and discussions of divisional or company operations, and a statistical section with footnotes. On opening the report, the reader is usually confronted with a table of contents and highlights, in both tabular and graphic form, of the most obvious financial data for the current year vis-à-vis the data of the previous year. A quick glance will show how earnings, dividends, sales, total assets, shareholders' equity, and so forth have increased or decreased during the latest year. If earnings have declined, the year-to-year percent comparison may be omitted, or if graphics are used, they may be presented so as to minimize the decline. Next comes management's letter to stockholders, which attempts to put the best possible slant on results. If the year was a poor one, the letter may focus on the company's future rather than on its past.

In the second section, which details operations, the report may discuss where the company is headed and how it stands in relation to others in the industry or to its own goals. If the company has expanded, entered new fields, or accomplished a technological breakthrough, these will be discussed here. A service company may expound on the efficiency of its staff, a gas utility on the miles of new pipeline installed, or a technology company on its vision of the future. In this section the company can elaborate on its strengths—sell itself, so to speak.

The third section provides facts and figures. The financial statements in this no-nonsense segment include the balance sheet, income statement, and changes in shareholders' equity, and a statement of cash flows. In addition, a 5- and 10-year summary of important financial and operational data, divisional operating results, a summary of common stock changes, and quarterly data may be included. Several pages of footnotes, a statement of accounting principles, and an auditor's report appear in this third and final section.

The Balance Sheet

The balance sheet shows the financial condition of the company on the last day of its fiscal year. Normally, the figures for the previous year are also included to facilitate comparisons. Note that the balance sheet for TCA Industries, our model manufacturing company, shows the assets, the liabilities, and the shareholders' equity, or capital, of the corporation.

The balance sheet will also yield the company's *book value.* Book value merely represents common stockholders' equity less goodwill, all other intangible assets, and preferred stock. In effect, then, book value is the amount of money stockholders originally invested in the company, plus profits the company has retained from year to year, subsequent equity offerings, and acquisitions.

Now let's go over the various categories of the balance sheet (not all of which will appear on our sample balance sheet for TCA Industries). *Current assets* are items that normally can be converted into cash within a year. *Cash* itself would include petty cash, checking accounts, and other demand or short-term bank deposits. *Marketable securities,* which are usually listed at cost, would be principally confined to short-term U.S. Treasury securities or commercial paper. If the company held *other investments*—for example, unconsolidated, partially owned subsidiaries or purchase mortgages on properties sold—these, too, would be listed. *Accounts receivable* are amounts payable by customers within a year for goods delivered or services rendered. Note that the figures are net of a stated allowance for bad debts. *Inventories* consist of raw materials, partially finished goods, and finished products. The accounting method used to evaluate inventories is described in the footnotes or statement of accounting principles.

Fixed assets are items needed for carrying out the company's business and might include factory buildings, machinery, offices, and land. Traditionally, these items have been shown on the balance sheet at their original acquisition

BALANCE SHEET FOR TCA INDUSTRIES

Assets

	Year Ending Dec. 31	
	(000 Omitted)	
	1990	1989
Current Assets		
Cash and temporary investments	$101,100	$ 66,900
Accounts receivable less allowances of $2,130 in 1990 and $1,900 in 1989	83,800	71,100
Inventories	128,000	124,400
Other	28,100	16,400
Total current assets	$341,000	$278,800
Fixed Assets		
Land	8,300	8,000
Buildings	71,200	67,200
Machinery and equipment	147,700	133,800
Less accumulated depreciation	(119,200)	(106,600)
Total	$108,000	$102,400
Other Assets		
Investments	83,300	96,100
Purchase price in excess of net assets of companies acquired	9,500	10,000
Property held as investment	9,000	11,100
Miscellaneous	25,500	25,100
Total	$127,300	$142,300
Total assets	$576,300	$523,500

Liabilities

	Year Ending Dec. 31	
	(000 Omitted)	
	1990	1989
Current Liabilities		
Accounts payable	$ 22,400	$ 19,300
Accrued salaries, wages, benefits	11,600	11,100
Accrued income taxes	26,200	21,800
Accrued other taxes	4,800	4,900
Dividends payable	9,100	7,200
Other accrued liabilities	27,300	24,000
Total current liabilities	$101,400	$ 88,300
Long-term debt	8,100	8,100
Other noncurrent liabilities	12,000	9,200
Deferred income taxes	27,000	25,300
Stockholders' Equity		
Common stock, $5.00 par value: Authorized—87,000,000 outstanding—28,120,000 and 26,992,000	140,600	135,000
Additional paid-in capital	72,800	32,800
Retained earnings	216,700	227,500
Unrealized loss on investments	—	(800)
Cumulative translation adjustments	(2,300)	(1,900)
Total shareholders' equity	$427,800	$392,600
Total liabilities and shareholders' equity	$576,300	$523,500

cost. Now some of the largest companies are required to show in their 10-K statements the estimated replacement cost of these assets.

Accumulated depreciation is deducted from *gross plant and equipment* to reflect the fact that these assets have been declining in their useful value each year. Land, though, is never depreciated. Its balance sheet value doesn't change. Several depreciation methods for plant and equipment are still in use; the footnotes will indicate which one has been used.

Intangibles usually refer to patents, franchises, or goodwill. While these assets may have a very real value, some companies follow conservative accounting practices and assign them only a nominal value. A *goodwill* value results when one company acquires another for a price exceeding its book value. The difference (goodwill) becomes an intangible asset that must be written off within 40 years.

Prepaid expenses refer to items that have been paid for but have a useful life beyond the next 12 months. *Deferred charges* refer to items the company has chosen to add to the balance sheet (capitalize) rather than treat as expenses that are shown only on the income statement. Some questions might arise if the deferred charge account has been increasing rapidly and is now shown as a substantial asset.

Current liabilities are items payable within a year. *Accounts payable* are sums owed to the company's regular vendors and suppliers. *Accrued expenses* refer to unpaid wages, insurance premiums, and so forth. *Notes* and *loans payable* refer to short-term money owed to banks and other creditors. *Long-term debt due within one year* is self-explanatory.

Accrued income taxes are federal, state, local, and foreign income taxes, also due within one year. Sometimes a deferred tax account is set up as a short-term, long-term, or other liability that may be due in future years. These deferred taxes arise from the fact that companies can employ different accounting procedures for shareholder and for Internal Revenue Service purposes. Thus they may report and pay less tax to the government than is reflected in the income statement for shareholders. There is nothing illegal about this, and the company, in fact, may never actually have to pay these additional taxes. But the quality of *earnings* would be diminished for a company with a large tax deferral account.

What is referred to as the capital structure or capitalization of a company will include such different securities as straight and convertible bonds, straight and convertible preferred stocks, common stocks, and warrants. *Long-term debt* usually consists of bonds and bank debt due more than one year from the date on the balance sheet. The interest rates and payment schedules for debt securities can be found in the footnotes.

Shareholders' equity includes preferred stock, so to compute book value or earnings on shareholders' equity the preferred stock and dividends payable on it must be subtracted. The principal categories under common stockholders' equity are *common stock, capital surplus,* and *retained earnings.* These three items in total show the amount of equity or ownership that the common stockholder has in a corporation. *Common stock* is shown on the balance sheet at *par value.* But this is an arbitrary figure having no relation to market or liquidation value. *Capital in excess of par value* is what it says—the amount in excess of par value that shareholders have paid for their stock. This account would be set up when shares were initially sold. It would be increased after any subsequent new issues of stock. *Retained earnings,* also sometimes referred to as *earned surplus,* is the accumulation of profits remaining after payment of dividends on all outstanding securities. Another item that appears under shareholders' equity is *cumulative translation adjustments.* As the international operations of U.S. companies become more widespread, this adjustment will become increasingly common. It reflects the difference between the currency exchange rate used for income and expense statements and that used to value foreign-based assets and liabilities. The former is the average rate of exchange during the year, the latter the rate at year end.

Analyzing a Balance Sheet

Many investment analysts maintain that the balance sheet is more important than the income statement in assessing a company's prospects. Yearly increases in certain balance sheet items are good indicators of the company's growth potential.

There are a number of rather simple calculations you can make to help determine the financial strength of a company. Let's first consider the ability of a company to liquidate its debts and other obligations. This would logically come from current assets. Hence, to relate these two items, we employ the *current* (or *working capital*) *ratio*. This is computed by dividing current assets by current liabilities. A ratio showing current assets in excess of current liabilities by two to one is generally considered quite acceptable for the typical manufacturing company. But for certain other industries it might be either unnecessarily high or unacceptably low. Businesses require different amounts of working capital and liquidity. But where a company does have current assets in excess of current liabilities, that difference is available to reduce long-term debt or help finance growth.

It is also worth noting if working capital is expanding from year to year. A growing corporation probably needs expanding working capital.

A more exacting test for liquidity is the *quick ratio*, which is also called the *liquidity ratio* or *acid test*. This is figured the same way as the current ratio, omitting the inventory from the asset side. The rationale for this is that inventories may not be easily liquidated except at a discount. Cash on hand and that collected from receivables is used by a company to pay bills. If these sources are inadequate, operations may have to be slowed or bank loans floated in order to buy supplies or even to meet payrolls. A one-to-one liquidity ratio is reasonable.

To further test financial strength, long-term debt and preferred stock outstanding should be related to stockholders' equity. Creditors' and preferred stockholders' claims on assets in liquidation and on earnings for interest and preferred dividend payments have priority over those of common shareholders. Then, too, a relatively large amount of long-term debt or preferred stock may mean the company is burdened by these fixed-interest and dividend charges. This may help to leverage the company's earnings upward in years when there is rapid growth, but it works on the downside, too.

Capital structure varies from industry to industry. Utilities usually carry larger amounts of debt than manufacturing companies because of the stability of the former's operations. But generally speaking, shareholders' capital should total substantially more than long-term debt and preferred stock combined.

To determine whether a company's debt burden is reasonable you should look at its *debt to equity ratio*. This is often shown in the report's financial highlights, but you also can calculate it from balance sheet figures. Add the value of long-term debt and preferred stock to shareholders' equity to get total capitalization. Then divide long-term debt by total capitalization to get the *debt to capital ratio*. A similar calculation is made for the preferred and the common equity. The *equity ratio* should be larger than the combined debt and preferred to capital ratios.

The Income Statement

The *income statement* summarizes a company's performance for the current year and previous two years. The statement of our model firm, TCA Industries, appears on page 248.

Net sales represents money received by the company from the sale of its goods, minus any allowance for sales discounts or returned goods. *Cost of goods sold* includes raw materials, plant wages and salaries, utilities, maintenance, and other factory overhead costs. These expenses are directly related to the company's manufacturing operations. Cost of goods sold is subtracted from net sales to arrive at the company's *gross profit*.

Selling, general, and administrative expenses cover certain costs not involved directly in production and thus not shown under cost of goods sold. The expenses in this account would include such things as executive salaries, rent, miscellaneous office expenses, advertising, and travel. This is deducted from gross profit to determine *operating income*.

CONSOLIDATED STATEMENT OF INCOME
FOR TCA INDUSTRIES

| | Year Ending Dec. 31 | | |
| | (000 Omitted) | | |
	1990	1989	1988
Net sales	$668,800	$614,200	$581,100
Cost of goods sold	(450,400)	(407,600)	(385,200)
Gross profit	218,400	206,600	195,900
Selling and administrative expenses	(113,400)	(109,200)	(106,200)
Operating income	105,000	97,400	89,700
Other income			
Investment income	15,200	11,600	9,200
Interest expense	(700)	(800)	(600)
Other income or (expense)	(2,700)	(1,800)	900
Total	11,800	9,000	9,500
Income before taxes	116,800	106,400	99,200
Provision for income taxes	(37,400)	(35,100)	(36,700)
Net income	$ 79,400	$ 71,300	$ 62,500
Earnings per share	$ 2.82	$ 2.64	$ 2.20

Listed under *other income* are income sources other than operations—investments, for example. Interest expense is deducted here. This is the amount paid during the year to bondholders and other creditors. Since interest paid is deductible it is listed before income taxes. These items are added to or subtracted from operating income to calculate income before taxes. Taxes—federal, state, local, and foreign —are subtracted next and the resulting figure is *net income.* In the course of business, a company will report a nonrecurring item—the sale of a plant, discontinuance of a business, an insurance award, or a foreign expropriation. The adjustments would be made here. *Earnings per share* are listed next, and if a nonrecurring item is to be reported, net per share also is calculated after that adjustment.

The calculation for *net income per common share* involves subtracting from the net income figure any dividends paid on preferred stock during the year and dividing the result by either the number of shares outstanding at the end of the year or a weighted average of the number of shares outstanding during the year. If companies have sufficient convertible bonds, convertible preferred stocks, warrants, or options outstanding to dilute per-share earnings by more than 3 percent, they must also show *primary earnings per share* and *fully diluted earnings per share.* The primary earnings per share figure is arrived at by dividing net income after preferred dividends by common shares outstanding plus dilutive common share equivalents. The latter are those securities whose dividend or coupon rate at the time of issue was less than two-thirds the prime rate at that time. Since options and warrants have no payment, they are regarded as common stock equivalents at all times. The fully diluted earnings per share figure assumes the conversion of all outstanding securities that would reduce earnings per share.

Analyzing the Income Statement

There are a number of ratios you can use to derive information from the income statement. Some of these involve determining profitability, such as the amount of each dollar of sales the company is able to bring down to net or pretax income, or how much the company is able to earn on stockholders' equity.

In establishing the return on sales, you could calculate a *pretax profit margin,* a *net income profit margin,* an *operating profit margin,* and a *gross profit margin.* The pretax profit margin is computed by dividing pretax income by net sales. This may be a more significant number than the net income profit margin, because the latter can be distorted by sharp changes in the tax rate. The operating profit margin would be operating profit before interest expenses and, sometimes, depreciation, divided by net sales. The gross profit margin is the income that remains after only cost of goods sold is deducted from net sales, and again this figure is divided by net sales.

There is likely to be a sharp increase in profit margins in the years when sales have risen markedly. Also, industry leaders tend to have higher profit margins than their smaller competitors. A deterioration in profit margins might reflect more severe price competition or certain expenses temporarily running out of control. Some industries or businesses are inherently more profitable than others, so the ratios you calculate for the company you are examining should be compared with those of firms in similar fields.

A common stockholder also should be concerned about how much money the company is able to earn on his investment. The return should be much better than that which he could obtain from a bank savings account, for example. So the *return on equity* is an important ratio. This figure is calculated by dividing net income for the common stockholder (what's left after preferred dividends have been paid) by the previous year's common stockholders' equity. You use that figure to see what the company was able to earn on the stockholders' equity available to it at the beginning of the year.

If return on equity seems high it might mean that the company was using substantial amounts of borrowed funds (so-called leverage) and preferred stock instead of common stock. So check back in your analysis of the balance sheet to see what the common stock or debt to equity ratio was.

Some other items worth checking are the *tax rate* and the *inventory turnover* and *accounts receivable turnover*. The tax rate is taxes paid as a percentage of pretax income. As part of the Tax Reform Act of 1986, corporate tax brackets were reduced from five to three, and the maximum corporate rate was lowered from 46 percent to 34 percent, effective July 1, 1987. Most U.S. corporations are taxed at the maximum rate. Earnings from foreign operations are usually subject to a much lower tax rate, and the company might have substantial overseas business. The investment tax credit, by which corporations could temporarily reduce taxes in a year of heavy buying of equipment, is no longer available. Also, a much lower tax rate might reflect the presence in a particular year of tax-loss carry-forwards stemming from some earlier deficit years. That credit may not be available in subsequent years, either.

The *inventory* and *accounts receivable turnover* ratios are meant to show how liquid the company's inventory and accounts receivable are. The inventory turnover ratio is usually derived by dividing net sales (or, to be more exact, cost of goods sold) by the year-end inventory figure shown on the balance sheet. A high ratio would suggest strong demand for the company's products. A low ratio might indicate either severe competition or inventory obsolescence. These ratios, though, will depend on the business. A food chain is likely to have a much faster inventory turnover rate than a heavy-machinery company. The accounts receivable turnover ratio is net sales divided by receivables. A low ratio might indicate that the company has poor collection procedures.

Other Lodes to Mine

After you have gained an understanding of a balance sheet and an income statement, you would do well to examine two other related financial statements in the annual report.

The first, the *statement of cash flows,* was seldom seen in annual reports before 1988, when the Financial Accounting Standards Board made them mandatory. Cash flows are reported separately for the firm's operating, investing, and financing activities. Whereas operating activities increase cash flows, investing and financing activities usually decrease them. But some of the items under the latter two categories can also contribute to cash flows. When a corporate raider casts his net for a new catch, he is particularly attracted to companies with a high cash flow to use in financing a leveraged buyout. Shareholders should study these statements. A company that has a good rate of liquidity (cash flow) is better able to finance continued expansion. These figures tend to show a skewed picture of banks, brokers, lending companies, and other financial institutions because their operating income is understated and expenses are emphasized.

Most, but not all, annual reports include a breakdown for *changes in shareholders' equity.* It reveals how and from what source equity has been depleted or increased. Shareholders' equity is derived from the par value of common and preferred stock, retained earnings, surplus or excess over par value, less treasury stock at cost. It can be increased annually by net income, the issuance of common stock for the exercise of stock options, the conversion of preferred shares or bonds, or additions to an employee benefit plan. When dividends

**CONSOLIDATED STATEMENT OF CASH FLOWS
FOR TCA INDUSTRIES**

	1990	1989	1988
Cash Flows from Operating Activities			
Net income	$ 79,400	$71,300	$62,500
Adjustments to reconcile			
Depreciation and amortization	16,600	15,000	14,200
Deferred income taxes	400	2,600	4,200
Other, net	2,600	1,800	1,700
Changes in operating working capital			
Accounts receivable	(12,700)	(3,900)	(1,000)
Inventories	(3,600)	(17,900)	(5,900)
Other current assets	2,000	1,100	(1,900)
Current liabilities	11,200	6,700	8,400
Net cash from operating activities	95,900	76,700	82,200
Cash Flows from Investing Activities			
Additions to property, plant, and equipment	(21,500)	(17,200)	(18,700)
Noncurrent investments bought	(10,700)	(36,000)	(48,400)
Noncurrent investments sold	13,100	20,900	23,500
Sale of business	—	—	6,500
Other, net	(100)	(1,700)	(1,400)
Net cash used in investing activities	(19,200)	(34,000)	(38,500)
Cash Flows from Financing Activities			
Payment of dividends	(33,000)	(27,400)	(24,100)
Acquiring treasury shares	(12,200)	(12,900)	(14,300)
Exercise of stock options	2,700	3,500	3,600
Other net	—	(500)	(500)
Net cash used in financing activities	(42,500)	(37,300)	(35,200)
Increase (decrease) in cash and temporary cash investments	34,200	5,400	8,500
Cash and short-term investments			
Beginning of period	66,900	61,500	53,000
End of period	$101,100	$66,900	$61,500

are paid or treasury stock is bought it reduces shareholders' equity. The payment of a stock dividend is a wash—adding to common stock and additional paid-in capital, but reducing retained earnings. In our fictional company the effects of currency translations can change equity in either direction, depending on exchange rates of U.S. dollars vis-à-vis the foreign currencies involved. Although our example carries information for only two years, three years are usually carried in annual reports.

CONSOLIDATED STATEMENT OF CHANGES IN SHAREHOLDERS' EQUITY FOR TCA INDUSTRIES

For the Two Years Ended December 31, 1990

	Series C Preferred	Common Stock	Add'l Paid-In Capital	Retained Earnings	Cumulative Translation Adjustments
Balance at Dec. 31, 1988	$ 2,800	$128,200	$ 600	$230,200	$(2,700)
Net income				71,300	
Conversion of preferred	(2,800)	1,400	1,100		
Exercise, stock options		900	2,600		
Acquisition, treasury shs.		(1,900)	(11,100)		
Cash dividends declared:					
Common stock ($0.99/share)				(28,000)	
Preferred ($1.03/share)				(100)	
Stock dividend declared		6,400	39,500	(45,900)	
Translation adjustments					800
Balance at Dec. 31, 1989		135,800	32,800	227,500	(1,900)
Net income				79,400	
Exercise, stock options		600	2,100		
Acquisition, treasury shs.		(1,600)	(10,600)		
Cash dividend declared ($1.24/share)				(34,900)	
Stock dividend declared		6,700	48,500	(55,200)	
Translation adjustments					(400)
Balance at Dec. 31, 1990		$140,600	$ 72,800	$216,700	(2,300)

Let us now turn to some of the other sections of the annual report that are mandated by the SEC. One of these is *management's analysis of operating results.* The SEC requires that material developments during the last two fiscal years, particularly those relating to the income statement, be discussed in considerable detail. Some corporations might extend the discussion back over the past five years. The SEC expects companies to be more factual and objective in this section than they might typically be in their letter to shareholders. However, this section likewise is unaudited, so it, too, should be read with some degree of skepticism.

The SEC also requires an unaudited five-year *statistical summary.* The summary normally will carry key items from the income statement and balance sheet, as well as some of the important ratios we have already discussed. Many companies expand this table to cover a 10-year span, which shows how the firm has responded to more than one economic cycle. This helps to establish significant trends in the company's fortunes. But, as an actual or potential investor, you're primarily interested in trying to predict the company's future.

Let us suggest here some of the trends you might look for. Have sales shown a sharp increase over the past 5 (or 10) years? If so, have the sales gains been consistent or erratic? Have earnings generally moved in line with sales? If not, can you find the reason in various expense items or the tax rate? Do the sales and earnings trends seem consistent with the general business picture and industry performance in that same time period?

You might also look to see if earnings per share have matched the improvement in net income. If not, it may mean the company has been "buying" earnings (through acquisitions) for stock and the effect has been dilutive. Have dividends ever been omitted or reduced? Have there been increases in the total dividend payments every year?

As far as the balance sheet items are concerned, we have already noted the importance of increases in working capital. But has long-term debt also increased substantially? Has long-term debt risen more than shareholders' equity? Has book value risen markedly? Other items worth looking at are changes in the number of employees and capital-spending trends.

The push by the SEC and the Financial Accounting Standards Board for fuller corporate disclosure in annual reports has resulted in companies being required to include (1) a breakdown of sales and earnings for at least five different product lines, if there are that many; (2) a price range of securities; (3) dividends, if any, paid during each quarter of the two most recent fiscal years. The product line breakdown can be helpful in revealing that some operations are considerably more important to earnings than they are to sales, or vice versa, than one might expect after reading the earlier textual material.

Analyzing a Common Stock

There are still other ratios with which you should be familiar. The *price-earnings ratio* is the market price of the common stock divided by earnings per share for that stock. You are likely to find some variation in price-earnings ratios for the same company's stock, because newspapers tend to use the latest 12-month earnings figures that are available, whereas investment analysts generally prefer estimated current-year results. Also remember that price-earnings ratios will fluctuate over time, with the general psychology of the market, anticipated earnings growth, dividend yield, marketability, volatility, and the quality of the earnings per share.

The *dividend yield* is the indicated annual dividend rate divided by the current market price. By relating this return to a bank savings rate or the yield on AA or AAA corporate bonds, you can get some indication of the stock's appeal for income purposes. On the other hand, too high a yield may indicate that the dividend is shaky.

The *dividend payout ratio* is arrived at by dividing indicated dividends per share by the latest available annual earnings per share. This shows what percent of earnings is paid out in dividends. The *earnings retention rate* is found by subtracting the dividend payout ratio from 100 percent. If the payout ratio is 40 percent, the retention rate would be about 60 percent. That is, the company is reinvesting about 60 percent of its earnings. Some analysts suggest that if you multiply the retention rate by the percentage amount that the company returns on stockholders' equity, you get a good indicator of the future earnings growth for the company. What they are saying is that the company's growth will be determined by what it is able to earn on the new money it is retaining. So if the rate of return on stockholders' equity is 10 percent and the retention rate is 60 percent, future income growth might be about 6 percent. While some companies obviously are interested in pleasing their stockholders by boosting dividends, many prefer to retain as much of their earnings as they can in order to facilitate the corporation's growth.

The Footnotes Are Important

The footnotes undoubtedly constitute the most yawn-inspiring reading in the annual report. But they shouldn't be skipped. Fortunately, SEC rules require their type size to be at least as large as the numbers in the financial statement. The footnotes are important for several reasons. For one thing, they often explain the accounting methods used. There are a number of methods available that would meet an auditor's approval, each of which produces a different bottom-line result. Furthermore, most companies employ one accounting procedure for stockholders and another for Internal Revenue Service purposes. This point is generally elaborated upon in the footnotes.

Here are some of the other items frequently covered in the footnotes:

Inventories, as computed for cost of goods sold and carried in the asset section of the balance sheet, can be assigned widely different values. Many analysts believe that in a period of rising prices the most conservative accounting treatment for inventories is LIFO (last in, first out) as opposed to FIFO (first in, first out). In figuring the cost of goods sold, LIFO assumes that the latest items added to inventory, which should be the most expensive in a period of inflation, are sold first. That means assigning a higher value to inventories in cost of goods sold. The effect is to increase expenses and reduce income. Lower income means lower taxes. It also means, though, that in expensing the latest inventory figures, the corporation will be carrying a lower inventory value on the balance sheet than the real figure.

Various acceptable methods are also available to compute depreciation, depending on when the asset was placed in service. Some of these allow writing off more of an asset's worth in its earlier years than in later years. Most companies use straight-line depreciation for stockholder purposes because it tends to reduce income less, and accelerated depreciation for tax purposes in order to reduce the amount of income subject to a tax bite. If corporations use the two different methods, they are subject to the alternative minimum tax on half the difference in earnings. A more conservative accounting practice is to use accelerated depreciation for both stockholder purposes and tax purposes.

Companies are now required to state in the annual report their pension accounting and funding policy, as well as the pension charge for the preceding year and the unfunded vested liabilities. For some corporations, these numbers are already large, and for others they are increasing rapidly. Some companies even have unfunded pension liabilities that represent a substantial percentage of stockholders' equity— or may even exceed stockholders' equity. As a result of strong investment performances and employee attrition, many company pension plans are *overfunded*. Finding this information in annual reports and other published reports is not easy. However, overfunded pension plans are a "hidden asset" and often a factor in takeover or leveraged buyout bids.

The annual report also must disclose any potential legal problems. You should be somewhat wary of these even though the company might indicate that in its opinion a suit against the corporation is "without merit." Adverse settlements in an era of growing "consumerism" have proved expensive for many companies.

As a rule, the footnotes contain a detailed breakdown of long-term debt by type of security and schedule of maturity.

Many companies lease rather than own equipment, and

these leases can then become a substitute for longer-term debt incurred to purchase that equipment. Use of leases is sometimes referred to as *off balance sheet financing*. But under new regulations of the Financial Accounting Standards Board, these leases must be capitalized and shown as a liability on the lessee's balance sheet, albeit on a phase-in basis. FASB rules prohibit a company from capitalizing research and development outlays on the balance sheet and writing them off gradually against income over a period of years. Instead they must be expensed in the year incurred.

Some annual reports reveal in the footnotes stock options granted officers and other employees, plus intercompany transactions. Whether a company is still amortizing its investment tax credit may be revealed. Also detailed in the reports of multinational companies is the impact of certain currency changes.

Companies are also now required to carry in their annual reports a statement reconciling any differences between a tax rate for stockholder purposes and the statutory U.S. tax rate. Foreign taxes, state and local taxes, and the investment tax credit are some of the items that might account for such a difference.

The Accountants' Report

Every public company must have its accounting records reviewed and audited by a firm of certified public accountants. That firm will also issue an opinion regarding the veracity of the financial statements in the annual report. The accountants' report is definitely worth reading, if only to see whether the auditors include some qualifications or exceptions or note changes in accounting procedures that are material. The investor should be concerned about any departures from what is normally a routinely worded statement. The corporate examination by the auditors will generally include a review of bank statements, a physical counting of the inventory and an estimate of its salability, and a confirmation of receivables.

As you can see, if you've only been looking at an annual report's photographs you haven't been getting half the picture. The text, the financial tables, and the footnotes can tell you a lot about the companies you own or contemplate owning—if you take the time to read them right.

CHAPTER 24

Analyzing Specific Industries

UNTIL NOW, WE have been discussing in general terms how to go about analyzing a company as a potential investment. Obviously, certain tests will be more important for companies in one industry than for those in another. Some industries are by nature cyclical. The ebbs and flows of their fortunes are tied closely to the ups and downs of the economy. Others are more stable. They follow the same path regardless of what business in general is doing. Still others are mature. They have grown just about as much as they ever will and, in fact, may even be declining. Others are emerging. New technology and changing life-styles are bringing them into prominence.

How do you know what tests to apply to which industries? Common sense is a good starting point. It is often easy to surmise which industries will be affected by rises and falls of the economy and which will not be. Then there is performance. There's a good chance that patterns occurring in the past will be repeated in the future. Finally, there is awareness. Careful study depends on keeping up with events and trends that might affect an industry. These broad categories, of course, embrace the many finer points of the financial analyst's art and science.

Financial analysts, in fact, spend most of their time poring over figures, reading extensively in the various industries they cover, and talking with key executives in those industries. Because of the vast amount of material that they must keep under surveillance, most analysts confine their efforts to a limited number of industries. Indeed, some devote their entire careers to a single industry, becoming as knowledgeable as many leaders in the industry itself.

To give you an idea of what you should be looking for in the industries that interest most investors, the analysts on our staff at Babson-United Investment Advisors have provided the commentary that appears in this chapter and the next. They won't get into the fine details, but they'll tell you the important things they themselves look for as they analyze their industries and the companies in them.

The Basic Industries

Automotive, chemical, coal, construction, machinery, metals, oil and gas, paper, textiles. These are the basic industries —"smokestack America," as it were. Without these industries, our way of life would be primitive indeed. For all the abuse that is heaped upon the steelmakers, the oil moguls, and the auto producers, theirs is no bed of roses. Between the demands of labor, the restrictions of government, the protests of environmentalists, foreign competition, and the exigencies of business, they do well to keep their heads above water, let alone turn a profit for their shareholders.

All these industries suffer to some extent from the cyclical nature of their markets. Some lead the economy, others follow it, and the rest move in close conjunction with the ups and downs in the business cycle. The ability to fine-tune capacity and output to demand is an important aspect of a company's profit record. These are capital-intensive companies, but some groups have less trouble generating sufficient cash flow to meet their capital needs than others.

While the investor can reap long-range profits from investments in basic industries, he must be willing to sit through the dry spells or be able to jump in and out with facility.

AUTOMOBILES AND TRUCKS. This industry, which includes manufacturers of parts and components, is one of the most pervasive influences in our lives. Not only is it the nation's single largest employer after the federal government, but it also affects the prosperity of such industries as steel, nonferrous metals, chemicals, tires, and glass. When consumers are in a car-buying mood, the economy prospers; when demand for new cars ebbs, the entire economy suffers. Because the automobile has become such a necessity in the lives of most of us, it would be easy to conclude that demand is always high. The truth is, this is a highly cyclical industry, studded with peaks and riven with valleys. Personal income trends, the jobless rate, and consumer sentiment in general play major roles in the strength or weakness of auto sales.

Because theirs is, in the final analysis, a consumer industry, auto manufacturers must be able to anticipate taste trends, buying fads, and domestic and foreign competition. Then they must market products that will fulfill the fantasies and needs of their customers. Poor judgment or a misreading of the public's tastes can spell disaster, since model changes are not easily made. A manufacturer also must be able to gauge accurately the level of sales for a model year. Overproduction can be nearly as disastrous as misjudging style preferences. So can underproduction, for that matter.

Major factors affecting auto sales today include credit availability and cost, consumer confidence, used-car trends, foreign demand, and scrappage levels. Tied closely to sales is the cost of production. Is a union contract about to come up for renegotiation? Are costs of raw materials rising? When rising costs are coupled with sluggish sales, the industry is heading for hard times.

The greatest fundamental change in the domestic auto industry is the increasing penetration by foreign auto makers. Market shares for these manufacturers have been rising steadily. The domestics are often cited as manufacturing a more competitive vehicle now that improved production and higher quality have been emphasized. Also, there is increasing reliance on foreign parts and production. Nevertheless, the auto maker best able to accommodate the public's ever-changing demands will be of most interest to investors.

CHEMICALS. This industry is more truly an aggregation of many subindustries—organic and inorganic commodity chemicals, intermediates, functional specialties, and various product groups not strictly classified as chemicals, such as plastics, fertilizers, industrial gases, synthetic fibers, minerals, and carbon black. Within each of these subgroups, different forces are at work. The supply-demand balance, competition, price-cost differentials, geographic advantages, and alternative processes vary from one product area to another. Thus, the product mix of an individual company must be studied before assessing other information bearing on its prospects for the future. The subindustries vary widely in cyclicality, from the sustained growth of specialty chemicals or industrial gases to the feast-or-famine swings of fertilizers.

Once the analyst has determined a company's product mix, he can see what portion of the business is in mature product lines and what portion is concentrated in expanding fields. While a company should have a sizable stake in growth areas, its more mature business areas are likely to produce a substantial cash flow, not only for current income but also for investment in the growth ventures. However, a company must be willing to recognize and phase out those weaker lines that are no longer generating sufficient cash flow. A key consideration is the company's market share in each subgroup, since market leadership is the prime determinant of profitability and growth for a chemical company.

A highly important factor for many firms today is the status of their fuel supplies and raw-material feedstocks. How a company handles long-term supply contracts, process changes, and conservation requirements is a clue to the ability of its management. How well it manages captive resources and moves to alternative resources is also vital. Other considerations include environmental legislation, research, technical services, pricing strategy, foreign currency devaluations, cash flow versus capital requirements, and the upgrading of returns on investment.

Chemical stocks can be profitable investments if caught at the low end of a cycle. Yields are reasonable and price-earnings ratios usually below average.

COAL. Only a handful of coal companies are still privately held; most have gone public or been acquired by larger companies. While there are enormous reserves of coal in this country, domestic use is clouded by coal's polluting characteristics. Moreover, the value of U.S. coal in the export market is diminished by the presence of abundant reserves in Australia, South Africa, and Latin America.

Metallurgical coal, mined in many parts of Appalachia, is the highest-value coal because its BTU is high. Both domestic and foreign steel producers are willing to pay a premium for it. Second in value is the Eastern high-BTU, low sulphur and ash coal used by the electric utilities. Burning of this coal is controversial and the subject of clean-air legislation.

Western-mined coal has a lower BTU and a low sulphur content, but its ash content is high. Its price is significantly lower than that of Eastern coal. Because it is open-pit-mined by nonunion labor, it is less costly to produce. Nonetheless, transportation costs limit its markets to the West Coast, Gulf Coast, and Mid-Continental areas.

There is a growing consensus that sulphur emissions must be controlled and acid rain reduced. Scrubbers, used following combustion, are the most widely accepted antipollution devices. Newer, more effective techniques, such as fluidized beds used during combustion, are meeting resistance from utilities. Not caring to risk their huge capital-intensive plants on a new technology, the utilities have sought support from labor and politicians to preserve the status quo.

CONSTRUCTION. Although this is a cyclical field, many of the industry groups that compose it have tended to move before the swings in the economy in general. The classic pattern has been that when the economy is running full steam—when interest rates are high, savings are depleted, mortgage money is tight—then housing begins to suffer. Conversely, toward the end of a downturn, interest rates decline, savings rise, the money supply increases, and building loans are easier to obtain. Building activity turns the corner as a result and signals a turn in the economy.

Some 10 percent of the gross national product is derived from construction spending, making the industries involved one of the economy's most important sectors. Because stimulation from Washington may create artificial swings in the housing-start figures, the analyst must be aware of any pump priming from this source. Shifts in housing trends—from single-unit to multiple-dwelling housing, from suburban to urban, and so forth—must be watched.

These trends can have a significant impact on the types of building materials that are in demand. Population shifts, such as the rush to the Sunbelt, also can make or break regional suppliers.

Conditions in the building industry were favorable during most of the decade of the 1980s. Housing starts were above average for several years, although still shy of the baby-boomer and inflation-driven peaks of the late 1970s. Widespread acceptance of variable-rate mortgages and an active secondary mortgage market have helped to soften the restraints on housing during periods of high interest rates.

Though pushed and pulled by lower interest rates and curbs on public spending, commercial and public construction has remained fairly stable, while industrial construction expenditures have lagged since the 1980–82 recession. These trends have impeded producers of construction equipment. However, any weakness in the dollar should make domestic construction-equipment makers more competitive with foreign manufacturers.

Remodeling and renovation of existing homes is a key segment of the building industry. It is from this sector that the industry derives a stable and continuing revenue base. Those firms that supply the commercial as well as do-it-yourself remodeling market have generally better records for consistent growth than the volatile home-building companies.

MACHINERY AND MACHINE TOOLS. While these two allied industries are cyclical, their cycles are dissimilar. Machine tool orders are often used as a bellwether of business upswings. Conversely, orders for the machinery industry lag behind in an upturn, sometimes by as much as six months. The key to this dichotomous behavior lies in the nature of their respective markets. Hard-goods manufacturers in anticipation of better times must tool up to meet the expected increase in demand; hence machine tool orders rise even though business in general may still be in the doldrums. Machinery makers serve the heavy industries—auto and truck, oil, coal, construction, utility. The huge outlays required for this type of equipment can be postponed until a recovery is well under way, creating a lag in orders for machinery.

Prosperity for tool and machinery manufacturers depends on real growth in gross national product, a good level of capital spending, and customer confidence in the direction in which the government is steering the country. Order levels can swing by 50 percent or more in one year. Within the industry itself, capital spending plans hinge on long-range economic forecasts. If these prove too optimistic, machinery and tool makers are left with excess capacity, which can play havoc with profits.

In analyzing an individual company, you should determine whether it is a market leader in its specialized line, if its research program has been productive, its sales and marketing efforts effective, its service organization strong, and its markets expanding. A company should be geographically diversified, with worldwide sales, and it should be vertically integrated. In looking at order backlog figures, you should note, if possible, whether order levels are up across the board or only in certain segments of the company's operations.

METALS. This is another lagging industry; it picks up steam only after the economy is well on its way to recovery. But unless economic conditions are sufficiently robust to support the industry at near-peak capacity, these companies get caught in a squeeze between rising costs and falling prices for their products. As a whole, the industry sells in large volumes and operates on razor-thin margins. The demise of inflation hurt profitability. However, a better supply-and-demand situation due to increased industrial activity reversed that trend.

Following much bloodletting at the beginning of the 1980s, steel companies have markedly improved their position by cutting work forces, shutting down or renovating aging and costly facilities, and gaining relief from competitive imported steel. Specialty producers managed to avoid much of the bloodbath by carving out individual niches in the high end of the market. Even with import quotas, however, the major steelmakers will have to stay vigilant on costs and capacity use.

In terms of price and demand, copper companies have had the most volatile record. Historically, domestic producers have raised capacity in response to demand increases and rising prices only to see demand dry up—creating an inventory excess and sagging prices. Here, too, imports have become increasingly troublesome for domestic producers, who are being pitted against lower-cost producers in developing nations. Some of the latter are government-owned and not always operated with profit as a primary motive.

Demand for aluminum has increased since the mid-1980s, but prices, particularly for primary ingot, peaked in 1988, then backed off. While the value of aluminum is influenced by currency fluctuations, demand is sensitive to interest rates, as more than 40 percent of the industry's shipments go to the construction and automotive industries. The trend toward lighter, more fuel-efficient cars bodes well for the white metal. In fact, each year auto manufacturers use more aluminum to fabricate their products, to the detriment of the steel industry. Other areas where the use of aluminum is on the rise include building, containers, and electrical products.

Throughout the metals industry companies have had to cut costs to compete with foreign producers. When the dollar is strong, foreign companies compete in the U.S. market, but with the slide in the value of the dollar the competitive situation has eased. In addition, major wage concessions granted by labor unions, plant modernization efforts, and the closing of obsolete and inefficient production facilities have enabled domestic producers to reduce costs and operate more efficiently. However, it is still wise for investors to keep close tabs on when labor contracts are due for renegotiation, not only for the obvious reason—to assess the possibility of a strike or a major concession from management—but also to gauge whether demand reflects true market conditions or prestrike stockpiling.

Over the long run, metal stocks tend to sell at a discount to the market, due to below-average demand growth and vulnerability to cyclical swings in economic activity. Market share leaders, low-cost producers, and broadly diversified companies usually represent the best opportunities for investors seeking cyclical stock market profits.

OIL. Obviously one of the major sectors of the economy, this industry accounts for 10 to 15 percent of the value of the stock market, including many of the country's largest companies.

To many, the key reason for investing in oil is its future price, a rationale that was underscored by the Iraqi invasion of Kuwait. Oil pricing is a classic study in supply and demand. The role of the United States in this truly worldwide market is important, but by no means overwhelming. World consumption is distributed as follows:

United States	26%	Other Free World	25%
Europe	20	Soviet Bloc	22
Japan	7	Total	100%

Demand for the product is growing at the slowest pace in the mature industrial countries, where conservation and the development of alternative energy sources are significant. Oil demand growth is most rapid in the developing nations, where its low cost and flexibility in use is most advantageous.

There is ample oil in the world, but the cost of finding and extracting it varies widely. In the mature industrial countries, the oil that can be extracted at low cost has already been tapped. In frontier areas, large pools of oil remain to be discovered, but finding rates are erratic and costs are frequently high. Costs in the United States are $5 to $10 per barrel, because of the low output from individual wells. In the Middle East, a $1 to $2 per barrel cost is customary because the wells are so prolific. Unconventional sources—tar sands and oil shale—are readily available but expensive to develop and to extract oil from. Unless oil were to reach and stay at $30 a barrel, it would not be commercially feasible to tap these sources.

The bulk of the world's oil comes from the OPEC countries, the Middle East and Persian Gulf nations in particular. Given the size of their reserves, they are likely to increase their shares over the coming decade. The Gulf War caused wide volatility in the price of crude oil. Despite the short duration of the war a flood of oil hasn't come on the market, depressing its price. It is to be hoped that the petroleum-rich OPEC countries, such as Kuwait, Saudi Arabia, and the United Arab Emirates, will in future be less inclined to overproduce their quotas at the expense of their poorer partners. Moreover, private and other national oil companies will be more inclined to diversify their sources of supply to more stable, albeit expensive, producing areas.

The oil industry has a voracious appetite for capital. Not only do existing reserves have to be replaced and existing facilities upgraded, but building new facilities also consumes enormous amounts of both time and money. For many companies, buying out a competitor's known reserves and plants is a better way to expand than dealing with the uncertainties of exploration and the costs of building new plants. Consequently, takeovers, restructuring, and consolidation within the industry are probable.

In looking at individual companies, look beyond earnings and dividends. Because the industry is so capital intensive, study the company's cash flows to determine its ability to finance growth internally. Look for a well-balanced company, an important attribute in a volatile industry. Then check to see if management invests its capital in ways that will increase the company's net asset value.

PAPER AND FOREST PRODUCTS. This is a relatively concentrated industry, in which the top dozen or so producers now account for more than half of industry output. A few of the companies produce paper only, buying pulp and selling in bulk, whether the output is newsprint, kraft, or bleached white printing or writing papers. But most companies in the industry are vertically integrated in varying degrees. They may grow their own pulpwood, which they convert into corrugated cartons, paper bags, computer output forms, disposable diapers, food packaging, or specialized coated papers to be used in making such things as this book's cover and papers for electrical condensers. In addition, many produce lumber and plywood for the building trades.

The entire industry is highly capital intensive, requiring

huge expenditures for new plant capacity and upgrading papermaking machines. The expense of air- and water-pollution control equipment has burdened the industry in the last decade, but this was mitigated somewhat by the availability of low-cost, tax-exempt industrial revenue bonds for financing this equipment. Analysts must assess closely the unfilled spending requirements of individual firms, as well as their financing ability.

Probably the most consistent and profitable sector of the paper industry has been the tissue market—facial and toilet tissue and paper napkins and towels. Along with production efficiency, marketing and consumer brand awareness are important to these companies. Although domestic market growth in recent years has only slightly exceeded population growth, industry leaders have shown strong and consistent profit trends based on market share gains, broadened product lines, and increasing penetration of largely untapped foreign markets.

For general producers of stock for the packaging and printing markets, capacity use of plant and equipment is watched closely as a clue to the industry's pricing flexibility. In the past, as output rose to 90 to 92 percent of capacity, paper companies were generally able to raise prices by more than their relatively fixed capital and operating costs, leading to substantial profit leverage. This was usually reflected in good relative performances for the companies' shares. Because modern equipment and controls can be operated for longer periods without maintenance shutdowns, capacity use has become a less reliable indicator in recent years. Currency exchange rates, which bear heavily on the success of foreign competition, are another factor in the fortunes of domestic firms.

The forest products industry represents an important sector of the economy, one that should remain strong as population and economic growth put increasing pressures on resources generally. Because of the cyclical nature of many of the industry's products, investors should look for companies with well-diversified positions, sizable market shares in several product lines, creative management, and aggressive marketing strategies.

TEXTILES. While this industry remains fairly fragmented, a considerable amount of consolidation has taken place. Serving such cyclically sensitive markets as apparel, home furnishings, and industrial fabrics, the textile industry tends pretty much to feast or famine. To help reduce this inherent vulnerability to overall economic conditions, the industry has undergone a considerable technological, managerial, and marketing face-lifting in recent years. Major automation should serve as a buttress against foreign competition in the 1990s.

Along with the trend toward consolidation, textile manufacturers have been placing increasing emphasis on cost control, with particular attention being given to all-important inventory controls. When heavy inventory accumulation occurs along with sluggish business activity, the result is product markdowns and reduced profits. Research and development has also become a top priority as companies search for new technologies to increase productivity, reduce costs, and meet constantly changing fashion trends.

Raw-material costs account for more than 50 percent of the value of all textile shipments. Synthetics are a good deal more stable in price than cottons and wools and have gained good consumer acceptance for their durability and easy care. Manufacturers are diversifying both inside and outside the textile area. So, when choosing a textile issue, the analyst must be particularly alert to such items as cost control, use of advanced technology, product mix, and diversification. Some of the major difficulties facing the textile industry are import competition, labor costs, and the growing need for capital to modernize facilities. It is most important to keep these in mind when analyzing individual companies.

The textile group historically has moved in line with the industrial averages. Growing in importance is the individual company's dividend policy. Since the textile group's profits can be volatile (owing to its cyclicality), the analyst should look closely at the company's record of consistency of dividend payments. Stability of cash flow should also be examined, as modernization often depends on the amounts of such internally generated funds.

Science and Technology

Aerospace, data processing, electronics, and health care. The industries in this segment have several characteristics in common. Their shares have traded historically at a premium over the market; dividend payouts tend to be modest, research and development expenditures large, and earnings growth rates well above average. New-product development costs are huge, yet necessary, as product obsolescence is a constant threat. However, the rewards for technological breakthroughs are sufficiently large to offset these risks.

The long arm of the federal government reaches into almost every facet of operations, in the form of product, price, and advertising regulation, safety and environmental standards, and funding. Cyclical influences are less apparent in technology companies than in the basic industry group. In some areas, in fact, members may move in a countercyclical pattern.

Investors willing to take on a degree of risk with these stocks are often rewarded by an above-average return. At the same time, more than the usual degree of selectivity is essential when investing in this premium-priced group of industries.

AEROSPACE. The aerospace industry frequently moves counter to the prevailing business cycle, a phenomenon that has its roots in government funding. As an employer of 5 percent of all manufacturing workers and as the source of equipment vital to the nation's defense, the aerospace industry encounters little resistance from Congress in obtaining huge fund allocations, particularly in bad times. In recent years, sales of military equipment to foreign nations, most notably the Arab bloc, also have been a significant factor in supporting the industry through economic downturns.

Military spending accounts for 60 percent of total aerospace revenues. Six major companies control the bulk of this business. Defense spending began to accelerate in the mid-1960s, picked up momentum in the mid-1970s, and then eased. In the 1987–90 period defense spending leveled at about $300 billion annually. Meanwhile commercial sales are revving up again and should remain strong through the mid-1990s, somewhat offsetting any "peace dividend" cuts in defense spending. Warming of East-West relations is not likely to yield much by way of a peace dividend—for the balance of the century a loss of 1 percent of one year's GNP is probable. A repeat of earlier buying binges by airlines of new equipment seems likely for the next several years.

In looking at individual companies in the industry, the analyst must always keep in mind the possibility of a major new military contract award or cancellation. Product diversification, as well as the military-commercial balance, are areas he should study. Also important in this industry are the amount of aggressiveness a company displays in pursuing new contracts, its research program, and its ability to finance new products.

DATA PROCESSING. As an industry, data processing is a virtual infant compared with such graybeards as shipbuilding and railroading. Mushrooming growth in recent years has seen one technological breakthrough after another as applications and use expanded hand in hand with declining product prices. Computer use has become so prevalent today that even home computers have moved from the realm of science fiction to the shopping-center shelf.

The industry is divided into four major segments, but there is considerable overlap. The mainframe market is dominated by a few large companies, with International Business Machines doing two-thirds of the business. Software is marketed by all the majors, by publicly owned smaller companies, as well as myriad privately and individually owned enterprises. Add-ons, or peripheral equipment, are packaged and sold by the mainframe manufacturers and also by many others, large and small, some concentrating in this one area and others offering it as part of a widely diversified product line. However, the number of players in the fields of software and peripherals has been substantially reduced in the last few years by takeovers, mergers, and bankruptcies.

Microcomputers, the newest segment of the business, were made possible by developments in microminiaturization. Again, some of the majors have reached down to expand the bottom end of their lines into the fast-growing mini and micro fields. Although a few specialists control this end of the business, competition from the other entrants is intense and has squeezed out some of the weaker, undercapitalized companies.

Cyclical influences such as capital spending have the biggest impact at the heavy end of the business—large mainframes. Manufacturers operating in this area spend heavily for product development; IBM alone expends $1 billion annually on research and development. Foreign operations also bulk large, often accounting for one-half to two-thirds of a company's sales. However, currency fluctuations, governmental restrictions, and labor relations can affect profits from overseas operations, while competition from foreign manfacturers has adversely affected profits in domestic operations.

In line with other high-technology stocks, computer issues have long commanded premium price-earnings multiples. Similarly, the bulk of earnings has been plowed back rather than distributed to shareholders. But market conditions and industry maturity have wrought changes so that price-earnings ratios have worked down significantly in recent years. Selected issues in this area are attractive for long-term growth.

ELECTRONICS AND ELECTRICAL EQUIPMENT. In discussing this industry, it is difficult to generalize, since it covers manufacturers of such diverse products as citizens' band radios, television sets, massive power generating equipment, semiconductors, and highly sophisticated scientific instruments. While one segment may be seriously hurt by a business downturn, another may not be. Some areas may require large infusions of capital to stay afloat; others are characterized by the ease of entry for new companies. Those companies that primarily produce household appliances and home entertainment equipment will be subject to the same influences as other consumer product companies, while those fabricating expensive capital equipment will move in line with the cyclical basic industries. Of course the larger companies may have a stake in both ends.

The future health of these producers is assured by the massive sums that will have to be spent by industry and government to reduce the nation's dependence on oil, to improve mass transportation, to develop alternative energy sources, to automate manufacturing, to explore the universe, and to advance our technological applications. The government is also pouring billions into electronic warfare devices, intelligence and surveillance equipment, and improvement of the nation's retaliation capabilities.

In analyzing individual companies, you should look at the competitive position, marketing expertise, patent position, product diversification, government-commercial product mix, and research leadership. Many of the larger firms in this industry are multinational and subject to the usual considerations of currency stability, regulation, and political climate. As a whole, these issues are attractive investments.

HEALTH CARE. Key factors in the appraisal of health care securities include federal regulation, research, and marketing strength. For some companies, especially the major drug firms, international business also involves significant considerations. Actually, more than half of the health care dollar goes to nonprofit hospitals and to doctors. But investor-owned businesses also bulk large; here is a partial list: ethical pharmaceuticals (with promotion directed toward the medical profession), proprietary drugs (consumer advertised), medical supplies and equipment, wholesale distribution, diagnostic products, and health care services. (Investor-owned hospitals, nursing homes, and health maintenance organizations are notable areas.) Diversification is another aspect of investment appraisal, since many companies cover a broad range of health care fields.

A common denominator for appraising companies in this industry is federal regulation. Even the merest rumor of Congressional committee hearings can have a marked impact on the price of their stocks. Although the government underwrites a sizable chunk of our medical bills, soaring costs to some extent have been fostered by Washington's efforts to improve the quality of health care and the safety and efficacy of health care products. These costly standards are forcing smaller companies out of business and concentrating activities into fewer, stronger companies. At the same time, ironically, the Federal Trade Commission (FTC) periodically engages in antitrust litigation aimed at preventing such concentration.

The key regulatory agency is the Food and Drug Administration (FDA), which has unusually strict standards for new drug clearance. Several years and close to one hundred million dollars must be expended to bring a new drug from its initial research stage, through animal and human testing, to final FDA clearance. The clearance of new medical devices has been somewhat less difficult, but still more costly than small companies can generally afford. Hence, an analyst is essentially concerned with tracking the research progress of the larger companies, including the cost-effectiveness of the research approach and the progress of products through the various test stages. Moreover, he must keep abreast of the technological competition among the companies in every major health care field.

Marketing strength is another important facet. In ethical drugs, a company's basic marketing force is its detail staff, people who keep physicians and pharmacists informed on products and their use. In proprietary drugs, the marketing effort is centered in advertising and promotion directed to the consumer. Another government watchdog, the Federal Trade Commission, steps in here to see that advertising doesn't get out of bounds.

International business plays an important role in the operations of health care companies, particularly for the major drug manufacturers. Because Japan is second to the United States in total health care expenditures, it is an especially significant market. Europe also figures prominently here and should become increasingly important when the European Community (EC) emerges in 1992. Other international aspects include the handling of currency fluctuations and tax shelters.

Thus far, we have touched on a few of the general considerations that apply to the appraisal of several segments of the health care industry. In weighing the specifics of a given company within that industry, the analyst must start by knowing how the business is divided. What are the company's major products? What services does it provide? Where are its geographical markets?

Then each of these factors is appraised with regard to competitive strengths, basic earning power, and potential for future growth. Yesterday's success may become a company's Achilles' heel due to intensified competition or harmful side effects. A new product may well bring new life to a sleeping giant almost overnight.

As in other industries, ultimate considerations include the quality of earnings, the overall growth trend in terms of profits and dividends, and the relative price-earnings ratio of each individual stock of the companies within that industry.

For the investor, health care stocks have above-average long-term potential. The demographics of an aging America will be a positive force in the decades to come for well-positioned health care companies.

Transportation Industries

Airlines, railroads, and trucking. The movement of goods and people is big business, but it also is a business that has been, and will continue to be, in a state of flux. The trucking industry has significantly increased its share of the freight-hauling market, to the detriment of the rails. The airlines have made major inroads into the passenger-hauling market, once dominated by the railroads. In recent years, another contender for freight revenues has come into its own, intermodal shipping or container leasing.

In general, the transportation industries are cyclical, reflecting changes in the level of freight being moved and in the amounts being spent for travel. All are capital intensive, while most are also labor intensive. Profits are often highly dependent on prevailing fuel costs, particularly oil prices. Deregulation and mergers have changed the number and names of industry participants as well.

AIRLINES. This capital-intensive industry's sensitivity to economic conditions has produced a boom-and-bust earnings pattern over the years. Scheduled air carriers dominate intercity public transportation, holding at least 85 percent of that market. That dominance is not likely to be challenged in the foreseeable future.

Potential investors should seek information on a carrier's overall financial strength, as debt ratios vary widely. Planned equipment purchases and options to buy new planes are also valuable indicators of future financing needs. Equipment use rates, load factors, passenger yields, and degree of exposure to business and tourist markets are also important tools in the investment selection process.

Passage of deregulation legislation in 1978 gave airlines greater rate-setting flexibility while easing entry requirements on new and existing routes. The Civil Aeronautics Board's authority over domestic rates, mergers, and acquisitions ended in 1981, while the CAB was abolished in 1985. Deregulation temporarily brought on considerable changes in the operating environment, including intensified competition on lucrative routes, rampant fare discounting, and abandonment of marginal short-haul service by many of the trunk lines. Meanwhile most regional carriers and start-ups have, for the most part, been acquired or failed. This has fueled critics' charges that industry consolidation has boosted fares too far, especially in smaller cities, which are part of the hub and spoke system.

Perhaps the most important recent trend is the domestic carriers' rush to expand into international service. With the European market developing rapidly, and trade increasing between the United States and the Pacific Rim cities, all major domestic airlines are expanding abroad.

Historically, airline stocks begin to outperform the market before the trough of a recession, in anticipation of renewed traffic growth. Investors are cautioned that stock action, like profits, tends to be volatile, with fast-paced movements on both the upside and the downside.

RAILROADS. Few industries are as closely linked to business cycles as the railroads. Fluctuations in such basic industries as autos, steel, mining, coal, and capital goods have a decided impact on carloadings. As the revenue ton-mile (movement of one ton of freight one mile) performance is the analyst's basic tool for measuring traffic growth, these variations are crucial. In one major business cycle of perhaps two years' duration, these figures can vary by 100 billion tons. Fixed costs are high, so operating profits are hard to come by in recessions. Thus, when reviewing this industry, current and projected economic trends are important factors.

Rails are among the most labor-intensive of industries, with wages accounting for a huge percentage of total revenues in the mid-1980s. Therefore, it is important to keep tabs on the timing and content of union contracts. Other major costs include maintenance of way, structures, and equipment, and transportation accounts (fuel, loss, and damage). By measuring a carrier's transportation expenses against revenues, the analyst can compare the efficiency of one road with that of another. A similar comparison can be made with maintenance costs and revenues to get information on the condition of fleet and property.

Another important consideration is the railroad's geographical operating area. The industry is generally reviewed in three segments, Eastern, Western, and Southern. Operators in each area have many similarities, but they have important differences in weather conditions, types of freight hauled, and their areas' growth prospects.

Deregulation has also been in the cards for the nation's rails and the Interstate Commerce Commission has loosened the regulatory noose around the industry. The Railroad Revitalization and Regulatory Reform Act of 1976 provided the initial catalyst to the ICC's increasingly constructive stance on questions of track abandonment, rate setting, and mergers.

A flurry of mergers in the early 1980s added a unique shading to rail investment decisions. More recently, a number of carriers moved to release hidden asset values from their holdings. Vast mineral rights, valuable tracts of real estate, and other such holdings have been sold piecemeal, allowing some rails to remain independent. Further similar activity is possible in the future.

TRUCKING. A substantial amount of the freight moved within the country is carried by truck. In view of the prominence of the trucking industry in transporting raw materials to manufacturers and manufactured products to the market, it is not surprising that the industry tends to be an economic bellwether. Changes in the weekly intercity truck tonnage figures, whether they are changes in direction or changes in velocity, often signal a shift in the business climate. For this reason, the group is important to the analyst trying to ferret out clues to business trends.

The industry is labor intensive, with personnel costs taking a huge bite of every sales dollar. As with the airlines, fuel oil prices are important in determining profits for these firms. Equipment and terminal maintenance costs have risen sharply in recent years and are significant expense items for the motor carriers.

The Motor Carrier Act of 1980 provided for significant changes in trucking regulations, including relaxed entry requirements, reduced operating restrictions, greater pricing flexibility, and a phaseout of single-line collective ratemaking. That legislation, combined with the dynamic changes already taking place in other transportation sectors, suggests that realignment of the nation's transportation industries will continue in response to the ever-present demands for maximum energy efficiency.

When the dust from deregulation finally settles, many transportation specialists expect large intermodal companies —with important trucking components—to emerge as the most viable competitors in coming years. An investor considering trucking firms should therefore keep in mind the sweeping changes affecting the nation's transportation system and the likelihood of an acceleration of mergers and acquisitions.

For the next decade financial strength, professional management, and access to capital are the key elements to success in this industry.

This industry can provide some exciting rides for the investor. The shares generally are volatile and, caught at the bottom of a cyclical swing, can be rewarding investments.

CHAPTER 25

More on Specific Industries

THE INDUSTRIES REVIEWED in the previous chapter were largely those that make the things we use and those that transport the goods to market. In this chapter, we shall look at the industries that most closely touch our own everyday lives—the consumer-oriented segment of the economy. It's a large segment; personal consumption expenditures make up nearly two-thirds of our gross national product.

Consumer Products and Leisure Time

Food processing, the media, motion pictures, personal care, recreation equipment, and retailing. How each of us chooses to spend his disposable income has a strong influence on these industries. Thus, competition is intense and top profits often go to those companies with the greatest marketing skill, highest advertising budgets, or most innovative products.

A constant parade of new products designed to dazzle and bewitch the consumer into parting with his cash is a necessity for survival in these industry areas. To some of these companies, product obsolescence is a continuing threat.

281

Shifting demographic patterns and new fads and trends can have a pervasive influence on the entire group.

FOOD PROCESSING. Because of their relatively stable earnings growth and history of rising dividend payments, food processing stocks historically have been attractive as both defensive and growth investments. Since food is literally the world's most basic need, it stands to reason that this industry would enjoy rising demand for its products. Since the United States is the largest producer of foodstuffs, the long-range potential for domestic food processing companies is impressive.

While the overall industry outlook is undeniably favorable, the rate of growth of any individual company hinges on several important factors. One of the most important considerations when analyzing a food stock is the company's vulnerability to and ability in dealing with the volatile commodities markets. Since ingredients are a major consideration, knowledge of present and future commodities price projections and supply-demand prospects is important.

Profit margins can narrow if demand weakens in the face of growing supplies. The same is true when the supply is low, since higher prices often lead to consumer resistance. So a company's ability to keep tight control of ingredient costs is of the utmost importance in determining its earnings potential. A diversified product line helps protect a company from the risk of oversupply or undersupply of any one ingredient. Many of the larger companies have expanded into nonfood areas to further reduce their commodity-related risks. When inflation rates ease, commodity prices tend to stabilize or even decline, allowing the food-processing company to increase margins and profitability.

Other major operational costs include energy, labor, packaging, research and development, and advertising and promotion. Research and development, marketing, and advertising and promotional capability are vitally important contributors to the success of companies operating in this highly competitive environment. A successful food processor is one that is able to identify growing markets, has the research and development skill to come up with products that will meet these new demands, and has the advertising and promotional expertise to gain an adequate market share.

Because of the stability of the group, the stocks of the top-quality multiproduct diversified companies tend to be very attractive to conservative investors. On the whole, food company issues have limited downside risk even under adverse economic conditions and are appropriate defensive investments.

THE MEDIA. This industry is composed of somewhat diverse segments—broadcasting and publishing, including magazines, books, and newspapers. Broadcasters and newspaper and magazine publishers depend more specifically on their advertisers than on the public for their bread and butter. Although readership and audience figures are vital to their marketing success, revenues are derived largely from advertisers.

Both broadcasters and newspaper publishers enjoy high operating margins, leverage, and profits; small volume gains can generate significant profit increases. For publishers, the increasing use of automation and photocomposition equipment has reduced labor costs. Because broadcasting time is limited, advertisers are reluctant to cut back on their TV and radio commercial messages even during recessions. Thus the broadcasters are not as subject to cyclical influences as are the large metropolitan newspapers. In good times, there is a mad scramble among advertisers to secure time slots on the highest-rated network programs. Quite the opposite is the case for newspaper ad linage, which is highly sensitive to business cycles.

Cable TV is experiencing strong growth, but some reregulation benefiting subscribers may be in the works. Viewer choice is no longer limited to the fare of the three major networks. New developments such as satellites, cable TV, and pay cable are ushering in an era of "narrowcasting"—programming geared to the special interest of select audiences. Television has become more interactive, permitting such activities as shopping from your TV, using a home computer. Many media companies (particularly newspaper publishers) are now diversified, so that representation in more than one area can be obtained in one stock.

This industry is generally an attractive one for the investor. There are companies appropriate for the speculator and others more suited to conservative tastes.

MOTION PICTURES. Though the motion picture industry bears little resemblance to its former self, it is likely to be around for many years, despite continuing prophecies of doom. There will still be a demand for the type of entertainment that only the movies can provide. We suspect, too, that many people will continue to prefer seeing movies on a theater screen. Even with rising ticket prices, movies will probably be less expensive than many other forms of entertainment. The increased popularity and affordability of the videocassette recorder (VCR) has cut into moviemakers' profits somewhat, but most of the companies are capitalizing on this trend by preselling video rights in order to finance movies. Also, movie companies with huge libraries of old, popular films have found that they are now sitting on gold mines. Cash generated by the eventual release of these films will be substantial. Revenues from overseas rights can also go a long way toward determining a film's eventual success.

The movie stocks, however, almost defy analysis. In fact, there are only a few smaller movie stocks. Gone are the days of the big studios and their stables of stars—their properties, as it were. Some of the major film companies are now divisions of large foreign companies and some have evolved into vast entertainment complexes with important stakes in recorded music, publishing, and cable television, and are now supplying the industry's old archenemy, television, with most of its prime-time product. Those remaining few movie companies with the least diversification seem eager to explore other growth avenues.

For most of the smaller companies, individual motion pictures can have an enormous impact on earnings. With one major box office smash, a company's earnings can mushroom, its cash position improve significantly, and its stock price rise dramatically.

For every hit there are usually many misses, though the

industry is trying to elevate its batting average by releasing fewer but bigger movies and a greater number of sequels. Furthermore, vast sums of money are now financing, or being risked on, many films. Nevertheless, the hefty guarantees that are demanded from exhibitors actually assure a profit for some films. The industry must anticipate what its public will want to see many months in the future. This is dangerous business—for the movie moguls themselves, for the analyst, and for the investor.

PERSONAL CARE. The personal care industry is highly competitive, with a score of large firms vying for 75 percent of the total dollar volume. A company's success or failure is largely determined by its marketing and merchandising ability. Huge amounts are spent annually trying to capture consumers' dollars and product loyalty. Advertising, packaging, new-product development, and promotion are major expense items. Spending for personal care products has been on the rise in recent years, reflecting the increase in the number of women working outside the home, a bulge in the number of persons in the 25–40 age bracket (a prime age for this type of spending), and the rise in disposable income. These favorable demographic factors and market trends are expected to continue.

There is a wide difference between the world of cosmetics and that of toiletries. Each has its own distinctive characteristics. Channels of distribution, advertising methods, packaging, promotional expenses, and competitive climates are different, and the analyst must approach them separately. Sales and earnings should be studied division by division so these differences can be taken into account. Cosmetics are at the top end of the industry with medium- to premium-priced products, high profit margins, and fashion-related product lines. The more mundane toiletry business includes such pedestrian products as shampoos, deodorants, toothpaste, shaving products, and hair coloring.

While the industry as a whole is fairly recession-resistant, inflation does have a stifling effect on growth. Periods of high inflation necessitate increased consumer spending for food and shelter and reduce the demand for personal care items.

At the same time, manufacturers are forced to pay higher prices for raw materials and supplies. The combination can seriously squeeze profit margins. Alternatively, a dramatic decline in the inflation rate can be quite beneficial. Then companies enjoy rising profits as a result of a leveling off and possibly a decline in raw materials costs. Because so many of these companies are multinational, it is imperative to determine how much of a company's business comes from overseas.

New products are the lifeblood of this group's growth. A company's record of developing and marketing new products may be a clue to its potential. A strong and creative management that recognizes new consumer trends and is willing to make the changes necessary to accommodate these new ideas is one key to success in this highly competitive industry. Diversification efforts have further enhanced the outlook for many personal care firms. Health care firms have been favorite targets for acquisition, given the compatibility of their operating requirements and marketing channels with the personal care sector.

RECREATION EQUIPMENT. This fragmented group includes manufacturers of boats, bowling equipment, sporting goods, video games, snowmobiles, and camping equipment. Thus, conditions that might hurt one company might not hurt another. However, the industry as a whole is sensitive to changes in the economy and in the level of disposable income. In line with some other leisure-time groups, recreation product manufacturers are among the last to be hit in a recession and the first to recover as business heats up.

Demographic conditions favor this group for the next few decades. The 35–54 age group—where most of the big-ticket recreation equipment purchases originate—is expected to increase by more than 60 percent through the year 2000. Americans are enjoying rising discretionary incomes, longer vacations, shorter workweeks, a reasonable level of employment, and excellent retirement benefits, all of which are spurs to recreational activities.

Important to the success—or failure—of a company are its product research and development, its ability as a marketer, its skill in keeping costs down in an inflationary climate, and its product reputation. Because recreation equipment often tends to be seasonal, oriented to a particular population segment, easily duplicated, and short-lived in popularity, a broadly diversified product line is vital to a company's stability.

These stocks, bought in an up cycle, can be highly rewarding. Leisure is big business, and the choices for investments are varied. However, those companies with strong managements, broad product diversification, and products that can be used near the home seem to have the most attractive prospects.

RETAILING. An overview of retailing involves considering the business cycle, inflation, unemployment, consumer disposable income, installment debt, and savings. This industry is affected by seasonal factors, fashion trends, the promotional environment, and consumer buying habits.

Retailing covers a wide range of merchandising, which is generally separated into food and nonfood groups. In the latter group, general merchandisers are studied separately from the specialty stores. But even within these broad categories, there is considerable overlapping. Supermarkets are adding more and more shelf space for nonfood items, and specialty stores are dealing in health and beauty aids. These two types of stores are not only competing with each other, but are encroaching on the business of the general merchandisers.

Central to all retailing is the competitive position of the individual company in its given segment. The supermarket seeks to balance low prices with quality and convenience. The convenience chains stress their round-the-clock neighborhood shopping convenience and underplay their higher prices. A specialty apparel store may appeal to a shopper's desire for service, high fashion, and top quality. Some retailers play all ends of the mass/class market, with boutique, off-price, and discount outlets. In recent years, super stores and membership warehouse clubs have evolved, creating new competition for the traditional service-oriented departments stores. Site location is often the key to the store's ability to achieve this success.

In appraising managements, you must consider how well

central control and local autonomy are balanced. Chain stores do their buying from a central location on information fed from decentralized outlets.

One measure of a company's progress is sales growth, which may come through acquisitions, adding new stores, or replacing outdated units. The yardstick here is the annual figure for square feet of retail floor space and sales volume per square foot.

In appraising retailers' earnings, look at gross margins. This figure is derived by subtracting the cost of goods sold from total sales volume. Inventory control is an important factor in maintaining a favorable level of gross margins. Frequently there is considerable shrinkage between the initial markup and gross margin, reflecting pilferage, errors, and markdowns. Major investments in computer-assisted systems are contributing to improved profitability.

Though retailing for the most part is a mature and intensely competitive field, the group offers some excellent growth selections for the judicious investor.

Financial Services

Banks, insurance companies, and savings and loan associations. For those companies that provide financial services, interest-rate trends are an all-important key to their fortunes. The spread between short-term and long-term rates, or between the rate of interest earned and rate paid, can make the difference between a profit and a loss.

Investments made by these financial companies turn the wheels of American industry, fund most of the housing, and keep the various levels of government operating. They tend to make stable, consistent investments with modest yield and good growth potential.

BANKING. An understanding of the banking industry requires an in-depth study of balances—balances between loans and deposits, between interest rates paid and interest rates earned, between deposit inflows and disintermediation, between short-term loans and long-term loans, and so on. The prosperity of the industry can often swing in either direction on no more than a quarter-point change in the prime lending rate. Thus it is important for the analyst to understand the subtle nuances of these balance and ratio relationships.

To facilitate study, banks generally can be segregated into two groups—money-market-center banks and regional banks. Within these categories are banks whose focus is wholesale, retail, domestic, or international—or any combination thereof. Money-center banks, which are more wholesale in nature, react dramatically to changes in the business climate. Regional banks, with their longer-term portfolios, more stable deposit bases, and better-balanced customer mixes, are in a more advantageous position to withstand economic cycles. Not surprisingly, their stocks display a similar pattern, offering the investor stability, modest yield, and good appreciation potential.

Money-center banks, which are heavily dependent on commercial and industrial loans, can be hard pressed when the demand for such loans dries up, reflecting customers' increased use of cheaper money from commercial paper, notes, and other sources. Banks in need of loan customers often accept less attractive risks. Examples of this are the loans to highly leveraged corporations and commercial real estate developers that have resulted in large losses in the industry.

When analyzing individual bank stocks, important items to examine include loan volume and quality, the health of the regional economy, operating expenses, and noninterest income. The last, generated by account service charges and credit card, data processing, and trust fees, has become an increasingly important component of bank earnings in recent years.

Banking is one of the few industries in which book value or net worth per share has any substantive meaning. Unlike a manufacturer with large amounts of capital tied up in inventory, a bank has assets that are usually of a type that can be easily turned into cash.

Banks' earnings can be analyzed by looking at operating income, which includes profits from operations only, and net income, which includes operating income as well as gains or losses from year-end security portfolio transactions. The first figure is the one generally used in comparing statistics on banks.

Stocks in the larger banks can provide you with an equity position to cash in on favorable interest-rate swings. But, because these bank stocks tend to be more volatile than those of the regionals, you'll have to keep a closer eye on them. Regional banks provide an opportunity to include some close-to-home investments in your portfolio.

INSURANCE. Until the late 1970s, life insurance companies were able to generate steadily rising annual income streams. However, the deregulation of interest rates and high rates of inflation permanently altered profit trends for this segment of the insurance industry. Traditional whole-life premiums, which provided low rates of return to policyholders, failed to appeal to consumers. Through policy loans and terminations, funds flowed out of policies into financial products paying substantially higher rates of return. Slow to adapt to the change, life insurers eventually developed competitive products, such as investment-oriented single-premium and annunity contracts.

Today, the life insurance industry is highly competitive. When analyzing these companies, look at premium growth, mortality experience, lapse rate, reserve position, and operating expenses. The policy mix—ordinary, term, and group —is important, since each type has its own characteristics. Nonlife revenues generated from annuities and accident and health insurance are also important sources of profits.

The earnings trend of property-casualty insurers has always been characterized as cyclical. When companies are experiencing strong profit growth, there is a tendency to cut premiums to garner greater market share. At present, the industry is nearing the bottom of a four-year downturn in the underwriting cycle. An upswing in underwriting profits is anticipated for the 1990s.

The key to evaluating a company's underwriting profitability is its combined ratio. This statistic is made up of a company's loss ratio (losses to earned premiums) plus its expense ratio (expenses to premiums written). Other items to examine are investment income, incurred losses, and loss reserves. The last figure represents funds set aside to cover unpaid losses, estimated future claims, and costs related to these payments. Reserves should be larger than necessary to avoid unpleasant surprises on future earnings. New accounting standards separating gains/losses from investment income should help in the analysis of income statements.

While intense competition has contributed to the woes of the property-casualty industry, jury awards have also affected profits. Both Congress and state legislatures are now taking steps to correct this problem. Federal tort legislation is expected to be enacted; some states have passed bills, and several are considering tort reform measures. Government reform will be welcomed by property-casualty insurers, as long as insurance premiums aren't capped.

SAVINGS AND LOAN ASSOCIATIONS. S&Ls are a major source of home mortgage capital in this country, despite current industry troubles. Mortgage funding is generated primarily from the deposits of savers, but advances from the Federal Home Loan Bank are a secondary source. Earnings are derived from the spread between the interest costs on deposits and the return from mortgages outstanding. Origination fees on new mortgages are also a source of income. New funds are also raised by the sale of mortgages and participations in existing mortgage portfolios.

Because mortgages tend to be written for the long term, and deposits are frequently short term, S&Ls can be in the unenviable position, under high-interest-rate conditions, of having to pay as much or more for borrowings as they are earning on portions of their loan portfolios. But, because of deregulation, products such as money-market accounts, CDs of all sizes and maturities, and adjustable-rate loans, the industry has become more insulated from problems associated with interest-rate swings.

Conversely, deregulation also has been a culprit in the recent S&L debacle. Diversification of loan portfolios into real estate development and junk bonds, for example, has largely been a failure, creating the need for the costly thrift bailout by the Bush administration. Reregulation, a merger with the FDIC, product diversification, and matched balance sheets should provide the S&Ls with a more stable operating environment over the long term.

Public Utilities

Electric power, natural gas pipelines, telephone companies. The tie that binds these three public utility groups together is regulation, at both federal and state levels. Indeed, the only growth some companies can expect will come from rate increases granted by the regulating agencies that control them. This is particularly true for some of the poorly situated electric power companies and for those pipeline companies that have failed to diversify. Of the three industry areas, the telephone companies have suffered the least from regulatory manipulation, only because they require rate boosts less frequently.

In general, investors turn to these groups for generous yields, gradual growth, and better-than-average stability. The electric utilities are particularly liberal in their dividend payments; the integrated natural gas distributors are the least generous.

ELECTRIC UTILITIES. As members of the most capital intensive of industries, electric utility companies are vulnerable to interest-rate swings, shifts in the money supply, and inflation. The industry has to combat such problems as fuel availability, rate regulations, and pressure from consumer and environmental groups. Because electric power companies all face these difficulties, there is a tendency to view them as a homogeneous unit. There is, however, a wide variation in the investment opportunities represented within the group.

One of the most important criteria in evaluating the group is the regulatory climate under which the company must operate. Is the regulatory agency sympathetic to the needs of the company, with decisions rendered promptly and a reasonable return on equity allowed? (A 12 percent return on equity is a workable figure.) If construction work in progress is included in the rate base, so much the better.

In comparing company earnings, an analyst must pay close attention to the quality of those figures. If a large percentage of profit comes from allowance for funds used during construction, the quality of these profits is questionable.

A utility's financial position is particularly important, since the company's future depends heavily on its ability to raise new capital economically. Two important ratios are *fixed charges coverage* and *debt to equity.* A fixed charges ratio of two times is desirable—that is, earnings that are twice as great as total bond interest and preferred dividends. In the debt to equity ratio, when debt moves up to account for more than 60 percent of capitalization, the balance begins to get unhealthy and equity financing becomes the obvious alternative. If, however, the stock is selling below book value, equity financing will result in heavy earnings dilution. The greater the percentage of capital requirements that can be generated internally from cash flow, the healthier the utility.

The fuel used by an electric utility has an important bearing on its attractiveness. Hydropower, coal, and nuclear energy have been the preferred generating fuels in this era of more costly oil and less abundant natural gas. However, the near-disastrous malfunction at the Three Mile Island nuclear plant in Pennsylvania in 1979 precipitated a controversy that cast a cloud over the future of nuclear power. Stringent safety guidelines were subsequently imposed on nuclear power plants. More recently, concern over acid rain emissions and the attendant cost of cleaning up "dirty" plants has forced a reevalution of coal as a fuel source. Thus, fuel risk has evolved as a significant criterion in evaluating securities within the utility group. A final measuring stick to apply to these companies is their comparative earnings and dividend growth rates.

As long as inflation remains within bounds and interest rates remain relatively stable, electric utilities offer above-average current yield, reasonable dividend growth, and moderate price appreciation.

NATURAL GAS—PRODUCERS, TRANSFORMERS, AND DISTRIBUTORS. This is a complex industry with a multitude of participants, but it can be readily divided into three categories: producers, transporters, and distributors. Two characteristics are common to all—they operate largely in the United States and traditionally have been subject to a great deal of government regulation.

Unlike oil, which is ubiquitous in its use throughout the economy, natural gas is used more narrowly, reflecting its physical properties. It is distributed to the consumer through a maze of large- and small-diameter pipelines. This infrastructure is very expensive to construct, but efficient to operate. Canada is increasingly a major part of this network, whereas Mexico is not. Since gas can be liquefied at cryogenic (super cold) temperatures, it can be transported by ship almost anywhere. Liquefying facilities are particularly complex and expensive, and are located primarily in the Far East.

Demand for natural gas is increasing in the United States, while the proven supply is shrinking. It is the cleanest of the hydrocarbon fuels. In an era of environmental consciousness, gas has been singled out for increasing use. It fuels power plants to generate electricity and provides heat in a variety of industrial processes, and in the home it fuels stoves, hot water heaters, and furnaces. In the 1950s and 1960s, natural gas was plentiful. Because it sold at a discount to oil on a BTU-value basis, it was very affordable. However, low prices and neglect of exploration led to shortages and sharp price increases in the 1970s. The introduction of government regulation in the 1980s cured the price problems to the satisfaction of politicians and consumers, but did nothing for supplies. The story for the 1990s will be deregulation, higher prices, and, one hopes, an increased supply.

Such developments present the greatest opportunities for the explorers and producers. There is a consensus that more gas remains to be discovered and developed, but only at great depths or in tight formations. Therefore, higher prices will be required to encourage production. Once the price outlook improves, we would expect independent producers, as well as large integrated petroleum companies and pipelines, to increase their activity. Those independents who can exploit the financial and marketing resources of the latter entities will be the strongest companies in the 1990s.

The interstate pipeline companies have taken the brunt of

the regulatory burden over the past decade. They were beset both by producers who were reluctant to sell their gas too cheaply and by distributors who hesitated to make long-term commitments to buy expensive gas given the availability of cheap spot-market gas. Unsuccessful efforts by the government to deal with this turned investors away from the industry. It appears that in the future the pipeline industry will become transporters rather than contractors of energy. Companies will compete with one another over the cost of their services, which will be determined by the value of the particular franchise and the efficiency of the operation.

Although returns for natural gas distributors are limited by state regulators, companies that can sell more gas to existing customers and entice others to switch from alternative energy sources will be the leaders. The growing awareness among consumers of the shifting balance between gas and oil as fuels will make these goals difficult to accomplish. Because of regulation and the limited growth in gas resources, the stocks of distributors will probably continue to be bought by investors seeking high quality and income.

TELEPHONE COMPANIES. These utilities are in a better position than most of their regulated colleagues. Although they are not completely immune to inflationary cost pressures, future capital needs are manageable. Costly pollution controls, customer conservation measures, and soaring fuel prices have not affected the communication companies. Earnings quality is generally high, reflecting conservative accounting practices and limited allowances for funds used during construction.

Although telephone companies are dependent on favorable treatment on rates, improved industry fundamentals should lessen the amount of rate assistance needed in the future. In general, costs have been well controlled in the industry, while direct distance dialing and electronic switching equipment have provided more efficient operations and lower maintenance costs. Revenue growth has been accelerated by the increase in household formations and the installation of second phones, which have outpaced population growth.

The seven regional holding companies created during the breakup of the old American Telephone & Telegraph system dominate the industry, servicing 80 percent of U.S. telephones. Servicing of the remaining 20 percent, or one out of five telephones, is parceled out among numerous independents. However, the five largest—GTE Corp., United Telecommunications, Continental Telecom, Southern New England Telephone, and Centel Corp.—serve well over three-quarters of all non-Bell telephone users.

While the Bell regionals are located in the more densely populated areas, the independents generally cover the smaller but more rapidly growing rural and suburban sections, where phones are being added and toll use is rising at a fast clip. Thus, the threat of bypass is not nearly as prevalent for the independents as it is for the Bell regionals. The Bell companies are restrained from entering certain businesses under terms of the Modified Final Judgment handed down at the time of the divestiture. However, the Bell regionals are slowly chipping away at these restrictions. Most of the independents offer broad diversification beyond the area of basic telephone service.

As a general rule, as a telephone company becomes more diversified, the percent of earnings paid out annually in the form of common dividends decreases. This is due to the nature of the businesses into which telcos diversify—telecommunications equipment manufacturing and sales, financial services, and software development and marketing are a few. The nature of these industries requires that earnings be plowed back into operations to fuel growth. Therefore, within the industry, there are a variety of choices for the right combination of current income and growth potential.

Regulation for telephone companies has generally been less of a problem than for electric utility companies, and there is little to suggest that this is likely to change. Indeed, telcos have been at the forefront of efforts to negotiate new, alternative rate structures that reward efficiency. These so-called incentive rate plans generally give the company greater pricing flexibility and allow it to share with ratepayers whatever extra earnings it can generate through cost cutting and productivity improvements. However, investors should be aware of changes in the regulatory climate that could affect future earnings.

CHAPTER 26

Cashing In on the Future

A MODERN INDUSTRIAL economy, free-world style, is a constantly changing body. New industries emerge, and old industries disappear. Some regions advance, while others fall behind. Cities decline, and suburbs grow. The crucial industries that provide power and transportation undergo transformations.

Some sources of change in the economy are the result of legislation. Others may reflect such influences as wars or weather changes. Many major changes, however, are generated within the system itself.

Many years ago, the Austrian-born economist Joseph A. Schumpeter identified the process of innovation as the primary source of internally generated change. In furthering understanding of the complexities of a modern economic society, the work of Professor Schumpeter, probably the most neglected of the great twentieth-century economists, has major contributions to make.

Dr. Schumpeter's first writing on the subject of innovation was published in 1911 in Germany. This work was not translated into English until 1934. In 1939, while at Harvard, Dr. Schumpeter expanded upon and further developed the ideas of his youth in a two-volume work called *Business Cycles.*

Innovation, in Dr. Schumpeter's system, takes four forms:

the introduction of a new product, the use of new methods of production, the opening up of new sources of supply, and the development of new forms of business organization. Examples abound.

New-product innovation may be illustrated by such diverse examples as the automobile, antibiotics, the microwave oven, and the videocassette.

New methods of production may be illustrated by developments in the steel industry, from the Bessemer process through the open-hearth furnace to the modern basic oxygen process. The jet engine powers airplanes by means superior to the internal combustion engine.

Food processors have found new methods for preserving foods by spraying and freeze-drying them. Dry packaging, which is cheaper than glass and metal containers, has been developed for liquid food products.

Innovative new sources of supply are illustrated by Alaskan oil, iron ore from Labrador, electronics from the Far East, and fresh produce from South America and Europe.

Finally, new forms of business organization have evolved, such as the limited-liability corporation and the one-bank holding company, the "full-service" bank, and the master limited partnership.

Innovation Versus Invention

The business innovator or entrepreneur should be distinguished from the inventor. First, many innovations, such as the supermarket or the medical clinic, have little or nothing to do with invention. The inventor's skills are likely to be of a mechanical or scientific nature, while the innovator's strengths lie in the ability to conceive better production methods, products, and business organizational forms. The innovator may start a new business, select a site, obtain the capital, hire the people, provide the raw materials, and sell the product. Like many inventions, a particular innovation may come to nothing, but the hallmark of successful innovation is the earning of profits.

The profits of innovation will attract new entrants into the field. Sometimes the competitors have to circumvent patents or copyrights, or attempt to offer a superior product. In other cases, entry may be possible by duplicating the activity elsewhere, say, in some other location. The entry of competitors will stimulate plant and equipment spending and increase output and employment. The increase in output will bring down prices and reduce profits. Eventually the innovating industry becomes mature. Firms in the industry may attempt to sustain themselves by superior management, by consolidation, and by making minor innovative adaptations of the basic product.

The Effects of "Future Shock"

Superimposed on Dr. Schumpeter's ideas is the acceleration of change that has now reached such proportions that there is hardly anyone in our midst who can escape its effects. "Future shock," Alvin Toffler called it in his 1970 book by the same name. Mr. Toffler's claims are hardly an exaggeration. Think of all that has been discovered, invented, produced, and experienced in the brief span of years we have been around. Today's 25-year-old will see more changes by his fiftieth birthday than today's 50-year-old has experienced since he was 25.

While all this is apparent and interesting, what is more to the point is how we can profit by this acceleration of change. Perhaps those among us with the imagination of Jules Verne find it easy to envision a world a quarter-century into the future. But most of us are not such visionaries. Our feet and minds are firmly planted in the here and now; we think we're doing well if we can anticipate a week, a month, or a year ahead.

Given the limitations of our prophetic powers, perhaps we should turn to the past for some clues. What were the conditions that fostered the growth of such an industrial giant as International Business Machines? From its humble beginnings as a manufacturer of scales and cash registers in St. Louis, Missouri, in 1911, who could have foreseen its rise to a behemoth grossing over $65 billion a year?

By 1954, when IBM marketed its first large-scale stored-program computer, it already had achieved a commendable growth record, with annual sales well over $400 million and net income approaching $50 million. To some analysts, who failed to comprehend what the future held for the computer, IBM was already a maturing company. Anyone venturing to buy 10 shares of stock at that time—which would have cost less than $3,000—would have owned 363 shares worth almost $100,000 at the close of 1977.

This success story has less to do with technical leadership —Sperry Rand, now merged into Burroughs Corp. to form Unisys, beat IBM to the market with a large-scale computer —than with recognizing the product potential and creatively moving to capitalize on it. The leadership of Thomas J. Watson, the development of an outstanding marketing organization, and access to adequate financing were also major factors in the company's growth.

Why Some Companies Succeed

A study of IBM's modus operandi reveals a number of factors that contributed to the company's success. Early on, it established a strong position in the computer industry; by 1964, it had sold 75 percent of all computers in place at the time. It worked hard to build a solid customer relationship, providing programs, hardware, peripheral equipment, installation, and services. It nurtured strong customer loyalty, effectively disarming the competition. It built up a large base of future revenue by renting as well as selling its equipment. It worked to make its customers "dependent" by generating a steady stream of new products and supplies to operate, expand, and upgrade the old.

Gillette and Polaroid are other examples of companies that were able to capitalize on the "captive customer" situation by coming up with new products that consumed company-produced supplies. American Telephone & Telegraph was another past master of this technique, first supplying the apparatus required to use the service, then providing the service, and finally creating broader and broader applications of that service. Had it been less successful in its integration, it might not have been broken into its component parts by the government. The lesson, then, is that you must not only find companies capable of producing goods and services for the next new era, but you must find companies with the imagination to provide for and capture the markets for those goods and services.

Watch for Trends

In any search for future profit opportunities, then, you must give thought to the changing trends of our society. For example, there has been a shift toward later marriage, fewer babies, and single-parent households. The increase in demand for energy-saving devices and supplies has created new areas of opportunity. People are working fewer hours. Women are working away from their homes. Which are the industries that will benefit from these shifts and which will be hurt?

A classic example of a company that felt the pinch of later marriages and the declining birth rate is Gerber: "Babies are our business—our only business." In a series of defensive maneuvers, Gerber branched out into other areas—life insurance, day-care centers, and a broad line of products for infants—then quietly retired its long-standing slogan. Conversely, delayed marriages and more single-parent homes have tended to increase the demand for apartments, furnishings, and other consumer products. The upsurge of women in the workforce has had a noticeable impact on the sale of convenience foods and on the growth of the fast-food business. As a result, old-line food packagers have been among the most sought-after merger candidates in recent years.

Another demographic change that is being felt in sundry ways is the increase in the number of people among us aged 60 and older. The Sunbelt states were the first to feel the effects of the older people in their midst. The population explosion in these areas has far outpaced growth in the more northern states as retirees flocked there to escape the cold.

Longer life spans have benefited the life insurance companies, the leisure industry, travel-related companies, and consumer products firms. Increasing at an even greater rate is the population segment made up of persons 80 and older. This trend benefits the broad spectrum of health care services and extended-care nursing facility companies.

Because people are living longer, they are becoming more aware ever earlier in life that they want those later years to be secure. They also want to be physically fit so those years can be enjoyed. Long life is no boon for those too unhealthy or too poor to benefit. Good nutrition and exercise are subjects that are attracting more than lip service. Companies that cater to these needs, such as H. J. Heinz, with its Weight Watchers division, or Nike and L.A. Gear, makers of sports shoes, have benefited from these trends.

Profits in "Cleaning Up"

While there has been a "graying of America," there has also been a "greening of America." We as a nation have become aware of the finiteness of our environment and are bent on preserving it. Hazardous-waste cleanup has provided profits for some companies while creating expenses for those who have been judged guilty of fouling the environment. Investors who assess these situations accurately stand to do well with their portfolios.

Consumerism will have its effects on business and investments. Some companies will falter as the market for their products dries up. Other companies will be formed to provide newly demanded consumer services. Some companies will meet the new challenges with creativity and will wax; others will ignore the trends and will wane.

We've already alluded to the prospects for health services in an aging society. But the area should be singled out for some special consideration, for it represents a field containing a potentially bountiful harvest for the canny investor. Not only must products and services be made available for a population that is growing older, but they must be provided for one that is bent on remaining as young, fit, and healthy as possible for as long as possible. Ethical drugs, hospital supplies, medical appliances, physical fitness equipment, and electronic diagnostic equipment all provide potential avenues for profitable investment.

Cashing In on "Getting There"

Vancouver's Expo '86 had as its theme transportation and communication. Which of its futuristic visions of people movers and word transmitters will actually come to pass? Will a space shuttle become a reality? Will picturephones replace telephones? Will electronic equipment make commuting to an office a thing of the past? Will a computer do most of your driving for you? Some of these concepts have already moved from the drawing board to the production line. Picturephones are available, at a price. Computer chips control an increasing number of functions in your car. And those same chips, plus the FAX and the modem, allow a rapidly increasing number of people to work from their homes.

These areas could provide major investment opportunities as demand for such products increases. Someone has to supply the chips, the phones, the electronics, the computers, and the training for the users. Someone has to provide the capital and, in turn, reap the rewards for undertaking the risks.

Making Money on Money

Technological changes may have a greater impact on the future of the financial services industry than on most other groups. Automated teller machines (ATMs) have gained widespread consumer acceptance and have replaced their human counterparts in many locations. Electronic funds transfer (EFT) and direct deposit have also wrought significant changes in the banking industry. So-called debit cards, powered by semiconductor brains (implanted chips), may eventually replace cash, checks, and credit cards. And home computers may make it possible to perform any type of financial transaction from the comfort of your own living room.

How can you profit from these trends? The companies that will benefit most will have to be more forward-looking and innovative than their competitors. But they will need substantial capital support. Individuals willing to invest in the industry's future delivery systems should be well rewarded over time.

Some Guidelines

So now we get down to the real nub of this chapter. How do you break out of the rush of today's events so you can cash in on tomorrow's investment winners? From the foregoing brew, let's distill a few guidelines.

First, look for companies in the process of developing new products or new ways of doing things. Look for companies on the ascendant in their fields, not those that have matured or passed into a declining phase or those entrenched in a mature industry.

Second, look for companies that have the managerial expertise necessary to capitalize on their innovations.

Third, examine the basic trends in our society. Look for the real changes in direction that are already occurring and that are likely to occur in the years ahead, based on what is happening today. Then, look for companies already positioned to take advantage of the trend.

Fourth, don't confuse a fad with a trend. We've already cautioned you to exercise diligence in distinguishing between a substantive change in cultural or economic direction and a passing fancy. Sometimes it's not easy to tell the difference, particularly at the outset. Once you have discerned a bona fide trend and invested accordingly, keep an eye on your investment to be sure that conditions do not develop to jeopardize the trend or the position you have staked out in it.

CHAPTER 27

Where to Get Advice

"WHERE DO I get investment advice?" That's a difficult question to answer, because the answer depends on what kind of advice you expect to get. If you want panaceas, secrets to surefire success, or that one key that unlocks all the mysteries of the stock market, you'll find them aplenty; they litter the road of broken investment dreams. You need but ask— friends, relatives, passersby in the street—and you will be deluged with all manner of theories, explanations, and "wisdom." It is no wonder that a new investor so often finds himself reeling under the barrage of information and opinion available. The intelligent and experienced investor who has delineated his investment objectives stands a better chance of obtaining usable advice. He has been around long enough to know the superficial, appreciate the possible, and recognize the charlatan. For the novice, this chapter attempts to highlight the major categories and sources of investment information.

Some investment sources present facts only and leave interpretation to the reader, while others provide an interpretation of the facts and specific advice. Most investors, without substantial time to devote to the formulation of their portfolios, prefer the latter. No matter what sources you choose, the most important prerequisite for successful investing is the formulation of a specific goal. The retiree, dependent on his dividends for "eating money," should think twice before acting on a speculative recommendation, no matter how reliable he perceives the source to be.

Your Broker and the Bank

Your broker can provide good information if he has a large research department to back him up. Many sizable houses publish market letters as well as company and industry studies for which they charge. Other investment houses put out literature that is available to clients free of charge. Some will analyze a portfolio and make suggestions in line with a given investment objective. An important caveat, however, is that brokers survive on commissions and thus are under pressure to advise change. If you are not an aggressive trader, watch out for excessive switch recommendations.

Many banks also offer a number of services. The simplest is a custodial arrangement under which the bank maintains physical care of the securities, keeps accounting records, and executes transactions at the owner's request. No advice is included. Some banks offer more extensive services, ranging from periodic portfolio reviews and recommendations to continuous supervision. Most banks tend to be conservative in their recommendations and thus are not really appropriate advisors for the aggressive speculator. However, larger money-center banks now offer portfolio management aimed at specific financial goals, including more aggressive growth, with assets allocated accordingly.

Standard & Poor's and Moody's

Two financial publishing firms, Standard & Poor's and Moody's, are in a class by themselves. Both offer a wide range of services. Standard & Poor's provides more than a dozen—from *Corporation Records,* which includes factual descriptions of all important corporate and many public issuers of both listed and unlisted securities, to *The Outlook,* a weekly advisory letter. Especially valuable for the individual investor are S&P's monthly paperback publications, *Stock Guide* and *Bond Guide*. The *Stock Guide* shows earnings, dividends, yield, capital structure, working capital, and market price data. The *Bond Guide* gives ratings, interest dates, form (bearer or registered), redemption provisions, earnings, prices, and both current yields and yields to maturity. Occasionally brokers and dealers distribute these to active customers free of charge.

Moody's publishes large reference volumes on listed industrials, over-the-counter industrials, utilities, Governments, and financial companies. It also offers many other services, including a weekly *Bond Survey*. Moody's and S&P are the major rating agencies for corporate and municipal debt offerings. Most of their publications are relatively expensive but are available in major university and public libraries.

Advisory Services

Advisory services vary widely in their scope and slant. Some rely on technical factors and try to gauge the likely short-term movement of the market as a whole and of individual securities. Others recommend fundamentally strong companies with only secondary emphasis on the near-term outlook for the market. Some seem consistently to presage doom; others tend to look mainly on the bright side.

The *Value Line Investment Survey,* one of the larger and better-known advisory services, covers more than 1,700 stocks. Each stock in the list is reviewed comprehensively every three months, and each week the service covers four to six industries, on a rotating basis. Stocks are rated for safety and expected performance. The service each week also covers the outlook for the stock market and the economy, and highlights certain individual stocks. Sometimes other special studies are included. The service is relatively expensive but is available in many libraries.

The weekly *United & Babson Investment Report* is among the oldest and largest of these services. It presents a concise summary of economic and business news, and includes coverage of commodity price trends, as well as industry or topical studies and specific buying and selling advice on individual securities. In the first issue of each month, it publishes a supervised list of common stocks, divided by investment objective. It is generally upbeat and steers its clients toward quality and investment for the longer term.

Standard & Poor's *Outlook,* which we mentioned earlier, is another of the larger and better-known investment letters. It plots an investment course similar to United's, though its content is more fully devoted to securities investment rather than including broader commentary on economic, business, and financial affairs, as does United's.

Many other advisory publications are available, some of which are general in nature, such as *Indicator Digest* and *The Primary Trend.* Still others embrace particular investment philosophies. These include *Dow Letters* and *Dow Theory Forecasts,* which use the Dow Theory as their springboards; Robert Prechter's *Elliott Wave Theorist,* which analyzes the market based on Elliott's studies of cycles; *The Dines Letter,* which follows gold and gold-related securities; *The Prudent Speculator,* which advises on a value and technical basis; and the *Professional Tape Reader* and *Zweig Forecast,* which recommend stocks on the basis of strict technical models. Another technically based newsletter, which covers more general information than the last two, is *The Astute Investor,* written by Robert Nurock.

Many of these services are one-person, one-desktop-publisher affairs. The Investment Advisors Act of 1940 requires all such advisors to be registered with the Securities and Exchange Commission. However, the registration is designed to guard against fraud; it does not indicate any particular expertise or guarantee favorable results.

We should mention here another type of service available: chart books. Although their publishers generally do not provide specific investment advice, their products can be useful in showing you past performances and price, earnings, and dividend trends of various stocks. Such charts are particularly helpful in discerning technical market trends. Securities Research Company, a division of Babson-United Investment

Advisors, Inc., publishes a monthly chart service of listed companies, another for OTC stocks, and quarterly *Cycli-Graphs,* as well as quarterly wall charts of market averages and an annually issued 35-year stock chart book. Daily Graphs, R.W. Mansfield Company, and Trendline provide similar services.

Investment Advice in the Computer Age

Within the realm of computerized market advice, there are as many variations as there are in the field of hard-copy investment advisory services. All that you need to play in this field are a PC with a graphics card, a spreadsheet program, a modem, a dot matrix printer, and the wherewithal to pay for the program, real-time or delayed quotes, connection charges, and telephone time.

The fees depend on the type of service you buy. Some of the discount brokerage companies offer software programs with real-time quotes, news, research, and portfolio management systems at excellent prices. The reason for the competitive price is that you can buy and sell securities using their programs and their brokerage services. For a novice in the field of computerized portfolio analysis, the low cost of broker-sponsored programs makes them an attractive way to begin. But keep in mind that in addition to the software, you will have to pay a cable fee or subscription fee to download quotes to the program—unless you plan to enter prices manually.

Although investment programs are "user friendly," learning to operate them to best advantage will require time and patience. You must also be aware of which programs operate on which type of computer—IBM PC, IBM XT, Apple II, Compaq, AT&T 6300, and so forth. Will the program be compatible with DOS 2 or some other operating system? Most investment programs are written for IBM and IBM-compatible machines, with a narrower variety of programs available for other PCs. Many programs require 256K RAM and at least one hard drive to operate.

Computer portfolio programs come into their own in the

area of technical analysis, enabling the market trader to do in a wink what it would take hours to do by hand. Some of the programs in the field are *Winning on Wall Street, The Active Investor, The Dow-Jones Analyzer Plus, MetaStock, Savant,* and *Trendline II.* The cost of such software is in the range of $250 to $500, for starters.

Because of the mass of data required for in-depth fundamental analysis, fundamentals-based programs are more costly than the technical ones. To reduce the cost, data are recorded on diskettes. Value Line and Standard & Poor's sell floppies with data on around 1,500 stocks on each disk. An annual subscription costs $200 and up. Programs that allow the investor to do fundamental screening include Savant's *Fundamental Investor,* Value Line's *Value/Screen Plus,* S&P's *Stockpak II,* and Dow-Jones's *Market Microscope.*

In addition to these computerized stock and portfolio analysis programs, there are many telephone hotline services that take advantage of the fee-for-call 900 numbers. For a minimum charge of two dollars a minute, you can get the latest market or stock analysis from a "pro." So far we aren't aware of any services for stock market advice via FAX!

Before leaving the realm of advisory services, some mention of the sources of information available to the mutual fund investor is in order. *The Wiesenberger Investment Company Service,* published by Warren, Gorham & Lamont, provides an annual compendium of information about mutual funds and investment companies, and an explanation of their functions and various uses to the investor. Data are included on the background, management policy, and salient features of all leading companies, including income and dividend records, price ranges, and comparative operating details. A similar but newer publication is the *Mutual Fund Source Book.* This quarterly softcover is put out by Morningstar, Inc. Again, these relatively expensive publications are available in many libraries.

A valuable statistical source on the fund industry as a whole is the *Mutual Fund Fact Book,* published and updated annually by the Investment Company Institute, 1775 K Street, N.W., Washington, DC 20006.

The *United Mutual Fund Selector* provides a wealth of

information on mutual funds. Published twice monthly by the Babson-United Investment Advisors, Inc., the *Selector* in one issue provides comparative tables that track the recent and longer-term performance of more than 1,000 funds. It also includes a supervised list of mutual funds and provides specific recommendations in line with different objectives. Every issue contains general features about the industry, detailed discussions of certain funds, and other timely recommendations.

The Financial Press

The financial press is brimming with valuable information. Most daily newspapers provide some sort of financial section, which generally includes price quotations as well as business highlights and sometimes commentary. *The Wall Street Journal,* the most widey read national daily business and financial newspaper, provides much more extensive coverage of financial news, including, in addition to comprehensive price quotations, news about companies, industries, commodities, financial affairs, taxes, labor, and public policy.

A relatively new national financial newspaper, *Investor's Daily,* is full of charts and computer screening results. It features a full-page analysis of one stock daily, including charts of daily, weekly, and monthly highs and lows. This paper is well organized; précis of the day's stories are carried on the front page. The five cover stories are continued on the back cover.

The New York Times publishes a comprehensive business and financial section daily. *The Journal of Commerce* is an excellent resource for the commodity investor and also includes extensive business news, with emphasis on national and international economic developments.

Barron's, published weekly by Dow Jones & Company, provides a good wrap-up of the preceding week's economic and stock market happenings. It includes an extensive section on stock and bond quotations, economic and market statistics, timely articles on various companies and current economic events, and a section on commodities. Editorial commentary is liberally interjected.

Magazines

Many magazines available on the newsstand or by subscription can provide up-to-date information. *Business Week, Financial World, Forbes, Fortune, Money Magazine,* and *U.S. News & World Report* are examples. *Financial World* and *Forbes* are more heavily weighted with investment news; *Money Magazine* is oriented toward financial planning for individuals; the others deal more with general business topics. For investors with a strong interest in a particular industry, there are trade journals such as *Supermarket News, Electronic News,* and *Women's Wear Daily.*

Government Publications

U.S. government publications can yield clues to economic trends that might affect the investment climate. *Business Conditions Digest* provides data on the cyclical indicators. *Economic Indicators* is a monthly compendium of statistics on gross national product, employment, production, prices, money and credit, federal finance, and international trade. The *Survey of Current Business* is another comprehensive statistical source that includes detailed commentary on various economic subjects. The Federal Reserve Bank of St. Louis publishes *Monetary Trends* and other excellent bulletins on the money supply and interest rates, available at no cost. For labor and employment trends and developments, there is the *Monthly Labor Review,* published by the Department of Labor. Many of these publications may be available at your local library.

Investment Counselors

For the well-to-do investor who wishes to leave the research and decision-making to someone else, there are investment-counseling firms. Their annual fees, as a rule of thumb, will run 0.5 to 1.0 percent of the value of the portfolio being managed. Most firms handle large accounts only, those valued at $300,000 and up. They provide in-depth investment advice, watch clients' portfolios continually, and notify them when changes appear warranted. Major companies in this category include David L. Babson; Loomis Sayles; Scudder, Stevens & Clark; and United Investment Counsel, a subsidiary of Babson-United Investment Advisors, Inc.

Some investment counseling companies handle smaller accounts. For example, Babson's Registered Investors, an arm of Babson-United Investment Advisor, Inc., supervises portfolios of $150,000 and over. Companies that provide counseling for accounts of less than $100,000 generally either pool funds or restrict portfolios to stocks on a master list or the S&P 500. Thus, technically, their counsel is not individualized. The annual fee is usually 1 or 2 percent on the managed assets, with a minimum in the vicinity of $100 to $200. Danforth Associates is an example of a company providing such services.

There you have it: a sampling of the wide spectrum of investment advice and information available to you. With experience, you'll be able to tell how much digging you want to do on your own, how much you're willing to pay others to dig for you, and whose advice best suits your own investment needs and philosophy.

PART V

Mastering the Strategies and Tactics

CHAPTER 28

Five Rules for Investors

UNTIL NOW, THE focus of this book has largely been on the definition and analysis of various savings and investment vehicles. Now it's time to start applying this body of information to the construction and maintenance of your own program. As with any other undertaking, you will be better served if you set down some rules ahead of time.

We have five that tend to crystallize the investment philosophy we at Babson-United Investment Advisors have pursued for more than half a century. We believe they will serve you well, too. After reading our earlier chapters, you should find none of them surprising.

The thoughts have all been expressed at least once before in this book; some will be expressed again. By bringing them together here, we provide a yardstick against which you can measure future investment decisions. Read them carefully. Commit them to memory. Recite them whenever you have an investment decision to make. If you are a compulsive investor, tempted by every hot tip that comes your way, tattoo them to the back of your hand. Ignore them at your peril.

The five: Set your goals. Buy the best-known companies. Invest for the long term. Avoid fads. Diversify.

Set Your Goals

RULE NUMBER ONE. Set your goals. Decide what you want your savings to do for you. You wouldn't buy long underwear for a trip to the Bahamas, nor would you travel by way of the Yukon when you finally set out. But you'd be surprised at how many investors pack their portfolios with inappropriate garb and travel needlessly circuitous routes to their investment destinations.

Before you plunge into your savings and investment program, sit down and list your objectives on paper. College education for the children? How long before they'll need it? How much will they need? Retirement fund for yourself? When will you want to start drawing on it? Next year? Three years from now? Trip to Europe? New car? Emergency fund?

The answers to these questions are important, for they will determine whether you should invest for capital growth or current income. Most of the time you will have to accept one or the other. Rare indeed is the investment that offers a generous helping of both. The answers, too, will tell you how much risk you can reasonably assume—and which type of risk.

Suppose you're a mid-career salaried individual who can divert to savings regular amounts of income from your family's spending stream. Your aim is a retirement fund to supplement your company's pension. As with most of us who labor in the corporate vineyard, the Internal Revenue Service enjoys a generous share of your income. Since you're already earning enough so you can set some aside, and since your objective is relatively long term, there's no reason for you to shoot for investment income now. It would only have to be shared with Uncle Sam. What you want is capital growth and little or no current income.

Furthermore, since you have a secure job and considerable time before retirement, you're in a position to assume some market risk in the chance of making better-than-average capital gains. That's because if you should lose, you would still be in a good position to replace those lost dollars from regular earned income. So you concentrate your investment efforts on building a portfolio of growth stocks.

Now, suppose you have a maiden aunt in her middle years whose pay just barely covers her needs. Let's further suppose that she inherits or otherwise comes into a $125,000 windfall. Not only is this a sum larger than anything she had ever known before, but it is a bit of fortune that is not likely to be repeated.

What should she do? Her first objective would be to preserve that capital, since her ability to replace it is negligible. So she chooses investments that will provide the highest posssible current return and the greatest possible "safety." Savings certificates and bonds, both corporate and government, spring immediately to mind. But there are common stocks that also fit the description. These would provide some chance for dividend growth and capital appreciation at minimal risk to her nest egg, all the while giving her a substantial current return, which, of course, she immediately reinvests.

Your uncle the doctor, his children through college, his retirement approaching, would take still another tack. He would have to reevaluate his investment program, gradually shifting it from the growth orientation of earlier years to an income orientation to provide his "eating money" in retirement. Again, because his working years are drawing to a close, he would have to concentrate on preservation of principal, since his opportunities for replacing it are fast closing.

The doctor's case illustrates another point you should keep firmly in mind. Your investment goals can—and usually do —change as you proceed through life. Therefore, you should subject your program to periodic review to see that its objectives remain consistent with your needs.

Buy the Best-Known Companies

RULE NUMBER TWO. Buy the best-known companies. Stick with the tried and true. There is far too much risk in trying to unearth tomorrow's Compaqs. The mortality rate of these ventures is staggering, and you'd do best to leave this kind of financial wildcatting to someone else.

There are plenty of firmly established companies around that offer attractive investment possibilities. Bristol Myers,

General Electric, and PepsiCo still can add zip to a portfolio despite their maturity.

There are promising lesser lights like Genuine Parts, Millipore Corp., and Waste Management with good survival records despite the vagaries of the economy and the stock market. They have been in business for a long time, their products are well known, their markets firmly established, and their financial condition solid. They're not necessarily blue chips. Some, in fact, have a clearly speculative tint. But because they have demonstrated an ability to survive, they should not be overlooked.

Equally important, their stock prices are reasonable in relation to such fundamentals as assets, earnings, and dividends. In short, there are plenty of attractive, reasonable investments that offer the promise of real and substantial profit someday for the investor who can take the risk.

Invest for the Long Term

RULE NUMBER THREE. Invest for the long term. Patience with the stock market is more than a virtue. It is a must. Things rarely work out overnight on Wall Street, and when they do, almost everyone is taken by surprise. So, when you buy a good stock, buy it for the long pull. Consider yourself a part owner of the business. You have become one because you believe the business is fundamentally sound and the prospects excellent. Therefore, you don't have to watch the daily gyrations in your stock's price with fear in your throat when it is down and exultation in your soul when it is up.

Take Anheuser-Busch, for example. The investors who bought this stock in late 1976 probably were motivated by the company's still-premier position in the brewing industry and, perhaps more important, the fact that the shares were selling at only about a third of their old high. However, earnings had been battered earlier that year by a strike, and Philip Morris's Miller Brewing was becoming an ever more formidable competitor. The value was there, to be sure, but so were the risks.

Over the next three years, the stock essentially went nowhere despite a surge in earnings and further gains in industry market share. Those investors not liberally endowed with patience undoubtedly bailed out. But in early 1980 the stock began to move. And move it did, more than tripling by 1983. Following a 10-month breather during which the shares lost less than 10 points, the stock took off, tripling by mid-1987. In the crash later that year, Anheuser-Busch lost about one-third of its value. But the lost ground was recovered by mid-1989, and the shares went on to make new highs in 1990.

The key was patience. Those who waited prospered. Those who wanted instant rewards lost out, as they usually do in the stock market.

It might help you to develop patience if you think of your commitment in a stock as you do your investment in your own home. You bought your house to fill a specific need after applying certain qualifying tests. As long as your living requirements remain the same and nothing seriously wrong develops with the structure or the neighborhood, you stay put.

You don't regularly check with your real estate broker for the current value of your home, and you shouldn't need to be constantly concerned with the day-to-day price fluctuations of your stocks. Even if you read in the real estate section of the Sunday newspaper that "Home Values Slump," you don't rush out and sell. You realize any such slippage in price will be temporary. Think long term with your stocks just as you do with your home.

Avoid Fads

RULE NUMBER FOUR. Avoid fads. Stay clear of the crowd, even when it looks right. This is one of the most important rules of successful investing—and one of the most frequently violated, to the ultimate chagrin of legions of hapless violators. If everyone seems to be rushing out to buy stocks in a particular industry group or company, let them. But don't do it yourself. If a particular stock seems to be the darling of the day, don't compete. Let the others have it.

Fads come and go on Wall Street just as they do on Madison Avenue, Seventh Avenue, or Main Street U.S.A. One big trouble with fads is that it's sometimes hard to tell when something is just that—a passing fancy—or if it's truly a technological or sociological breakthrough and represents something that will become a fixture in our everyday lives. The distinction is particularly difficult to make in the early stages, when the temptation is greatest to "get in on the ground floor."

Who could have foretold, for instance, back in the 1950s, that a photocopying device being toyed with by a little firm known as the Haloid Company out of Rochester, New York, would change the lives of nearly all of us and in the process firmly affix the word "Xerox" in our lexicon? The spectacular success of that xerographic photocopier made fortunes for its supporters, who, corporate legend tells us, included cabdrivers and bartenders.

Or who could have known that an instant-picture camera developed by Dr. Edward Land would catapult a manufacturer of polarized-lens sunglasses to the forefront of American industry in the days following World War II? Investors in Polaroid in those days were surely involved in a gamble. They won, and some of them won big.

But for each legendary corporate success, how many "hot ideas" have failed, leaving their gamble-oriented investors holding the bag? More to the point, how can you—or anyone —separate the Xeroxes and Polaroids from the failures? The plain fact is that few can. And since your chances of riding a loser are tens or hundreds of times greater than climbing aboard a winner, you'd do best to let the out-and-out gamblers play those odds. There will be ample opportunity for reaping substantial returns from the winners once they have become established, as thousands of investors in Xerox and Polaroid have learned over the years.

Consider those who perceived a great new day as digital timepieces began to replace the world's conventional wristwatches, and invested accordingly. The watches caught on all right, but electronics companies thronged to that marketplace in such numbers that many fell helplessly aside and were trampled in the stampede, their backers with them. The same thing happened with Coca-Cola's "New Coke," polyester and discos. The same thing happened with pocket calculators, double knits, and citizens' band radios. It will happen again with something else. And again. And again.

It sometimes happens with the stock of an established company. A new product or new process is announced, and before its true market worth has been established, eager investors are beating a path to their brokers' offices to grab a piece of the action. Remember the Cabbage Patch doll? Coleco Industries made millions with it in the mid-1980s, when it accounted for 85 percent of their sales. Unfortunately, the company failed to hedge its bets with other products. When the market for Cabbage Patch dolls faded, so too did Coleco.

When such a situation develops, the stock's price eventually rises above its intrinsic value and the "greater fool" theory takes over. Those who play that game purchase shares in the hope of eventually selling at a profit to a "greater fool." Pity the "greatest fool"—the one finally left holding the bag. That is not a risk with which you need burden yourself.

Diversify

RULE NUMBER FIVE. Diversify. Spread your risks, for few "sure things" prove to be such. Someone once said that the way to make money is to put all your eggs in one basket and then watch that basket like a hawk. That's fine, as long as the stock you choose soars; as it does, so will your fortunes. The corollary, of course, is that if the stock plummets instead, your fortunes vanish. Even if you know a company intimately and its industry inside out, you still stand to lose, for luck is very much a part of the game. Too many things can happen that no amount of research will foretell.

Take microcomputer maker Commodore International. Its prospects in the much touted home computer field appeared bright in the late 1970s. Investors were eager to share in the bonanza, and Commodore looked like a good choice. Rapidly rising earnings propelled the shares from one high to the next, with the stock splitting five times in four years. A softer-than-predicted demand for computers for home use and competition from the proliferation of small manufacturers took some of the euphoria from the home computer market during 1983, and Commodore shares began their decline. From a June 1983 high of 60, the stock had dropped to about 6 three years later.

One young acquaintance of ours, in his enthusiasm for his own PC, put his entire $25,000 inheritance in Commodore early in 1983. The stock was then trading at 42; when it hit 60 he was elated. He had made $10,000 in just a few short months. When the stock started to drop, in spite of continuing earnings increases, he remained confident. The 1984 December quarter report released early in 1985 showed a sharp earnings decline; then our friend sold. The stock was selling at 13, and his inheritance was worth less than $8,000.

The lesson is clear. Even if you have only a little to invest, spread it around. Diversify your holdings to reduce the overall risk. If one element in your portfolio goes sour, the others should hold it up.

There are several ways to do it. One, of course, is to buy securities of a variety of companies. By choosing well-diversified firms you can spread the risk even further. Or you can buy mutual funds. Even here, you should diversify, buying several different funds.

Besides diversifying as to companies and funds, be sure to spread your investments over a number of different industries as well. Look for promising industries, though; don't buy into a dead-end field just for the sake of diversifying.

Your diversification will likely restrict your portfolio to an "average" or even "mediocre" performance. You will miss the thrill of instant riches. So also will you avoid sudden financial disaster. But you will sleep better at night.

So there you have the five key rules for successful investing. Here they are again, all in one place for your quick review:

1. Set your goals.
2. Buy the best-known companies.
3. Invest for the long term.
4. Avoid fads.
5. Diversify.

CHAPTER 29

How the Stock Market Works

ONCE YOU HAVE set your investment objectives and promised yourself to stick with the best companies, be patient, avoid fads, and diversify your holdings—that is, to abide by the five rules outlined in the preceding chapter—you're ready to start polishing your investment techniques. An understanding of the basic workings of the stock market and of your buying and selling choices within that framework is essential to your mastery of successful investing.

To provide that background, we shall discuss briefly in this chapter the various securities markets, the major stock exchanges, the types of orders you can use in executing your buys and sells, and, finally, some important considerations regarding the timing of your buying and selling.

The Role of Investment Bankers

When a company originally offers new securities for sale, it does so through the *primary markets*. In recent times, the primary market has been dominated by new bond issues, with a smaller ratio of common stock offerings. Securities are sold in the primary market either through private placement or public offering. In either case, the details are usually handled by investment bankers. Private placement is a choice made by the company for a variety of reasons; privacy, economy, and circumvention of certain registration requirements are the most common. Since there is no public participation in private placement, nothing more need be said about it here.

On public issues, investment bankers use three basic methods of bringing the securities to market: standby agreements, agency marketings, and purchasing-distributions. *Standby agreements* are usually employed when companies seek to sell more stock or bonds to their own security holders by way of a "rights" offering. Since most of the rights will be exercised, there is little market risk to the investment banker handling the details. But since the company wants all of the capital from the issue as soon as possible, it arranges with the banker to buy up any rights that are not exercised. The investment banker, in turn, will market those securities to the public.

The *agency marketing* procedure is used when the investment bankers perceive some difficulty in marketing an issue, either because of its size or because of its doubtful reception by the public. Or it might be employed because the issuing company is confident that the issue will sell and there is little marketing risk involved. In this instance, the investment banker may take an issue on a "best effort" basis. The bank will receive a commission on that portion of the issue which it makes its "best effort" to sell, but it does not actually buy the issue itself for resale. In effect, the investment banker merely serves as the "broker," seeking to match buyer and seller.

However, most of an investment banker's business comes from *purchasing-distribution,* where the banker buys the entire issue outright and resells it to the public. The banker then assumes the marketing risk associated with the underwriting. Sometimes a syndicate of underwriters is formed so that no single firm assumes full risk on the issue.

When you as an individual investor buy original-issue securities, you pay no commission on them; the fee has already been worked into the selling price. However, you are more likely to be buying "previously owned" securities than new issues. In that case, and likewise when you yourself sell any securities you hold, you'll be dealing in the *secondary market*. Trading in existing securities occurs in the organized exchanges and the over-the-counter (OTC) markets.

The organized exchanges are actually auctions where traders and investors negotiate by setting "asking" prices and making "bids" on thousands of different securities. The New York Stock Exchange (NYSE) is by far the most important of these auction markets. The annual volume on the NYSE is in excess of 40 billion shares. Other auction markets include the American Stock Exchange (AMEX), the Midwest Stock Exchange (MW), the Pacific Stock Exchange (P), and the Philadelphia Stock Exchange (Ph). The over-the-counter market is actually second to the NYSE in size, but it is a negotiated rather than an auction market.

The New York Stock Exchange

The New York Stock Exchange was formally established in 1792, though it was not known by its present name until 1863. Often called the "Big Board," it is a corporation with more than 1,200 members, each of whom has purchased a "seat" (membership) on the exchange. This membership gives its holder the privilege of trading on the floor of the exchange; no one else is allowed to do so. Members of the NYSE include member-firm corporations, specialists, floor brokers, and registered traders. Each type of membership is designed and regulated to assure the continuation of an efficient, liquid market.

Member firms are the various brokerage houses that do commission business with the public. Their seats are usually filled by general partners or holders of substantial amounts of common stock in the firm.

Specialists are the exchange members responsible for maintaining orderly markets in the stocks of specific companies. Each of the more than 1,700 companies listed on the NYSE is assigned to a specialist. Each specialist rides herd on a number of these assigned stocks, making sure to avoid excessive spread in the bid and asked prices in the auctioning process. In maintaining an orderly market for their assigned securities, the specialists may buy and sell for their own accounts. Their operations are governed by the statutes and regulations of the Securities and Exchange Commission (SEC) and the exchange itself. In addition, specialists execute orders that other exchange members have left with them. In this capacity, they are acting as brokers or agents.

Floor brokers help commission brokers when they become swamped with orders to execute. In this way, they protect the customer against the possibility of missing a market because of an overburdened stockbroker.

Registered traders buy and sell stocks strictly for their own personal accounts. The activities of these traders are monitored by the exchange, which requires that their transactions contribute to the market's liquidity.

In order for a stock to be listed on the New York Stock Exchange, certain criteria must be met and maintained. Among them: a demonstrated earning power of at least $2.5 million annually before taxes for the most recent year and $2 million for each of the two preceding years under competitive conditions; net tangible assets of $18 million, though greater emphasis will be placed upon the aggregate market value of the common stock; at least $18 million in market value of publicly held common stock; at least 1.1 million common shares publicly held; at least 2,000 holders of 100 shares or more.

The listing agreement between the New York Stock Exchange and the company is designed to assure timely disclosure to the public of earnings statements, dividend notices, and other data that can affect security values and hence investment decisions. A company is not guaranteed continued listing on the exchange.

AMEX and the Regional Exchanges

The American Stock Exchange had its start in the 1850s, though it was not known by its present name until 1953. Before that, its name was the New York Curb Exchange, reflecting its earlier history, when trading was done outdoors at a number of New York City street corners. The Curb Market moved indoors at Trinity Place in 1921.

The AMEX follows procedures much like those of the New York Stock Exchange, although listing requirements are not as stringent as those of the NYSE. Companies traded on the AMEX are generally less mature and seasoned than those on the NYSE.

NASDAQ: A Major Presence

In addition to these organized exchanges there is a huge and active over-the-counter market. It consists of broker-dealer members of the National Association of Securities Dealers, a self-regulatory organization and operator of the NASDAQ, an automated quotation system. In addition to the 11,000 or so "pink sheet" stocks that trade through the NASDAQ system, some 4,500 of the larger OTC stocks are listed on NASDAQ's National Market System. In recent years a growing number of securities listed on the major exchanges have been trading OTC as well. This so-called "Third Market" is being used increasingly by index arbitrage program traders to avoid the restrictions placed on such trades by the exchanges during periods of rapidly rising or falling prices. Securities are bought and sold over the counter on the basis of negotiated prices. The spread between the "bid" and "ask" prices represents the dealer's profit on a trade.

Listing requirements for NASDAQ's National Market System are: a net income of $300,000 in the last fiscal year or two of the last three fiscal years, public float (not including shares held by officers, directors, or other insiders) of 350,000 shares, a market value for floating shares of $2 million, and a minimum bid of three dollars.

A Central Securities Market

Since the early 1970s, the Securities and Exchange Commission has been moving toward the formation of a central marketplace. In 1975, Congress, by amending the securities laws, provided the SEC with the power to take the necessary steps to implement such a market. Congress's objective in ordering the changes was to increase competition among the NYSE, regional exchanges, and over-the-counter traders and to ensure that investors get the best possible price for their transactions.

In 1978 a pilot program was initiated. This Intermarket Trading System (ITS) linked the New York and Philadelphia stock exchanges for trading eleven issues. More securities were added to the ITS roster, and other exchanges joined the electronic network. In 1982, the National Association of Security Dealers (NASD) automated dealer trader system (CAES) was connected to ITS. By the end of 1989, the network linked eight markets and traded about 2,100 separate issues.

Twenty-four-Hour Trading

One by one the various securities markets have announced that they are in the process of developing expanded trading hours. First to announce the extended trading plan was the National Association of Securities Dealers. Its global electronic trading system—NASDAQ International—was scheduled to begin operations late in 1990. Trading would commence at 3:30 A.M. Eastern time in the United States. However, the start-up of the system was delayed by the SEC's requirement that greater disclosure of trading data be provided. The NASD program is designed to attract overseas traders who aren't accustomed to the stringent U.S. regulations. A pilot program may be allowed to operate for a year or so to determine the feasibility of a full-scale program.

The Big Board quickly came up with its own announcement of an after-hours trading system. A plan for a limited system is pending at the Securities and Exchange Commission. However, full implementation isn't expected before 1995. Eventually, the expanded system would allow orders to be entered all night, with computers matching buyers and sellers three times during the night, at 8:00 P.M., midnight, and 5:00 A.M., Eastern time.

Following this news the American Stock Exchange and the Chicago Board of Options Exchange, in tandem with the Cincinnati Stock Exchange and Reuters, released their plans to inaugurate nighttime trading, first in options and later in stocks. The start-up date isn't until 1993. The Chicago Mercantile Exchange and Reuters plan to name their system for trading futures after hours GLOBEX.

In addition to the SEC's concern about disclosure, some institutional investors worry about the liquidity and volatility of off-hours markets. Other money managers, who already invest globally, see continuous global trading as a logical extension of computer automated trading. But for individual investors, particularly those with long-term goals, all-night trading will have little significance. Investors worried that they might get caught by late-breaking news could protect their portfolios against market drops with stop limit orders.

The Gulf War stimulated overnight trading by institutional investors who do their buying and selling through the already existing third market system known as Instinet. This computer network, owned by Reuters Holdings PLC, allows buyers and sellers to anonymously negotiate trades.

Types of Orders

Investors have at their disposal several types of orders they can use in executing their purchases and sales of securities. A full understanding of the uses and advantages of these various orders can help you become a more successful investor.

The most frequently used orders are the market order and the limit order. When you place a *market order,* you are instructing your broker to execute the desired transaction at the prevailing market price. He is obliged to consummate the trade at the most advantageous price to you. This means that in the case of a buy order he seeks the lowest price, while in the case of a sell order he seeks the highest price.

Market orders are particularly valuable in that they are executed rapidly at a price close to the last sale price. This characteristic is particularly desirable in a rising or declining

market. In effect, this order protects you against the possibility of missing a market. The obvious disadvantage of a market
order is that you cannot be certain of the exact price at which
your order will be executed. This factor can be crucial in an
erratic market, because you cannot be certain that your order
will be executed anywhere near the most recent sale price.

Limit orders are used when you indicate to your broker
the price at which you wish the order executed. These orders
are placed "away from the market," in that the broker leaves
the order with the specialist assigned to the particular stock.
The specialist enters your limit order in his books, according
to the time he receives it, along with others left with him. If
the stock reaches the limit price, the specialist will execute
the order according to when it was received. Obviously,
some limit orders are never executed. If and when the limit
order is executed, the specialist informs your broker, who in
turn relays that information to you.

A limit order is useful because you can specify the price
"or better" at which you wish the transaction to occur. Issues
with limited markets and wide price spreads are the most
appropriate candidates for limit orders. Over-the-counter
stocks frequently display these characteristics.

The principal disadvantage of a limit order is that you can
miss a market completely over a fraction of a point. For instance, when an investor buys a cyclical stock XYZ Machinery at 100 and simultaneously places a limit order to sell
at 120, his order might never be executed, although the stock
could sell at 119½ or 119¾. Even if the price did reach the
$120 limit price, there could be insufficient buyers to cover
all the limit orders on the books at that price.

A limit on the buy side is always placed at a price below
the current market. A sell limit is above the current price.
When buying a stock that is moving down, you place the
limit in hopes of a better price. If the stock is moving up, you
use a market order.

When selling a stock that is declining rapidly, you would
sell at the market. But in selling a stock that is rising, a limit
order might get you a better price.

Several other types of orders are available, too. Although
they are more valuable to those who trade frequently or tend

to tinker with their portfolios than to those who choose good stocks and hold them for the long term, you should have some passing acquaintance with them.

Stop orders, or *stop loss orders,* specify a particular price at which a stock should be bought or sold. A buy stop is always above the current market and a sell stop is below. The buy stop—at a price above current market—limits the loss or protects a gain on a short sale. The sell stop—below market—protects a gain or limits a loss on a long position. When the issue reaches the specified price, the stop order automatically becomes a market order and is executed. But, as we said earlier, a market order is executed at the most favorable price near the last sale price, and there is a chance that when execution occurs, there will be a substantial spread between the execution price and the last sale price. A large backlog of stop sell orders can touch off a price break sharp enough for trading to be suspended.

Stop limit orders are a hybrid form of stop and limit orders. A specified limit is indicated that the buyer or seller will accept, should the stock reach the stop price. For instance, an investor wishes to sell 100 shares of XYZ Machinery at 90 stop, limit 89½. In other words, if the price of XYZ Machinery falls to $90 per share, his stop order becomes a market order to sell. But if the order is not executed by the time the stock reaches $89.50, the limit order takes effect and no transaction occurs.

Market-if-touched orders are similar to stop orders in that they become market orders if the specified price is reached. They differ from stops in that a buy market-if-touched order is set at a price below current market and a sell market-if-touched order is entered above the current market. The order is then filled at the specified price or the next best price to it.

Day orders are orders that are only good for one day. Hence, if it has not been executed, the order expires at the end of the day on which it was placed. All market orders, obviously, are day orders. Limit orders are also day orders unless the customer places them as open orders, which is usually the case.

Fill or kill (FOK) orders are price- as well as time-limited; if they cannot be filled immediately at the set price, they are killed and the current price level of the stock is reported to the buyer for reconsideration.

Open orders can be placed for a specified period or can remain effective until executed or canceled.

GTC orders (good till canceled) run indefinitely. However, the NYSE requires that all GTC orders be confirmed with the floor specialist on a semiannual basis. GTC orders pose certain risks, in that an investor could forget that he has them outstanding or they could be executed at a time the investor finds unsatisfactory.

Finally, an investor can place a *discretionary order.* In this case, the broker determines the timing for buying and selling as well as the selections and number of shares to be bought and sold. Under these circumstances, the investor is using a complete discretionary order. This order must be given in writing to the broker and then must be approved by an officer of the broker's firm. A limited discretionary order allows the broker to decide only the price and timing. In using discretionary orders, it is absolutely essential that the investor have an established and trusting relationship with his broker.

Special Timing Situations

There are times when the price of a stock is affected by the impending distribution of a dividend or stock right. Buying or selling at these times requires the consideration of information an investor does not usually have to evaluate. Take *ex-dividend,* a term we discussed in Chapter 5. As we explained, the declaration is the date a company's directors vote on the dividend. The date the checks will be mailed to shareholders is the payment date. The date a shareholder's name must be on the corporation's record books to receive a dividend is the record date. Finally, the ex-dividend date is the date that determines whether the buyer or the seller receives the dividend.

The exchanges and the over-the-counter markets have determined that investors must purchase a stock five business days before the record date to be eligible for the dividend payment. In other words, a purchaser of stock must buy before the stock trades ex-dividend in order to receive the dividend payment. Otherwise, the previous owner will receive the dividend.

When a stock sells ex-dividend, the market price will drop by an amount approximating the dividend. Hence a buyer will pay less for the stock but will not receive the dividend. Once the stock comes out of ex-dividend, the market price will rise to its prior level, other things being equal.

Should the investor buy or sell during ex-dividend trading? As an overall rule, it is best to execute purchases before ex-dividend trading begins. That way, you are entitled to the dividend payment. While the price will decline during ex-dividend trading, it will probably return to its former level shortly after ex-dividend trading stops. An exception is the investor in a high tax bracket. The lower price level of the stock trading ex-dividend is preferable to receiving the dividend, on which income tax will have to be paid.

Sales are best executed after ex-dividend trading, since the stock probably will recover the amount it declined during ex-dividend, and in addition you will receive the dividend payment.

When a company decides to issue new securities through a rights offering to its shareholders, it issues *stock rights*, also known as *preemptive rights*. These are short-term options granted to shareholders to purchase new stock issues, generally at reduced price levels. Stock rights are distributed to shareholders in certificate form. The shareholder can either exercise the rights and purchase the stock at the designated price or he can sell the rights in the open market. Rights are issued for common stock and debentures (especially convertibles). You can determine the market value of the rights with this formula:

$$\frac{\text{Stock Market Price} - \text{Subscription Price}}{\text{Number of shares required to buy one share at subscription price} + 1}$$

Hence, a stock selling at $30 per share, with rights to purchase one share at $20 for every three shares owned, means that the rights themselves are worth $2.50 each, or:

$$\frac{\$30 - \$20}{3 + 1} = \frac{\$10}{4} = \$2.50$$

An investor should exercise rights to purchase stocks solely on the basis of the prospects for the stock generally. The attitude that rights should be exercised because they offer a "bargain" is not valid, since the rights themselves can be sold.

The term *ex-rights* denotes when a stock is selling without rights, the rights having been retained or exercised by the seller. As with dividends, you must own the common stock before it trades "ex-rights" to be entitled to the rights. The price of a stock will also decline by the value of the rights on the day the stock trades ex-rights. Once a stock trades ex-rights, the amount of the decline is determined by the following formula:

$$\frac{\text{Stock Market Price} - \text{Subscription Price}}{\substack{\text{Number of shares required to buy one} \\ \text{share at subscription price}}}$$

Hence, in the situation already described, the stocks decline by a value of $3.33 when ex-rights trading begins. According to the formula:

$$\frac{\$30 - \$20}{3} = \frac{\$10}{3} = \$3\frac{1}{3} = \$3.33$$

A stock might sell at depressed levels throughout a rights offering, but normally it will recover after expiration of the rights. This period can be regarded as an attractive purchasing opportunity, providing overall prospects are sound.

Buying Low and "Taking Profits"

Fortuitous investment timing is probably an even more difficult endeavor than deciding what securities to buy. The most naive investor recognizes that the fastest route to stock market success is to "buy low and sell high." But even the most seasoned professional is hard pressed to pick market tops and bottoms with any degree of consistency. Experienced hands don't even try; they leave that game to novices driven more by greed than common sense.

They also know that when the market in general is down, even the bluest of the blue chips will likely go down, too. But because the decline is the result of a general market drop and not due to any fundamental changes in the individual company's stock, experienced investors recognize this as a buying opportunity, and they add to their portfolios accordingly. They know that once the market starts back up, the quality issues will probably bounce back faster than others.

So much for buying "low." What about selling "high"? If it is considered advantageous to put money into a good stock when it is down, then shouldn't it be sold when the market is up? Generally, we would say no. In stock market parlance, this is called "taking profits." Presumably, the reason you want to do so is to allow you to reinvest the proceeds in another stock, which you hope you'll be able to run up into a similar profit. How will you do this? If the market is "high," so then are most quality stocks. Putting the money into anything less would be like gambling. Putting the money into the bank while you wait for the market to go down again into a "buying range" would foreclose the opportunity for further capital gains should the market continue to rise. Not only that, in your profit taking you would incur a capital gains tax liability, thus eroding the real size of the gain.

If you want to sell a stock, do so because you question its long-term prospects, not simply because you have a profit. Or do it because you have an overconcentration in a certain area and wish to diversify your holdings. Or do it because you have some capital losses against which you can offset these gains and thus upgrade your portfolio.

Dollar Cost Averaging

You don't have to wait for the market to hit its low before adding to your investments. There is an investment strategy that will give you good results over a long period of time. It is called dollar cost averaging and it is a simple technique that sidesteps altogether the issue of market timing. All it

ABBOTT LABORATORIES

	Amount	Price (Adjusted)	No. Shares Bought
January 1975	$ 1,000	3	333.33
1976	1,000	6	166.67
1977	1,000	6	166.67
1978	1,000	7	142.86
1979	1,000	9	111.11
1980	1,000	10	100.00
1981	1,000	14	71.43
1982	1,000	14	71.43
1983	1,000	19	52.63
1984	1,000	22	45.45
1985	1,000	21	47.62
1986	1,000	33	30.30
1987	1,000	25	40.00
1988	1,000	23	43.48
1989	1,000	29	34.48
1990	1,000	33	30.30
	$16,000		1,487.76

1,487.76 shares times 44 (9/1/90 price) = $65,461

PHILIP MORRIS

	Amount	Price (Adjusted)	No. Shares Bought
January 1975	$ 1,000	3	333.33
1976	1,000	2½	400.00
1977	1,000	3½	285.71
1978	1,000	3½	285.71
1979	1,000	4½	222.22
1980	1,000	4½	222.22
1981	1,000	5½	181.82
1982	1,000	6	166.67
1983	1,000	7	142.86
1984	1,000	9	111.11
1985	1,000	10	100.00
1986	1,000	11½	86.96
1987	1,000	21	47.62
1988	1,000	21	47.62
1989	1,000	25	40.00
1990	1,000	40	25.00
	$16,000		2,698.85

2,676.23 shares times 45½ (9/1/90 price) = $122,798

requires is that at regular intervals you make investments of a constant dollar amount in a stock or a variety of stocks that have generally favorable long-term prospects. Your dollars purchase fewer shares when the market is up, but they buy more when it is down. Because the market is fluctuating a certain amount even during a period of relatively flat price movement, this technique can bring a profit. For instance, if you had put $1,000 each into shares of Abbott Labs and Philip Morris in January of every year from 1975 to 1990, the value of your holdings would be $188,259 in 1990. You would be $156,259 ahead of the $32,000 you had invested.

In Conclusion

Proper timing of your buys and sells can get to be a complicated matter if you let yourself become preoccupied with it. Obviously, you should give it some thought as you adjust your portfolio, but in general you should place greater emphasis on sound values. When you do that, it is almost impossible to lose over the long term. Good stocks go down with everything else in bear markets, but they tend to bounce back faster. We don't believe you will profit in the long run by jumping from stocks to cash and back to stocks again with the ups and downs of the market. The experience of mutual funds and major banking trust departments confirms the assertion that investors with the most money and experience tend to remain fully invested in the best stocks most of the time.

While you might be advised to lighten up your portfolio at critical junctures in the stock market, you'll find that if you stick with the best stocks they will rise more often than they will fall. This, over the long pull, is where your brightest profit opportunities lie.

CHAPTER 30

Capitalizing on Global Markets

THE STAFF ECONOMIST for *United & Babson Investment Reports* stated in one of his weekly "Economic Perspective" pages, "There is no turning back the clock on our growing interconnectedness in—and vulnerability to—the global village." In this age of technology, information speeds almost instantly from one side of the world to the other and back. Cultures that were once viewed as exotic have now become familiar, thanks to television. We see Russians lining up outside McDonalds, Cokes being drunk from Iceland to Fiji, and U.S. products in markets worldwide. TV also has brought the Middle East into our homes, with minute-by-minute accounts of the Gulf War. The flow of products moves both ways; U.S. consumers' appetite for foreign-made goods seems virtually insatiable.

How does the average investor prudently tap this flow of money and goods between the United States and other countries? There are several means open to the individual, some more speculative than others. Direct investment in foreign stocks is one possibility, investing abroad through American Depository Receipts (ADRs) is another. A somewhat less risky approach to participating in foreign markets is through mutual funds that invest in overseas companies. Holding shares of U.S. companies with large foreign sales is still another means of tapping economic growth abroad.

From Eurosclerosis to Europhoria

Just a few years back, Europe had been consigned to the minor leagues of national economic vitality. GNP growth during the 1980s had averaged only 2 percent annually in Europe versus 2.8 percent in the United States. However, three events now promise to accelerate that growth to about 3 percent, while in the early 1990s the U.S. growth rate has slowed to a sluggish 1.2 percent. These events are: the 1992 completion of the European Community market, the reunification of Germany, and reconstruction of Eastern Europe. The rebuilding of Kuwait and Iraq in the aftermath of the Gulf war should stimulate U.S. and European markets.

EC '92 has attracted the attention of investors, corporate boardrooms, and the press. There are, after all, 320 million consumers represented by the EC. Some of the largest U.S. corporations have been actively seeking a stake in Europe through mergers and acquisitions—Ford Motors bought British carmaker Jaguar; General Electric purchased a Hungarian light bulb manufacturer, Philip Morris acquired Jacobs Suchard, a Swiss firm and a leading marketer of chocolate and coffee. Investors were so eager for the single-country closed-end funds in the late 1980s that they bid the funds up to excessive premiums over their net asset values. However, this early "Europhoria" failed to take into account the major problems that still had to be overcome to transform Eastern Bloc countries from centralized to market economies.

Rapid Growth Ahead in the Pacific Rim

The rise of Japan and the "Four Tigers"—Korea, Taiwan, Hong Kong, and Singapore—was the story of the 1980s. In this decade, these nations will have to cope with the political consequences of their successful economic development and with the new "tigers" as they appear. Also, Asia has its own, darker version of 1992; 1997, when Hong Kong reverts to control by the People's Republic of China. Nonetheless, Asia will continue to chalk up the most rapid growth rates in the 1990s, probably double those in the more industrialized West.

Throughout East and South Asia, rising incomes have meant rising demands from the populace for greater political participation. Taiwan is moving slowly but successfully in that direction. Although the political transformation in Korea has been chaotic, U.S. interests in the region and the prospect of reuinification with North Korea should be beneficial. There seems to be little inclination for change in repressed but efficient Singapore. Funded by Japanese capital, Thailand was the region's and the world's fastest-growing economy in the late 1980s. However, because of rising costs and infrastructure problems in Thailand, the Japanese have begun to eye other areas for investment. As for some other Pacific Rim nations, political calm will be essential before economic development can proceed.

Buy American

One of the safest ways to participate in the economic growth of other countries is by investing in the U.S. companies that derive a significant portion of their sales and earnings from overseas business. In addition to those whose foreign sales are through export business, there are a number of corporations that have production and distribution facilities abroad. This eliminates the difficulties involved in surmounting trade barriers, which are more of a problem between the United States and a foreign country than they are from nation to nation within Europe or the Pacific Rim.

Coca-Cola, Dow Chemical, General Electric, International Flavors & Fragrances, and International Business Machines are but a few of the corporations with foreign facilities. The companies on the following list all derived at least 35 percent of their 1989 sales overseas.

U.S. COMPANIES WITH LARGE FOREIGN PRESENCES

Company	Foreign Sales/ Total Sales	Company	Foreign Sales/ Total Sales
Datapoint	86%	AMP	55%
NL Industries	80	Black & Decker	55
Microsoft	76	Dow Chemicals	54
Exxon	75	Boeing	54
Mobil Corp.	73	Merck	47
Int'l Flavors & F.	68	Warner Lambert	46
Coca-Cola	66	Minn. Mining	45
Measurex	63	DuPont	44
Raychem	63	Ford Motors	43
Amer. Brands	62	Pfizer, Chas.	42
Perkin-Elmer	61	Lilly, Eli	41
Gillette	61	General Electric	40
Millipore	58	Corning Glass	40
Ashton-Tate	57	Kellogg	37
CPC Int'l	56	Archer Daniels	37

Use American Depositary Receipts

Another way to tap the growth of overseas companies is through American Depositary Receipts (ADRs). Usually each ADR represents one share of the underlying stock, but in some cases it equals only a fraction of a share. There are ADRs now available on approximately 800 different companies, but that number should continue to increase. These represent companies from 30 countries, with the largest number coming from Australia, the United Kingdom, Japan, and South Africa.

The purpose of an ADR is to simplify foreign investing for Americans. The ADR is denominated in dollars, so dividends are paid in dollars, less any foreign taxes and fees. A non-domestic company interested in having its shares available for U.S. investors can arrange with a U.S. bank to act as a sponsor. The company pays the bank a fee for servicing its ADR holders by paying out dividends and forwarding financial reports to them. If the ADR isn't sponsored, the shareholder pays the fee, which is deducted from dividends. Foreign taxes paid on ADR dividend distributions by U.S.

citizens can be recovered by filing Form 1116 with Form 1040.

Although ADRs trade on several exchanges, the bulk of them are listed on the American Stock Exchange. In addition, a separate list of about 25 ADR quotes is carried daily in *The Wall Street Journal.*

Double Risk in Foreign Stocks

Foreign stocks also can be directly purchased by U.S. investors. However, these issues are denominated in the currency of the country where the company is headquartered. Quotes on the most widely held foreign stocks are listed daily under the country of domicile in *The Wall Street Journal.* These prices then need to be translated to U.S. dollars in order to track the current value of the investment. If the foreign stock declines at the same time that country's currency declines against the value of the dollar, the U.S. investor is hit twice. Thus, you face not only market risk but also exchange rate risk when you invest abroad.

Aside from the political instability of some foreign countries, accounting standards and financial reporting requirements vary widely from nation to nation. Regulation of the exchanges abroad is usually far less stringent than regulation in the United States. Rules on insider trading also may be more lenient, more as they were in this country several decades ago. Therefore, most individuals would do better letting professionals do their foreign investing.

Diversify with Mutual Funds

Open-end, closed-end, sector, Asian, European, global, international, and one-country funds—you name it and the mutual fund industry has it. Going the fund route for your foreign investing has many advantages. First, you tap the expertise of professional fund managements; second, you participate in a diversified portfolio, thereby spreading your risk; and third, you will be relieved of worry about exchange rates and foreign taxes.

By and large, the single-country funds are closed-end or publicly traded funds, which usually sell at premiums over the net asset value of the underlying portfolio. Investing in these means that you are concentrating all your money on the success of one economy. Frankly, we favor hedging your bets with a regional or worldwide fund. Moreover, we see little justification for paying a premium to participate in a portfolio. It does make sense, in a world that daily becomes more interdependent, to have a stake in the global economies. The following table lists load and no-load funds that invest worldwide.

GLOBAL/INTERNATIONAL FUNDS

No-Loads

Freedom Global Fund	Scudder Global Fund
Freedom Global Income Fund	Scudder International
MFS Lifetime Global Equity	Thomson McKinnon Global
Pru-Bache Global Fund	Transamerica Global Growth

Load Funds

Amer. Funds, New Perspective	Putnam Int'l Equities
First Investors Global	SLH Global Opportunities
John Hancock Global Trust	Templeton Global Fund
Lexington Global	Templeton Growth
Merrill Lynch Int'l Holdings	Templeton World
Oppenheimer Global	Tyndall-Newport Global
Paine Weber Classic Atlas	Van Eck World Trends

CHAPTER 31

How to Use Options in Trading

REGARDLESS OF WHAT may be written to the contrary, options trading is not an exact science. No amount of studying, charting, planning, or figuring will guarantee favorable results. By planning a carefully programmed strategy and observing a few rules, you can reduce your losses and increase your chances for gains. Options trading is less costly but more risky than investing in the underlying equities. The mathematically inclined may derive much comfort from setting up elaborate systems of charting and calculating options trades. For others, a more simplified approach should produce satisfactory results.

A few rules that apply to all types of options trades should be adhered to. First, diversify. Start out by limiting yourself to only one option on any one expiration date. Second, before making any commitment, set upper and lower limits at which you will cover. This will limit gains but, more important, will limit losses. Third, if you are a buy-'em-and-forget-'em type, go no further—options are not for you. Fourth, buy calls or sell puts only after several days of down markets. Conversely, buy puts and sell calls only after several rising trading sessions.

Buying Calls

The simplest option transaction to understand is the purchase of a call. Say, for one reason or another, you expect "ABX Corp." to rise in price. Your capital is limited, but you still want a piece of the action, so you decide to buy a call. This is the classic motivation for call buyers—leveraging their capital. The stock is trading at 65, but there are calls available at premiums of 13¢ a share (⅛) up to $15. Striking prices range from 50 to 75, and expiration dates are October, January, and April. (For a review of the mechanics of options, see Chapter 14.)

CALL OPTIONS ON "ABX" SELLING AT 65

Striking Price	Premiums on Options Expiring in:			
	October	*January*	*April*	
50	14⅞	15⅜	—	In the money
55	10⅜	11⅛	—	In the money
60	6¼	7⅜	8	In the money
65	3¼	4½	5⅜	At the money
70	1½	2½	3½	Out of the money
75	⅜	—	—	Out of the money

This set of quotations presents a wide range of choices. How should you decide where to put your money? There are rules that help narrow the choices. First, don't buy a call that is far "out of the money" (striking price above trading price). In the example, the price of ABX stock would have to rise 15 percent to reach the 75 striking price. Second, let time improve your odds by choosing an expiration date two to five months away. In our example, the January call series qualifies for this. Third, limit your risk by buying an option with a striking price not more than 10 to 12 percent above the stock price. In the example, the selection rules narrow the choice to the January 65 or 70 options. In the case of the January 65 call, the premium of 4½ represents time and is a pretty steep price to pay. The January 70 call will participate in any rise in ABX shares at a lower premium cost, and because of the leverage factor should produce a larger percentage gain.

By reducing the premium to a cost-per-week basis, you will have a better idea of the time value. Rather than reaching for the moon, you should decide beforehand that you will sell once you have a reasonable profit on the call. On the loss side, you should also make a decision to close out the trade when the premium drops below a preset level. In any case, it is always good policy to be out of the position at least a month before expiration. Remember that 70 percent of options expire worthless, so buying calls in expectation of a short-term profit is risky business.

Selling Calls

Why do investors sell calls? To maximize their return. In addition to obtaining dividend income, the seller pockets the call premium. Unlike the buyer, who usually buys calls on high-volatility issues, the seller chooses low-volatility, high-yield stocks. He is willing to settle for the smaller premium this type of stock commands in order to increase his return.

Since your objective as a writer is to increase income while retaining your stock, you will choose to write the option with the highest striking price if you expect your stock to rise in price. Your premium may be only $100 on 100 shares of $30 stock, but on an annual basis your income has been increased by $400, for a 13.3 percent return. Should you anticipate a drop in the stock price, you would get greater protection by writing the in-the-money option with the highest premium. A price reversal would mean you would lose your stock yet still make a profit.

An investor who does not actually own the underlying stock may sell what is known as a "naked call." This strategy takes courage, for the downside risk is potentially unlimited. The speculator in naked calls sells an option on stock he doesn't own but which he may have to deliver at a price well below the market. For example, a speculator sells a call at 50 on a stock trading at 48 and receives a $300 premium in return. The stock rises sharply to 58 and he is called on to deliver. He must purchase shares for $5,800 to deliver at $5,000. His loss is $800, minus the $300 premium, or $500. To prevent this type of squeeze, a simultaneous GTC (good till canceled) order is placed to cover the option if the premium rises to $600, limiting his loss to $300, the amount of the premium received when the call was sold.

Another means of reducing risk is to sell only calls that are far out of the money, where the stock is trading below the striking price. In the highly volatile markets of recent years, the odds against a seller of call options are very high.

Trading Puts

The put buyer expects to profit by a drop in the trading price of the underlying stock. He may make his profit by delivering his shares at a price above market or by covering the put. And he may be either long or short the shares, since the choice of whether or not to exercise is his. If he is short the shares, he will probably elect to cover, as it is generally more profitable. The long buyer is protecting his shares against a drop in price. If the market moves up, the put buyer's loss is limited to the premium paid for the option. This loss may be reduced by selling a covering put before expiration.

The put buyer has effectively locked in a profit—or limited a loss—at the exercise price. Unlike the placer of a stop loss order, which may be executed at a price lower than specified on the order, a put buyer is guaranteed receipt of the striking price at exercise.

The put seller agrees to accept delivery of shares at the striking price and receives the option premium in return. For an investor interested in acquiring a particular stock that he considers too high priced, selling a below-market put may accomplish his purpose. Suppose you like the long-term prospects of XYZ Industries but at 48½ think it is currently overpriced. You can write a put at 45, receive $200 in premium income, and if the option is exercised your shares will have cost you $4,300, plus commission. The shares will have been acquired at 10 percent below current market. Should the stock fail to drop below the striking price, you would not acquire them but would be ahead by the $200 premium income.

As a put seller, you should observe some very basic rules. First, be sure the stock is one you wish to own—and at that striking price. Second, be certain you have the cash or the buying power in your account to take delivery on the shares. Third, remember that if the stock drops in price and you have only the minimum collateral required, you could be faced with a margin call for additional capital.

Hedging Strategies

One of the most frequently employed strategies is the "straddle," the purchase of a put and a call on the same underlying stock having identical striking prices and expiration dates. In an uncertain market, this tactic allows the trader greater latitude for error. If the stock rises or drops substantially, he will be a winner. Sideways price action, of course, would mean a loss on both options. For example, you would buy a November 30 call on Volatile Manufacturing (market price 33) at 5 and a November 30 put at 1¼, spending $625 plus transaction costs. A rise in the stock's trading price to above 36¼ or a decline to below 23¾ would produce profit. In either case, one option would expire worthless, while the other would generate the profit. Obviously, in actual practice the losing side (leg) could be cut short by the sale of a covering option.

In trading straddles, you should choose stocks with a high "beta" coefficient—that is, those whose prices tend to be volatile. These issues have a greater probability of moving far enough and fast enough to make a straddle profitable. Choose options with striking prices close to the trading price of the underlying issue. Also select higher-priced issues, since the premiums on these usually represent a smaller percentage of the stock's trading price. You will also add to your chance for success if you place your straddle on an issue that has an established price range. For example, on a stock trading in a channel between 80 and 100, the options would be at a 90 striking price. An issue with a clearly defined resistance and support level gives you better odds for success.

Because stocks fluctuate, the straddler will generally have ample opportunity to cover both options at small profits before expiration date, particularly if the underlying security has a high beta. As a trader in straddles, you must keep on top of your investment at all times, making new moves as indicated by market conditions. At the point where the premium on either the put or the call leg is sufficient to make the entire straddle profitable, that leg should be sold out and the proceeds reinvested. This procedure is known as "leg lifting."

On the opposite side is a straddle seller, an investor who anticipates only a narrow movement in the chosen stock over the life of the straddle. As a straddle seller, you wish to enlarge on the premium you would receive by selling only a call or a put. Concurrently, you subject yourself to the risks of both positions. Should the stock break out of its trading channel on the upside, you will be forced to deliver your shares at the lower-than-market exercise price. However, since you retain premiums from both the call and the put (which has expired worthless), you have a greater margin for profit than with either option alone. If the stock drops, the call expires unexercised. But you will have to take delivery on stock put to you at the above-market strike price. Again, downside protection from a straddle is greater than from the put alone, reflecting the premiums from both options.

The further a stock moves in either direction from the striking price, the greater the amount of equity required in the margin account. A substantial cash backlog is a must for dabblers in straddles.

Spreads—Bullish and Bearish

Spreads may be accomplished using either put or call options. As a spreader, you would buy a call (or a put) and simultaneously sell a call (or a put) on the same stock, using options with the same exercise date and different striking prices to transact a price spread. For a calendar spread, you buy and sell options with the same striking price but different exercise dates. A bullish spread using calls might entail buying an at-the-money call (strike and trading price similar) and simultaneously selling a call that is out of the money. Should the stock advance as anticipated, a profit is made on the buy side, and the call that was sold is covered, leaving a limited profit. If the market drops, the call that was sold expires worthless, and the call that was bought may be covered to limit the loss, for a smaller loss on balance.

A bullish put spread requires buying a put with a striking price below trading price while selling one with a higher strike price and the same expiration date. When the premium on the long put (the one purchased) exceeds the proceeds from the one sold (short), the spread is termed a "credit"; the reverse situation results in a debit spread.

Price spreads that use options bought and sold with the same expiration dates and different striking prices are also referred to as "vertical" or "perpendicular" spreads. When the expiration dates differ, the spread is a "calendar," "horizontal," or "time" spread.

Bearish investors wishing to spread may do so with either puts or calls. Using calls, the trader inverts the technique used by the bull, by buying an out-of-the-money call and selling an in-the-money call. Should the stock drop as expected, the call that was bought expires worthless and its cost is deducted from the proceeds of the call that was sold. While this limits the profit when the market price of the stock moves as anticipated, it also limits the loss if the stock rises counter to expectations. A bearish put spread involves selling a put with a lower striking price than the one on the put that is purchased.

Since margin rules relating to puts and put spreads are complex, you should become well versed in them before using these strategies. A long put (one that is purchased) must be paid for in full and has no loan value in a margin account. Furthermore, to qualify for put-spread margin treatment, the long side must not expire before the short side of a spread. These and other special margin rules are explained in the prospectus of the Options Clearing Corporation, a document that your broker will furnish. One of the main advantages in using options is the additional leverage they provide the trader, so understanding the margin rules is a must.

Still another technique, called "ratio writing" or "variable hedging," involves selling calls on more shares than are actually owned. A ratio writer holding 100 shares of Cyclical Steel trading at 65 would sell one covered and two naked calls to gain greater income as well as greater downside protection. For example, he could sell three January 70 calls on his Cyclical Steel to receive a premium of $750 ($250 per call). This gives him downside protection to 57½ rather than to 62½ with one call. But a rise in the stock to above 70 leaves him vulnerable to three exercise notices and the need to satisfy them with 200 shares bought at the market. Even though his break-even point is 77½ on the Cyclical Steel, he would still face having to raise the capital to deliver the shares. The trader, of course, would cover before getting into this situation.

Covered Combinations, the No-Decision Strategy

This strategy is best employed when market volatility is high, which typically causes option premiums to expand. You don't know whether to buy, hold, or sell, because there is no clear indication of where the economy is heading. To execute this strategy to cover some of your blue-chip holdings, you sell a call with a strike price above the current market price while selling a put with a below market strike. Both have the same expiration date. If the price rises and the call is exercised you will have to deliver your shares. But you will have realized the market price plus the premium for a nice profit. Meanwhile the put will expire worthless. Should the market move down, you will be obligated to accept 100 new shares at the strike price. Your cost is the strike price less the premium. The call would expire worthless. A sideways movement in the shares would result in both options' expiring worthless and your profiting on both. The covered combination assumes that you are prepared to buy the shares when and if the put option is exercised and that you like the stock well enough to double your holdings.

Software for Option Trading

Evaluating options is a time-consuming, mechanical process that lends itself very neatly to the number-crunching skills of a computer. Because option software does so many calculations, these programs work faster when the computer is equipped with a math coprocessor. To get a worthwhile program expect to pay at least $300. Prices go as high as $2,000, but this is overkill for most investors. Two popular programs in the $300–$500 price range are *OptionVue IV* and *Options Valuation Model (OVM)*. *OptionVue IV* can evaluate a single strategy, several strategies with one or more limiting parameters, or all strategies. The evaluation can be given as a yield, annualized yield, and profit or loss. Results, which are displayed graphically or as a table, factor in transaction costs. Prices can be entered manually or downloaded from a database for either *OptionVue* or *OVM*. The less costly of the two programs, *OVM*, is available using either the Black Scholes or the Bookstaber pricing models. Both programs calculate theoretical market values for each option contract. *OVM* analyzes up to 12 different option strategies, with commission costs, margin requirements, and premiums either paid or received factored in.

Risk Versus Reward

The use of any combination strategy such as straddles, spreads, or variable hedges increases the cost of the transaction, thereby reducing profits. Furthermore, there are possible tax implications that should be taken into account before plunging. For example, buying a put in a stock you already own might change the long-term status of that issue. If the stock has not been owned long enough to qualify as a long-term holding, the purchase of a put would wipe out the time previously accrued toward that qualification. Until the put is liquidated, a new holding period will not begin. Conversely, calls may be used to turn a short position into a long position.

It is possible to provide considerable protection against investment risks through the informed use of options. But this is possible only if you have a complete understanding of the subject or have an investment advisor willing and able to guide you through the intricacies of the various maneuvers.

PART VI

Taking Care of the Housekeeping

CHAPTER 32

Choosing a Broker

BACK IN THE good old days, the broker you started with would probably still be handling your investments on the day you died. It was a lifetime decision, like choosing a family doctor, and one that could have considerable impact on your financial health. Today this decision is not likely to be so final. With the advent of discount brokers and brokerage-company mergers, lifetime associations with one firm and one representative are now a rarity. As a result, the criteria for selecting a broker have changed.

If you are starting your investment career from scratch, having never invested or had a brokerage account, you would probably like some guidance in developing a personal investment portfolio. In this case, an old-line, full-service company would be best. However, if you are planning to do your own research and require only efficient and economical execution of your orders, a discount brokerage firm would best fit your needs. It should be noted that these rules are not ironclad; today more and more discounters are offering expanded services, while full-service firms are extending discounted commissions to their clients. Therefore the best advice is to shop around, not only to get rate discounts, but also to fulfill your individual service needs.

Full-Service Houses

Obviously there are still legions of investors who are looking for service, the staple of the conventional brokerage firm. If you are looking for a company that will safeguard your certificates, forward dividend checks, execute specialized transactions, and service financial products such as tax shelters, IRAs, Keogh plans, insurance programs, and money-market funds, then a full-service firm is just the ticket.

A full-service firm will offer you all the above-mentioned services and will contact you from time to time to offer investment "suggestions." More stocks are "sold" to investors than are "bought" by them. Before acting on any of your broker's recommendations, you should be sure the stock he suggests fits your investment goals. Don't be sidetracked from your particular financial needs by the tempting visions of a quick profit, for these are few and far between and are seldom shared.

Speculation is no substitute for investment, and you should view with suspicion any broker who tries too hard or too often to get you to accept his profferings. Always keep firmly in mind that his motivation in persuading you to buy is not his desire to be a nice guy, but a piece of the commission you'd pay. On the other hand, a smart account executive is one who realizes he'll do best in the long run by giving his clients good advice and the kind of service they want.

Discount Brokers

Not all investors require the range of services offered by full-service houses. Many people don't see much point in paying for bells and whistles they don't use, so they use a discount broker, instead. These low-fee brokers now account for 25 percent of the $6 billion in retail brokerage transactions yearly.

Discount brokers came along when the Securities and Exchange Commission began putting on the pressure for negotiated commission rates. Until the mid-1970s, all brokers used a fixed schedule of rates, a situation the SEC regarded as a hindrance to free enterprise. It reasoned that if rates were unplugged from the schedule, competition among brokers would result in lower commissions. Despite its actual and philosophical proximity to the center of the free-enterprise system, the brokerage industry objected strenuously. The SEC proceeded in spite of the protests. Its first step was to rule that the commission on the portion of all trades above $500,000 could be negotiated. The limit was later dropped to $300,000. This did not help small investors, whose flight from the stock market had been a major factor in the financial straits that had beset many brokerage houses. So on April 1, 1974, the SEC started freeing up the other end. Trades of $2,000 or less were taken off the fixed schedule. Finally, as of May 1, 1975, the vast bulk of trades between these limits was included, and the move to fully negotiated rates was completed.

Did it help? Not much. In fact, in many instances investors found themselves paying more in commissions, as a percentage of the transaction, than they had under the fixed rates. Here is where the discounters emerged. By cutting out all extra services and by running tight, no-frills offices, they were able to offer substantial savings to investors seeking straight no-nonsense transactions. However, as a result of competitive pressures many of these discounters began to offer more than just transactions. Some will automatically sweep cash balances into money-market funds, service IRA and Keogh accounts, hold securities and collect dividend and interest, provide checking accounts, and provide 24-hour telephone service. Discounters who offer these extra services have had to raise their fees to pay for them. Thus, the distinction between these discounters and full-service brokers has eroded. Although discounters' fees are still only about half those of the full-service houses, there are deep discounters around who beat those prices by a good margin.

Deep Discounters

According to Mercer, Inc., a New York company that tracks 75 discount brokers, there are a number of companies around the country that still offer plain pipe rack brokerage business.

Deep discount firms are generally small, but their executions are comparable since they trade through the Individual Investor Express Delivery Service, which gives preferential treatment to individual investors. Not all of them are small. Fidelity Brokerage Services, a discount brokerage company, has started its own deep discounter—Spartan Brokerage. Just as full-service and discount brokers are covered by the Securities Investor Protection Corp., so too are the deep discount firms that engage in interstate business.

COMPARISON OF BROKERAGE COMMISSIONS

	Telephone	*Commission for 500 Shares at $20 Each*	*100 Shares at $30 Each*
Deep Discount Brokers			
Barry W. Murphy	800-288-1400	$31.50	$ 47.50
First National Brok.	800-228-3011	31.00	48.00
Kennedy Cabot	800-252-0090	35.00	50.00
Pacific Brokerage Sv.	800-421-8395	27.00	40.99
York Securities	800-221-2111	35.00	50.00
Discount Brokers			
Fidelity Brokerage	800-544-7272	48.00	98.75
Quick & Reilly	800-666-0388	49.00	84.00
Charles Schwab	800-832-5300	49.00	99.00
Full-Service Brokers			
Merrill Lynch		85.50	227.00
Shearson Lehman		75.50	237.75

How Much Should I Pay?

The developments outlined above are good news for you, for they place you in a better bargaining position. Full-service houses base their commission rates on the dollar value of the transaction. Their fees also reflect the overhead incurred by the firm in providing you with plenty of research material on specific stocks and industries. Even so, you still may be able to negotiate discounts with your account representative. Discounts at full-service firms will range anywhere from 10 to 40 percent depending upon how much and how often you trade. Also, the firm may offer a low minimum commission for trades of less than, say, $2,000. These fees are comparable to the price floors at discounters. The key to obtaining any type of discount or minimum rate is simply to ask for it.

Much like their full-service competitors, most discount brokers base their fees on the dollar amount of the transaction. However, some discounters base their rates on the number of shares of stock handled in a single transaction. If you buy and sell large numbers of high-priced shares, the difference between the two pricing methods can be substantial. The traditional dollar amount fee structure may be better for those trading in low-priced (under $40) shares. Oftentimes it is difficult to tell which pricing scheme a particular broker is using, especially since advertisements tend to focus on the most attractive schedules and rates. What you will want to do is study a number of brokers' commission schedules. Then choose the firm that offers the fee structure that best suits your kind of trading. Obviously you should shop around before deciding which broker to use.

Special Buying Programs

Many brokers, especially the conventional firms, offer reduced commissions through specialized investment plans. Perhaps the best-known of the brokers' specialized plans is the Merrill Lynch "Sharebuilder Program." This plan features discounts of 15 to 35 percent for purchases from a selected list of stocks in transactions of $5,000 or less. Dividends may be reinvested automatically as well. Some companies have reductions on commissions for "round-trip" trades; that is, on a stock bought and sold within 45 days, the fee for the sell side is cut in half. For an active trader, this type of account offers big savings, but for the long-term investor it is useless.

Some full-service brokerage firms and banks, which were allowed to establish or acquire discount brokerage operations beginning in 1982, have expanded their service lines to include overall money management. This smorgasbord of offerings includes free checking, low-interest loans, credit and debit cards, free travelers' checks, and consolidated monthly (and yearly) statements listing all financial transactions. Some cash management accounts require an initial deposit of cash or securities of $20,000 or more, others much less.

Two Groups Assist Individual Investors

The National Association of Investment Clubs (NAIC) is an institution that helps individuals to organize investment clubs and promote the principles of conservative investing. Investment clubs are usually composed of a group averaging 16 people who meet monthly to invest money regularly; they are not unlike a small mutual fund. The NAIC charges groups a nominal annual fee ($30 plus a $7.50 per member charge). It provides members with regular publications as well as low-cost investment plans that take advantage of dividend reinvestment plans offered by many corporations. In sum, an NAIC affiliation is an excellent introduction to the field of investments.

An organization geared to the individual shareholder is the American Association of Individual Investors. The AAII was formed for the purpose of "assisting individuals in becoming effective managers of their own assets through programs of education, information, and research." The AAII, an independent, nonprofit corporation, publishes a monthly investment magazine. The annual membership dues of $49 include the price of a one-year subscription to their investment periodical.

Making the Choice

If you live in or near a large urban area, you probably have access to offices of several of the major firms, plus some local firms. In deciding upon one, you can canvass friends and business associates who have had dealings with them. Your lawyer and banker might be able to help, too, particularly in providing insights as to the quality and extent of services offered.

It is not imperative that you live close to your broker's office; toll-free telephone numbers have eliminated that need. If you are a long-term investor, some distance might be advantageous, since it will tend to reduce the number of hot tips you receive. One advantage of a local broker is your ability to settle in person any problems that might arise.

Extensive comparison shopping is not necessary if you decide to go with a full-service firm. Their commissions vary little since they incur similar overhead costs. What will differ is the breadth of their product lines. Similarly, investors whose transactions are modest will find little variation in the commission rates of the major discounters. However, the more active investors, especially those with big-ticket trades, can reduce fees by dealing with more than one discount firm.

Whether you decide to choose a full-service or a discount firm, the broker should be a member of the New York Stock Exchange. You should select one that provides not only the $500,000 ($100,000 for cash) account protection insurance required by law through the Securities Investor Protection Corporation (SIPC), but also additional coverage.

Once you have made the choice of a brokerage firm and an account representative, you should take time to acquaint him with your investment goals. It is the only way he has of knowing your needs and how he can help you implement them. Don't hesitate to let him know exactly what you expect —and don't expect—of him.

Your next step will be to open an account. This involves filling out some forms, and there is not a great deal of difference from one firm to the next in what type of questions you'll be asked. But it's a simple process; opening a charge account at a department store is probably more complicated.

Besides supplying basic information such as full name and address, you will be required to give your Social Security or tax identification number. You will also need to instruct the broker as to how you wish him to handle your dividends and certificates and what type of account you are opening—joint, margin, or whatever. You'll have to provide the name of your bank and employer, too. For a margin account, you will have to complete and sign a customer's agreement and loan consent.

While you are completing the account forms, you may want to ask the broker about the bank from which dividends and other checks are drawn. Many brokerage firms draw checks on distant banks to take advantage of "the float." Until the check clears, which sometimes takes as long as a week, your money is providing the broker, the issuing banks, or both with an interest-free loan. Ask your broker to have your checks drawn on a local bank. Most firms are willing to do this. Once these forms have been completed, you will be ready to start on a new adventure in investing.

When You and Your Broker Disagree

If you have a problem with your broker that can't be settled between you, the next step is to escalate your complaint to the branch manager. He should be able to settle the dispute to your satisfaction. The firm's legal counsel may be asked to assist in reaching a mutually satisfactory resolution of your differences. Failing this, you may request that your differences be settled by arbitration. More than 2,000 disputes a year are handled by arbitration panels. The panel is composed of three members, of whom two come from the general public and one from the securities industry. About 50 percent of the cases settled by arbitration favor the investor. The losing brokerage firm must either file an appeal within 30 days of an unfavorable decision or pay the customer within that same period.

CHAPTER **33**

Safeguarding Your Securities

IMPORTANT AS IT is to select the right investments to meet
your financial needs, the protection of these assets once they
have been acquired is equally vital. The safeguarding process should begin even earlier, before any money has ever
been invested. Your choice of brokerage firm, how you elect
to have your securities held, and what records you keep are
all factors crucial to the safety of your investments. These are
also matters that can and should be decided before embarking on an investment program.

Holding Your Securities

There are four basic ways you can hold your securities.
You can obtain and safeguard the certificates yourself. You
can have them registered in your own name and have them
held by a bank, a lawyer, or someone else as custodian. You
can register them in your own name and keep them on deposit with your broker in a custodian account. Or you can
keep them in street name—this means leaving your certificates in your broker's name and in his possession.

Which way is best? The answer depends on your own psy-
chological makeup and the way you plan to operate your

brokerage account. If you prefer to keep a firm grip on your possessions, you'll probably want to take delivery of the certificates and see to their safekeeping yourself. This means you will have immediate access if you need them for such things as loan collateral. It also means some inconvenience, for you must be sure to keep them safe, preferably in a safe-deposit box at the bank. It means you must go down to the bank and remove them when you sell, then be sure they are safely delivered to the broker for transfer.

If you do a good bit of traveling or are away from home much of the time, you might wish to place them in your own name but have your bank or lawyer hold them for you. You might make such an arrangement temporarily if you go away on an extended trip. While you are away, you may effect a transfer merely by signing a stock power and sending it to the person or institution that is safeguarding your securities. Or you may sign a power of appointment beforehand.

Alternatively, you can have them registered in your own name but held by your broker. That way a sale can be executed by sending him a signed stock power. But in recent years, some brokers have experienced back-office logjams that have resulted in delays in obtaining certificates and even in lost certificates. Even though shares held by your broker in your name eventually would be returned to you in a brokerage house bankruptcy, there inevitably would be a delay. This could result in a loss of capital if the stock dropped in price before you were able to sell.

Street name accounts are popular with investors who trade their securities frequently. Shares held this way can change hands without being endorsed by the owner. However, besides running the risk of lost or mislaid certificates or bookkeeping mixups, in some cases you have no direct control over your securities. You would lose this control if you signed a hypothecation agreement, a document that gives the broker the right to pledge his customers' securities as collateral for loans the broker himself takes out. You need not sign such an agreement if you have a strictly cash account, but you must do so in order to open a margin account. Normally, such an arrangement would not cause any problems, but it could in a brokerage house bankruptcy. Thus, even with insurance against brokerage house failures, your street name investments could be tied up for a long time if something went wrong.

Are Stock Certificates on Their Way Out?

The SEC and the brokerage industry are seriously considering phasing out stock certificates and moving to a book entry system. The elimination of certificates would enable the industry to shorten the time period for settling transactions from the current five days to three days. The longer settlement period is necessary now because brokers must collect certificates in order to complete a transaction. It would be virtually impossible to go to three-day settlement as long as certificates were outstanding. Speedier settlements would reduce costs for brokers and create fewer liquidity squeezes on dealers.

Some in the industry are worried that such a change would drive the small investor out of the market. However, the Treasury has successfully weaned its bond, note, and bill buyers from certificates. Similar fears were expressed when banks eliminated passbooks for savings accounts. Those who fear that individual investors would not accept a book entry system overlook how pervasive computerized accounting has become. Moreover, certificates would still be available at a price for the diehards who cling to this evidence of ownership.

Does SIPC Protect You?

Creation of the Securities Investor Protection Corporation (SIPC) by Congress in 1970 was a boon to investors. Until then, when a broker went bankrupt it was catch as catch can for the investor whose securities were held in street name at that house. Under SIPC, brokerage accounts are insured for up to $500,000, of which $100,000 can be cash. SIPC does not protect customers against market losses from price declines, nor against a broker's fraudulent dealings.

An individual having several accounts with the same brokerage firm may or may not be covered separately for each account. For example, if you had an account in your own name, another as a trustee, and a third held jointly with your spouse, you would be covered to $500,000 in each. But if you merely had three different types of account in your own name only—cash, margin, bond, and so forth—coverage would be limited to a total of $500,000.

With the exception of those firms engaged solely in the distribution of mutual funds, variable annuities, insurance, or investment advice, all broker-dealers registered with the Securities and Exchange Commission must be members of SIPC. Funding for SIPC comes from assessments on member firms. It has accumulated a trust fund of $485 million and has a bank credit line of $500 million. The agency also may borrow up to $1 billion from the U.S. Treasury through the SEC. Once the SIPC determines that a brokerage firm should be liquidated, application is made to the federal district court for appointment of a trustee. The trustee, in turn, notifies all customers of the firm. Claims against the broker should be submitted directly and promptly to the trustee.

How well has SIPC worked? It was created at a time when a major shakeout was occurring in the brokerage industry. In its first 19 years of operation, SIPC has handled 212 brokerage failures, noncompliances, and so forth. Claims of $185 million have been paid to more than 200,000 customers. Experience shows that in segregated accounts, where the shares are fully paid and held in the customer's own name, restitution has been prompt. In margin accounts, the experience has not been as favorable. Margined shares are held in street name and may be held by a bank against a broker's loan. Thus, they might be sold off during a market decline to maintain the required collateral to cover the loan. This means that in a brokerage house liquidation, customers with margin accounts could be paid off in cash rather than securities. This, in turn, means they might have to accept a sizable loss. In addition, it sometimes takes considerable time to sort out the failing firm's affairs, and in a liquidation that occurs during a down or falling market—when most of them do occur—this can mean even deeper losses for the holder of a margin account.

For those with accounts in excess of the SIPC-covered amount, most brokers also have supplemental insurance coverage of $500,000 per account. If your account is in that range, make sure your broker offers the additional protection.

Good Records Are Important

Whether you hold your own certificates or they are held for you by your broker, it is important that you keep accurate records of what securities you own and where they are located. For each transaction you make you receive a confirmation slip, which carries all the information needed for your records and for filing your income tax return. The confirmation slip shows the number of shares bought or sold, the trade and settlement dates, price per share, total amount of the transaction, and the net amount. Because confirmation slips may get misplaced over the years, you should keep a chronological record of all your transactions. Certainly this record should list the number and cost of the shares held, the trade date, and the net received in a sale or the gross paid on a buy. If you hold your own securities, you should be sure to record the certificate number in case of loss.

Your broker will send you monthly or quarterly statements indicating the status of your account. These statements should be retained for a reasonable period of time, because they provide good records of your transactions. Another reason you should keep them is to provide you with corroborating evidence of a claim against the firm, either in a bookkeeping slipup or in the event of the firm's bankruptcy. Some firms include on the year-end statement the total margin interest charged to the account during the year.

Using Stock Powers

If you have taken possession of your own stock or bond certificates, you have the problem of delivering them to the broker when you make a sale. But you can safely do this by mail, using certain precautions. One way is to execute a power of substitution—a stock or bond power. Your broker, bank, or stationery store should be able to provide the necessary form. The power should be endorsed with your name appearing exactly as it appears on the face of the stock or bond certificates. No other information need be filled in on the power; your broker will complete it. After signing it, you will mail the power and the unendorsed certificate to the broker in *separate* envelopes. Another way is to endorse the certificate itself. You do this by affixing your signature and the brokerage firm's name in the appropriate places on the back of the certificate. An endorsed certificate should be sent only by *registered mail*. This is also true of bearer bonds— those that can be cashed in by anyone bearing them.

Although bonds now must be issued in registered form, previously issued bearer bonds are still outstanding. The cartoon of the rich old man sitting in a bank vault clipping his coupons is all but an anachronism these days. There are several advantages of registered bonds. For one thing, the bondholder's name is registered on the company's books, so interest checks are mailed directly to him. Notifications of calls, redemptions, and the like also are mailed directly to the holder. On the other hand, with coupon bonds he must watch for notices of such events in the financial press, since the issuing company has no other way of notifying him. However, if a bank or other institution is acting as trustee, custodian, or investment manager for him, it is responsible for keeping abreast of such developments. Registered bonds are not transferrable to another party unless they are endorsed. Bearer bonds, because they are so readily turned into cash, require special care in safekeeping.

When Certificates Are Lost or Destroyed

Replacing lost bond or stock certificates is a costly and time-consuming process, so a thorough and determined search should be made before initiating replacement proceedings. If certificates are destroyed in a fire or are stolen, it is possible that your insurance carrier may be responsible for underwriting some of the costs involved in getting them reissued. Be sure to check into this if you ever lose any this way.

Once you ascertain that a certificate is truly lost, not just misplaced, you should send written notification to either the bond trustee or the stock transfer agent. The trustee or agent will send you an affidavit of loss to complete, have notarized, and return. He then will place a stop on the security to prevent its sale. If you have been assiduous in your record keeping, you will have recorded the certificate numbers, which you can pass on to the trustee or transfer agent. You will be required to furnish a perpetual indemnity bond to protect the issuing company from loss if the certificate should subsequently appear. The surety bond costs 2 to 4 percent of the current face value of the security. Most brokers will underwrite the replacement cost for certificates that never reach the buyer. The issuer may impose other conditions before reissuing the certificate. Replacements should reach you within 3 to 4 months; until you receive them the shares can't be sold. If the original certificate does turn up within a year of purchasing the surety bond, half of the premium will be returned.

There are times when you must reregister a certificate. Again, it is the bond trustee or stock transfer agent who will make the change. The agent generally is a bank, but in some cases the issuing company acts as its own agent. The bond trustee will always be someone other than the company. In any case, the name and address of the agent appears in the company's annual report, and this would be another useful piece of information to add to your record book.

If your shares are held jointly as joint tenants with rights of survivorship, the survivor receives full title on death of the co-owner. Shares held as tenants in common have no such survivorship rights; the decedent's share goes into his estate. When the securities are held with survivorship rights, the survivor can have them reissued in his own name merely by forwarding a certified copy of the death certificate to the transfer agent. In some cases the transfer agent may require a residence certificate for tax purposes. It makes no difference whether the conjunction "and" or "or" is used between the joint owners' names, as long as the shares are held as joint tenants with rights of survivorship.

Are Old Certificates Valuable?

According to those who keep track of such things, five out of every hundred old stock certificates traced have some value. In 2 percent of the cases, the obsolete certificates have a worth of $1,000 or more. With odds like these, time spent doing some digging on your own or money spent on experts to do the digging for you can prove well invested. There are at least three firms that specialize in tracing old certificates: R. M. Smythe & Company, 24 Broadway, New York, NY 10004; Stock Search International, 1-800-537-4523; and Tracers Company of America, 39 Broadway, New York, NY 10006. If the shares turn out to have any value, you will receive information on how to collect. These companies are also useful if you should need to establish the date a security became worthless for tax-loss purposes. In the past, the Internal Revenue Service has considered them sufficiently authoritative to accept their information without challenge.

If you want to pursue the investigation on your own, your local library may be an invaluable source of information. Not all small libraries have an extensive business and financial section, but they might have arrangements with state libraries that can obtain books for you. Here are some books to look for: *Robert D. Fisher Manual of Valuable and Worthless Securities, Directory of Obsolete Securities, Capital Changes Reporter,* and *The "Questioned Stock" Manual. Valuable and Extinct Securities,* published by R. M. Smythe in 1934, might also be available.

Determining the value of old stock certificates is only the first step in receiving such windfalls. Not infrequently, they turn up in Great-Aunt Bessie's trunk, made out in her first husband's name. Before you can collect, you will have to establish your right to them. Of course, if they were issued in bearer form, it's finders keepers.

Should your old certificates turn out to be among the other statistical 95 percent—that is, they are worthless shares of a defunct corporation—don't be discouraged. Your search was probably worth the satisfaction gained in knowing for certain that you did *not* toss Great-Aunt Bessie's fortune out with the trash, and for the authoritative information you have collected for estate tax purposes. What's more, you may be surprised to learn that some antique certificates have value as collector's items—particularly if they are dated pre-1900, have decorated details and vignettes, or bear famous signatures. "Scripophily" is a growing specialty of the antiques and collectibles market. R. M. Smythe & Company is an expert in this area as well as in the tracing of a certificate's historical worth, and holds regular auctions in New York and London for scrip collectors. For the $20-per-stock research fee, Smythe provides a written appraisal of both the market and the antique value of the certificate.

Minority Shareholder Rights

Normally, a shareholder has the right to vote, to receive a portion of the profits, to inspect company books, to share corporate property, and to subscribe to subsequent stock issues. When a company goes private by buying up a majority of its outstanding shares, or merges with another company in an exchange of its stock for that of the acquiring company, usually 3 percent or less of its common stock remains outstanding. Owners of this remaining portion are known as minority shareholders. As a minority, they forfeit virtually all their shareholder rights. Numbers alone have silenced their voices. The best way to protect yourself and your investment against this problem is to avoid getting boxed into the position in the first place.

The most frequently given reason for getting into that spot is that the tender price of the stock was unfair. Yet the alternative to accepting the offer is equally unattractive—ownership of a batch of unmarketable shares. Attempts to obtain judicial redress are almost always unsuccessful. The usual court response to aggrieved shareholders is that they go through the appraisal system in effect in their state. This is frequently a complex procedure that yields varying results.

Just plain ignorance is another factor contributing to a shareholder's finding himself in a minority position. He received the tender offer but did not know what to do with it, so he ignored it. Most corporations make a concerted effort to buy back small batches of stock in such cases, so several offers are made before they close the books on such conversions. Once the major part of the stock has been tendered, the minority shareholder might as well face the facts—he is not going to get any more for his shares than the tendering holders received. If he continues to hold out, he might as well forget about dividends, too.

Shareholders occasionally have an opportunity to join in a settlement on a class action suit. If they held the stock during the critical time period, they should receive an application to participate in the settlement. However, unless they return the application by the stated date, with the required documents of proof, they will not share in the settlement.

Unless your investments are in a trusteed account or otherwise supervised, it is your responsibility to safeguard them, physically and otherwise. Although most publicly owned corporations will extend themselves within reason to protect and inform shareholders, it is up to you as an individual investor to read all company communications and take action when required. The small amount of time, care, and intelligence you must spend on your investments will pay off in the long run.

CHAPTER 34

Investing on a Shoestring

NOT EVERYONE IS financially able to invest a few thousand dollars at a time to buy securities in round lots. Fortunately, that isn't the only way they can be purchased. Several alternatives are available for the periodic investment of smaller amounts of money. Among the choices are monthly investment plans offered by brokerage houses, dividend reinvestment plans operated by individual companies, and mutual fund accumulation plans.

Besides these rather formally structured programs, you can, of course, design your own plan for making regular additions to your savings and investment program. You can have funds deducted from your salary and set aside for periodic investment. The bond-a-month payroll savings plan has proved a boon to millions in building a financial reserve of U.S. Savings Bonds. You can pick stocks in three or four—or a half-dozen—different well-diversified companies and by investing a predetermined monthly amount on a rotating basis build yourself a mini-mutual fund of respectable size in fairly short order.

The possibilities are endless, bounded only by your own imagination and desire to accumulate a savings and investment portfolio. We will discuss several alternatives in this chapter. One of these is the monthly investment plan offered

377

by many brokerage houses. These plans vary from one firm to another, but the concept is the same—to provide a systematic periodic method of building a stock portfolio. Generally, you're allowed to invest a regular monthly or quarterly amount in one or more stocks chosen from a list of 30 or 40 Big Board issues. Although there may be a discount of up to 25 percent from standard commission rates on these trades, the expenses can prove costly on small transactions. In addition, a small service fee may be charged. Usually a minimum of $20 can be invested.

Dividend Reinvestment Plans

Well over a thousand companies offer their shareholders the choice of having dividends automatically reinvested in stock instead of being paid directly to them. In addition, the plans allow cash to be added to the dividend to purchase more shares to build the pot faster. Many of the companies with such plans pay all or part of the commissions and bank fees involved. Others reinvest the dividends in shares at a 5 percent discount from the market price. Several companies have extended this discount to apply to shares purchased with shareholders' additional cash contributions. With a small initial investment to acquire a few shares through the customary channels, you can then enroll in the company's dividend reinvestment plan, add small cash infusions, and acquire additional shares at a reasonable fee or perhaps with no fee at all.

Here's how the plans work. Enclosed with your first dividend check should be application forms and information about the company's plan. Once you're enrolled, your dividends will be reinvested automatically in shares and fractions of shares (computed to three decimal places). Cash additions are generally limited to $20,000 or less a year, with a minimum addition of $10. If a pro rata commission is charged, your share probably will not amount to more than 1 percent of the amount invested. If a bank fee is charged it will be 4 to 5 percent of the invested amount, but only to a maximum of $2.50 to $3 per transaction. If you plan to make small cash additions, it would save on the bank fee to lump these annually or quarterly. Even after paying the bank fee and commission, your cost will be only about $4 per $100 invested, compared with the $7 or so it would cost by going through a broker.

To find out which companies offer such plans, you can ask your broker or check the Standard & Poor's *Stock Reports*, if your local library subscribes. Once you've zeroed in on a few companies that offer the plans, you can get the full details about each by writing the corporate secretary for a booklet. Your broker or the *Stock Reports* will provide the address.

Aside from being a painless and economical way to build a portfolio, dividend reinvestment plans have the built-in advantage of growth through compounding. From the initial investment forward, the reinvested dividends themselves earn dividends. This means that even if you do not add any more cash as you go along, your investment works harder for you with each passing quarter.

Participants in dividend reinvestment plans receive a detailed statement of their account after each investment is made. If you decide to make voluntary cash additions, you should send them shortly before the dividend payment date. Most companies accumulate participants' cash additions until collectively there is enough to purchase a round lot. That means your cash could sit around for a month or more without earning any interest.

Bank service charges are deductible for tax purposes if you itemize. Commission costs are handled in the usual manner by adding them to your cost basis. Even though the dividends are reinvested, they are taxable as income in the year received. In plans that reinvest dividends or cash or both at a discount from market price, the amount of that discount is taxable as income in the year received.

Mutual Fund Programs

Most mutual funds offer some kind of systematic investing program. In general, these fall into two types—contractual and voluntary. Contractual plans have earned a bad name with their front-end load. But some of the worst aspects were reduced with the 1970 revisions in the Investment Company Act. The plans work by committing an investor to pay a predetermined amount into the fund over a period of 10 to 15 years. Before the reforms were instituted, the unwary investor found that the lion's share of the load fee for the entire life of the plan was skimmed off in the first year. While this was wonderful for the salesman, it did little for the investor. Even with the 1970 revisions, the front-end load remains fairly heavy—as much as 20 percent of the first year's contribution can be allocated to sales charges, as long as the load fee is 9 percent or less of the total investment. In a 150-payment plan, more than half the total load is collected in the first 36 payments.

Operators of the plans point out that the penalty serves to encourage people to complete the programs. Furthermore, because a contractual plan is, in effect, "a letter of intent," the rate of the load fee could be lower than on a voluntary plan, if the total investment was large enough. The contractual plan offers the person who has trouble disciplining himself a form of forced investment program. Of course, there is nothing in the contract that requires completion of the plan, except the threat of forfeiting the large sales fee collected in the plan's early years.

Voluntary or systematic investing programs are looser than contractual plans. Often they are without any specified number of payments or amount to be paid. A simple notice is sent as a reminder at the appointed time. Terms and conditions of the various programs offered by a particular fund are set out in that fund's prospectus.

Stock Dividends and Rights

Another way to build your portfolio is to invest in companies that regularly pay stock dividends. By limiting your choices to such issues you could build a sizable portfolio in just a decade. For example, Archer Daniels Midland has paid a 5 percent stock dividend annually since 1977. This stock also split its shares three-for-two in 1981, 1987, and 1989. A

100-share purchase in 1980 would have grown to 574 shares by the end of 1990 as a result of the splits and eleven 5 percent stock dividends. Myers Industries split its shares two-for-one in 1984 and three-for-two in 1987, and paid a 10 percent stock dividend in the other six years from 1983 through 1990. A 100-share purchase in 1983 would have increased to 531 shares by the end of 1990.

Adding the small amount of cash required to exercise rights is another means of increasing your holdings. Rights offerings are a common method of raising capital in the utility industry. In the last few years, American Electric Power has offered shareholders rights on a 1-for-10, 1-for-9, 1-for-11, and 1-for-15 basis. Shares acquired through rights are free of commissions, and prices are under the market. In a six-year period, the owner of 100 shares of American Electric Power would have added close to 60 more shares if all rights had been exercised.

The Magic of Tax-Deferred Compounding

When you tuck money away toward retirement in tax-deferred investments, you win two ways. The first is through the magic of compounding—a phrase attributed to economist John Maynard Keynes. The second derives from the fact that earnings on the investment aren't taxed until they are withdrawn. Even after you retire and begin tapping your investment, the remaining funds continue to grow tax-free.

The chart on page 382 clearly illustrates how compounding increases the value of your investment. But, when investment earnings also are tax-deferred, the growth is even more dramatic. Our $2,000 is invested at a modest 6 percent, yet it grows at a compound rate of 13.2 percent annually, when held 25 years in a tax-deferred plan. A comparable fully taxable investment would grow only 7.5 percent annually after 25 years. Only a few tax-deferred investments are available; among them are commercial deferred annuities, EE Savings Bonds, and deductible and nondeductible IRA accounts. Each of these quite dissimilar investments has its own advantages and disadvantages. Their common attribute is that the earnings accrue tax-deferred until they are redeemed or transferred. EE bonds are discussed in the following paragraphs, while annuities and IRAs are covered in later chapters.

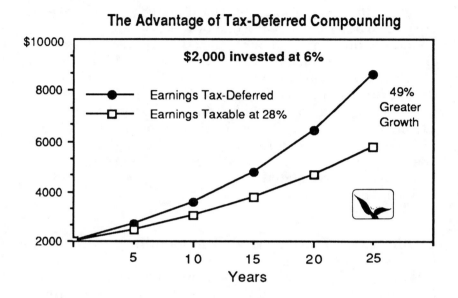

The Advantage of Tax-Deferred Compounding

$2,000 invested at 6%

— ● — Earnings Tax-Deferred
— □ — Earnings Taxable at 28%

49% Greater Growth

Years

U.S. Savings Bonds

Until now, this chapter has discussed alternative methods of acquiring and building assets with marketable securities. However, as a supplement to stocks, bonds, and mutual funds, well-rounded financial plans often include nonmarketable investments such as U.S. Savings Bonds, savings time deposits (time certificates), and annuities. While it is not always possible to adhere to a regular investment program, serial purchase has the advantage of producing income on a monthly or quarterly basis when the bonds are redeemed after your retirement. We provide an example of this type of purchase and redemption program using Savings Bonds in a later chapter.

U.S. Savings Bonds, in fact, should not be overlooked as you consider investment alternatives. Though these are snubbed by "sophisticated" investors, the Treasury sells around $8 billion worth of EE bonds annually. Their popularity lies in their safety, convenience, low denominations, state and local tax exemption, fair rate of return, and ease of their cost-free purchase and redemption. More than two-thirds of sales are made on payroll deduction plans, with close to 10 million workers enrolled in such a plan. To enroll, a worker need only agree to invest $50 or more per investment period.

Series EE bonds replaced Series Es, which were no longer marketed after 1979. EEs are priced at 50 percent of their face value. In the past, the term to maturity varied according to what interest rate the government wished to pay. In 1982, Congress authorized the Treasury to periodically change the interest rates on EE bonds. Although the interest is adjustable, it can't be reduced below the guaranteed minimum rate at the time of purchase on bonds held five years. That minimum on bonds sold since November 1, 1986, is 6 percent. Every six months the EE bond rate is adjusted to equal 85 percent of the average yield on five-year Treasury notes. Series EE bonds are issued in denominations of $50 to $10,000.

You need not redeem Series E or EE bonds at maturity; they shift automatically into an extension period. However, all EE bonds reach final maturity after 30 years. E bonds issued up to November 1965 have a 40-year life; those issued after that time reach final maturity in 30 years. Once a bond reaches its final maturity, it no longer earns interest. If you wish to avoid paying taxes on the accrued interest, matured E or EE bonds can be exchanged for Series HH bonds, which pay currently taxable interest.

The stated return on Series E and EE bonds is an average return; in the early years it is well below the guaranteed rate, thus providing an incentive to hold them at least to maturity. The income generated by Savings Bonds is subject to federal income taxes, but not to state and local taxes. On Series E and EE bonds, interest is compounded semiannually but is not actually paid until the bonds are redeemed. Likewise, tax on that interest need not be paid until it is actually received. Hence, a Series E or EE bond is a means of deferring income taxes and qualifies as a "tax shelter." However, if you desire, you may pay the tax on the interest annually as it accrues.

The tax liability on accrued interest is an important factor in deciding what to do with bonds that you have held for a number of years. By cashing them in, you could subject yourself to a large tax bite. If after retirement you expect your tax bracket will drop, waiting until then to cash your Savings Bonds makes sense. There's another way to do it and continue to defer the tax on your stored-up interest. That is to exchange the E or EE bonds for HH bonds.

The main difference between EE bonds and HH bonds is that the latter pay interest currently, rather than compounding it. They don't necessarily pay the same amount of interest, either. As with Series EE bonds, interest on HH bonds is less than the stated rate when these bonds are redeemed in the first five years of their life. Today these bonds are only available in exchange for E or EE bonds having a total redemption value of at least $500. HH bonds mature in 10 years, but are guaranteed to pay interest for 20 years. Interest on them is paid by electronic funds transfer semiannually and is taxable in the year paid. However, the tax on the accrued interest on any E or EE bonds exchanged for HH bonds is not payable until the latter are sold, disposed of, or have reached final maturity. Denominations for HH bonds are $500, $1,000, $5,000, and $10,000.

Since Savings Bonds are registered securities, no one but the actual owner may cash them. This also means they can be replaced if lost or destroyed. To replace bonds, write the Bureau of the Public Debt, Parkersburg, WV 26106-1328. Provide as much information as possible about the missing bonds—their registration numbers, date and place of purchase, names and addresses of owners, and the like.

Savings Bonds are not transferrable or acceptable as collateral on loans. Partial redemption of E bonds of over $25 face value, EE bonds of over $50, or H-type bonds of over $500 is allowed; the reissued portion will carry the original issue date. Smaller denominations may be exchanged for bonds of larger denominations only when you are making another change, such as a revision in ownership form or name. Again, the original issue date is applied to the reissued bonds.

Redeeming a bond you own is almost as easy as buying

one. All you need is your signature and proper identification. On an E or EE bond, you will get your proceeds on the spot. H or HH bonds may be redeemed at a Federal Reserve Bank or branch office. Your signature must be certified by a qualified agent. The bonds then are forwarded to the Treasury for payment.

When a more complicated transaction is involved, such as changing the name of a beneficiary, adding the name of a co-owner, or changing the name on inherited bonds issued in a decedent's name, you will have to furnish certain documents. These changes cannot be made on the spot. Instead, the bond must be sent to a Federal Reserve Bank or the Treasury for payment or reissue.

Other U.S. Obligations

Other U.S. Treasury and agency securities are not as elaborately packaged for consumption by the general public. In fact, most members of that public rarely trade them, even though they often yield more than Savings Bonds. However, if you do decide that your program could use some "Governments," there are four ways you can buy them and three ways you can sell them.

For most investors, the most convenient channel for buying and selling is through a local bank. Bank fees vary but generally amount to a flat charge of $20 or $30, plus mailing expenses, per transaction for amounts up to $100,000, and an added fee of around $5 per $100,000 above that.

Alternatively, your broker can handle the business for you. Here again, the expenses vary widely, so it's best to inquire beforehand. Some brokers will fill the order on a net basis, that is, charge the asked price and derive the "commission" from the spread between the bid and asked price. Others charge a flat fee of, say, $25 plus another $25 if you want the bonds delivered to you rather than being kept by the broker.

For the investor who buys in round lots ($100,000 or more), a dealer in government bonds will charge the asked price and receive as his compensation the spread between the bid and asked price, just as is done by some brokers.

On new issues, you can buy directly from the Federal Reserve Bank in your district. Your order must be received by the stated deadline, accompanied by certified or cashier's check (or cash, if you go in person) to cover the amount of the offering price. There is no commission involved and the transaction can be handled entirely by mail. Contact your nearest Federal Reserve Bank for the necessary forms and information.

Thus, you can buy government securities from a bank, a broker, a bond dealer, and the Federal Reserve Bank. You can sell or redeem them through a bank, broker, or dealer, but not through the Federal Reserve Bank. However, you can "roll over" maturing Treasury securities into newly issued ones through the Federal Reserve Bank.

Are Your Savings Safe?

Although the sagging real estate market has caused problems for some banks as loans go sour, banks are on a far sounder footing than the savings and loan industry. Bank regulation is tighter and banks' capital reserves are higher. Because bank assets are shorter term than assets in the thrift industry, they are better able to balance borrowing and lending rates. The problems that have developed in the banking industry have depleted the Federal Deposit Insurance Corporation's insurance fund. FDIC reserves as a percentage of insured deposits are at a record low. In addition to the $13.2 billion in reserves, the FDIC can borrow up to $5 billion from the Treasury, a source it may have to tap.

Members of Congress are drafting or have submitted legislation calling for increases in the insurance premiums paid by banks, higher capital requirements, and tighter regulation. Although there is talk of reducing the amount of insurance coverage on deposits, any such reduction could only be implemented after a reasonable transition period. Deposit insurance coverage has been extended beyond the $100,000 limit beginning with the 1984 bailout of Continental Illinois. Since then it has been regularly broadened to cover institutional investments, pension fund deposits, and Bank Investment Contracts. By adhering strictly to its intended limits, the FDIC could improve or at least not worsen its reserve position. Your savings account is still insured for up to $100,000 as long as the bank is FDIC-covered. Nonetheless, it behooves you to put your savings in a bank with a conservative investment policy. Avoid those that offer well-above-average interest rates, because higher rates mean higher risk.

CHAPTER 35

Tax Pointers for Investors

WHEN IT COMES to tax laws, Congress is an inveterate tin-kerer. It is constantly adjusting, dismantling, and reas-sembling; adding new gadgets, altering old ones, and "reforming" rules that are "unfair." Yet it rarely succeeds in simplifying, even when it deliberately sets out to do so, as it did with the Tax Reform Act (TRA) of 1986. The key words in selling yet another "reform" were *fair* and *simple*. Did the final product, more than two years in the making, turn out to be either? Your opinion depends on how the 1,700-page act treated you. It was certainly "simpler" for those who were relieved of filing the long form. It was "fairer" for those whose tax bracket dropped to 15 percent. But for owners of burnt-out tax shelters or rental property producing passive income, TRA '86 complicated the filing process and elimi-nated write-offs. Owners of small businesses, the self-employed, parents of children having investment income, and investors in tax-deductible IRAs could certainly ques-tion both the simplicity and fairness of this monumental piece of legislation.

More Tax Changes

As long as Congress's appetite for spending continues, so too will it continue to seek ways to increase revenues through taxes. In each year since the passage of TRA '86, Congress has enacted a new law incorporating tax revisions. The Revenue Act of 1987 was no exception. The following changes affecting individuals were included: a limit on the amount of mortgage indebtedness that qualifies as deductible interest and a postponement to 1993 of the lowering of the maximum estate and gift tax rate to 50 from 55 percent. This law also addressed the problems faced by the Pension Benefit Guaranty Corp. (PBGC), by strengthening funding rules for defined-benefit plans and by nearly doubling the premium paid by plans.

In 1988, the Technical and Miscellaneous Revenue Act (TAMRA) was passed. TAMRA included a section on taxpayers' rights, which provided for an ombudsman and clarified penalties and assessments. Home office deductions were cut back and mutual fund expense deductions rules (so-called phantom income) were changed once again. TAMRA broadened the occupancy rules applicable to the over-55 exclusion and the nonrecognition of gain on the sale of a home. Moreover, it provided an interest exemption for Savings Bonds that are used to pay the costs of higher education, when the conditions of the exemption are met.

Congress enacted the Revenue Reconciliation Act and the Medicare Catastrophic Coverage Repeal Act in 1989. The latter relieved older (over the age of 64) filers of the involved reporting requirements and added costs imposed under the Medicare Catastrophic Coverage Act. The Revenue Reconciliation Act reduced the tax benefits of modified endowment contracts and other investment-oriented life insurance products. This law also dealt with tax compliance, penalties, and filing requirements. It repealed unenforceable nondiscrimination rules (Code Section 89) for employer-provided health care and group term life insurance coverage. The 1989 law allowed parents the choice of reporting their children's investment income on their own return or on a separate return for each child. But it required that a Social Security number be included for any dependent claimed who was at least two years old at the end of the tax year.

The Revenue Reconciliation Act of 1990 was finally passed after protracted battles in both houses of Congress. This act increased the number of tax rates from two (plus a 5 percent "bubble") to three. The three rates are 15, 28, and 31 percent. Taxpayers in the top 31 percent bracket with adjusted gross incomes (AGI) over $100,000 for single filers and $150,000 for joint filers lose part of their personal exemption(s). Regardless of filing status, taxpayers also lose $300 of deductions for every $10,000 of AGI over $100,000 for tax years 1991 through 1995. In addition, the 1990 act capped the rate for capital gains at 28 percent and increased the rate for the alternative minimum tax to 24 from 21 percent.

Once a new tax act is written, it goes through a year or so of settling, during which time its flaws become glaringly apparent. Congress then attempts to remedy the errors by passing a technical corrections act. In other words, there is seldom a time when tax law status quo is reached. As a result, investors are always making financial decisions on the basis of tax law that is either outmoded or soon to be so. For this reason, unless yours is the simplest of investment programs, you should probably seek the advice of a qualified professional to help you map tax strategies that mesh with and enhance your investment goals and personal financial plan. However, to get you started, here are five basic rules.

Don't Let the Tax Tail Wag the Investment Dog

The cardinal rule is to let the basic validity of the investment itself be the deciding factor in whether to acquire, hold, or sell. Thus, tax considerations should always play a secondary role in your decision. But once an investment decision has been made, you should examine its tax consequences. The Revenue Reconciliation Act of 1990 restored a modest differential between the capital gains tax rate and the top rate on other income, capping that rate at 28 percent. Timing the sale of securities can also be beneficial, with both long- and short-term gains taxed at 28 percent.

Capital gains and losses are netted, and net losses (both short and long) can be used to offset up to $3,000 of ordinary income, dollar for dollar. Any excess losses may be carried forward to be used in a later year. The old adage about taking losses and letting gains run is now good investment advice as well as good tax advice.

Give Uncle Sam His Due

Many investors who have enjoyed substantial capital appreciation on well-chosen securities are reluctant to cash in on these profits because of the tax liability involved. A large profit—even one in which Uncle Sam shares—is better than a smaller profit later (he'd get a piece of that, too) and infinitely preferable to a loss. When it's time to sell, sell—and give Uncle Sam his due!

As noted previously, you can blunt the tax effects of a substantial capital gain. Any capital losses taken in the same tax year or carried over from a previous year can be used to offset the gain, dollar for dollar. Thus, you can use the gain as an opportunity to weed out your portfolio by selling off investments in which you're showing losses and which should be unloaded anyway.

Suppose you took a flier on a "sure thing" last year and it has done so poorly you want to dump it. You also hold a blue chip that has been growing steadily for years and you have no intention of selling it. Why not use the loss as an opportunity to raise your cost basis in the blue chip? Sell the "sure thing" and at the same time sell an equivalent dollar amount of the blue chip. But while you're transacting that business, instruct your broker to replace the shares of the blue chip with an equivalent number. Not only does this strategy offset the tax-deductible loss with a taxable gain, but also it lowers the taxable gain on the blue-chip shares when they are sold by reducing their cost basis.

Don't Go to the Showers on a "Wash Sale"

Many investors play losses against gains by selling a position to establish a loss, then buying the shares back because they believe in the long-term soundness of the investment. That's fine, as long as you don't run afoul of the 30-day repurchase limitation, the so-called wash sale rule. That rule prohibits you from claiming a loss on any security that you've replaced with a substantially identical security within 30 calendar days before or after the sale of your original holding. The wash sale rule applies only to losses; you can repurchase immediately before and after establishing a gain.

Remember, the wash sale rule applies on either side of a loss sale. You may sell your holding first, then wait the 31 days to buy the replacement shares, or you may buy the replacements first, and then sell the original holding after the appropriate period has passed. The date of the sale is the date the loss is established. The wash sale rule applies even if the maneuver spills over from one tax year to the next. This has useful implications, for it means that with proper forethought you can establish a loss toward the end of the year or delay taking it until the start of the next, depending on which would be more advantageous for tax purposes.

Another point that's important to remember about the wash sale rule is that it may apply to more than the common stock itself. The rule says "substantially identical" securities, and this can mean the common stock, warrants, or options on the common. It can mean bond issues sold by the same company that have similar yields and maturities, even if the bonds are from a different issue. However, you probably would not run afoul of the wash sale rule if you sold common stock and bought bonds or preferred stock in the same company within the 30-day period, as long as these were not convertible into the common.

In fact, that is one way to avoid problems with the wash sale rule if you want to establish a loss yet retain a position in the company. Another way is to sell the securities to establish the loss, then buy a similar position in another company within the same industry group that possesses investment attributes similar to the stock you sold.

Don't Trip Over the Calendar

Much portfolio adjusting is done toward the end of the year as investors obtain a clearer picture of their gain-loss situation. If you do this, keep one eye on the calendar.

If you're a cash basis taxpayer, as most individuals are, you can sell a stock any time to the last day of the year to establish a loss. But to establish a gain, you have to sell at least five business days before the end of the year to allow the transaction time to clear. You have to watch the calendar, too, to avoid problems with the wash sale rule discussed above.

Don't Compare Stock Loss Apples with Tax Saving Oranges

Remember, a $1,000 loss does not mean a $1,000 saving on your income tax. If you're in the 28 percent tax bracket, it means a $280 savings; in the 15 percent bracket, a $150 savings.

Year-End Tactics

As the tax year draws to a close, you may be in the enviable position of owning shares that have appreciated substantially, but that you think are due for a correction. You would like to lock in the gain but defer the tax liability to the following tax year.

You can do this by "selling short against the box" in the current year, while delivering the shares in the following year. The holding period ends at the time of the sale, but the gain is not realized until the shares are delivered. For example, you sell 100 XYZ short on December 20 but don't deliver your shares (to close the short sale) until January 30 of the next year. Your tax liability is incurred on the latter date.

Buying a put on shares you hold at a profit is another means of locking in the gain while delaying the tax bill. As with a short sale, the holding period for the underlying stock ends with the purchase of the put. Your gain is reduced by the cost (premium) on the put, but should the stock go up in price, contrary to your expectations, you share in that gain. For example, you hold XYZ at a cost of $25, and it is trading at $50. In December, you buy a February 50 put for $3. If the stock drops to $45, you exercise your put and realize a gain of $22 ($50 − $25 − $3). If the stock rises to $60, your put expires worthless, giving you a $3-per-share short-term loss on the put. Your shares may then be sold for $60, giving you a $35-per-share gain.

Tax-Wise Charitable Donations

Gifts to charities are tax-deductible for taxpayers who file the long form (1040). However, there are some limitations on the type and amount of a gift that can be claimed as a donation in any one year. Understanding the tax rules that govern charitable donations and abiding by them will help you avoid having a charitable deduction disallowed.

Before making a sizable gift to a charity, be absolutely certain that the donee organization is truly tax-exempt. The following types of charities are qualified: The United States; states and other governmental units; religious, charitable, scientific, literary, and educational organizations; veterans' organizations; domestic fraternal organizations; and volunteer fire companies (Code Section 170[c][2]). Additional confirmation of exempt status can be obtained by checking the *Cumulative List of Organizations*, published periodically by the IRS. You should also request an affidavit from the charitable recipient confirming its tax-exempt status.

There are limits on the amount that can be deducted. The deduction limit is determined by the type of charity that is to receive the donation, the form of the donation, and how the donation is made—whether it is "to" or "for the use of" the charity. Gifts of cash or income property made "to" a *public* charity are deductible up to 50 percent of adjusted gross income (AGI). *Public* charities include the Red Cross, United Way, your church or college, and public broadcasting or television stations.

When cash or income property is donated to a *semipublic* charity (veterans' organization, fraternal group, nonprofit cemetery association, and so forth), the deduction is limited to 30 percent of AGI. The deduction limit for gifts to *private* charities is 20 percent of AGI. *Private* charities are defined as organizations that are neither operating nor distributing foundations or that don't maintain a common fund.

Gifts "for the use of" a charity are deductible only to 30 percent of AGI. A charitable donation of an income interest in an asset is an example of a gift made "for the use of" a charity. Gifts of appreciated property can be claimed only up to 30 percent of AGI. If monies are donated to all three types of organizations, the aggregate contribution limit is 50 percent of AGI. Any excess can be carried over to be claimed during the subsequent five years.

A donor must file Form 8283 for all noncash gifts in excess of $500. When the gift exceeds $5,000 for the item or for a group of similar items, the donee's acknowledgement of receipt and a qualified appraiser's certification of value must also be submitted to the IRS. When an art gift valued at $20,000 or more is claimed, an 8- by 10-inch color photo must accompany the appraisal. No appraisal is required for gifts of publicly traded stock or for closely held stock of $10,000 or less.

Gifts of Appreciated Property and AMT

A donor who makes a gift of a highly appreciated asset avoids paying taxes on the property's capital gain. Moreover, as long as the gift's fair market value does not exceed 30 percent of his AGI, it is fully deductible. For example, for a person in the 28 percent bracket the capital gains tax on an investment costing $1,000 and currently worth $10,000 would be $2,520. If that person gives the stock to a charity, the deduction would reduce taxes by $2,800. Thus, his cost for the $10,000 gift would be only $4,680. The cost of giving capital gains property is higher for persons in a lower tax bracket. The greater the appreciation, the lower the cost of the gift.

A partial gift of appreciated property also can be arranged using a procedure called a "bargain sale." For tax purposes the gift is split into two portions, the contribution segment and the sale segment. The donor must pay the capital gains tax on the sale portion (the portion he retains). The cost basis of the asset is apportioned according to the percentages of the two segments. For example, the donor sells to his church a piece of land at his cost. The land's current market value is $100,000 and his cost is $25,000. The deductible gift is $75,000. To determine the capital gains on the retained portion, he multiplies the tax basis of the property ($25,000) by his retained sale portion divided by the property's current market value ([$25,000 × $25,000] ÷ $100,000 = $6,250). That amount is subtracted from his retained portion to determine the taxable gain ($25,000 − $6,250.00 = $18,750). Had the property been sold he would have been liable for capital gains taxes on $75,000 rather than on $18,750.

The capital gains portion of a bargain sale or gift of appreciated property that is not taxable to the donor is a preference item under the alternative minimum tax (AMT). This means that it, along with other preference items, is included in the base of AMT taxable income. Even though the AMT rate is only 24 percent (for 1991 income), the fact that far more of a filer's income is taxable under AMT can result in an increased tax liability. If a donor of appreciated property uses a special election, he can avoid AMT. However, to do so he must forgo claiming the appreciation as a deduction. This special election allows the donor to take as a deduction up to 50 percent of AGI.

When a donor makes a contribution and retains a lifetime interest in or power over it, the gift will be includible in his estate. An income tax deduction can be taken at the time the gift is made and an estate tax deduction at the time the gift is distributed by will. A charitable remainder trust, if property structured, will generate both tax deductions. Similarly, gifts of life insurance can be arranged so that they meet both tax goals.

PART VII

Investments and Your Financial Plan

CHAPTER 36

Are Your Finances in Order?

WHEN WAS THE last time you gave your family's financial situation a thorough review? In the rush of everyday living, it's easy to let these things slip. Yet, when you stop to think about it, in the process of managing your income and outgo, you're running a sizable "business." How well or poorly you do it depends in large part on how thoroughly you have organized the job.

When you first started out, it was an easy task, and you could handle it efficiently on a week-to-week, month-to-month basis. Then came a house, with a mortgage running 20 years or so. And children. And the start of a nest egg for the future. The management task has become considerably greater as you have added more places for your money to go and have moved up the income scale.

Your acquisitions quite likely have come gradually—so gradually that you may not have recognized just how complex your affairs have become. No longer can the week-to-week, month-to-month approach suffice.

Then, too, there is the concern that your family might have to get along without you at some point. How well have you prepared for that possibility? If you were to duck out for good tomorrow, would you leave behind a jumble of records, some

399

here, some there, for your survivors to try to find as best they might?

If you are the well-ordered type, you probably have things well in hand. Even so, you might profitably run through this chapter in the event you have overlooked some point worth reviewing or reworking. If you feel your family's financial program needs some organization, you can use what follows as a starting point.

Finding Your Net Worth

The first thing to do is to find out where you stand. How much are you worth? Take a stab at the answer before you write anything down. Chances are, when you do the arithmetic, you'll find that your guess was on the low side.

"Well, let's see," you say. "I have some life insurance, we're buying a house, the car's almost paid for, we have a few stocks and bonds. That's about all. Guess I'm not worth much, am I?"

Using the work sheet opposite, you can create your personal balance sheet, carefully listing all your assets and liabilities. Most of the information should be in your files, but some data will require additional digging. Rather than relying on instinct or guesses in valuing your home (most people's largest single asset), consult a broker or check your newspaper's real estate section for current market values of similar properties in your area. Once the balance sheet is completed, you will have an overall picture of your financial condition.

The reason you might mislead yourself into believing you don't have much material worth is the state of your wallet. It's pretty flat most of the time for a good many of us. But think of what you're buying with what comes out of it. Sure, there are the necessities—food, heat, clothing, contributions, a night out once in a while. You don't have much to show for the shelling out on these items.

But what about the mortgage payment? A portion of that goes each month toward paying off the principal and increasing your equity in the property. This is like a savings ac-

CASH RESERVE ASSETS

Cash on Hand .... $ _____
Checking Accounts .... _____
Savings Accounts .... _____
Money-Market Accounts ...... _____
Credit Unions .... _____
CDs—Less Than 1 Year ...... $ _____

PROPERTY ASSETS

Residence .... _____
Vacation Home .... _____
Furnishings .... _____
Jewelry and Art .... _____
Automobiles .... _____
Other Property Assets ...... _____

EQUITY ASSETS

Realty Investments .... _____
Stocks .... _____
Mutual Funds .... _____
Variable Annuities .... _____
Business Interests .... _____
Other Equity Assets .... _____

FIXED ASSETS

Bonds:
  Government .... _____
  Municipal .... _____
  Corporate .... _____
CDs—More Than 1 Year ...... _____
Fixed Annuities .... _____
Other Fixed Assets .... _____

RETIREMENT ACCOUNTS

Vested Portion of Pension .... $ _____
Other Co. Savings Plans ...... _____
IRA .... _____
Keogh .... $ _____

Total Assets .... $ _____

LIABILITIES

Home Mortgage .... _____
Other Mortgage .... _____
Bank Loans .... _____
Auto Loans .... _____
Charge Accounts .... _____
Education Loans .... _____
Insurance Premiums .... _____
Taxes:
  Federal .... _____
  State .... _____
  Local .... _____
Other Debt .... _____

Total Liabilities .... $ _____

NET WORTH

Total Assets .... $ _____
Total Liabilities .... − $ _____
NET WORTH .... $ _____

count. The same is true, though to a lesser degree, of your automobile. Your life insurance policy, too, might be building some cash value each year—yet another form of "enforced" savings not immediately visible.

In fact, most of your net worth is "invisible." Or it's so visible that you don't really see it. Take your furniture. You probably don't think of that in terms of its material value. Yet, you laid out cash for it; it represents an investment. You'd have to lay out more cash to replace it if it were lost. Same thing for your home appliances. Add up their value— the refrigerator, dishwasher, clothes washer, dryer—just these major items represent a sizable sum in themselves. Of course, their value diminishes each year with their use, but as long as they are of use they have value. They are part of your assets.

Almost anything you own can be included among your assets—sporting goods, jewelry, cameras, boats, home workshops, garden tools, snowblowers, bicycles, art, and so forth. Of course you wouldn't forget to include the value of your vacation home. As you work up an inventory of such things you can see just how much you have accumulated along the way.

Your vested interest in your company's pension plan or profit-sharing program is an asset that is not always readily visible. Are you also contributing to a group term life insurance policy that will return these contributions when you leave the company or retire? You should check the status of your company benefits from time to time and add their value to your assets.

Don't forget to add savings and checking accounts and the current worth of your stocks and bonds. Since your house has probably increased in value since you bought it, include the full current market value on the asset side of your ledger. Now add everything up.

Chances are, you owe money, too. Get this all together. The balance due on your mortgage. On your car loan. On any other loans outstanding. Insurance premiums. Current household bills.

Subtract the total of these liabilities from the total value of your assets and you'll have your net worth. Not bad, you might conclude. By making an accounting at about the same time each year, you'll get an idea of how well you're progressing. You'll also have an idea of what your goals should be, where you should be devoting more or less emphasis. This provides an excellent chart of the family's financial progress.

Where Does the Money Go?

Great. But where does all your money go each month and each year? Find out by drawing up an income statement. Your checkbook is probably as good a data source as you can get, particularly if you write checks for most of your bills. If you don't pay by check, by the way, you ought to consider doing it, because it serves as an excellent record, and it can provide proof of payment if you're ever challenged on that score. Taking your most recent full-year period, go through your records and write down all expenses, putting them into such general categories as mortgage or rent payments, auto loan, heat, lights, phone, food, clothing, entertainment, and so on.

Next, jot down your total income, making note on the expense side of the amount taken out for taxes and Social Security. Work your figures over until the "income" and "outgo" sides of the ledger balance. This income statement gives you an idea of how much you're paying for what. It makes a good starting point for drawing a budget.

Controlling the Outgo

A budget is needed to keep future spending under control. It need not be cast in concrete at the start of the year; in fact, it should not be so rigid that it allows no flexibility. Your budget shouldn't run your life, but instead it should serve as a map of your financial trip through the upcoming year and as a chart to keep you on course.

Once you have these three basic tools—a balance sheet, an

income statement, and a budget—you're well on the way to getting your family finances under control. A couple of other things might be worth mentioning at this point. One is a household inventory. The other is an insurance checkup.

As you probably discovered when you added up your possessions for your net worth tally, you own a lot more than you realized. Should you be hit with a burglary or fire, it might be difficult to remember the specifics in placing an insurance claim or filing a loss deduction on your income tax return. It would be a lot easier to have a list made ahead of time. It wouldn't be a bad idea to keep a copy of that list somewhere other than in the house, say, in your safe-deposit box at the bank or perhaps in your insurance agent's file. You ought to update the list from time to time. Include specifics of brand and style, your cost, date acquired, and estimated replacement cost.

In an inflationary period, you are at risk, too, with your homeowner's insurance coverage if you don't add to it from time to time. One reason is obvious: If you have a total loss, you wouldn't be fully covered on replacement costs. The other isn't so obvious: If you're not covered to within 80 percent of the value of the property, your coverage for any partial loss will be reduced to the extent that full coverage falls short. To make sure that your coverage is up to snuff, you should give it a yearly checkup. You can also ask your insurance agent to write an inflation escalator clause into your policy, and coverage will be automatically increased each year in line with the rise in prices. You should be certain your other casualty and liability coverage, such as that on your automobile, is periodically upgraded as well.

Providing for Illness, Disability, and Death

While you're thinking about insurance, you should give your health and life insurance programs a going-over. Since it is not the purpose of this book to educate you on that score, we'll only mention in passing the need to take a look at them from time to time to make sure they still meet your needs, both immediate and long term. With medical bills rising constantly, one hospital stay alone would put you behind unless you're adequately covered.

If your family insurance program doesn't include disability coverage for the principal breadwinner, you ought to consider taking some on to provide continuation of income in the event of his incapacitation. This protection, frequently overlooked because of its expense, in some ways is more important for younger families than life insurance, since disabling illness and accidents are more likely prospects than death.

That does not mean life insurance should be ignored, either. How much coverage you carry depends on how you regard such protection, how much you think the family will need to function comfortably in the absence of the principal wage earner, and how much you can afford to lay out for premiums.

Again, without getting into an involved discussion, we believe that, in general, term insurance buys you more protection for your dollar than whole life, which shunts a portion of the annual premium into a "savings" program that builds up cash value. We believe that by investing the difference yourself you can do much better over the long run—provided you discipline yourself to put that money aside each year. Your term policies should have a guarantee that they will be renewable at the end of each term regardless of your health at the time, and you might do well to pay a bit extra for a guarantee that the premiums will be paid if you become disabled.

A Record-Keeping Checklist

So, now that you have your income and outgo under control and your insurance coverage checked, what other records need to be assembled? Here's a list to get you started.

Will. Note where copies are filed, when it was last drawn, and when any changes were made.

Safe-deposit boxes. Note where they are located and list their contents as of a certain date. Note where keys are kept.

Insurance. List all policies and their numbers, and note where they are located and whom to contact if needed.

Bank accounts. Note account numbers, location of passbooks, and other pertinent information on all family accounts.

Securities. Provide a complete current listing, including costs, and note where certificates are located.

Real estate. Maintain a list of capital improvements with supporting invoices for tax purposes; note basic expenses such as property taxes, utilities, and so forth, as well as mortgage data.

Income taxes. Retain copies of final returns for the past several years and keep complete data for the current year.

Professional advisors. List names of attorney, trustee, and executor of the estate, insurance agents, stockbrokers, tax counsel, physicians, and so forth.

Requests and recommendations. Provide notes on disposition of personal effects after death for sentimental or other reasons not specifically mentioned in the will; provide suggestions for survivors on how best to make sure of the resources and advisors; list obituary material.

Once these records have been assembled, don't keep them a secret. If you are married, go over them with your spouse, explaining each item and its significance.

But contemplation of death shouldn't be the only motivating force behind establishing a good record-keeping system. If you sell your house, it can help you establish costs so you can reduce capital gains tax liability on appreciated value. If the IRS challenges your tax return, you have your defense readily at hand. You can tell at a glance how your investment portfolio is performing. You can detect potential financial problems ahead of time and take remedial measures before they become expensive crises.

The earlier you start such a system, the more help it can be to you in preserving your hard-earned assets and making them work more efficiently for you. Now is the time to get on with it.

CHAPTER 37

Investing for a College Education

IF YOU HAVE children, chances are that one of your primary financial objectives is to provide college educations for them. If you haven't priced a college education lately, you're in for a shock. Tuition costs have been rising 5 to 10 percent annually for several decades and no relief is in sight. Tuition alone at private colleges averages close to $10,000.

The sooner you begin your college fund, the easier your task will be. It will be a twofold job: first, to provide the assets; second, to make sure these assets work as hard as they possibly can while they're waiting to pay the college bills.

If you have a chunk of cash you are able to salt away immediately, all to the good. A portfolio of good-quality growth stocks should appreciate sufficiently over the next decade to give you a solid start toward paying the bills.

Or you might have to set aside funds a little at a time. The secret to success is to do it on a regular basis. Such a program takes discipline, but it can pay off handsomely. By increasing the yearly contribution as your earnings rise, you should be in a reasonably good position to meet those college expenses.

It is well to keep firmly in mind as you start planning for your children's educations the importance of protecting your fund from inflation, because college costs are rising faster than prices in general and the trend is likely to continue for

407

the foreseeable future. That's why we have placed emphasis on common stocks. The earlier you begin your college investment program the greater will be the benefits from capital appreciation of good investments.

Gifts of Tuition Payments

One of the little-publicized rules in the Tax Code (Section 2503[e]) allows an unlimited gift tax exclusion for tuition and health care payments made on behalf of a donee. In order to qualify for the exclusion the donor need not be related to the donee, but the payment must be made directly to the educational institution or health care provider. Gifts to cover the cost of books, lab fees, board and room are not eligible for the tax break. Grandparents, godparents, and other benefactors should be made cognizant of this ruling.

Keeping the Tax Man at Bay

Whether you invest in a portfolio of growth stocks or prefer the comfort of investments that provide greater "safety" of principal, you must consider the potential effect of taxes on the nest egg. With growth stocks, the big bite comes when they're sold. And with the capital gains rate at 28 percent, they don't get much of a break. With income securities the bite is more gradual, a year at a time as the income is earned. However, there are still some ways to reduce the impact of taxes. The most effective ways use investments that allow taxes on the income to be deferred or that pay income that is tax exempt.

U.S. SAVINGS BONDS. Parents who meet the income and other conditions might want to take advantage of the interest exclusion allowed after 1989 on Educational Savings Bonds (EE) used to fund college tuition and required fees, minus scholarships. To exclude the interest from taxation, the bonds must have been purchased by a person who is at least 24 years of age and whose modified adjusted gross income when the bonds are redeemed is between $40,000 and $55,000 for single filers and between $60,000 and $90,000 for joint filers. A married person filing singly doesn't qualify for the interest exclusion. The tax break is only available when used by the buyer to fund his own, his spouse's, or a dependent's tuition.

Even if your income when the bonds are redeemed exceeds the limits for the exclusion, interest on those EE bonds will have accrued tax deferred while they were held. Bondholders do not have to pay income taxes on this accrued interest until they redeem or otherwise dispose of the bonds. If you buy bonds in your child's name, they will be taxable to the child. Since up to age 14 a child's unearned income (in excess of $1,000) is taxed at his or her parents' highest rate, EE interest should be deferred. When the child reaches college age the bonds can be liquidated to help defray expenses. Although the accrued interest on them will be taxable, it will be at the child's tax rate, presumably lower than that of the parents.

CUSTODIAN ACCOUNTS. While custodian accounts generally allow assets to be removed from your estate, they have the same income tax drawbacks as EE bonds. Above $1,000, any income earned on transferred assets is taxable at the donor's top rate. No gift tax is incurred as long as the value of assets transferred is $10,000 or under. When a husband and wife make a joint gift the exclusion is $20,000 annually.

However, there are some other things you should know about using custodian accounts. The first is that assets automatically go to the child, no strings attached, when he or she reaches legal age. In some states, that is 18. If that's the case in your state and you have any qualms about your child wasting the money on something other than college, you might consider another approach.

It is important to name someone else as custodian. If the donor names him- or herself as custodian and dies before the minor comes of age, the assets will be included in the donor's estate.

MUNICIPAL BONDS. One way of avoiding the "kiddie tax" is to buy tax-exempt bonds or their stripped version. Stripped municipal bonds are noncallable, and they are backed by Treasury and agency bonds. One advantage of strips is their low cost; they sell at deep discounts to their $1,000 face value. These are purchased under the Uniform Gift (or Transfer) to Minors Act and, as explained earlier, become the child's property.

SINGLE PREMIUM LIFE INSURANCE. Earnings from whole life (cash value) insurance grow tax-deferred until a policy is surrendered or lapses. These insurance earnings may be tapped by the insured at any age—by borrowing from the policy—without penalty or tax liabilities. A parent who buys a policy on his or her own life can, when the child reaches college age, take a policy loan to help fund educational expenses. Interest cost is low and up to 75 percent of the principal can be borrowed. When outstanding at the death, policy loans (and accrued interest) reduce the death benefit. If a policy is allowed to lapse or is surrendered, then the earnings are taxable, but when paid to a beneficiary, proceeds are tax-free.

Whole life insurance guarantees a minimum interest rate during the initial years, with annual adjustments thereafter. Buyers of variable life may invest in bonds, stocks, money markets, and other portfolios. If the insured chooses well and the account manager is skilled, policy earnings will prosper, but there is no guarantee. Either type of policy is suitable for meeting college expenses, but variable life, with its potential for gains and losses, is best used for long-term goals.

State-Sponsored Tuition Programs

Because the cost of higher education has escalated so sharply, a number of states have stepped into the breach to offer tuition payment plans. The plans have taken two distinct forms—tax-exempt, zero coupon bonds and prepaid tuition plans. The following states have one or the other tuition program in place or pending.

Arkansas	Missouri
Colorado	New Hampshire
Connecticut	New York
Delaware	North Carolina
Florida	North Dakota
Hawaii	Oklahoma
Illinois	Oregon
Indiana	Rhode Island
Iowa	Tennessee
Kentucky	Virginia
Maine	Washington
Michigan	West Virginia
Minnesota	Wyoming

BACCALAUREATE BONDS. Fifteen states have sold or are planning to sell these tax-exempt, zero coupon bonds. The bonds are sold at deep discounts to their value at maturity in 5 to 20 years. There is no guarantee that the bonds will cover the cost of the future tuition. The state of Illinois adds $400 to the face value of the bond at maturity if it is used to pay tuition at a state university. The difference between the cost of these bonds and their value at redemption is taxable at the child's rate when they are redeemed.

PREPAID TUITION PLANS. Prepaid tuition programs have been offered by about 10 states. These guarantee to pay full tuition for a two-year or four-year higher education at a school in the state university system. The price of the plan depends on the number of years until the child matriculates. Some states allow a plan to be transferred to a sibling, if the named child doesn't use it. A few states allow the funds to be used to pay tuition at a private college within the state. Most states allow only in-state residents to use their plans. Refunds on unused prepaid tuition plans vary, so the individual state's plan should be checked carefully. It is not uncommon for the state to refund only the original principal.

Privately Sponsored Payment Plans

COLLEGE-SURE CDS. A bank in Princeton, New Jersey, offers FDIC-insured College-Sure CDs. The interest rate on these CDs is pegged at 1.5 percent below the rate of increase for expenses at 500 independent colleges and universities. With those expenses increasing an average of 7 percent annually, you would get 6 percent on the CD. Unless college expenses increased at a double-digit rate, you could do equally well investing in a bank CD, money-market account, or money-market mutual fund. Assuming the account is held in custody for the child, interest in excess of $1,000 will be taxable at the parent's top rate until the child reaches age 14.

NATIONAL CONSORTIUM OF COLLEGES. A group of colleges and Hemar Corp. of Minnesota are working on a tuition prepayment plan. One advantage of the plan is that the tuition credits could be transferred to another participating school if the student did not attend the designated college. It could also be transferred to a sibling or first cousin. Should a refund be necessary, only the original investment would be returned. There are several SEC and IRS hurdles to be surmounted before this plan becomes available.

Doing It with Trusts

Grantor or reversionary trusts, such as the Clifford trust or the spousal remainder trust, have been virtually eliminated as family tax-planning tools. Income on these is taxable to the grantor, unless the grantor retains less than a 5 percent reversionary interest in the assets in the trust at its inception. Income from a grantor trust in existence on March 1, 1986, is not taxable to the grantor but to the beneficiary. However, if the beneficiary is under 14, trust income above $1,000 is taxable at the parents' top rate in any case. Capital gains taken within the trust are taxable to the grantor whether the trust is or is not grandfathered.

CHAPTER 38

Countdown to Retirement

RETIREMENT EVE IS no time to start wondering what you'll have for "eating money" once you bid your fond adieus to your job. Five to 10 years ahead is not any too soon to begin figuring. Probably you have a pension plan where you work. But do you really understand how it operates—and how much you are likely to get out of it once you hang up your tools? You're pretty sure to be eligible for Social Security when you retire. But do you have any idea how large the monthly checks will be?

If you're like the vast majority of workers, these two items will provide the lion's share of your retirement income. To make realistic projections about your financial needs in retirement you'll have to have a rough idea of how much they will give you. You'll also have to know early enough so you can start laying away some savings to provide extra income.

A ballpark figure is sufficient. It's impossible to get a precise fix anyway, because of the changes that will occur in your income and in the Social Security rules during your remaining years on the job.

The quickest way to estimate your potential retirement income situation is to assume you're retiring right now and compute your benefits on that basis. Ask your company what the pension plan would pay someone who retires this year at

413

your income level and with the number of years' service you'll have at retirement age. Then estimate the Social Security benefit you'd receive if you retired this year. Your nearest Social Security office can give you the figure.

Add the two together. In all probability, that's pretty close to what you'll get in dollars of equivalent buying power when you actually retire. Could you live on that sum? Make a quick calculation of your living costs in today's dollars under circumstances approximating those that will exist when you do reach retirement age. Remember, in retirement your income needs will be more modest than they are while you're working. No more expensive business lunches, not as many new clothes, no commuting costs, and so forth. If your mortgage is paid off at retirement age, your housing costs will be lower. With the children grown and gone, there will be fewer mouths to feed, no more college tuition bills to pay. Do the projected expenses fall within the projected income?

If not, you'll have to get cracking and (a) build some savings or (b) develop some ways of earning money in retirement or (c) both.

How Much to Save?

Because conditions may change drastically between now and the time you retire, particularly if you are relatively young, it is difficult to judge with any degree of accuracy how much you'll have to save to provide an adequate retirement nest egg. But remember, inflation must be factored in both during your saving period and after retirement when you will be drawing down the account.

Just to give you an idea of what you're up against, let's assume that inflation averages 5 percent. At that rate, prices double in roughly 14 years. (The consumer price index doubled in the 10 years to 1985.) To provide, at a 5 percent inflation rate, the same buying power for $1,000, you'll have to have $1,276 if you retire in 5 years, $1,629 in 10, $2,079 in 15, and $2,653 in 20. Remember, too, that during retirement that same process will continue; think what the effects will be on a nest egg that has to last three decades or so. Or what will happen to your life-style over that period if you don't have such a reserve.

Obviously, the earlier you start saving, the easier the task will be. Suppose you decide you'll need $100,000 on which to retire comfortably at age 65. If you're 45 now and your assets grow at a 10 percent rate (including income and appreciation), you'll need to save $1,746 a year for the next 20 years, or $140 a month compounded. If you're 55 now, you'll have to sock away $501 a month to meet your goal. The moral is obvious.

Savings Alternatives

After you've estimated how much retirement income you'll need and how much you must save to get it, you have to draft a retirement program.

It's stating the obvious to say your aim in providing a retirement nest egg is to build your assets as large as possible within reasonable bounds of risk. It's something else again to come up with a program that meets this goal.

The list of alternatives is well known, and we won't belabor it here. Basically, your choices divide into three general categories: *savings* (bank accounts, cash value life insurance, annuities, bonds, and so forth); *equities* (business ownership, real estate, and common stocks); *speculations* (oil-drilling participations, futures trading, options trading, and so forth).

Weighing the obvious risks, you can quickly trim the list substantially at the outset. Unless you have funds you can really afford to lose, we'd suggest you leave the speculations to wealthier investors. Unless you're ready and able to undertake management of a business or real estate, we suggest likewise for these. Most retirees aren't interested in spending the time necessary to manage a business or keep tabs on rental property. That leaves stocks, bonds, bank accounts, insurance, and annuities for most.

By limiting your choices to these, you have substantially reduced, but not eliminated, the risk factor. Let's review our earlier comments on risk. Most likely your first thought is of the risk that your assets will shrink in the face of a decline in the securities markets just when you need to liquidate. That's a valid concern, and it should not be overlooked.

But there are other kinds of risk, and they are as important to consider. We have just demonstrated the risk of lost buying power as inflation erodes your savings. Then there is the risk that you'll get yourself locked into some investment to the extent that you can't easily or economically shift into a more lucrative one should the opportunity arise. Finally, there is the risk that the investment to which you entrust your savings will turn sour and fail altogether.

Ideally, you'd like an investment that would keep your capital intact, that would grow sufficiently fast to overcome inflation, that would be flexible, and that would not go down the tubes. Unfortunately, no single investment or savings vehicle exists that can guarantee all these goals at once. There will always be some element of risk involved. The trick is to get that risk under reasonable control and to spread it out to minimize its effects on your total program.

How do you do this? First, you determine which risks you can most easily live with. If you're nervous about putting your capital on the line, you'll have to live with the risk of shrinking buying power as you indulge in the "safety" of fixed-income investments. If you're more aggressive, you'll have to face the risk that your investment in equities might even decline in value in a bear market.

Isn't there some happy medium? We believe there is, and we've been preaching it for a good many years. It's called diversification. Don't put all of your retirement nest egg savings into the same investment basket. Your "mix" will be largely determined by the length of time you have before retirement and the amount of risk you're willing to undertake in relation to your expected return.

What kind of mix do you need to yield the desired results? If you have 10 to 15 years before retirement, we'd suggest you go heavily on the side of common stocks, to minimize the risk of buying-power erosion. By choosing from only the strongest and best companies, you can select a portfolio of stocks that is highly resistant to market risk as well.

Don't make the list of stocks too long; keep it within manageable bounds. A half-dozen to a dozen companies should provide sufficient diversification.

How much of your savings should you devote to equities? We would say 70 percent and still feel conservative, dividing the remaining 30 percent among bonds and savings certificates.

To retain flexibility, select bonds with maturities five or six years out, rather than those of longer term. This will minimize market risk should you wish to shift investments along the way.

As you move to within five years or so of retirement, you could begin to tilt portfolio acquisitions more toward fixed-income securities. You shouldn't start any wholesale shifting of equities already in your portfolio, though; there might be tax consequences that could be reduced if action is delayed until after retirement, when your taxable income and possibly your tax bracket will be lower.

As you make the transition into retirement, you might have a portfolio consisting of 60 percent equities and 40 percent fixed-income assets. Because the inflation risk is likely to be present during all of your retirement years, you should think seriously about retaining a solid position in equities to help offset the constant rise in the cost of living.

Making Savings Grow

There's more to the creation of a nest egg than just putting funds aside. You must make them work as hard as possible while they wait for you to retire.

We've talked about determining how much savings you'll need for retirement and the various savings options open to you. Now let's look at some ways to make the retirement fund grow.

The first, and most obvious, way is to make regular additions to it. You've got to discipline yourself to do this, or your plan is doomed from the start. Play tricks on yourself, if you must. Have pay deducted from your salary so you never "see" it. Write yourself a check each month and deposit it to your retirement account. Start a regular investment program with your broker or with a mutual fund.

Another way to make savings grow is via compounding. Be sure all of your assets—including the income generated by them—are working for you all of the time. Keep dividends reinvested, rather than cashing and spending the checks; enrolling in dividend reinvestment plans will expedite this. Pay any taxes out of pocket rather than out of the fund. Choose savings accounts that offer the most attractive compounding.

A third way is to defer taxes wherever you can. By putting off tax obligations until you pass into a lower tax bracket, you'll obviously have a lower tax bill. Not only that, you'll have the advantage of compounding with the earnings that otherwise would have gone to pay current taxes.

There are several ways of deferring taxes. If you are self-employed, you can start a Keogh or a SEP plan. Depending on your income level, you can also invest money in a tax-sheltered individual retirement account (IRA). You can buy an annuity, where tax on the income generated by your contributions is deferred until you begin to draw benefits out. If you choose the appropriate option on your ordinary life insurance policy, the dividends it earns accumulate without any current tax liability.

You should take maximum advantage of any pension plans, savings programs, stock options plans, or salary deferral arrangements offered by your employer. While not all these plans will include a current tax benefit, they will provide you with a regular and disciplined savings program.

Equities Have a Unique Advantage

But perhaps the greatest potential available to you for deferment of taxes lies with equities. The most convenient way to establish an equity position is through common stocks, and the best way to defer taxes via stocks is to choose those that emphasize capital growth. You pay taxes on dividends as received, but you don't have to pay any tax on appreciated value of the stocks until you sell them.

If you want to go whole hog and you're up to it, you can establish an equity position via outright ownership of a business or of rental real estate properties. If you possess the necessary know-how and talents, and if you do your homework properly, these could provide you not only with an appreciating asset but with a continuing source of income in retirement and a new "career" in the bargain. But it's risky, and not something that you should plunge into with all of your resources, for a loss could be disastrous and your time for recouping is severely limited.

Supplementing Retirement Income

If you think you'll need to generate extra cash to make ends meet in retirement, you should lay the groundwork before you get your gold watch. Whatever your motives for pursuing a postretirement career, the earlier you start preparing for it before you actually step down from your primary job the better are the chances for its success.

For one thing, you might have valuable contacts in your profession that will not be as readily available once you retire. For another, there might be some resources available to you; more and more companies are helping their older employees prepare for second careers. Sometimes these can constitute major incentives for stepping down early to clear the decks for younger managers on the way up. At any rate, an early start can give you the chance to work out a lot of the kinks before you actually have to start depending on the income from the new career. And you should count on plenty of kinks.

The first step, naturally, is to decide what you'll do. Explore the possibilities carefully. Check your potential market —be sure there's really one out there for whatever it is you consider, be it as modest as a garage fix-it shop or as ambitious as a globe-girdling consultant practice.

As you do your planning, don't forget to take the Social Security rules pertaining to taxes and earnings limitation into account. Remember that if you work, are 65, and collect benefits, for every three dollars you earn above the limit you will lose one dollar of your benefit. At age 70, you are no longer subject to the earnings limitations. However, if added earnings push your adjusted gross income above the $25,000 (single) or $32,000 (couple) base, half your Social Security will be added to your AGI for tax purposes.

Choose a business in which you have some demonstrated

expertise—either professionally or via a well-developed avocation. Remember, the odds of failure of small businesses are very high. The more savvy and management skill you can bring to the job, the better the chances of making a go of it.

Guard your resources. Zero in on something you can try in a small way first, so if it doesn't work you won't have lost all your savings. Remember, your ability to replace lost wealth after retirement will be severely limited, if not nonexistent.

If you don't like the idea of putting your savings on the line, you might consider working for someone else instead. You might find your expertise affordable to a small business on the less than full-time basis you'd be able to provide.

But remember, you'll be "retired." Unless it's really what you want, be careful not to replace one all-consuming career with another. By shaking things down before retirement, you can get an idea of how to pace yourself, what kind of time the new venture will take.

CHAPTER 39

Employee Benefit Plans

ALTHOUGH MAJOR PENSION legislation passed by Congress in 1974 made it possible for most of the nation's 92 million workers to be eligible for retirement benefits funded by their employers, only 46 percent of the workforce is actually covered. If you are one of these workers, it's important that you be as familiar as possible with how your plan works. What type of plan are you enrolled in? How long do you have to work before your benefits are fully "vested"? What payment options do you have at retirement?

How important are employee benefit plans? When you did the retirement income calculations outlined in Chapter 38 you probably found that your projected pension is greater than your estimated Social Security benefits, if you are covered by a defined-benefit plan. For those covered by a defined-contribution plan, the retirement benefits may not be as generous. A 1989 survey of retirees 65 and older found that Social Security benefits provided over half their incomes.

The rapid growth of employee benefit plans since 1974 has not been without effect on the nation's businesses and financial markets. Not only do the plans provide employment for a bevy of lawyers and fund managers, but they also have become an important source of investment capital. Private

421

and public pension funds now hold about 15 percent of all outstanding corporate bonds and 23 percent of the nation's publicly traded stock. Their combined assets at the end of 1988 were worth over $2.2 trillion.

ERISA Set New Standards

Why was 1974 such a watershed year for employee benefit plans? That was the year that Congress passed the Employee Retirement Income Security Act, more commonly referred to by the acronym ERISA. Although the act did not force employers to offer pension benefits to employees, for the first time it spelled out several regulations governing all employer pension plans.

What are ERISA's major provisions? Most of the act's regulations establish standards for pension fund eligibility, contribution limits, vesting, and funding. For example, ERISA generally requires that if an employer sponsors a pension plan, all employees must be eligible to participate in the plan after reaching age 25 and serving one year with the company. The rules also prohibit plans from discriminating on behalf of any group of employees, such as owners or management.

While ERISA allowed companies to choose from one of four vesting schedules, the Tax Reform Act of 1986 mandated that companies adopt more rapid vesting schedules. The revised schedules, which became effective in 1989, required vesting at a 20 percent per year rate. Employers may start vesting with the first year the employee enrolls in the pension plan or delay it for two years. Thus, the employee's pension assets would be his property after five to seven years. The law also lowered the age at which employees must be covered by the company plan from 25 to 21.

The funding requirements are designed to assure that adequate capital is available when an employee begins to draw benefits. How reliable is a pension when its sponsor has been negligent about the plan's funding? Employer contributions must adhere to a certain schedule. This prevents "backloading" of plans as employees approach retirement age.

Pension Benefits Insured

What happens to your pension if your employer goes bankrupt? In its infinite wisdom, Congress created the Pension Benefit Guaranty Corporation when it passed ERISA. The PBGC guarantees vested pension benefits in much the same way the FDIC insures bank deposits. At the end of 1989, PBGC had $1 billion in liabilities from terminated pension plans under its supervision. Of the 100,000 pension plans PBGC insures, over half are 150 percent overfunded. However, underfunded plans represent a potential $20 billion to $30 billion liability. The insurance protection is funded by plan sponsors, who must pay a premium of $16 (as of 1990) to the PBGC for each plan participant.

From this brief overview of ERISA, you can see that the regulations are a problem for plan sponsors. For most companies, the cost of complying with the regulations has been tremendous. Since 1974, therefore, many corporations have either cut back on the scope of their pension plans or altered them to shift more of the costs onto workers.

What's What in Pension Plans

Sorting out the post-ERISA world of employee benefit plans is made more difficult by the lexicon peculiar to the field. For example, do you know what CODAs and ESOPs are? Or what distinguishes a target benefit plan from a profit-sharing one?

All employee benefit programs can be classified as either "defined-contribution" plans or "defined-benefit" plans. The latter type, covering 31 percent of workers, includes pension and annuity plans. If you participate in such a plan, your retirement benefits will likely equal a fixed dollar amount or a set percentage of either your "career pay" or "final pay."

As noted previously, the ERISA regulations have become a major disincentive to funding pension plans. And a 1982 change in the law has further curtailed the use of defined-benefit plans. The maximum annual defined benefit that can be funded in 1990 is limited to the lesser of $108,963 (indexed to 1991) or 100 percent of the average compensation during your three highest-paid years. But 1986 legislation reduced the maximum benefits that early retirees could receive. At age 55 the maximum benefit a retiree can receive is $48,436; at age 60 it is $72,654; and at 62 to 65 the limit is $87,185. These figures include cost-of-living increases through 1991.

Defined-contribution plans can take several shapes: profit-sharing plan, stock bonus plan, money purchase plan, and target benefit plan. Because defined-contribution plans aren't subject to all of the ERISA regulations, they are less expensive to administer than pension plans. Furthermore, they transfer much of the risk to the participant. The employer need only provide the accumulated contributions and earnings on them to the worker at retirement or separation from the company, rather than a pension for the rest of the worker's life.

Stock bonus plans provide benefits in much the same way as profit-sharing plans, with the company setting up a trust for the benefit of employees. In these plans the contributions for each participant must be in direct proportion to his or her salary for the plan to be judged nondiscriminatory. But in contrast to a profit-sharing plan, employer contributions can be in the form of company stock and are based on a set formula rather than on profits.

Contributions to money purchase plans are determined by formula—8 percent of each participant's salary. Again, they are not tied to the company's profit, but are otherwise similar in form to profit-sharing plans.

Employers having target benefit plans contribute by a formula, placing in each account sufficient money to provide the worker with a "target" benefit.

Some Companies Sponsor Several Plans

It is possible to be covered by a defined-benefit and one or more defined-contribution plans at the same time. There is a complex formula for determining the overall limit placed on aggregate contributions. But for the majority of workers these employer contribution limits will be well above the aggregate contribution made on their behalf. When an employer has several defined-contribution plans, the aggregate contributions to them on your behalf are limited to the lesser of $30,000 or 25 percent of your compensation.

In addition to contributions made for you by your employer, one of these plans may permit voluntary employee contributions. Your tax-qualified plan contributions are limited to $8,475 (indexed for 1991) for all plans. For contributions to be made from pretax dollars the plan must meet IRS requirements on funding, vesting, distributions, discrimination, and so forth. Your employer may also sponsor a thrift plan enabling you to invest after-tax dollars in a savings plan, the earnings on which are tax deferred. These are often made in conjunction with a matching contribution from the employer to encourage participation.

ESOPs and CODAs Are Popular Plans

These defined-contribution plans can use profit-sharing, money purchase, or stock bonus funding rules. A cash or deferred arrangement (CODA) is also known by its Code Section number, 401(k). The employee may elect to take cash or make an equivalent contribution to a tax-qualified plan. Contributions are limited to $8,475 (indexed). But this limit applies to voluntary contributions to all tax-qualified plans in which the worker participates. The plan participant is 100 percent vested from the first contribution. CODAs may permit withdrawals in case of hardship to meet heavy medical bills or educational expenses. They also may be drafted to allow the participant to borrow against his plan assets.

Employee stock ownership plans (ESOPs) may take the form of a stock bonus plan, but not all stock bonus plans are ESOPs. They frequently are set up as profit-sharing plans. Unlike CODAs, vesting is not usually immediate, but follows the vesting schedule elected by the employer. When plan assets are distributed, they may be paid out either in cash or shares, at the employer's option.

Calculating Your Benefits

To avoid confusion, we have so far stayed away from too much detail on each type of plan. From a retirement-planning perspective, what is most important is that you make a yearly approximation of how much your accumulated benefits are worth. If you are covered by one or more of the defined-contribution plans discussed above, making such an estimate is fairly simple, because employers send out annual statements summarizing these accounts.

But making the same evaluation of your pension plan benefits is almost impossible. Employers are not always willing to divulge all of the information you need to make such a careful appraisal. However, they must supply you with answers to the following questions:

Who manages the plan? Depending on the fiscal health of your employer, it could be advantageous if a bank or insurance company manages your pension plan assets and administers the payment of benefits.

Is the plan contributory or noncontributory? If it is contributory, the company's only responsibility is to match your contributions to the plan. But if the plan is noncontributory, the employer is required to make contributions on your behalf at a level based on a percentage of your salary.

What formula is used to determine the size of your retirement pension? Your benefits might be based on your salary at retirement, the average of your highest-paid three years, or average career earnings and your years of service to the company.

How are benefits distributed? Many plans offer several options, including a lump-sum distribution, a payout in installments over a preset period, or a joint and survivor annuity. Most pensions are reduced if you retire early. Depending on the options you and your spouse choose, your benefits may or may not continue for your spouse. However, as a result of the Retirement Equity Act of 1984, unless a spouse signs a written statement requesting otherwise, a married retiree's benefits are automatically based on a joint and survivor annuity.

Tax Changes and Pension Plans

TRA '86 changed many aspects of pension laws. Because the pension rule revisions were substantial, employers were given two years to bring their plans into compliance. The rules determining whether a plan is "top-heavy" (unfair to the rank and file) were tightened. The definition of "key employee" was broadened and clarified. It also placed a limit on the aggregate amount that an employee can collect from all plans. If the annual distribution exceeds $136,204 (indexed for 1991), a 15 percent excise tax is levied on the overage.

Reform also reduced the contribution limits and changed the taxation of distributions from 403(b) tax-sheltered annuities. These are the retirement plans that cover employees of nonprofit organizations. The contribution limit is the lesser of $8,475 or 25 percent of the employee's salary. Elective contributions may be made to 401(k) plans up to the same limit, but will reduce the 403(b) contribution. When the employee retires and annuity payments commence after 1986, he or she will no longer be able to receive a portion of the payment tax-free indefinitely. Using the IRS tables, the exclusion ratio is calculated, and once the annuitant's cost is recovered, remaining payments are fully taxable. If the retiree dies before recovering his cost, then unrecovered costs are deductible when the final income tax is filed.

Collecting Plan Benefits

Here, too, Congress busied itself to disallow previously bestowed tax breaks. The tax treatment of lump-sum distributions was significantly changed. Both 10-year averaging and capital gains elections will disappear eventually. Ten-year averaging was replaced with 5-year averaging except for those persons who had reached age 50 by January 1, 1986. This age-qualified group can elect 10-year averaging, using 1986 tax rates, or 5-year averaging, using 1987 or later tax rates. The election can be made before reaching age 59½, but if the 10-year method is chosen, it can be used only once.

Capital gains treatment of contributions made before 1974 is being phased out, so that after 1991, that election will no longer be available. The rules governing lump-sum rollovers to IRA accounts were left intact. This method for handling lump-sum distributions is the most popular, because it allows continued tax-deferral.

What should you do now that you have all of this background information on pension and employee benefit plans? Keep two things in mind. First, remember that the pension tax laws are not set in stone but are subject to change at the whim of Congress. Second, know that few people can afford the luxury of choosing between employers based on the merits of their retirement plans. And fewer still are in a position to influence management's selection of plans. But by knowing the advantages and drawbacks of all your company's plans, you'll be in a better position to select those best suited to your present and future financial needs and through planning to offset any shortfalls. Investigate all of your options.

CHAPTER 40

Retirement Plans for
the Self-Employed

In 1962, when the Keogh Act was enacted, self-employed persons and unincorporated businesses were granted modest tax breaks on retirement savings programs. Before that time, their retirement nest eggs had been laboriously built with after-tax dollars. Once the Keogh Act (HR-10) was enacted by the 87th Congress, it wasn't many years before unincorporated businesses were allowed most of the same retirement savings tax breaks that corporate employees had long enjoyed.

In its original form back in 1962, the Keogh Act did not provide much of a tax incentive. It allowed a self-employed person to set aside the lesser of $2,500 or 10 percent of his earned income each year, and to deduct from current taxes half that amount, or $1,250 on a maximum contribution. Furthermore, it provided penalties—stiff to the point of being confiscatory—for excess contributions and premature withdrawals. The stringency of the rules is a mark of the political price the opponents exacted before agreeing to let the legislation pass.

The benefits were liberalized in 1968, and again in 1974 when the contribution limit was raised to the lesser of $7,500 or 15 percent of earned income. Penalties for excess contributions and premature withdrawals were eased. The contribution limit was doubled in 1982, and retirement benefits for unincorporated businesses were finally brought into alignment with those of corporations in 1984. Participants in Keogh plans were allowed to invest the lesser of $30,000 or 25 percent of earned income.

How Keogh Plans Work

So much for the evolution of Keogh plans. Suffice it to say that as a result of the Tax Equity and Fiscal Responsibility Act (TEFRA), for the years after 1983, contribution limits and benefits for Keogh, S corporation plans, and Simplified Employee Plans (SEPs) were brought into line with those of corporate qualified employee plans. But since Congress has a habit of changing laws every few years, you should check the latest information before setting up a Keogh plan.

Who qualifies for a Keogh? Basically, if you file Form SE to pay a self-employment tax (Social Security), you qualify. But if you establish a plan for yourself you will also have to contribute the same percentage of earnings for any full-time employee (one who works 1,000 hours or more per year) who is 21 years of age or older. Contributions you make for employees (but not for yourself) are 100 percent tax deductible as a business expense.

As we said before, you can set aside up to 25 percent of your earned income (after the Keogh contribution) to a $30,000 limit annually. Both your contributions and all Keogh earnings are exempt from federal taxes as they accrue. Taxes on them are deferred until withdrawals start. Voluntary nondeductible contributions of up to 10 percent of your aggregate compensation for all years since you have been in the plan are also allowed.

Since 1976, self-employed individuals have been able to initiate defined-benefit plans that allow them to shelter more than the allowable limits under a defined-contribution Keogh. Under a formula based on earned income and age at entry in the defined-benefit plan, the maximum benefit that can be funded is the lesser of $108,963 (indexed for 1991) annually or 100 percent of average compensation for the three highest consecutive years as a plan participant. Essentially, what these "Maxi Keoghs" do is allow a participant to make annual payments to a straight life annuity to the same extent he could if he were covered under a corporate defined-benefit plan. While too complicated to detail here, these plans can be very beneficial for highly compensated professionals. Before you decide which plan is best for you, your tax advisor should be consulted.

As we indicated earlier, there are some penalties against which you must guard. You can be penalized for making early withdrawals. That penalty is 10 percent and is added to the ordinary income tax levied on the premature distribution. However, if you have made voluntary contributions to your plan, you may withdraw those assets at any time without incurring a penalty.

To make it easier and less expensive for you to begin a Keogh program, "master plans" and "prototype plans" have evolved. Under a master plan, several individual plans are grouped together, funded, and administered in common by a bank or insurance company. A prototype plan is individually administered under sponsorship of a professional association or a regulated investment company. A much more expensive alternative would be to have your advisors draft your own individual plan, which then would have to obtain Internal Revenue Service approval before your contributions could qualify for deduction.

Investment Alternatives

There are three basic investment alternatives available for Keogh plans. The first is to contribute to an insurance company's qualified annuity plan. The annuity contract might guarantee a fixed or a variable rate of return over the life of the Keogh. However, any portion of the Keogh funds used to purchase separate life insurance protection is not exempt from taxes.

The second alternative is to deposit Keogh funds with a bank or a trust company. They act as custodians for the retirement funds and usually manage them as part of a professionally invested pool of pension funds. A third alternative is to invest in a mutual fund program through a custodian.

If you are so inclined, you may act as trustee for your own Keogh plan, saving red tape and costly trustee fees. If this is not permitted by your state, or you are not so inclined, you may use an institutional trustee or custodian and still make investment decisions for the plan by using a self-directed arrangement.

Banks have been the traditional repositories for self-directed plans, but insurance companies, savings and loan associations, and credit unions have a sizable share of this business. Some brokerage houses have custodial arrangements with banks, so that you can set up a self-directed Keogh through them.

When considering a self-directed plan, weigh the advantages of control, flexibility, and modest cost against the disadvantages of having to do your homework in maintaining a solid portfolio. You should also remember that when the plan includes employees, you assume fiduciary responsibility for the entire Keogh plan if you manage it yourself.

Can you switch from one investment alternative to another? For the most part, yes. If you are in a mutual fund program, it's no problem to shift assets from one type of fund to another. You can also shift from a mutual fund to a trusteed account with a bank for investment in common stocks or other securities of your choosing. The greatest difficulty arises when you try to exit from an insurance annuity program. The best way to do this is to stop funding the annuity, that is, freeze the assets, and divert future contributions elsewhere. Note that any "rollover" of Keogh assets from one type of plan to another must be completed within 60 days. Otherwise you immediately subject the account to taxes.

Collecting Your "Benefits"

When may benefits begin? Keogh assets cannot be withdrawn before age 59½ without incurring penalties. An exception is made if you become severely disabled or die before that age. Assets can also be withdrawn penalty-free before age 59½, if they are taken in equal payments over your life expectancy. If your plan permits them, voluntary nondeductible contributions may also be withdrawn at any time without penalty. Withdrawals from a Keogh must begin after you reach 70½.

What is the tax status of the benefits you have built up over the years when the time comes to convert them into a retirement income program? Uncle Sam did not "excuse" the taxes you avoided during the contribution years, you can be sure of that. What he did was to allow you to defer them until you started using the assets you salted away. Besides the advantage of compounding we mentioned earlier, this also means that when you start drawing out the "benefits" you're generally in a lower tax bracket. Thus, the tax bite is not as great as it would have been had you paid it during your earning years.

Withdrawal Options

Once you are eligible to begin withdrawing Keogh assets, you have several choices as to how you do it. You may take a lump-sum distribution or, under an annuity arrangement, you may choose to withdraw assets over your own lifetime, or over your lifetime and that of your spouse or other named beneficiary.

If you opt for a lump-sum distribution, you may roll it over to an IRA, use 5-year averaging, and in some cases 10-year averaging or capital gains treatment. The 1986 Tax Reform Act eliminated 10-year averaging and phased out, over a six-year period, capital gain treatment for lump-sum distributions. To replace these favorable distribution methods, 5-year forward averaging for lump-sum distributions received after age 59½ was adopted. This works the same way as 10-year averaging, only the lump-sum distribution is treated as if it had been received over a 5-year period. Thus, the single filer rate is applied to 20 percent of the distribution and the result is multiplied by five.

Individuals who were age 50 by January 1, 1986, could elect to use special transitional rules allowing 10-year averaging once before age 59½. This precludes its use again after age 59½. Capital gains treatment, if used by these individuals, is at a flat 20 percent rate. However, the phase-out rules on capital gains treatment of the pre-1974 portion of a lump-sum distribution will no longer be available after 1991. It is applicable to 50 percent of a lump-sum payment in 1990 and 25 percent in 1991.

When distributions are made under an annuity arrangement, part of each payment is treated as a tax-free recovery of voluntary contributions, if any were made. The balance is treated as ordinary income. If benefits cease before recovery of all voluntary contributions, the unrecovered portion may be taken as a deduction on the annuitant's final-year tax form.

Distributions After Death

If you die before distribution of plan assets has begun, then they must be distributed within five years of your death. But there are exceptions to this. The five-year distribution rule does not apply if plan assets are to be paid to a named beneficiary over his or her lifetime and will begin within one year of your death. The rule doesn't apply if assets are to be distributed to a surviving spouse over his or her lifetime. In this case the distribution must begin by the year you would have reached 70½. If distributions had commenced before your death, then the assets must continue to be paid out to the named beneficiary at least as fast as previously.

There are tax implications for Keogh benefits received on the plan participant's death. In plans using retirement income, endowment, or other life insurance contracts, the entire cash value of the contract at the time of distribution must be included in the recipient's income, unless within 60 days of receipt it is irrevocably converted into an annuity. If conversion to an annuity is not elected, the cost basis of the insurance paid from voluntary contributions can be recovered. It is subject to the same tax treatment as other lump-sum distributions. When policy proceeds are ultimately paid they will not be taxed to the beneficiary. In addition, the participant may transfer the policy so that proceeds will not be included in his or her estate. The first $5,000 of the distributions received from a plan may be excluded from the beneficiary's income as a death benefit.

SEP: A Low-Cost Pension Plan

A self-employed person or the owner of a small unincorporated business also should consider Simplified Employee Plans (SEPs). These offer most of the same tax advantages as Keogh plans, while entailing low start-up and administration costs and minimal fiduciary responsibility.

A SEP is a retirement plan based on IRA principles. Although contributions are made to each participant's plan, the funding vehicle, be it a mutual fund, annuity, CD, or brokerage account, is chosen by the participant. Employer contributions are excluded from the employee's income for income tax and Social Security purposes. When funds are distributed from a SEP they are taxed as ordinary income. Five- or 10-year forward averaging tax treatment, available on lump-sum distributions from qualified employee retirement plans, is not available on SEPs.

In order to make the procedure as simple as possible the IRS provides two model agreements—5305-SEP and 5305A-SEP. The former is used for a regular SEP built only with employer contributions; the latter is used if salary reduction or other elective contribution SEP is desired. A 14-line Form 5305-SEP, which requires the employer to fill in six blanks, is completed and presented to each plan participant. It is not filed with the IRS. The plan must comply with Code Section 408(k).

Contributions to a regular SEP are limited to the lesser of 15 percent of compensation or $30,000. Because the 15 percent limit is allowed only on wages after the SEP contribution, you should use 13 percent as a rule of thumb for determining the maximum contribution. The same percentage must be contributed for all employees. Salary reduction SEP elective deferrals are limited to 15 percent of earnings up to $8,475 (indexed for 1991).

Advantages and Disadvantages of SEPs

SEP contributions aren't taxable to an employee until that money is withdrawn from the account. Earnings on the SEP also compound tax-deferred. Money in the SEP can be withdrawn at any time by the employee or it can be transferred to another plan if the employee changes jobs. However, premature distributions will be subject to income taxes and a 10 percent penalty. If the worker isn't satisfied with the financial institution where the account is lodged, he can switch it to another one. SEP contributions may continue after a covered employee reaches age 70½, but withdrawals based on life expectancy also must commence at that time.

For the employer, these plans have a few disadvantages that should be considered. First, once the contribution is made to a participant's account it is fully vested. Therefore, the employee can withdraw it immediately if he wishes. If that withdrawal is premature, that is, if the employee is under age 59½, the participant will be subject to income taxes and a 10 percent penalty on the amount withdrawn. Second, virtually all employees must be included in the plan. Permitted exclusions are: employees who have not worked for the company during three of the last five years; those earning less than $363 (indexed for 1991) annually; employees under 21 during the contribution year; nonresident alien workers; and employees covered by collective bargaining agreements.

CHAPTER 41

Individual Retirement Accounts

WHEN FIRST INTRODUCED in 1975, IRAs were an instant hit—more than 1.3 million taxpayers established accounts. Yet at that time these retirement savings accounts were only available for workers who were not covered by any other pension plan. Furthermore, contributions were limited to 15 percent of wages up to a limit of $1,500. In 1981, IRAs were opened to all workers and their nonworking spouses, regardless of participation in another qualified or government pension plan. The contribution formula was also enhanced, so that a worker could defer 100 percent of wages up to $2,000 in an IRA. In 1987, just 12 years after they were introduced, participation restrictions were placed on IRA plans once again.

How IRAs Work

Individuals who aren't active participants in tax-qualified pension, profit-sharing, or stock bonus plans, in 401(k), 403(a or b), Simplified Employee Plan (SEP), or government pension plans may contribute up to $2,000 tax deferred to an IRA. An active participant is defined as an individual who is covered by any tax-qualified plan for any part of the year. Furthermore, a worker who meets his or her company's plan

437

eligibility requirements is considered an active participant whether he or she is enrolled in the plan or not.

Wage earners who are covered by one or more tax-qualified plans may still be eligible to make a *tax-deferred* IRA contribution if their adjusted gross income (AGI) is within prescribed limits. The limits are $25,000 for a single person and $40,000 for married couples. AGI for the purpose of determining IRA eligibility is the amount after passive losses and taxable Social Security benefits, but before IRA deductions.

Reduced IRA contributions are also allowed for singles with AGIs no greater than $35,000 and for couples whose AGIs don't exceed $50,000. The contribution is reduced ratably (to a floor of $200) according to the amount by which AGI exceeds the limits. However, when one spouse participates in an employer's retirement savings plan, the other spouse is not eligible for a *tax-deferred* IRA contribution even when his or her employer has no tax-qualified plan, if their AGI exceeds $50,000. For example, John Doe, who is covered under his employer's pension plan, earns $30,000. His wife, Jane, earns $15,000, so she can make a tax-deductible IRA contribution of $1,000. If her AGI were $20,000 she would not be eligible for a tax-deductible IRA contribution whether her employer had a pension plan or not.

An additional $250 may be contributed to a spousal IRA for a nonworking husband or wife. Before the passage of the 1986 Tax Reform Act, spousal IRAs were not allowed if the spouse had *any* earnings. The 1986 law allowed the $250 IRA contribution if earnings were $250 or less. However, when a couple's AGI exceeds $40,000, the spousal IRA contribution is reduced at the same rate as the wage earner's. Thus, if the couple's AGI was $42,000, the wage earner could add $1,600 to his or her IRA and the nonworking mate could contribute $200 to the spousal IRA.

A New Class of IRAs

Individuals who don't qualify for deductible IRAs may still make IRA contributions, but these must be designated as nondeductible. Deductible and nondeductible contributions together cannot exceed the $2,000 or $2,250 (spousal) annual maximum. Although these IRA contributions aren't deductible, earnings on them accrue tax-deferred. If nondeductible contributions are made they must be designated as such on that year's income tax form. In addition, the total of all nondeductible contributions made to date that have yet to be distributed, the year-end value of all IRAs, and the amount of distributions in that year must be reported on the income tax form.

Because earnings on nondeductible IRAs accrue tax-deferred, these IRAs have merit, particularly for young wage earners. However, at a 31 percent maximum tax rate, a taxpayer must earn $2,898 to make a $2,000 nondeductible contribution to an IRA. Conversely, contributions that *are* deductible *save* taxes. The following table shows the comparative after-tax costs of contributing $2,000 to a deductible versus a nondeductible IRA.

Tax Rate	Deductible	Nondeductible
31%	$1,380	$2,898
28%	1,440	2,778
15%	1,700	2,353

A $2,000 investment that grows tax-deferred at 8 percent per year will be worth $9,300 in 20 years. But if that same $2,000 were invested in a fully taxable account it would be worth only $6,100 if its owner was in the 28 percent bracket.

Flexible Investment Options

How can you invest your IRA funds? There are three basic types of individual retirement savings programs—individual retirement accounts, individual retirement annuities, and trust accounts established by employers or employee associations.

An individual retirement account must be a domestic trust

or a custodial account created for the exclusive benefit of an individual or his beneficiaries. The trustee or custodian must be a bank, a savings and loan association, an insurance company, a federally insured credit union, a mutual fund, or any person who can demonstrate to the satisfaction of the Internal Revenue Service the ability to administer the account in accordance with the law.

To make it easier and more economical to establish an IRA, the Internal Revenue Service has created model trust and custodial agreements. By using Form 5305 (Individual Retirement Trust Account) or Form 5305A (Individual Retirement Custodial Account), you can establish an IRA almost as easily as a bank account.

Depending on the trustee or custodian selected, you have a wide degree of flexibility in choosing the investments that fund your IRA. Most banks will set up an IRA using savings certificates. Most mutual funds will set one up using shares in the fund as assets. Stockbrokers, working with banks, can set up an account funded with stocks, bonds, mutual funds, and savings certificates. The latter self-directed accounts allow you to have an active hand in managing your investments.

Gold and silver coins minted in the United States were added to the approved IRA investment list beginning in 1987. The coins that qualify for IRAs are gold U.S. one-ounce, half-ounce, quarter-ounce and tenth-ounce pieces and U.S. one-ounce silver coins. The coins must be held by the plan trustee, not by the individual planholder.

No part of a trust or custodial IRA can be invested in life insurance. However, IRA monies may be invested in annuities provided the death benefit, if the annuity has one, is not tied to mortality assumptions. Your interest in the account must be nonforfeitable, and the account's assets may not be commingled with other property except in a common trust fund or common investment fund.

An individual retirement annuity is a contract (either an annuity or an endowment policy) issued by a life insurance company in your name for your exclusive benefit or for that of your beneficiaries. As with custodial or trust accounts, your interest must be nonforfeitable. Furthermore, to assure that payments will be used for your retirement, contract terms must provide that the annuity is not transferable and cannot be used as security for a loan. The annual premium cannot exceed the lesser of 100 percent of your earned income or $2,000, and any premium refund must be applied toward the payment of future premiums or the purchase of further benefits.

If you purchase an endowment contract, you can deduct only that portion of the premium allocable to retirement savings; any portion of the premium that pays for current life insurance is not deductible. However, if there is a difference between the cost of the retirement savings portion of the premium and your maximum allowable deduction, you may invest the balance in a separate IRA. The insurance company will provide you with an annual statement indicating the portion of the premium allocated to life insurance that is nondeductible.

Another possibility that might be available to you is participation in a group retirement annuity. The group annuity contract will be treated as an individual retirement annuity, provided it meets all the requirements of such an individual annuity.

Note the Penalties

There are penalties for making excess IRA contributions, for withdrawing funds from the account too early, and for taking out too little or too much. You may not take a current income tax deduction on excess contributions. Furthermore, you are charged a 6 percent excise tax on them (this is not deductible on your income tax) for each year the excess remains in your account. You can avoid the penalty by removing the excess—and any earnings on it—from your IRA before the due date of that year's tax return. Excess contributions left in the account may be applied toward future years' contributions to reduce the impact of the 6 percent excise penalty.

The rules are equally explicit on premature distributions. If you receive a payment from your IRA before reaching age

59½, or becoming permanently disabled, it is considered a premature distribution. The amount withdrawn is included in your gross income for that year *and* you must pay an added 10 percent tax on the distribution.

You can be penalized for not taking enough out of your IRA, too. Once you reach age 70½, you must either withdraw the entire balance in your account or start a schedule of regular withdrawals based on your life expectancy. If you fail to take out a sufficient amount you'll be hit with a 50 percent excise tax on the underdistribution. For example, if your minimum withdrawal at age 70½ is $1,000, but you only take out $600, you will have to pay a $200 penalty (50 percent of the $400 you failed to withdraw from your IRA). If you can show that the underpayment occurred because of a reasonable error, or that you are taking remedial action to correct the error, the IRS will waive the penalty.

Taking too much from an IRA aggregated with all other retirement savings plans can cause problems. Distributions from IRAs, qualified retirement plans, and tax-sheltered annuities that exceed $136,204 (indexed for 1991) in any one year are subject to a 15 percent excise tax. Special higher limits apply for years when a lump-sum distribution is received. This penalty, which was new with the Tax Reform Act of 1986, became effective in 1987.

You'll Pay Taxes—Eventually

Uncle Sam's generosity has other limits, too. When he lets you set up an IRA, he does not forgive the taxes that you would otherwise have to pay—he merely allows you to defer payment of them. That deferral is operative until you start taking "benefits" out of your plan.

There are three ways in which you can take benefits from your IRA. The first option is to take all assets in a lump-sum distribution. If you choose this alternative, the total value of the account must be added to your taxable income for that year. However, now that income averaging has been eliminated, this election could trigger a prohibitive tax liability. A lump-sum payment can be taken any time after age 59½, even after installment payments have commenced.

The second method is to use the assets that have accumulated in your IRA to purchase a single-premium individual retirement annuity. Payment options vary on annuities. Usually the contract guarantees a specified return on the annuity's value over your lifetime or the lifetimes of you and your spouse. But once annuity payments begin, you generally cannot change payment options. If you are uncertain about your future income needs, it would be unwise to lock yourself into an annuity contract.

The third, and most flexible, alternative is to arrange to receive distributions from the custodian in installments. The payments can be made as frequently as you see fit, perhaps monthly or quarterly, and are limited only by the total worth of your IRA. If your income requirements change, you may take the remaining assets in a lump-sum payment. Installment payments and annuity distributions are also taxable as ordinary income in the year they are received. If you elect to take installment payments remember that assets remaining in the account will continue to compound tax-free.

Nondeductible Contributions Complicate Distributions

The real confusion on nondeductible IRAs begins when distributions commence at or after age 59½. Since there is no tax due when nondeductible contributions are withdrawn (distributions of deductible IRA assets are taxable), it would be advantageous to deplete these assets first, or at least be able to determine from which account assets should be withdrawn. However, a foresighted Congress circumvented this potential tax advantage by writing complex distribution rules into the new law. These rules are especially disadvantageous to those who have large rollover IRAs.

When an individual has made both deductible and nondeductible IRA contributions, distributions will be counted for tax purposes as coming from both. The distribution will be taxable in the same ratio as nondeductible contributions bear to the value of the account at the year end, plus the distributions made during the year. All IRA and SEP accounts are aggregated to make these calculations, and withdrawals are totaled for each year.

Take, for example, a taxpayer who contributed $2,000 annually to an IRA for six years, the latest of which was a nondeductible contribution. Two years later, when the account is worth $16,000, he begins taking out $100 a month. At the end of that year the account's value, assuming 6 percent growth, is $15,724. To determine how much of the $1,200 in annual withdrawals is taxable, he adds $1,200 (total of monthly withdrawals) to the closing balance of $15,724 for an account value of $16,924. Next he finds the percentage of the total that his nondeductible contribution constitutes ($2,000 ÷ $16,924 = 11.8%). Therefore only $142 (11.8% of $1,200) of the $1,200 withdrawn from his IRA account is nontaxable.

As IRA assets are gradually depleted by distributions, the nontaxable portion of withdrawals increases. The following table, using the assumptions above (6 percent growth, $2,000 annual contributions, $1,200 in annual withdrawals, and so forth) shows a dozen years of this progression. At the end of the twelfth year, $1,945 of the $2,000 in after-tax contributions has been recovered under the new formula. An increasing portion of distributions will be tax-exempt in the ensuing years until the account is entirely exhausted.

Ending Value	Amount of Withdrawal	% Taxable	Withdrawal Amount Taxable	Withdrawal Amount Nontaxable
$15,724	$1,200	11.8	$1,058	$142
15,431	1,200	12.0	1,056	144
15,121	1,200	12.3	1,052	148
14,792	1,200	12.5	1,050	150
14,444	1,200	12.8	1,046	154
14,075	1,200	13.1	1,042	157
13,683	1,200	13.4	1,039	161
13,267	1,200	13.8	1,034	166
12,827	1,200	14.3	1,028	172
12,403	1,200	14.7	1,024	176
11,911	1,200	15.3	1,016	184
11,390	1,200	15.9	1,009	191

At age 70½ withdrawals *must* commence. Furthermore, you can no longer contribute to your account even though you may still be working. However, you can continue to contribute $250 to a spousal account for a younger, nonworking spouse. You have until April 1 of the calendar year following the year in which you attain age 70½ to begin taking distributions. Thus, if you are 70½ any time in 1991, then you must withdraw the minimum required amount by April 1, 1992.

The minimum distribution would be based on your account's value at the end of 1991. If an account holder is a male, then one-twelfth of the total value would have to be taken out by April 1, 1992; if a female, one-fifteenth of the value would be required. These withdrawal fractions are from IRS Form 5329 (Return for Individual Retirement Arrangements Taxes). When withdrawals are made over two life expectancies, an IRS annuity table is used to determine required amounts. Publication 590 (Individual Retirement Arrangements) includes this table as well as the unisex actuarial table described below.

Unisex Actuarial Table

Using the withdrawal timetables mentioned above, many retirees will outlive their IRA assets. When the IRA includes funds from a pension plan rollover, outliving those assets can create a serious financial bind in old age. To correct this inequity, the IRS adopted a new, unisex table of life expectancies, based on actuarial experience more recent than had been used previously. The new unisex table is more advantageous to retirees. The following table shows the differences in the divisors, amount of withdrawal, and the balance in the account using both life expectancy tables. Under the old rules, a retiree at age 82 would have collected $80,091 in distributions, exhausting his entire account. Using the unisex table, he is $12,547 ahead—his account is worth $36,920 and he has taken $55,718 in distributions since age 70. We assume the man's account has a $50,000 value at the start of his seventieth year and a 7 percent annual growth rate.

Age	Divisor		Amount Withdrawn		Year-End Balance	
	Old	New	Old	New	Old	New
70	12.1	16.0	$4,421	$3,344	$49,079	$50,156
71	11.1	15.3	4,731	3,508	47,783	50,159
72	10.1	14.6	5,062	3,676	46,066	49,994
73	9.1	13.9	5,416	3,848	43,875	49,645
74	8.1	13.2	5,796 ·	4,024	41,150	49,096
75	7.1	12.5	6,201	4,203	37,830	48,330
76	6.1	11.9	6,636	4,346	33,842	47,367
77	5.1	11.2	7,100	4,525	29,111	46,158
78	4.1	10.6	7,597	4,659	23,552	44,730
79	3.1	10.0	8,129	4,786	17,072	43,075
80	2.1	9.5	8,699	4,852	9,568	41,238
81	1.1	8.9	9,307	4,958	931	39,167
82	.1	8.4	996	4,989	0	36,920

Using Tax-Free "Rollovers"

So far, we have discussed individual retirement accounts whose primary aim is to serve as repositories for regular annual contributions. But the law allows them to serve another —and, as it turns out, extremely popular—function. IRAs may be used to channel retirement funds from one qualified pension program to another, with no immediate tax consequences to the employee. This is what has come to be known as a tax-free rollover. There are several ways you can use a rollover. You can use one if you change jobs and want to take your built-up retirement benefits with you. You can use a rollover to shift funds into an individual retirement account and leave them there to continue building up under your direction and management. If you wish, and if your new employer has a plan that can accept them, you may place the assets in his plan, where they will be handled as if they had been there all along.

You can also use a tax-free rollover to change your IRA investment vehicle. Say you have an IRA with a mutual fund and you're not satisfied with the fund's performance. You can roll the assets over into another mutual fund or into a custodial or trusteed plan where they will be invested in something else. You can also use a rollover to shift benefits into an IRA if your employer terminates his qualified plan.

Some Rules on Rollovers

Whether you use a tax-free rollover to shift assets from one plan to another, to shift them into your control, or for some other reason, you must observe certain rules. First, you must transfer the funds distributed from the old plan into the new one within 60 days of the distribution. Second, if property other than money is distributed, you must transfer that same property (usually stocks or bonds) or proceeds from the bona fide sale of that property to the new plan. Third, you may use the tax-free rollover provision only once in a 12-month period.

If you reinvest your retirement assets in a rollover IRA from a qualified plan, you must have terminated employment with the company operating the qualified plan. In other words, while you may stop participating in a company plan where you work, you cannot shift any assets built up in the account into an IRA until you reach normal retirement age, which is the age at which the company plan regularly allows workers to retire and start drawing benefits. Furthermore, if you have made any after-tax contributions to the company plan, those amounts may not be rolled over into an IRA, although earnings on them can.

As you have perceived by now, the rules surrounding IRAs are far from simple. What's more, they tend to change with alarming frequency. So, when you're ready to think seriously about an individual retirement account, you should check with your nearest Internal Revenue Service office for the latest rules. Ask for the most recent edition of IRS publication number 590, "Tax Information on Individual Retirement Savings Programs."

CHAPTER 42

Annuities as Retirement Fund Vehicles

THE MAIN PURPOSE of an annuity program is to eliminate the gamble that your retirement funds and life span will come out even. A secondary purpose—particularly for those still some distance from retirement—is to provide a vehicle for creating these retirement funds and for protecting them as much as possible against the ravages of inflation and taxes.

Since annuities are tied closely to the concept of life insurance, they are sold primarily by insurance companies. In fact, insurance companies are the only ones legally permitted to vend commercial annuities. Mutual funds and stock brokerage houses that have begun in recent years to market annuities with special "investment" twists do so through tie-ins with life insurance companies.

You can purchase an annuity all at once with a relatively large chunk of cash (called a "single-premium annuity") or a little at a time through regular installment payments (called an "annual-premium annuity").

An immediate annuity is a single-premium annuity that starts to provide income at once. (Payments must begin within a year of inception.) A deferred annuity is one you purchase, either as a single-premium or annual-premium annuity, on which income distributions begin at some future date as specified in the contract. The period during which

448

you are paying into the annuity but are not drawing income is called the "deferral period" or "accumulation period."

Annuities as Savings Vehicles

Deferred annuities, whether single-premium or annual-premium, have long been popular repositories for savings that someday will be used to provide retirement income. One reason for this popularity is that an annuity program provides a discipline for regular savings. Another is that, in general, the assets thus set aside may be confidently regarded as "safe."

It's because of this safety that the government has encouraged the use of annuities in personal retirement savings programs. By law, annuity earnings are not subject to income taxes during the accumulation period. This makes annuities suitable for retirement savings either inside or outside Keogh and IRA plans. Since employees of charitable and educational organizations are allowed to contribute generous portions of their incomes to annuities, such contracts often form the backbone of these employees' retirement savings.

The tax features of annuities have become one of their greatest selling points. In fact, the increasing use of deferred annuities as tax shelters rather than as retirement savings plans has prompted Congress to rewrite the tax laws governing them several times, the most recently in 1986. Congress retained the tax deferral of annuity earnings, but revised the taxation of annuity payments.

During the accumulation period, your principal may be invested in a variety of ways, depending on the type of annuity selected. In a fixed annuity, the insurance company invests in bonds or debt instruments that return a fixed amount of interest. The company can therefore guarantee you both the safety of principal and the rate of return. In the initial accumulation years the interest rate may be a few percentage points above the minimum rate guaranteed for the annuity's duration. However, the guaranteed rate frequently falls below the rate of inflation and even in the best of times barely keeps ahead of it.

To overcome this drawback, insurers introduced variable annuities, which allow the buyer to allocate his investment among portfolios of money-market funds, bonds, stocks, and so forth. Your investment may be reallocated a few times during the year. Your principal enjoys the benefits—and pays the consequences—of ups and downs in the stock market. Earnings on the account also reflect the skill of the portfolio managers and your wisdom in making allocations among portfolios. You're trading a guaranteed result for the chance to obtain a higher total return, hence a better inflation hedge.

How an Annuity "Pays" You

Historically—and annuities date back at least to the ancient Phoenicians—sellers of annuities agreed to pay buyers a predetermined amount periodically for life. No more, no less. But over the years, various payment options have been woven into the annuity fabric. These have evolved largely because of the quirk in human nature that resists giving away assets irrevocably, and out of the strong desire of one spouse to assure continued financial security for the surviving spouse as long as she (usually) should live.

Once the annuity begins making regular payments to you it becomes an income annuity. When the time comes to shift from a deferred to an income annuity, you must choose your payment option with great care. Once income payments begin, you generally are not able to change options.

There are several options. A *straight life annuity* provides a predetermined amount of income for the life of the annuitant. Period. When he or she dies, all payments stop—even if they fall far short of the amount paid into the annuity.

A *joint and survivor annuity* is one that provides income for the lifetime of two persons, generally a husband and wife. It may continue income at the same level until the second spouse dies, or it may provide larger payments while both are alive and reduced payments after one dies.

A *life annuity with installments certain* provides income for the lifetime of the annuitant. In addition, it guarantees to make these regular payments for a specified number of years, paying them to a designated beneficiary if the annuitant should die within that period.

An *installment refund annuity* pays income for life to the annuitant. But if he should die before receiving as much money as he paid in, the payments will go to a beneficiary until that amount has been reached. A *cash refund annuity* does the same thing, except that instead of continuing regular payments to the beneficiary, it provides a lump sum equal to the amount of undistributed principal.

An important point to remember is that these various options do not provide the same amount of income. The more guarantees the annuity has, the lower the payments to you. Thus, in making the proper choice, your main task is to determine what your present and future needs are likely to be. Forethought is especially important, because, as we have said before, once you make a commitment on how you'll receive payments, the decision is generally binding.

How Much Will It Pay?

Your health plays no part in your ability to purchase an annuity—unless the annuity has some life insurance aspects tied to it. The amount of income an annuity provides is determined by your age at the time the income payments begin and by the type of annuity you choose.

The extent of the guarantees provided by the insurance company will also affect the payment level. The more guarantees, the lower the benefits. Thus, straight life annuities, which guarantee nothing beyond a steady income as long as you live, yield the highest return. But when you die, the payments stop, and your estate receives nothing, even if the payments fall far short of the amount you paid in. They go instead into the pool to provide benefits for those who live beyond the life expectancy of the age group. Simple enough logic.

A more common situation involves a husband and wife who desire to assure lifetime income for both. A joint and survivor annuity, which is simply a straight life annuity on two lives, answers this need for many.

Because of the multitude of individual variables involved, no one type of annuity is best for everyone. However, you should keep these considerations in mind as you pick your way to a decision:

Since an annuity's main purpose is to deliver the highest income possible, you should look for the one that does this best. A straight life annuity will usually win.

If you want to leave assets behind for your heirs, you can generally do it more profitably by means other than annuities. Divide your assets accordingly between annuity and estate.

Don't automatically assume a joint and survivor annuity would be best for you and your spouse. Where the wife is younger, which is usually the case, payments may be significantly reduced on a joint annuity, because it covers two lives. Even if she is two or three years older than her husband, the income level will probably be lower than that of a similar annuity for the husband alone. As you shop around, then, compare the income of a joint and survivor policy against the combined incomes of annuities purchased separately by husband and wife.

If you do choose a joint and survivor policy, consider taking one that reduces payments after the death of one spouse. Since living costs generally decline when one spouse dies, this arrangement would provide more income for both during their lifetime together.

Should You Use Annuities?

We've discussed the various options open to you as a potential annuity buyer. What should you do? If you are sold on the safety and dependability of annuities, you should probably allocate a portion of your retirement savings to them. If they are bought well in advance of retirement, their tax-deferral feature gives them a significant edge over investments that are taxable. But if you select a fixed annuity, it should be balanced by other equity-type investments that will grow sufficiently to keep pace with inflation.

Another reason to be wary of becoming locked into an annuity program is that the very tax-deferral feature that attracts you to it could later work against you. That's because the only way you can escape a hefty tax on the accumulated earnings of the annuity is to take them out on an annuitized basis, that is, at a regular rate based on your life expectancy at the time payments commence. As we noted earlier, this decision is an irrevocable one; once you've made it, you're stuck with it. You can no longer get your hands on the assets you've committed to this program, regardless of how desperately you may need them later.

What if you decide to redeem an annuity during the accumulation period? If you do, you'll have to pay a tax all at once on the accumulated income. And if such a withdrawal is made before age 59½, you will be liable for a 10 percent penalty as well. If you anticipate such a contingency, you would do better to ignore the tax advantage and put your cash in an investment that is accessible without penalty.

Consider a "Private Annuity"

When they think of annuities, most people think of the type purchased from an insurance company—commercial annuities, which we have just discussed. However, it is possible to enter into an annuity agreement quite independent of an insurance company contract. "Buying" one "privately" has much to commend it.

The provision of a lifetime income for the annuitant is only one of the motives for using private annuities. More often the use of these contracts is associated with estate planning. Because of their various advantages, private annuities might be put to good use in your financial planning program. However, there are certain disadvantages and potential pitfalls to avoid.

To create a private annuity, you (the annuitant) agree to "sell" a specified asset to another party (the obligor) in return for a promise to pay you a fixed amount of money at regular intervals over your lifetime or for a set number of years. This payback must have a direct bearing on your life expectancy and it must be in accordance with the IRS table for annuity valuation. Currently these tables are based on a 10 percent interest rate. This means that when a person aged 70 transfers an asset worth $100,000 under a private annuity arrangement, the annual payment has to equal $16,523 in order to escape estate taxes.

Private annuities are frequently undertaken within families, with the obligor generally someone younger than the annuitant, say, a son or daughter. A family residence and other appreciated real estate are often used to finance the annuity. Sometimes these annuities are used as a method for an employer to pass on his small business to family members or employees, with the business itself funding the annuity.

The deferral of capital gains taxes on appreciated assets is the major advantage of a private annuity. Instead of paying such taxes "up front," which is the case when assets are sold to fund a commercial annuity, the tax on the capital gain is paid gradually as the capital is returned to the annuitant. Thus, the tax can be stretched over a period equal to the annuitant's life expectancy.

Besides the deferral of capital gains and the prospect of having regular income over your remaining years, a private annuity offers the annuitant the following advantages:

The assets can be removed from your estate and thus reduce potential estate taxes and administration costs.

As long as the "present value" of the annuity equals the value of the property transferred plus interest, there will be no gift tax.

The transfer of the property frees you from investment and management responsibilities.

Where the obligor is a relative (but not a child under 14) and is in a lower tax bracket than yours, you lower the family's total tax liability on the income generated by the property.

The obligor, too, can reap benefit from such a transaction:

He assumes ownership of the assets and thus can take any tax deductions available on the property (but no deductions for payments to the annuitant).

He can use the assets to provide financial leverage.

He can sell or exchange transferred property without incurring any capital gains.

Proceed Carefully

There are, as we said, some potential disadvantages and opportunities for slip-ups that must be given consideration before committing your assets to a private annuity.

Foremost, the agreement must be carefully and expertly drafted in order to withstand a challenge by the IRS. Because of the complexity of private annuities and this need for careful drafting, you should undertake them only with the advice and help of competent legal and tax counselors.

It is also important for you to realize that you must choose an obligor in whom you have complete trust and confidence. At best, you are exchanging a valuable asset for an unsecured promise on the part of the obligor. If he should go bust or otherwise renege on his promise to repay you, you would have no way to protect yourself or your investment. (You can, however, cover yourself against his untimely death with a life insurance policy separate and apart from the annuity agreement.)

There are ways to avoid or minimize the drawbacks of private annuities, and your counsel can help you incorporate them into your program. In many cases the potential benefits of such private annuities far outweigh the hazards and make them worth the care and effort needed to create them.

CHAPTER 43

Retirement

ABOUT ONE YEAR before you actually retire, you should begin to make preparations, so that the transition from salary to retirement income will be a smooth one. At that time you are close enough to retirement to get a fairly accurate reading on how much your Social Security benefit will be. The same goes for your company's pension plan, if you're included in one. Those two items are pretty much fixed by rules and policies beyond your direct control, but are influenced by your decision to retire before or after age 65. In deploying the assets you've built up in your own private retirement nest egg, you'll need to exercise much more judgment.

Social Security

But before we get into that, let's talk a bit about Social Security. It forms the backbone of the retirement programs of nearly all working Americans. It is frequently the largest single source of retirement income. Company pension plans are often tied directly to it.

For those receiving its retirement benefits, Social Security provides a basic monthly payment for life. It provides extra for a qualifying spouse, and it provides for that spouse after the primary beneficiary's death. It meets certain medical expenses under its Medicare program. It reduces the benefits of recipients who retire early and of those who earn more than a certain amount in retirement.

That much is generally understood. But beyond that, most people's knowledge begins to get hazy. Here is a nutshell description of how your individual benefit level is determined. To qualify for full benefits, you must have at least 40 quarters of "covered" service; that means you have to have worked the equivalent of at least 10 years in a job where Social Security taxes were deducted from your pay. These days, that means just about everyone except certain public-school teachers and civil servants, who are covered by other plans.

Having thus qualified, you are then subjected to certain rules to determine the amount of benefits to which you are entitled. Your *primary benefit level* is based on your "best" 40 quarters. Usually the most recent quarters are the "best" ones, because of rising income patterns and a rising wage base on which the Social Security taxes are computed. From these best 40 quarters, your individual average monthly wage is computed, and once this has been determined, henceforth and forevermore your Social Security benefits will revolve around this figure. If you choose to retire before the normal retirement age of 65—the rules allow you to start drawing retirement benefits at age 62—your benefits will be set at a lower rate than if you wait until age 65. If you work beyond 65, you can earn higher benefits.

Because the rules and benefit tables are constantly changing, it is impossible here to get very specific about how much your benefit payments will be. So, about a year before your projected retirement date, contact your nearest Social Security office and request a "Personal Earnings and Benefit Estimate Statement." It will take about a month to get back an estimate of your monthly benefit. You should start the actual application process for benefits about three months before retirement.

Then sit down with the people who manage your company's pension program and get a line on what to expect from that source. If you've been keeping tabs over the years, you'll have some general idea, and there should be no shocks or surprises there.

Next, take a pencil and calculator to the family budget to see where and how it will change after your retirement. If you're typical, your present living expenses should drop about one-quarter or one-third after retirement. Now, put your expected retirement income figure next to your projected operating budget. You'll probably find a gap. As we mentioned previously, it's a gap that's likely to widen with the years, too, because of the persistent rises in prices.

The wherewithal to fill that gap will come from the savings program you have been building and nurturing during your working years. The size of your nest egg will depend largely upon how conscientious you have been in adding to it and making it grow for you. The size of the nest egg in relation to the size of the gap will be a major factor in determining how best to deploy it.

What are your options? Annuities. Bank savings accounts. U.S. Savings Bonds. Bonds and other fixed-income securities. Real estate. Common stocks. Let's take a look, one by one.

Annuities

As you probably detected, we take a generally cautionary stance on the use of annuities as a source of retirement income. The main reason is that you must commit those resources irrevocably to the annuity, and therefore you strip yourself of a considerable amount of financial flexibility. You restrict your opportunities to juggle your assets around to meet changes in your situation. However, annuities have a specific utility as a tax-deferral tactic that is advantageous for building a nest egg.

We do concede that there are certain instances where annuities can serve well. So, we offer here some guidance on when and how to choose them. First—when might you consider the use of annuities?

When you want an assured income for life.

When you don't want to or don't feel you can manage your own investments—or if you seek such security for an heir.

When annuity "income" earns more than other investments in the marketplace.

When your health and condition make it likely that you'll live longer than the annuity tables.

Second—when should you not consider annuities?

When your age and other factors make the return on your annuity lower than those available from other securities.

When times are particularly inflationary.

When it appears likely that you won't outlive the annuity tables.

Generally speaking, the older you are when you take out an annuity, the higher the yield will be. That's because the insurance company writing the policy is taking less of a gamble as you advance in age. The return on a policy taken out at age 55 would probably be lower than that which those same assets could earn in many other good-quality investment vehicles. However, if you hold out until age 75, an annuity will yield considerably more—but keep in mind that the return is from both principal and interest.

That meshes well with the idea that during your younger retirement years, when you are still physically active and mentally alert, you should retain all the flexibility and control that you can over your assets. Then, as you grow older and less inclined to perform these tasks, consider investing some of your capital in an annuity.

But always remember: Once your annuity income payments begin, you cannot change your mind. Unless there is some refund feature, your heirs will receive nothing when you die. All too many annuitants—and heirs—fail to realize this, to their ultimate woe.

One other caution: Because annuities so severely limit your financial flexibility once you're committed to them, we firmly recommend that under virtually no circumstances should you convert all of your available assets to them. They should be regarded only as partial answers to your income needs.

In shopping for an annuity for guaranteed retirement income, do not assume that they all pay about the same. In one list of 39 different companies' straight life annuities, there was a 15 percent differential between the highest and lowest figure for monthly payments per $1,000. As you compare, you should also determine whether the companies charge a fee and, if so, how much it is. An unusually large one can significantly affect your return. Check, too, to see which companies offer discounts on larger annuities.

It may seem basic, but be sure that you compare the same type of annuity as you investigate each company. The straight life annuity generally offers the best income return, so that's a good place to begin. But if you feel another payout plan better suits your needs, obtain your comparisons on that plan.

Savings Accounts

Bank savings accounts can play a useful function in your retirement program. They can serve as repositories for capital on its way from one investment to another. They can provide a fund from which you can draw to meet financial emergencies. They can even be used to provide long-term income.

Let's turn our attention for a moment to that last function. As a rule, the longer you promise to keep your money in a bank account or term certificate, the higher the interest rate you will receive. A notable exception is the short-term money-market account, which under certain interest-rate conditions will provide a better return than some longer-term CDs. Because interest rates that financial institutions pay depositors are no longer regulated, a bank aggressively seeking deposits may sweeten its rates above those of its competition.

In looking for the best deal, note how the institution compounds interest. The shorter the compounding period, the more generous the yield. But also check when your deposits begin accruing interest—immediately or at the first of the next month? Does the bank impose a fee if the account drops below a certain limit? Are there restrictions on the number of monthly withdrawals? An extra interest point can be easily offset by unfavorable compounding terms, fees, or restrictions. In making comparisons, be sure to request a quote on the same type of interest rate from each institution. By getting the effective annual yield, you can more fairly compare accounts with different terms or compounding intervals.

There are certain advantages to keeping your money in a savings account. Foremost is safety. The deposits are fully insured; thus there is no loss if the institution should go broke. Second, savings accounts are simple to open—and to close—and there are no sales commissions or other expenses involved when making deposits or withdrawals, as there are when buying and selling securities. Third, they provide you with a source of ready cash when it is needed in an emergency.

But there are some drawbacks, too. Savings institutions impose penalties on time deposits that are withdrawn before the time specified in the agreement. Penalties are no longer regulated, so these too may vary. Be sure to inquire about these fines before investing in a term account. The "penalty" has no stigma attached to it; the money is yours to withdraw at any time, no questions asked. It just means that if you take it out before the agreed-upon interim, you don't get the agreed-upon rate, and you're assessed something for the bank's trouble.

The rate of failures in the thrift industry has been alarming. And although insured depositors in a failed institution don't lose their savings, they can suffer delays in gaining access to them. This can be inconvenient or even create hardship when funds are needed in an emergency.

When deciding whether to use savings accounts or term certificates, you must compare this return against what you would be able to get elsewhere. Sometimes corporate bonds will pay more and provide virtually the same safety of capital. Sometimes you'll want to link some prospects for capital growth to the income return on your assets, so you'll look at common stocks. Sometimes you'll have an opportunity to reap greater rewards with a real estate investment. We'll examine some of these on the following pages.

U.S. Savings Bonds

The savings aspects of U.S. Savings Bonds were covered in an earlier chapter. Now we will talk about using those bonds as a source of retirement income. Suppose you have been salting away a $50 E or EE bond each month for the past 30 years or so. As you make plans for your retirement, you'll want to consider the alternatives for turning this substantial savings bundle into a source of continuing income.

For purposes of illustration, suppose by the time you retire you have an even 30 years' worth of bonds purchased monthly—360 of them, at a cost of $37.50 each for the Series E and $25 for the EEs. Your total cash outlay was $12,000. At retirement, with the accumulated interest, your bonds are worth about $42,000. Here are four alternatives.

PLAN ONE. Cash in one bond a month, using the oldest ones first. In your first year of retirement your "income" would amount to about $2,700, with around $2,250 representing accrued interest, on which you'd have to pay federal income taxes. (Note that on Savings Bonds, as with most other U.S. Treasury and agency bonds, earnings are exempt from state and local taxation.) The annual income figures would rise somewhat in subsequent years as a result of the higher interest paid on newer bonds. Depending on your life expectancy, you might prefer to accelerate the program by cashing two years of bonds in one year.

PLAN TWO. Convert the E and EE bonds to HH bonds. The tax deferment on the accumulated E or EE bond interest would continue, but the semiannual interest payments from the H or HH bonds would be taxable as received. In converting the entire nest egg, you might have to add some cash in order to make an even exchange (HH bonds come in $500 minimum denominations). With interest on these bonds currently at 6 percent, you could expect to collect annual interest of $2,500.

PLAN THREE. Cash in all your Savings Bonds and reinvest the proceeds in better-yielding Treasury securities or corporate bonds. This may or may not be feasible, depending on interest-rate conditions when you retire. Of course, you would immediately incur a tax liability on the $30,000 or so of accrued interest.

PLAN FOUR. Cash in the E and EE bonds and reinvest the proceeds in a common stock portfolio. As in plan three, you'd have an immediate tax liability. After paying taxes ($8,400 if you are in the 28 percent bracket), you will have $33,600 to invest. The stocks you choose should provide an average annual total return of 11 percent, a performance widely regarded as realistically attainable for well-chosen common stocks held over the long term. By tilting your portfolio toward income stocks, you could obtain, say, 6 percent in dividend yield, with the remaining 5 percent representing capital growth. This would give you, on average, $2,000 in annual income in the early years, with increasing amounts as the years pass. But if your investments appreciate at the aforementioned rate of 5 percent each year, at the end of 10 years they will be worth $55,000, and $89,000 in 20, nicely hedging you against inflation. To do this, you must be aware that you might incur some risk, though that risk is minimized if you stick with investments in the highest-quality companies.

There can be variations of these plans, of course, or they can be employed in some combination. Then, too, the capital need not remain untouched under plans two, three, and four. It can be withdrawn gradually to provide steady income or it can be reserved to meet financial emergencies.

Here is a point to note when redeeming or exchanging E-type bonds. Proper timing of the redemption or exchange can prevent lost income. Unlike daily interest savings accounts, Savings Bonds do not accrue interest between payment dates. Interest is earned and reckoned every six months.

Thus, on a $25 E bond that has been held for 20 years or so, a poorly timed redemption could reduce earned income by as much as $2. Careful planning, especially when a large number of bonds are being cashed or exchanged, can pay off.

Say you have bought an E or EE bond each month over the past several years and now want to swap them for HH bonds to provide retirement income; you can do this most profitably by staggering the exchange over a six-month period. In January, exchange the bonds acquired in January and July of each of the past years; in February, the February and August bonds, and so forth.

If you start this exchange program six months before you retire, you'll begin receiving interest checks immediately after retirement, thus providing something to help fill the earnings gap right away and not six months down the road.

There's another benefit to employing this gradual exchange tactic. Since HH bond interest is paid semiannually, you not only avoid lost interest by using this serial redemption program, you also establish a schedule that provides you with an income check each month instead of only twice a year.

Corporate Bonds

We discussed corporate bonds extensively in Chapter 8, so by now you're familiar with how they work. But during the years you were building up your retirement fund, you probably did not give them much thought. Now, when income will become your primary investment concern, you may want to add some to your portfolio to provide assured income as well as safety of capital.

That's fine, and as we noted in the earlier chapter, you might even be able to build in inflation protection by acquiring some deeply discounted bonds that you can redeem at par when they mature.

As you consider bonds, look at those with "medium" maturities—those whose maturities aren't too far into the future. As we said earlier, bonds trade on the market near their par as they approach maturity. If you should have to liquidate some along the way, you'll want to do so at par or as close to it as possible.

But because their potential for capital growth is limited,

you probably won't want to commit all of your retirement funds to bonds. It depends on what your income needs are, of course, but we tend to believe that 20 percent or so in bonds is about right in most cases.

If you want instant diversification in the bond portion of your retirement portfolio, you can consider some bond funds; we discussed them in Chapter 13.

If you want more opportunity to provide capital growth but you still like the idea of bonds' safety and assured income, you can look at some convertible bonds. They were discussed in Chapter 9. They provide somewhat less yield than straight corporates, and somewhat less opportunity for capital appreciation than common stocks. But that's all part of the trade-offs we've been discussing throughout this book.

Real Estate

Unless you're looking for a new "job," or are willing to lay out money to a manager, the eve of retirement is not the time to start thinking about rental real estate as an investment. But there is this aspect: Rental income is not regarded as "earned" income as far as the Social Security earnings limitation rules are concerned, so no matter how much rental income you earn, it will not reduce your Social Security benefit.

What if you already hold real estate? Should you sell and reinvest the proceeds? Or should you keep the property, use the income, and call its appreciating value your inflation hedge? Several important factors will enter into your decision.

The best starting point would be to determine the true net yield on your investment—the amount realized after paying all expenses, using any tax offsets, and taking into consideration the amount of your own efforts expended in management. Then, compare that yield with the kind of yield the same assets would generate if diverted to other investments. (Remember, there would be some erosion of assets in making any switch—commissions, other sales expenses, and so forth —and probably some taxes.)

Next you must determine the future prospects of continued

ownership. Will the property continue to gain in value at least as fast as other, comparable real estate? Is the real estate market strong or is it in a slump? Will rent increases keep pace with inflation? Is there a chance the property could decline in value? Factors such as location, condition of property, and development trends of the community and neighborhood must be studied.

Then you must consider the personal aspects of continued management. Would it tie you down more than you wish? Would the management become too much of a burden as you grow older? Does ownership tie up too much of your wealth, creating the risk of loss in a "distress sale" should you suddenly need to liquidate to obtain funds? Does the real estate constitute too heavy a proportion of your investment portfolio to afford good balance? Would changes in the Tax Code make the property economically unsound?

Having considered these factors, you then must choose from several alternatives:

Retain the real estate and continue to collect rent.

Sell it all now and reinvest the proceeds in stocks and bonds.

Gradually divest yourself of the property, selling first the least desirable pieces, reinvesting proceeds as received.

Sell the real estate, but write the mortgage yourself. This would give you income as well as a gradual return of capital, while freeing you of the burdens of management and ownership. (Be sure if you choose this option to have the help of competent legal counsel to safeguard your interests.)

Obviously, there is no "right" answer. In general, though, it is our feeling that retirees should make their financial affairs as trouble-free as possible, within the bounds of good sense and sound judgment. It has been our experience that carefully chosen common stocks and bonds go a long way toward providing the sort of returns needed for current income and protection of buying power, while at the same time minimizing the management effort.

Common Stocks

Now you come to your common stock portfolio. During its accumulation years, you have been concentrating on growth, on building its value as much as possible, with little concern for how much income it was generating—or even making a studied effort to avoid income while your salary kept you highly taxed. Now, on the verge of retirement, you suddenly have to shift gears and find investments that will provide income to fill that "gap."

Because it takes time to make an orderly transition, we urge you to move slowly in this regard, as in all other investment decisions. In the first place, a wholesale shifting of "growth" stocks for "income" securities could increase your tax liability and eat heavily into your assets. In the second place, some of your "growth" stocks might also be perfectly good "income" securities, and therefore should be retained.

Don't feel that because you are about to retire you must completely divest yourself of common stocks and go entirely into "safe" fixed-income investments. When you think of the impact inflation has on the assets thus deployed, you have to wonder just how "safe" they really are.

On the other hand, wisely chosen common stocks, because they are equity investments, will tend to rise in value right along with—or even well ahead of—the rise in prices. Not only will their asset value rise, but so also should their dividends. Therefore, common stocks should play an important role in your investment picture after retirement, just as they did before.

How, then, does a retiree's investment portfolio look? It will depend, of course, on your own particular situation, but for the purposes of example, here is a fairly conservative approach to deploying a $100,000 nest egg for a couple retiring at age 65:

Amount Invested		Annual Income
$ 15,000	Bank accounts and term certificates for immediate needs and minor emergencies and a money-market certificate or fund for income. Average yield, 8%.	$1,200
50,000	Common stocks. A portfolio with somewhat less emphasis on growth than during the accumulation period, but not entirely committed to income. A representative income yield would be about 6%.	3,000
35,000	Corporate and government bonds and bond funds. Yields will vary according to current market activity, but a representative expectation would be around 10%.	3,500
$100,000	.... TOTALS	$7,700

Consuming Your Capital

Contrary to the old Yankee axiom that it's sinful to dip into principal, it sometimes makes very good sense to do so. The trick is to make the available capital last as long as you'll need it. There's no sure way of foretelling how long that will be, of course, but there are some rules of thumb that you can apply to the task. More on them in a moment.

First, there are some ways you can consume your capital in a rational fashion. One has to do with common stocks, as discussed above. Instead of taking your tax lumps to switch a growth stock to an income issue and then, to boot, paying taxes on the income generated by the new stock (not to mention the in-and-out brokerage commissions), why not sell off a few shares of the appreciated stock as you need the cash? You'll raise the income you require, you'll incur a small tax liability, and you'll still have a good part of your original stake left to continue growing. In terms of the number of dollars invested, you might well stay ahead.

Another way you can do the same thing is to invest in a mutual fund that has a cash withdrawal program. It will send you a regular amount each month, making up the required sum either from earnings on the assets or from the assets themselves. The rate at which the fund is growing and at which you withdraw from it will determine how long your assets will last.

If the combined earnings and appreciation of your stocks or mutual funds equal or exceed the rate at which you're withdrawing, your assets will last forever, of course. But what if you must consume your capital faster than it's growing? To get an idea of how long your capital should last, start by checking longevity figures.

Life Expectancy Table

Age	Male	Female	Age	Male	Female
50	25.4	31.1	68	12.7	16.6
51	24.6	30.2	69	12.2	15.9
52	23.8	29.3	70	11.6	15.2
53	23.0	28.4	71	11.1	14.5
54	22.2	27.6	72	10.6	13.9
55	21.4	26.7	73	10.1	13.2
56	20.7	25.9	74	9.6	12.6
57	19.9	25.1	75	9.1	12.0
58	19.2	24.3	76	8.7	11.3
59	18.5	23.4	77	8.2	10.8
60	17.8	22.6	78	7.8	10.2
61	17.1	21.9	79	7.4	9.6
62	16.4	21.1	80	7.0	9.1
63	15.8	20.3	81	6.7	8.6
64	15.1	19.5	82	6.3	8.1
65	14.5	18.8	83	6.0	7.6
66	13.9	18.1	84	5.6	7.2
67	13.3	17.3	85	5.3	6.8

Source: National Center for Health Statistics (1982).

As a safe rule of thumb, about one and a half times the indicated life expectancy should be enough cushion for estimating your own longevity. Then, using the following table, determine the number of years your assets will last if they are growing at a slower rate than they are being withdrawn. For example, a widow aged 65 with a life expectancy of 19 years should plan on making her capital last for about 28 years. That means that on assets that are earning and appreciating at a combined 8 percent annual rate, she could safely withdraw 9 percent of her principal each year.

Withdrawal Rate	Annual Growth Rate of Funds									
	5%	6%	7%	8%	9%	10%	11%	12%	13%	14%
6%	36						number of years			
7%	25	33					principal should			
8%	20	23	30				last			
9%	16	18	22	28						
10%	14	15	17	20	26					
11%	12	13	14	16	19	25				
12%	11	11	12	14	15	18	23			
13%	9	10	11	12	13	15	17	21		
14%	9	9	10	11	11	13	14	17	21	
15%	8	8	9	9	10	11	12	14	16	20

In Conclusion

We've covered a lot of alternatives in this chapter, and you can be forgiven if you are somewhat confused by the array of options open to you. Don't panic. But it's because of the number of decisions you'll have to make that we suggested at the outset of the chapter that you start considering them at least a year in front of your retirement date.

We can't tell you exactly how to make these decisions, of course. What we've tried to do here is lay out the options, note their pros and cons, and give you an idea of what they'll do—and won't do—for you.

You have to put together a package you're comfortable with, one that doesn't keep you awake at night worrying about the risks, and one that isn't so complicated that you have to stay up nights managing it. Some people can live with more risk than others, so they won't lose sleep over a plan that would turn the next guy into an insomniac. Others really enjoy a plan that gives them something to do, such as managing an investment portfolio or a piece of rental property.

We suggest that you retain as much flexibility as you can in your plan, so you'll be able to roll with any punches that come your way, and so you can change the program to meet any changing needs that come with advancing age.

CHAPTER 44

Planning for Death

EVEN IF YOU have done a good deal of estate planning—and most of us have done at least some—there's a chance you haven't gone over your program lately. If that's the case, it could well be out of date. An estate plan isn't something you can do and, having done it, say, "That's that." It needs adjustment from time to time to take into account changed conditions in your family and business. Furthermore, estate planning must be a continuing concern regardless of the size of your estate or the seeming simplicity of your individual situation. Finally, your estate is something that quite likely needs the help of a variety of qualified advisors—your attorney, banker, accountant, insurance agent, and investment advisor.

This chapter will give you a starting point for a full-scale review of your own program. It will help you spot areas that need special attention. After this preliminary work, you'll be in a better position to call upon your various advisors for specific application.

The best place to start the review is to find out how much you're worth. Besides determining how much you're currently worth, as we discussed in Chapter 36, you ought to find out how much your estate would be worth. The difference can be substantial, of course, because of proceeds from insurance policies and other death benefits, plus lump-sum distributions from pension and profit-sharing programs where you work.

Net estate worth is the starting point from which estate taxes will be calculated. How much of a bite these taxes—federal and state—take will largely rest on how well you have designed your program. The difference between taxes on an estate subjected to little or no planning and one that is carefully thought out can be staggering.

Keeping Your Will Current

After you find out how much your estate would be worth, you have to think about what you want done with this wealth. The front line of protection in this regard is a will. You do have one, don't you? Is it current?

Dying intestate—that is, without leaving a will—could be one of the most thoughtless, tragic, and expensive errors in your estate planning. It means that the courts, using an impersonal and rigid formula set out by state law, will decide who gets what, regardless of how you or your heirs might have wanted things.

Almost as bad is leaving behind a will that is so far out of date or so carelessly planned as to be inadequate, invalid, or inappropriate to your own current wishes and family's best interests. No matter how simple or clear-cut you think your situation is, you ought to spell out with a will your desires regarding the disposition of your wealth as specifically as possible. Another thought: although you can draw up your own will, there's a better than even chance that such a home-made document will not stand up in court. It's always safest to have the work done by an attorney.

Choosing an Executor

Choosing the right executor is nearly as vital as drafting the proper will. Yet the choice of an executor is too often left to chance and sentiment rather than to common sense. A hasty and ill-considered decision ultimately can undo much of your otherwise careful planning and estate-building efforts.

Many persons almost automatically name their spouse, another close family member, or a friend as executor, with little contemplation of the risks that will fall to this individual or the qualifications with which he would confront them.

On the other hand, a bank or trust company or an attorney specializing in estate management might not be as close to the family situation as a relative or friend, and might make decisions quite alien to your own desires or, possibly, to the real needs of the family.

But there is a way to have your cake and eat it too. That is to name your spouse or other relative as coexecutor with a bank or trust company. In such an arrangement, you could give your kin the final say in any decision, thus providing continuity in your family's life-style, while the professional executor would provide the good management, attend to the details, and be available to offer expert counsel.

As with other things, there is a difference in the quality of service between one institution and another. The better you know the bankers in your community, the better you'll be able to decide which one to choose. Your family lawyer can help you, too. Another way many persons get a feel for how a trust department would handle their estate is to establish a living, revocable trust, with the bank as cotrustee. The way the bank handles that trust is a good indication of how it would handle the estate.

An executor's task is not one to be taken lightly. In a small estate, with no major complications, where the will's intentions are clearly spelled out and there is not much property to dispose of or heirs to offer dispute, the job can be relatively easy. But in an estate of any substance, where there are children or elderly dependents and their continuing financial security to consider, or where family quarrels erupt, the job can be far from routine.

In such cases, the availability of an executor could be required over the span of several years. Can you be sure the person of your choice would meet this test? He could die or move away or be otherwise unable to carry on. In this event, a new executor would have to be appointed, at considerable expense to the estate. One way around this eventuality would be to name a successor executor at the time you draw up your will. Unless you designate an alternative choice, a court-appointed replacement might handle the estate, at a variance with your wishes.

Furthermore, an executor should have experience in this type of work. He should have the ability to conserve the estate's assets and administer them prudently. He should also be financially responsible. To be sure, an executor can be held legally responsible for the estate's assets if he carelessly handles them or illegally diverts them. He can be held liable for actions he fails to take as well as for oversights that result in losses. However, if he is financially unable to make restitution, the heirs will be the ultimate losers.

You are in the best position to know who will serve your family's interests well in your stead. But you should make the choice only after considerable thought, and possibly with some advice from professionals. Your decision can be as important as the care you take in preparing your will.

You Should Have a Living Will

Most of us have a horror of living in a vegetative state, kept alive by machines, fed by tube. While we usually associate this misery with the frail elderly, car accidents can leave even a formerly healthy young person comatose. Providing the state with "clear and convincing evidence" that a person had previously indicated that he wanted to die rather than live as a vegetable is facilitated by the existence of a living will, supported by a power of attorney for health care decisions. These documents must be executed while a person is mentally able to make a rational judgment.

Between 1976 and 1989, 41 of the 50 states enacted living will laws. Even in the nine states with no specific statutes pertaining to an individual's "right to die," case law has favored that right. While in some states, the law allows only the removal of life support equipment, in others the withdrawal of artificial feeding and hydration is permitted. In only seven states do laws specifically prohibit the removal of tubes supplying food and liquid. You can obtain a living will declaration form that satisfies the laws in your state from the Society for the Right to Die, 250 West 57th Street, New York, NY 10107.

Who Needs a Power of Attorney?

A power of attorney can be designed to serve your general business and financial needs or to accomplish a specific purpose. The person you appoint as your "agent" can act in your stead to carry out the tasks you specify in the power. Regardless of the wording used in the document, the power is revoked at your death. This prevents an unscrupulous "agent" from depleting the assets in your estate. To avoid possible misuse of the power during your life, you or your attorney should retain physical possession of it until it is needed. Once a person is mentally incapacitated it is too late to execute a power, since the person is deemed incompetent to make such a judgment. Without a previously drawn power, your assets are frozen until a conservator or guardian can be appointed by the court; then you would have no say in their selection. Most husbands and wives prefer to name their respective mates as agents, because they have interests in common. An adult child is also an appropriate choice when a spouse is dead. Whoever is chosen should be informed of your intentions, of the powers being granted, and of the location of the document.

A durable, general power of attorney is the broadest and most potent. The durable power, as opposed to a nondurable one, remains in force despite subsequent mental or physical incapacity. Nondurable powers are revoked at that time. Durable powers are allowed by all 50 states, but aren't permitted in the District of Columbia. When the power is a general one, the agent can file your taxes, sign your checks, sell your securities, run your business, and otherwise act for you in most business and financial matters. A special power of attorney enables the agent to act on your behalf for the particular duty stated in the document. That duty may also be limited to a specific time period. For example, you might grant your broker the power to buy or sell stock for you while you are out of the country.

Is a Trust for You?

We mentioned trusts above. Do they have a place in your estate plan? They are not only for the super-rich. More and more persons of modest means are using trusts to accomplish a variety of estate-planning aims, from lowering taxes to helping charities.

The first step in deciding whether trusts are for you is to determine just what you want them to accomplish. The second is to understand some of the basic differences between various types of trusts.

Here are some of the things trusts can do for you: provide financial support for a relative; divide an estate among heirs; retain family privacy; help minimize estate taxes; provide professional management of assets; protect a family business; make gifts; assure bequests of specific property; help charities.

There are basically two kinds of trusts: those that are in effect while you are alive, or "inter vivos trusts," and those that become operative upon your death, called "testamentary trusts." Living trusts can be revocable (in which you retain control of the assets) or irrevocable (in which you permanently give up control). The distinction is an important one, particularly in estate planning.

Trusts can be used to assure a lifelong stipend for a spouse or other relative from the income generated by the trust assets, with the assets themselves going, say, to a child or grandchild on the income beneficiary's death. This serves two valuable functions. First, it assures an income for someone who might not otherwise possess enough financial acumen to use the capital wisely. Second, it can save a good deal in estate taxes because, in effect, the assets are taxed only once, while serving twice.

Short-term trusts can be used to provide income for an aged parent or other older dependent. These revocable trusts are of no use in reducing your estate, since if you die while one is in force, the assets are counted among your own. This is the case with any revocable trust, that is, any trust that you retain the power to dissolve, or the provisions of which you retain the power to change.

However, if the trust is irrevocable, its assets will not be counted in your estate, because you have given them away totally and permanently. You might find that you incur a gift tax liability when establishing and contributing to such trusts.

Where can you get specific advice about trusts? A good place to begin is with the trust department of your local bank. They can tell you whether your idea has merit, perhaps offer alternatives if it's questionable. They can also give you a picture of total cost. You should also talk with your lawyer early on; you'll need one for just about any kind of trust you set up. You might want to bring your tax counsel into the talks, too. He could have some insights into your financial picture that the lawyer might not have.

Pros and Cons of Joint Ownership

There are many valid reasons for married couples to hold property jointly. If their total estate is so small that taxes would be minimal or avoided entirely, many of the negative effects of joint ownership probably would be nonexistent— and possibly even be more than offset by certain benefits.

Here are some advantages of joint ownership: It can give a sense of family security. It can provide a safe and easy way to maintain and liquidate bank accounts. It can reduce estate administration costs and speed up the settlement of the estate, since property passes at once to the survivor. It can reduce or eliminate the need for probate.

One important thing you should realize about joint ownership is that it does not take the place of a will. Whether you choose joint or separate ownership, each spouse should have a will; that's the only sure way of seeing that your wishes are carried out after death.

There are many types of joint ownership, and a quick review here might prove useful. *Joint tenancy* permits co-ownership of real estate and other types of property, with right of survivorship. In other words, the survivor receives total title of ownership at the death of the other co-owner. *Tenancy by the entirety* is limited to joint ownership by husband and wife, and in many states to real estate only, with the right of survivorship. *Tenancy in common* permits two or more persons to own undivided shares in real or personal property; co-owners' shares pass to their heirs or beneficiaries, not to surviving co-owners. *Community property* is the assumption, in force in eight states, that each partner in marriage has an automatic right to half the couple's assets, regardless of who provided how much. (The eight community property states are Arizona, California, Idaho, Louisiana, Nevada, New Mexico, Texas, and Washington.) Business arrangements such as partnerships, syndicates, and joint ventures are yet other forms of joint ownership.

For most married couples, joint ownership means joint tenancy or tenancy by the entirety, where right of survivorship is a principal element, or both. Many couples believe this arrangement is all they need in the way of estate planning. Here are some reasons why that can be a dangerously shortsighted assumption:

It restricts your estate-planning options. Because assets pass automatically from one spouse to the other on the death of one, you cannot spell out in a will conditions under which your "share" of the property can be distributed.

It can be inconvenient. Both owners must give their OK to any changes in the property—changing the ownership status, disposing of it, and the like. This means signatures of both will be required when, say, selling jointly held stocks and bonds.

It could increase estate taxes. Although the gift and estate tax laws have been liberalized with regard to the marital deduction and joint ownership, there are circumstances where maximum use of the tax provisions cannot be made because property is held jointly.

What, if anything, can be done to unspring these potential traps? First, it isn't such a bad idea, under most circumstances, to keep the house in joint names. That way, the survivor acquires it at once on the spouse's death. Likewise for a savings account with enough money in it to carry the survivor over the first rough months until the estate is settled, or at least sufficiently organized to permit the disbursement of some funds. Second, you could decide to divide all other property equally, including securities and other real estate, by changing from joint tenancy to tenancy in common, dropping the right of survivorship. This way, each can dispose of his or her share by will. As with other such maneuvers, the guidance of professional counsel is advised.

How Gifts and Estates Are Taxed

Determining how large the taxes on your estate will be should provide ample inspiration for formulating an estate plan that minimizes federal taxes. But before delving into the how-to's of cutting estate taxes, it's important that you have a general understanding of the current estate tax code. Of course, Congress has a habit of updating and changing the rules, which makes it impossible to be too specific here.

The first thing to remember about the federal gift and estate tax structure is that it is progressive. The tax rate is incremental, increasing as a percentage as a taxable estate gets larger. Therefore, even modest efforts to reduce an estate's taxable size can have a significant impact on its total tax liability. This is an important fact to remember as you set about planning your estate.

Because taxpayers have a built-in incentive to reduce the size of their taxable estates, the Internal Revenue Service has evolved a body of rules governing the way in which these reductions can be made. Basically, the IRS wants a share of your estate and forgives taxes on it only begrudgingly.

Although Congress has been liberal regarding estate taxes, the need to boost revenues has led to tightening in this area, beginning with TRA 1986, which made such terms as "kiddie tax," "generation-skipping transfers," and "GRITS" familiar additions to the tax lexicon.

Changes in Estate Taxes

How has the estate tax code changed? In 1976, Congress scrapped the separate gift and estate tax schedules. It replaced them with a unified tax rate on both and instituted a unified tax credit in place of the separate tax exemptions. In effect, the new unified credit exempted more estates from taxes by raising the minimum level at which taxation begins.

Congress further refined the Tax Code in 1978. Then, as part of the Economic Recovery Tax Act of 1981, it again made sweeping changes in the estate tax code. The unified credit, which offsets gift and estate taxes on a dollar-for-dollar basis, was again increased. The top estate tax rate was lowered. Joint property rules were simplified and the so-called marital deduction was made unlimited.

TRA 1986 signed the death warrant for all short-term reversionary trusts by making income from them taxable at the parent's top rate for beneficiaries under age 14. Estates and trusts were required to file quarterly estimated taxes and were made liable for the alternative minimum tax levy. Direct transfers to heirs two or more generations removed (from grandparent to grandchild) from the transferor were liable to estate tax at the maximum rate (currently 55 percent).

The Revenue Act of 1987 delayed the scheduled 1988 estate tax rate reduction until 1993. A 5 percent easing of the maximum rate to 50 percent had been scheduled. This act also added subsection (c) to Code Section 2036 limiting the benefits available from estate freezes. Where an older person holding a substantial interest (10 percent or more of the voting power or income) in an enterprise transfers a portion of it to a younger family member, yet retains an interest in it, the value of the transferred property will be included in the transferor's estate. Liberal interpretation of the code section would result in many gifts' being included in estates at their appreciated value years after the gift was made.

The 1988 revenue act (TAMRA) attempted to clarify the scope of 2036(c) and provide an "escape" period (from December 17, 1987, to January 1, 1990) for corrective action to undo transactions. Nonetheless, as this ruling now stands many transfers by gift could be affected. With fewer and fewer items left for Congress to tax, estates will become increasingly attractive as a potential source of additional revenue. Lowering the tax-free transfer floor from $600,000 to $250,000 would add more than $3 billion to revenues annually.

Marital Deduction

How you decide to apportion your estate will depend on personal circumstances and wishes. But from a tax savings perspective, primary consideration should be given to an estate plan that employs the unlimited marital deduction. Use of this deduction usually forms the backbone of most couples' estate planning strategies. It allows you to transfer all or part of your estate to your spouse tax-free at death. The marital deduction also allows you to make unlimited gifts to your spouse while you are alive. But for an estate to qualify for the deduction, a couple must be married at the time of death of one spouse. Divorced persons may not claim a marital deduction.

An estate plan should not overwork the marital deduction. Sometimes its use can be counterproductive in the long run, saving taxes in your estate only to have substantially larger taxes imposed on your spouse's estate. This is particularly true when each spouse has considerable wealth of his or her own. When planning your estate, don't assume that the spouse with the most property will die first. Above all, your estate plan should be flexible. If you plan to bequeath all or part of your estate to your spouse to make use of the unlimited marital deduction, your will should also contain contingency plans in the event your spouse predeceases you or your deaths are simultaneous.

A well-structured estate plan should make maximum use of both the unlimited marital deduction and the increased unified credit. It's possible to use both techniques to assure the financial security of your surviving spouse while at the same time reducing the total taxes on both estates. Here's an example of how this can be done. Assets of $600,000 are used to fund a testamentary trust benefiting your surviving spouse. The testamentary trust's assets escape taxation in your estate and, upon your spouse's death, pass tax-free to your chosen heirs.

The balance of your estate could be left to your spouse in the form of an outright bequest or in a terminable interest trust. Both qualify for the marital deduction in your estate and, when your spouse subsequently dies, for the unified credit in his or her estate. By maximizing use of the unified credit and marital deduction in such a manner, it is possible to bequeath as much as $1.2 million to your heirs tax-free.

A Program of Planned Gifts

What else can you do to reduce estate taxes? Individuals with potentially taxable estates should consider making life-time gifts to their future heirs. Gifts of up to $10,000 per donee per year may be made without incurring a gift tax liability. Married couples can give up to $20,000 per donee. In most cases, gifts made within three years of death are no longer considered made in contemplation of death, and thus are not included in an estate's value for tax purposes.

Remember, too, that both lifetime and testamentary gifts to charity also reduce your taxable estate. A program of planned giving can accomplish noncharitable goals as well. By funding a charitable remainder trust in your will, you can reduce estate taxes while also providing beneficiaries with a lifetime source of income.

Changes in the tax laws, new regulations, and court rulings continually add new shadings to the vast and complicated body of the estate tax code. These changes, as well as the specifics of your family situation, make periodic reviews of your estate plan necessary. Consult your tax advisor for suggestions on how best to meet your planning objectives while minimizing estate taxes.

PART VIII

Speaking the Language of the Bulls and the Bears

An extensive glossary of investment, economic, business, legal, and financial terms of importance to investors.

Glossary

accrual basis. One of the two major accounting methods. Revenues are assigned to the year in which they are earned regardless of when the earnings are received. Expenses are recognized when incurred regardless of when the cash is dispensed in payment of the expense. *See* **cash basis.**

acid test (also known as quick assets ratio or liquidity ratio). The ratio of current assets less inventories to current liabilities. The acid test provides a better test of a firm's current operations than the current ratio, since inventories often do not prove liquid enough to service current debt. *See* **current ratio.**

adjustable rate bond (or adjustable rate preferred stock). A security on which the interest rate (or dividend) is adjusted each payment period in relation to a recognized market rate such as the prime or that on Treasury bills; there may also be a maximum or a minimum, or both, on the adjustable rate.

adjusted gross income (AGI). The gross income received by an individual taxpayer, less business expenses, expenses attributable to property held to produce rent and royalty income, alimony payments, and contributions to Keogh or SEP accounts.

advance-decline index. The net result of all advances and declines on the NYSE or other exchange since a particular starting point. The ratio derived from relating advances to declines provides an overbought/oversold index.

advisory service. An organization offering information, generally buy and sell advice, to investors for a fee.

AMBAC—American Municipal Bond Assurance Corp. A consortium of leading insurance companies that guarantees principal and interest payments on municipal bonds. Evidence of the insurance is printed on or attached to each bond. Since the initials are part of the description of the bond, they should appear on the broker's confirmation and statement.

American Depositary Receipts (ADRs). Negotiable receipts issued by an American depositary bank stating that a certain number of foreign shares have been deposited with the overseas branch of the depositary or with a custodian. Since foreign stock is often in bearer form, the ADR facilitates such matters as the receipt of dividends by the shareholder.

American Stock Exchange (AMEX). The second-largest securities exchange, located in New York City. The AMEX's volume is approximately as heavy as that of all the regional exchanges combined.

amortization. The gradual liquidation annually of the cost of an intangible asset such as a patent or a debt. Amortization is a bookkeeping entry and does not require an outlay of cash.

annual report. The formal financial statement issued yearly by a corporation to its shareholders.

annuity. Payment made to an annuitant at some regular interval for either a specified or indefinite length of time. Annuity contracts are sold by life insurance companies. "Annuity" also refers to the contract under which the payments are made.

arbitrage. The act of purchasing a particular security or commodity in one market and simultaneously selling it in another market at a higher price. The arbitrageur profits when the price differential between the two markets exceeds the cost of the operation. Also, the purchase and sale of related securities—common, options, and convertible bonds or preferreds—for profit on price differentials.

assets. Physical properties or intangibles of value owned by an individual or a business.

authorized stock. The maximum amount of stock that can be issued by a corporation according to its certificate of incorporation, which may at any time be amended by stockholders' vote.

balanced fund. A mutual fund that diversifies its portfolio holdings over common stocks, bonds, preferreds, and possibly other forms of investment. Holdings of defensive securities are proportionately increased when the market outlook appears unfavorable, and aggressive positions are stressed when the market seems to be headed upward.

balance sheet. An accounting statement showing the amount of a company's assets, liabilities, and owners' equity as of a given date.

bar chart. A form of chart used extensively by technicians. The horizontal axis represents time and the vertical axis represents price. Vertical lines are drawn at each time period, with the top and bottom of each bar plotted at the high and low prices for the period. A small horizontal line is drawn across the bar at the closing price. Many charts also include a vertical scale at the bottom depicting trading volume.

basis point. A unit used to measure changes in interest rates and bond yields. One basis point equals .01, or one-hundredth of 1 percent.

bear. One who believes that the market is headed downward. One theory of the term's origin holds that the old proverb "to sell a bear's skin before one has caught the bear" describes what the short seller (bear) is doing, because the short seller does not own the stock he is selling. The terms "bull" and "bear" were both used on the London Stock Exchange in the early eighteenth century. *See* **bull.**

bearer bond. A bond that does not have the name of the

owner registered in the books of the issuer, but on which interest and principal are paid to the bearer. Although new bonds have not been issued in bearer form since December 31, 1982 (under terms of the Tax Equity and Fiscal Responsibility Act of 1982), many previously marketed bearer bonds are still outstanding. *See* **coupon bond, registered bond.**

beta. A measure of the sensitivity of a stock's price to fluctuations in a particular average. A volatile stock has a high beta, and a low-risk stock generally has a low beta. If a stock tends to move the same as the average, it has a beta of one.

bid price. The highest amount a prospective buyer is willing to bid or pay for a security at a given time.

Big Board. Another name for the New York Stock Exchange.

blue-chip stocks. High-quality stocks of major companies that have long, unbroken records of earnings and dividends, good growth prospects, well-regarded management, and a conservative financial structure.

Blue List. A daily trade publication for dealers in municipal bonds listing the names and amounts of municipal bonds that dealers all over the country are offering for sale.

blue sky laws. Laws various states have enacted to protect the public against securities frauds.

bond. Evidence of a debt on which the issuing company usually promises to pay the bondholders a specified amount of interest for a given length of time, and to repay the loan at the maturity date.

book value. A company's total assets less its liabilities and the liquidating value of its preferred stock. The result is divided by the number of common shares outstanding, to put the measure on a per-share basis.

broad tape. A machine operated by Dow Jones & Co. that prints important financial news on an enlarged form of the ticker tape. *See* **ticker.**

broker. An agent who handles buy and sell orders for securities or commodities for a commission charge.

bull. One who believes that the market is headed upward. One theory of origin holds that the way a bull tosses things up with its horns describes the action of a bull on the exchange. *See* **bear.**

business cycle. Regularly recurring periods of economic activity encompassing prosperity, recession, depression, and recovery.

businessman's risk. The risk involved in securities transactions that a businessman appears able to undertake. The term generally denotes securities entailing greater than average risk, but not so much as speculative issues.

cafeteria plan. A written employee benefit plan that allows participants to select the benefits desired. A plan must offer a choice of at least one taxable benefit and one nontaxable one.

callable. A bond or preferred issue all or part of which may be redeemed by the issuing corporation under definite conditions before maturity. Many high-coupon bonds are vulnerable to call in periods of declining interest rates.

call option. A contract that allows its owner to buy a certain number of shares of stock at a specific price, within a given period of time. The term also refers to commodity contracts.

call premium. The amount of excess over par value that a company must pay when it calls in a security.

capital gain or capital loss. Profit or loss from the sale of a capital asset. Tax considerations are different from those on ordinary income.

capital goods. Material goods used in the production of other goods.

capitalization. The total amount of securities (bonds, preferred stock, and common stock) issued by a corporation, plus its retained earnings.

cash basis. One of two principal methods of accounting. Using the cash basis method, income is reported when received and expenses are deducted in the year paid. *See* **accrual basis.**

cash flow. The reported net income of a corporation plus the amount charged off for depreciation, depletion, amortization, and other charges that are bookkeeping deductions and that do not entail actual payout of dollars and cents.

certificate. The actual piece of paper that is evidence of ownership of stock in a corporation.

certificate of deposit (CD). A certificate for money deposited in a commercial bank for a specified period of time and earning a specific rate of return.

Certified Financial Planner (CFP). A designation conferred by the College for Financial Planning upon individuals who have completed a series of comprehensive exams. Other qualified institutions offer similar study programs.

channels. A technical analysis term. Channels are drawn on a chart by connecting a series of highs and a series of lows to make parallel lines. Characteristically, a stock will trade within ascending and descending channels.

Chartered Financial Analyst (CFA). A professional designation awarded to those financial analysts who have passed a series of three examinations requiring knowledge of accounting, financial statement analysis, economics, and finance, as well as competence in investment management and securities analysis.

Chicago Board Options Exchange (CBOE). A market established in 1973 for the formalized trading of put and call options.

Chicago Board of Trade (CBT). One of the oldest and largest organized commodity exchanges in the United States. Officially chartered by the Illinois state legislature in 1859, the CBT provides facilities for trading in selected cash and futures markets.

churning. Excessive trading in a customer's account without adequate or proper justification. Churning is usually done to generate additional commissions.

clearinghouse. A corporation that takes the opposite side of all trades. The clearinghouse becomes the buyer to all sellers and the seller to all buyers.

Clifford trust. A short-term trust. Assets placed in the trust return to the donor after a specified period, as long as that period extends at least 10 years and one day, or upon the death of the beneficiary. The benefits of this trust were phased out by the 1986 TRA.

coincident indicators. Economic indicators that tend to move directly with the business cycle. *See* **lagging indicators, leading indicators.**

commercial paper. Unsecured short-term negotiable promissory notes of well-known business concerns and finance companies.

commission. The amount paid to a broker or other agent to buy or sell securities or commodities.

commission broker. A broker who owns a seat on the exchange and executes transactions on the floor for customers of his member firms.

commodity contract. A firm legal agreement between the buyer or seller and the commodity exchange's clearinghouse.

commodity futures market. A market in which contracts for the future delivery of commodities or foreign currency are bought and sold. The most important function of the futures market is that it provides a means of insurance against the risk of adverse price fluctuations between the time of the production of the commodity and its use.

Commodity Futures Trading Commission (CFTC). The agency created in 1974 by the federal government to regulate the commodity business, as the SEC oversees the securities industry.

common stock. Securities that represent ownership interest in a corporation. Preferred stock normally has prior claim in regard to dividends and, in the event of liquidation, assets. Stockholders of the common assume greater risk for potentially greater reward.

common stock equivalent. All stock options and warrants, plus all convertible securities that at time of issue have a cash yield of less than two-thirds of the then current prime rate.

confirmation. A formal memo delivered to a client of a brokerage house that bears all data relevant to a securities transaction executed for the client.

conglomerate. A diversified corporation with operations in a number of varied industries.

constructive receipt. This term is used by the IRS to indicate income that, though not actually received by a taxpayer, could be demanded by him. An example of this is interest accrued on a bank deposit or on a zero coupon bond.

contractual plan. A plan under which a mutual fund investor signs a contract agreeing to invest a specific sum of money in a particular fund at regular intervals for a definite period of time. Since, according to law, 20 percent of the first year's investment may be deducted as a sales charge, there is a monetary loss in dropping out of the plan before completion.

conversion parity. The point at which the price of a convertible security is equal to the value of the common shares into which it can be converted.

conversion value. The worth of a convertible bond, preferred stock, or warrant if it were converted into common stock under the terms of the conversion privilege and if the common stock obtained by conversion were sold at its current market price.

convertible security. A bond, debenture, or preferred stock that may be exchanged by the owner for common stock or another security, usually of the same company.

cost basis. The cost of an asset owned by a taxpayer. It is used to determine a capital gain or loss when the asset is sold and is used to calculate depreciation.

coupon bond. A bond with interest coupons attached. The coupons are clipped as they come due and are presented by the holder to a bank for payment. *See* **bearer bond, registered bond.**

covered option. An option written against securities already owned. *See* **naked option.**

cumulative preferred. Preferred stock on which unpaid dividends accrue. Dividends in arrears on a cumulative preferred stock must be paid before any common dividend.

current ratio. The ratio of current assets to current liabilities. This measure is used to evaluate a firm's liquidity. *See* **acid test.**

cushion bond. A premium bond, selling above its call price. Because of the possibility of call, it does not tend to rise as much in price as other bonds of a similar maturity when interest rates decline. It therefore does not decline as much when rates rise. Thus price action is cushioned by the call feature.

custodian account. An account—brokerage, bank, Keogh, mutual fund, and so forth—held in the name of the custodian for the benefit of another.

cyclical stocks. Stocks of companies whose earnings fluctuate with the business cycle. Cyclical industries include steel, cement, paper, machinery, and autos.

day order. An order to buy or sell that is good for one day only.

dealer. An individual who acts as principal, in contrast to a broker, who acts as an agent. A dealer buys securities for his own account and then sells them to a customer from his own holdings. Profit or loss is the difference between the price he paid for the security and the price at which he sells it.

debenture. A promissory note backed by the general credit of a company and usually not secured by a mortgage or lien on any specific property.

debt to equity ratio. The relationship of long-term debt and other long-term liabilities to common shareholder's equity. This measure is commonly used to indicate leverage.

defensive stocks. Stocks of companies in steady businesses that are relatively unaffected by the ups and downs of the business cycle. Examples of defensive industries are electric and telephone utilities and food suppliers.

deferred annuity. An annuity purchased as a single-premium or annual-premium annuity on which income distributions begin at some future date.

deferred sales charge. Also called a back-end load, this fee is used to discourage investors trading in and out of mutual funds too frequently. The charge declines the longer the shares are held.

depletion. Charges against earnings to reflect the gradual exhaustion of natural resources, such as ore, oil, and timber. It is a bookkeeping entry and does not require a cash outlay.

depreciation. Charges against earnings to write off the cost, less salvage value, of an asset over its estimated useful life. Like depletion, it is a bookkeeping entry.

discount. Amount by which a security may be purchased that is below its redemption value, as in Savings Bonds, Treasury bills, and some corporate bonds.

discount broker. A broker who charges a smaller commission than that of a full-service broker. Generally no investment advice is given by a discount broker.

discount rate. The interest rate the Federal Reserve Board charges member banks for loans.

discretionary account. An account in which the broker determines the timing for buying and selling as well as the selections and number of shares to be bought and sold.

disintermediation. The outflow of money from savings banks and other financial institutions to higher-yielding investments.

diversification. Spreading investments among different companies in a variety of industries, or among different types of securities or investments, or both, in order to spread risk.

dividend. A payment designated by the board of directors of a corporation to be distributed to shareholders on a pro rata basis.

dividend payout ratio. The percentage of earnings that is paid out in cash dividends.

dollar cost averaging. An investment plan under which an investor purchases an equal dollar amount of a given stock or stocks at regular intervals.

double tops and bottoms. A technical analysis term that refers to chart formations in which the stock fluctuates, hitting the same top or bottom on two and sometimes three or four successive occasions. The breakout from such a pattern is the clue to the action to be taken.

Dow Jones Industrial Average. An average of 30 blue-chip stocks. The average was originally published in 1897, based on 12 stocks. Adjustments in the divisor are currently used to reflect stock splits or stock dividends.

Dow Jones Transportation Average. An average of 20 transportation stocks.

Dow Jones Utility Average. An average of 15 utility stocks.

Dow Theory. A theory of market analysis based on performance of the Dow Jones Industrial and the Dow Jones Transportation averages. According to the theory, the market is in a basic uptrend if one of these averages advances above a previous important high, accompanied or followed by a similar advance in the other. When the averages drop below previous important lows, a confirmation of a basic downtrend occurs.

downtick. A transaction made at a price lower than the preceding transaction in a particular stock.

dual funds. Publicly traded investment companies with two classes of stock—capital shares and income shares. Capital shareholders are entitled to all of the capital appreciation but no income. Income shareholders receive all of the income from the portfolio of holdings.

dual listing. The listing of a stock on the NYSE as well as on another exchange.

efficient market. The theory that holds that stock prices always reflect all available relevant information.

Employee Retirement Income Security Act of 1974 (ERISA). The law that created a uniform federal standard for fiduciary conduct relating to the establishment and maintenance of corporate employee benefit plans.

exchange privilege. The right to exchange shares of one mutual fund for shares of another fund under the same sponsorship at net asset value or at a reduced sales charge.

ex-dividend date. The date when the stock sells "ex," or without the dividend. On or after this date, which is the fourth full business day preceding the record date, the buyer receives the stock "ex," or without the dividend.

fair market value. The price that a willing buyer will pay and willing seller will accept for an asset.

federal funds rate. The interest rate charged on overnight loans from one member bank of the Federal Reserve System to another.

Federal Reserve Board. The seven-member board of governors of the Federal Reserve System, the central bank of the United States.

FIFO (first in, first out). The method of inventory valuation in which those goods purchased first are assumed to be sold first. *See* **LIFO**.

financial futures contract. A contract under which an investor agrees to buy or sell a financial asset at a given future date and price.

fiscal policy. The use of a government's spending and revenue-producing activities to achieve certain objectives.

fiscal year. A corporation's accounting year. Because of the nature of their particular business, some companies do not use the calendar year for their bookkeeping. Retailing concerns, for instance, generally end their year on January 31, because of the Christmas rush.

flat. A bond that trades flat is one that trades without interest accruals. Bonds that are in default of interest or principal are traded flat. Income bonds trade flat, since interest is not paid on a regular basis but only when earned. Most bonds trade "plus interest," with the buyer paying the seller the interest that has accrued since the previous payment date.

floating supply. The proportion of the listed capital stock of a corporation available for trading purposes; usually excludes shares closely held by management.

flower bonds. Certain U.S. Treasury bonds that can be purchased at a discount and turned in at par for payment of federal estate taxes if the bonds are actually owned by the decedent at the time of death.

Form 10-K. A report that a corporation must file with the SEC within 90 days after the end of each fiscal year. The 10-K contains certified financial statements and is more detailed than the annual report.

fully diluted earnings. The earnings figure that gives effect to all securities that could be converted into common stock and that would reduce earnings per share. *See* **primary earnings per share.**

fundamental analysis. The study and evaluation of such basic elements as earnings and dividend growth potential, and the varied impact of economics and politics on the market as a whole or on a particular industry or company.

general obligation bond. A major type of municipal bond backed by the full faith and credit of the issuer.

good-till-canceled (GTC) order. An order to buy or sell that remains in effect until it is either executed or canceled.

Government Retirement Bonds. A special series of U.S. individual retirement bonds issued by the federal government under the provisions of the Second Liberty Bond Act. The government discontinued the sale of these bonds in 1982.

grantor trust. A trust over which the grantor retains control of income or principal, or both.

gross national product (GNP). A measure of the nation's total output of goods and services.

growth stock. Stock of a company whose sales and earnings are expanding faster than the general economy. Retained earnings are largely plowed back into the business to facilitate expansion.

head and shoulders. A technical formation whose name is derived from the appearance given by the pattern of a head and right and left shoulders. If a stockholder has not previously sold on the higher, "head" level, he should take advantage of the rally that forms the right shoulder, because price deterioration on reduced volume can set in quickly.

hedge. To try to minimize risk by taking certain steps to offset the risk. In commodities, hedging is taking a position in the futures market that is equal to but opposite from an existing or soon-to-exist position in the cash market.

hedge funds. Mutual funds that always keep a portion of their portfolios in a "short" position.

high-technology companies. Those companies engaged in, or developing products that require, high-level scientific research. Drug, electronic, defense, aerospace, communications, and computer companies are examples.

holding company. A corporation that owns the majority of stock or securities of one or more other corporations for purposes of control rather than investment.

hypothecation. The pledging of customers' securities as collateral for loans to brokers and dealers.

income bond. A bond that promises to repay principal but pays interest only when earned.

income stock. Common stock that pays out a relatively large portion of earnings in dividends, and thus provides a high yield to investors.

indenture. A written agreement under which debt securities are issued. It sets forth the maturity date, interest rate, call provisions, security, and any other factors affecting those bonds.

index funds. Mutual funds whose portfolios either duplicate the structure of the S&P 500 or other selected average or consist of 100 or more S&P issues to track the average.

The indexing concept concedes that since it is difficult to beat the average consistently, analysis and investment fees should be reduced and the performance of the average matched.

Indicator Digest Average. Equal dollar investment-type average of all stocks traded on the Big Board.

individual retirement account (IRA). A tax-deferred retirement savings account available to workers not covered by an employer's plan and in limited amount to nonworking spouses and divorced spouses.

insiders. Directors, officers, and principal securities holders of a corporation. Principal holders are those who own 10 percent or more of a publicly traded company's stock. The SEC requires insiders to report their initial position and details of any significant change in their holdings.

installment method. The method of reporting payments from the sale of an asset as they are received. Unless the taxpayer elects not to use this method it is mandatory for tax purposes.

institutional investor. An institution, such as a bank, life insurance company, or pension fund, whose investments constitute an important part of overall operations.

intestate. Without a will.

investment banker. The intermediary in the money markets who assists corporations in raising capital from investors. A profit is made on the difference between the price paid to the corporation and that at which the securities are sold to the public.

investment company. A corporation that sells its own securities to the public and invests the proceeds in other securities in keeping with an indicated objective. *See* **mutual fund.**

Investment Company Act of 1940. The basic federal law governing the registration and regulation of investment companies.

investment tax credit. This credit against taxes is given for the purchase of business equipment. Congress legislates the credit as a means of encouraging spending to spur the economy. When revenue-raising needs become more important than pump priming, Congress limits or withdraws the credit.

IPO. Acronym for initial public offering of a security.

joint and survivor annuity. An annuity that pays income over the lifetime of two individuals.

junk bonds. Lower-quality bonds, generally below investment grade, that provide exceptionally high yields with commensurately high risks.

Keogh plan. A retirement plan set up under the Self-Employed Individuals Tax Retirement Act of 1961 (HR-10). Self-employed persons and their employees can set aside a stated percentage up to a maximum dollar amount in a tax-sheltered retirement account. The dollar and percentage amounts are altered by Congress from time to time.

lagging indicators. Indicators of economic activity that change direction after moves in overall economic activity.

leading indicators. A group of indicators of economic activity that tend to turn up or down in advance of general economic activity.

leverage. The effect obtained when borrowed funds are added to invested equity in a financial venture.

liabilities. Claims against the assets of a corporation or individual.

LIFO (last in, first out). The method of inventory valuation in which those goods last acquired are assumed to be sold first. LIFO reduces earnings in periods of rising prices. *See* **FIFO.**

limited partnership. A form of investment often employed because of favorable tax consequences. The limited partnership limits both the risks and the rewards of the investor but puts the planning and decision making in the hands of a professional management team.

limit order. An order in which the buyer or seller indicates to his broker the specific price at which it is to be executed. A limit order to buy specifies a price below the market; a limit order to sell indicates a price above the market. *See* **stop order.**

liquidation. The process of converting securities or other property into cash.

liquidity. The cash or near-cash position of a corporation. The term may also refer to the ability of the market in a particular security to absorb a reasonable amount of buying or selling at reasonable price changes.

listed stock. Stock of a corporation that is traded on a securities exchange.

living trust. A trust that is in effect during the life of the testator, also called an inter vivos trust. A living trust may be revocable (control is retained over assets) or irrevocable (control is permanently forfeited).

load. The sales charge a buyer of mutual funds may have to pay in addition to the actual net asset value of the shares.

management fee. The fee deducted from the gross income of an investment company before any distributions to shareholders. Generally it amounts to one-half of 1 percent of the fund's net asset value. Also, the fee charged by an investment counselor for his service.

margin. The value of securities and cash in a brokerage account against which an investor may purchase more stock. Margin requirements in the past 20 years have ranged from 40 percent of the purchase price to 100 percent. In commodity jargon, margin refers to funds put up as security or guarantee of contract fulfillment.

margin call. A call from a broker asking for additional cash in order to bring the equity in a customer's margin account at least up to the margin maintenance requirements stipulated by the exchange. The margin call is made when the value of securities in an account declines.

market maker. A brokerage firm that buys and sells securities for its own accounts and risk at stated bid and asked prices.

market order. An order to buy or sell a stated amount of a security at the most advantageous price obtainable after the order is presented on the trading floor.

maturity. The scheduled date for repayment of the principal amount on a bond or other debt instrument.

MBIA—Municipal Bond Investors Assurance. A consortium of leading insurance companies that guarantees principal and interest payments on municipal bonds. Evidence of the insurance is printed on or attached to each bond. Since the initials are part of the description of the bond, they should appear on the broker's confirmation and statement.

monetary policy. The management by a central bank of a nation's money supply to assure the availability of credit in line with national objectives.

money market. The arena in which short-term funds (less than one year) are channeled. Money-market instruments include promissory notes and bills of exchange, commercial paper, bankers' acceptances, Treasury bills, short-term tax-exempts, dealer paper, and negotiable certificates of deposit.

money-market funds. Mutual funds that invest in money-market instruments.

money supply. The sum total of money stock. Common measures are M1, which is currency in circulation plus demand deposits (checking accounts), and M1A, which is adjusted for seasonal variations.

mortgage bonds. Bonds secured by a conditional lien on part or all of a corporation's property.

moving average. One of the popular methods for determining market and individual stock strength or weakness. A moving average is obtained by adding the prices for a certain number of days and dividing the total by the number of days involved. For the next figure, the price for the earliest day or week is dropped and the current one added.

municipal bond. A bond issued by a state or political subdivision, or by a state agency or authority. Interest from most municipal issues is exempt from federal income tax and in some cases from state and local taxes.

mutual fund. An investment company that enables its shareholders to pool their capital into a single professionally managed account. *See* **investment company.**

naked option. An option written against stock that is not currently owned. *See* **covered option.**

NASD (National Association of Securities Dealers). A national organization that provides for the self-regulation of the over-the-counter market.

NASDAQ (National Association of Securities Dealers Automated Quotation system). A computerized communications system that collects, stores, and displays up-to-the-second quotations from a nationwide network of over-the-counter dealers making markets in stocks included in the NASDAQ system. Certain requirements must be met in order for a stock to be included.

net asset value. The total market value of a mutual fund portfolio less liabilities, divided by the number of shares of the fund outstanding.

New York Stock Exchange (NYSE). The largest national securities exchange.

New York Stock Exchange Index. The unweighted average of all stocks listed on the New York Stock Exchange.

odd lot. A trade of fewer than 100 shares. *See* **round lot.**

offering price. The price for which mutual fund shares may be purchased. It includes any load fee.

open-end investment company. An investment company in which the price is determined by the per-share net asset value of the portfolio. There is no fixed number of shares. These funds make a continuous offer of shares for sale to the public, and at any time will buy back outstanding shares at net asset value.

open market operations. The purchase or sale of government bonds in the open market (mostly in New York) by the Federal Reserve Board. Open market operations are the chief stabilizing tool of the Fed.

option. The right to buy or sell specified securities at a set price within a stated time period.

option clearing corporation. The organization that acts as buyer to all sellers and vice versa for all traded options.

over-the-counter market. A negotiation market, which has a dollar volume greater than the total of all stock exchanges.

par value. The amount stated on the face of a bond, preferred stock, or common stock. Interest or dividends are often stated as a percentage of par in the case of bonds and preferreds, and bonds are generally redeemed at par on their maturity date. In the case of common stock, however, par value bears no real relationship to the market price or underlying value of the shares.

Pink Sheet. A daily publication of the National Quotation Bureau. Prices on over-the-counter securities are listed along with the names and telephone numbers of those firms that make a market in them. Prices quoted by these firms are not definite bids and offers.

pit. The trading floor of a commodity exchange where traders and brokers stand as they trade in particular commodities.

point and figure chart. A technical chart that shows a compressed picture of significant price changes. These charts are designed to show strength of price movement and to emphasize changes in direction.

portfolio. The total securities held by an institution or a private individual.

preferred stock. A class of stock that has preference over the common stock of a corporation regarding the payment of dividends. In the event of liquidation, preferred shareholders have priority over common shareholders in the distribution of assets.

premium. The amount by which a security, bond, convertible, and so forth sells above its redemption or conversion value.

price-earnings multiple. The current market price of a share of stock, divided by earnings per share for a 12-month period. (Also called price-earnings ratio.)

primary earnings per share. Net income after preferred dividends, divided by common shares outstanding plus the shares that would be outstanding if common stock equivalents were actually converted.

primary issue. The original sale of stock, where proceeds revert to the issuing company.

prime rate. The rate of interest charged by commercial banks for short-term loans extended to their best customers.

private placement. The selling of securities directly to one or more large investors, without the services of an underwriter or an SEC registration.

profit margin (pretax). Pretax income divided by net sales. This figure is a measure of the efficiency of a company, although profit margins vary from industry to industry and company to company.

prospectus. A printed communication that offers a security for sale. The prospectus contains salient parts of the registration statement, which gives all information relevant to the issue.

proxy statement. Information required by the SEC to be given stockholders as a prerequisite to solicitation of proxies for a security subject to requirements of the Securities Exchange Act of 1934.

prudent man rule. The rule that enables a trustee to use his own judgment in making investments as long as he acts in a prudent manner. The rule comes from an 1830 court decision.

put option. A contract giving the right to sell a certain number of shares of stock at a specific price, within a defined time period.

random walk. A theory that states that the size and direction of a stock market or individual stock price action cannot be predicted from the size and direction of previous moves.

ratio writing. Writing calls on more shares than are actually owned.

real estate investment trust (REIT). A professionally managed portfolio of real estate properties or mortgages, or both.

record date. The date on which a shareholder must be registered on the books of a corporation to receive a declared dividend or vote on company affairs.

redemption fee. A 1 percent or 2 percent charge that mutual funds sometimes levy on shares liquidated within the first year of purchase.

red herring. A preliminary prospectus that does not include the price at which the securities are to be offered to the public. It is issued to obtain an indication of interest in an offer. It gets its name from the statement, printed in red ink on its front cover, that it is a preliminary prospectus.

refunding. Replacing an outstanding debt obligation with a new obligation.

registered bond. A bond that is recorded on the books of the issuer in the name of the owner. It can be transferred only when endorsed by the registered owner. *See* **bearer bond, coupon bond.**

registered representative. An employee of a securities broker or dealer who, having passed examinations and met other requirements of the SEC or NASD, or both, is authorized to receive buy and sell orders for securities from public investors.

registrar. A trust company or bank charged with the responsibility of preventing the issuance of more stock than is authorized by a company.

regular way transaction. A transaction in which delivery of a stock certificate is made at the office of the purchaser on the fifth full business day following the transaction date.

relative strength. The relationship of the price of a stock to the Dow Jones Industrial Average or some other market average. The resulting percentage, multiplied by a factor to bring the plotting closer to the price bars on the chart, shows by the direction of the curve whether the stock is performing better than, worse than, or the same as the market average used.

replacement cost accounting. An accounting concept that espouses valuing assets at their replacement, or current, cost.

repurchase agreement. A cash loan to a bank or broker in exchange for or collateralized by securities (usually U.S. Treasury or agency), which the borrower agrees to repurchase at a specific price on a future date. These are not deposits; therefore they are not insured.

resistance level. A price area that attracts selling sufficient to keep the price of a stock from rising above it on repeated occasions. Once it has been broken through on the upside, the old resistance area becomes a new support level. *See* **support level.**

retained earnings. Profits remaining in the company after payment of preferred and common stock dividends. Retained earnings provide an important internal source of capital for business expansion.

return on equity. Net income available for the common stock divided by the previous year's shareholders' equity.

return on total capital. Earnings before interest and taxes, divided by total capitalization.

revenue bond. A municipal bond on which interest and principal are payable from receipts obtained from the operation of the project they finance rather than from general tax receipts.

revocable trust. A trust in which control of assets is retained.

rights (preemptive). Short-term options granted to existing shareholders of a company to purchase new stock issues, generally at reduced price levels.

ring. *See* **pit.**

round lot. Normally 100 shares of stock; for bonds, $100,000 face value.

Savings Bonds. Nonmarketable bonds issued by the U.S. Treasury. Now sold as Series EE, a discounted bond, and Series HH, a current-interest issue.

Securities Act of 1933. The law that states what information is required in a registration statement and prospectus.

Securities Exchange Act of 1934. The law that created the Securities and Exchange Commission. It requires registration with the SEC of many organizations dealing in securities and sets down rules for hypothecation of customers' securities.

Securities Investor Protection Corporation (SIPC). An insurance corporation organized under the Securities Investor Protection Act of 1970 to protect the assets of brokerage accounts in the event of a brokerage company bankruptcy. Operating funds are provided by assessments on brokerage firms' earnings.

selling against the box. Short selling against stock that is owned by an investor. The short sale may be covered by purchasing additional shares or by delivering the shares already owned.

semilogarithmic chart. A chart drawn on semilogarithmic graph paper. On this paper, the horizontal scale is drawn arithmetically, but the vertical scale is constructed so that equal distances represent equal percentage changes.

serial bonds. A bond issue that is sold with serial maturity dates and commensurate interest rates.

short interest ratio. The figure obtained by relating the monthly short interest (total number of shares sold short) to the average daily trading volume in the period concerned.

short selling. Selling stock one does not already own, in the belief that the price will decline. The broker borrows the stock so that he can deliver the shares to the buyer. Later, the short seller must cover his position by buying the same amount of stock borrowed for return to the buyer.

single-premium annuity. An annuity contract purchased with only one payment, or premium.

sinking fund. Money set aside by a company to redeem its bonds, debentures, or preferred shares periodically as specified in the indenture or charter.

specialist. An exchange member whose first function is to maintain an orderly market in the stocks in which he is registered as a specialist. To do so, the specialist is expected to buy or sell for his own account when there is a temporary disparity between supply and demand.

special situation. A term that encompasses several types of unusual investment opportunities, including merger or takeover candidates, new-product development, spin-offs, or liquidations.

speculation. The assumption of above-average risk in anticipation of commensurately higher return.

speculative index. The relationship of American Stock Exchange volume to New York Stock Exchange volume expressed as a percentage. Presumably, the lower the figure, the closer the market is to a bottom, and the higher the figure, the closer it is to a peak.

spin-off. The division of an existing corporate entity into two or more separate operating units, with shares of the new company being distributed—"spun off"—to shareholders of the predecessor.

Standard & Poor's 500 Composite Stock Price Index. Average of 500 stocks, consisting of 400 industrial, 40 financial, 40 utility, and 20 transportation stocks.

standing margin (commodities). The amount of money a clearinghouse member keeps on deposit with the clearinghouse for each net open position at the end of the trading day.

stepped-up basis. The revised cost basis of an asset to the new owner when transferred by a decedent's will.

stock dividend. A dividend paid in securities rather than cash. It may be additional shares of the issuing company or shares of another company (usually a subsidiary) held by the company.

stockholders' equity. *See* **book value.**

stock split. The allotment of additional shares to stockholders to represent their ownership interest in a corporation. Often stock splits are designed to broaden interest in a high-priced stock. A shareholder's proportionate interest in a company is not altered by a stock split.

stop order. An order that specifies a particular price at which a stock should be bought or sold. A stop order to buy specifies a price above the market; a stop order to sell indicates a price below the market. A stop order automatically becomes a market order once the security reaches the specified price.

straddle. The purchase of a put and a call on the same underlying stock having identical striking prices and expiration dates.

straight life annuity. An annuity that provides a predetermined amount of income periodically for the life of the annuitant. *See* **joint and survivor annuity.**

straight-line method. A method of writing off (depreciating) the cost of an asset in equal amounts over its useful life.

street name. Securities held in the name of a broker instead of the owner's name. Sometimes this arrangement is done for convenience; stocks bought on margin must always be left in a street name.

striking price. The price at which a call or put option is written. In the case of a call option, it is the price at which the stock named in the contract may be bought; in the case of a put, it is the price at which the stock may be sold.

STRIPS. An acronym for Separate Trading of Registered Interest and Principal of Securities. These STRIPS are authorized by the Treasury and are available to individuals through banks.

subordinate debenture. A debt issue whose claim on corporate assets comes after that of debentures in a liquidation.

support level. A technical analysis term that denotes a price area in which there is demand for a stock sufficient to keep the price from dropping below it on repeated occasions. Once there is a break below the area, a new support level is created. *See* **resistance level.**

sweep account. A savings or checking account in which funds over a specified minimum balance are invested in money-market instruments.

syndicate. A group of investment bankers formed to underwrite and distribute a securities issue. Also, a group of individuals or concerns who combine to undertake a particular investment. *See* **investment banker.**

tax-free rollover. Using an individual retirement account to channel retirement funds from one qualified pension program to another, with no immediate tax consequences.

tax loopholes. Gaps in the tax structure through which clever taxpayers and special-interest groups can maneuver. Use of tax loopholes is not illegal.

tax shelter. Any means whereby income receives preferential tax treatment.

technical analysis. The study of phenomena internal to the market, such as patterns of price movement, in an attempt to forecast the future movement of the market as a whole or of individual stocks.

tenancy in common. The title jointly held by two people, usually unmarried, to a given piece of property. Each person retains control over his individual share of the property.

tenancy by the entirety. The form of property ownership that exists when the names of both husband and wife appear on the deed to the property, with rights of survivorship.

tender offer. An offer by a corporation to buy back its own shares, or an offer to buy up shares in a company by an outsider interested in acquiring control.

ticker. The electronic system that prints prices and volume of security transactions in cities and towns throughout the U.S. and Canada within minutes after each transaction.

"Tiger"—Treasury Investment Growth Receipts. One of several pooled investment vehicles offered by major brokerage firms combining the advantages of zero coupon bonds (no interest payments but assured compounding of yield) with the safety of U.S. Treasury securities of a given maturity.

transfer agent. A bank or trust company that keeps a record of the name of each registered shareowner, his address, and the number of shares owned, and that sees that certificates presented to it for transfer are properly canceled and new certificates issued in the name of the transferee.

Treasury bills. U.S. government securities maturing in one year or less, usually in three months or six months. They are sold at weekly auctions at a discount from par and are redeemed at par.

Treasury bonds. U.S. government securities with a maturity of more than 10 years.

Treasury notes. U.S. government securities with a maturity of 2 to 10 years.

treasury stock. Stock issued by a company but later reacquired by the same company and held in its treasury.

trend line. Line drawn on a chart that indicates the direction in which a particular stock or the general market is trending.

trust. An agreement whereby the person who establishes the trust gives property to a trustee to invest and manage for the advantage of the beneficiary.

trustee. An individual or institution designated to oversee the handling and distribution of a trust fund.

12b(1) plans. Mutual funds using this plan are allowed to cover their marketing and distribution costs and brokerage charges from the fund's assets.

unit. A trading entity that is composed of more than one class of security but that trades together as one—for example, common stock or bond with warrants attached.

unit trust. An investment entity that issues only redeemable certificates that represent individual interests in a fixed portfolio with a specified life span and no continuing management.

unweighted average. Stock market average in which higher-priced issues do not have more influence on the average than lower-priced issues. This type of average is also called an equal-weighted average. *See* **weighted average.**

upside-downside volume. Tabulation of the shares traded on the New York Stock Exchange at prices higher or lower than the previous day's close.

uptick. A transaction made at a price higher than the preceding transaction in a particular stock.

Value Line Index. An equal-weighted average based on equal dollar investments in a list of around 1,700 stocks.

variable annuity. An annuity in which a specified portion of the principal is invested in common stocks.

volume. The number of shares traded in a given market (unless stated as consolidated, which would aggregate trades from all markets) during a given period of time.

warrant. A certificate giving the holder the right to purchase securities at a stipulated price within a specified time limit or perpetually.

wash sale. A wash sale is said to occur if securities or options to buy them are obtained within 30 days before or after a sale of substantially the same securities. No tax loss may be taken in such cases.

weighted average. An average that gives greater weight to stocks with a higher market value—S&P, NYSE averages. This type of average may also be called a value-weighted average.

"when issued." A new issue of securities that has been authorized but not actually issued to purchasers in a split. Shares are bought and sold in the market, with all transactions settled only when, as, and if the securities are finally issued.

withdrawal plan. An arrangement under which investors in mutual funds can regularly receive monthly or quarterly payments of a specified amount.

working capital. Current assets minus current liabilities. Working-capital needs vary among industries and among firms in the same industry.

yield. The dividends or interest paid on a particular security expressed as a percentage of the current price or as a percentage of cost price, or as related to the maturity of a bond.

yield to maturity. The return earned on a bond if it is held to maturity.

zero coupon bonds. Bonds on which there are no periodic

interest payments before maturity, but that are sold at a deep discount from their face value so that the principal payment at maturity provides an effective yield on the amount originally invested.

Index